Subversive Sites

Subversive Sites

Feminist Engagements with Law in India

RATNA KAPUR
BRENDA COSSMAN

SAGE PUBLICATIONS
New Delhi/Thousand Oaks/London
in association with
The Book Review Literary Trust
New Delhi

First published in 1996 by

Sage Publications India Pvt Ltd
M–32 Greater Kailash Market I
New Delhi 110 048

Sage Publications Inc
2455 Teller Road
Thousand Oaks, California 91320

Sage Publications Ltd
6 Bonhill Street
London EC2A 4PU

Published by Tejeshwar Singh for Sage Publications India Pvt Ltd, phototypeset by Line Arts, Pondicherry, and printed at Chaman Enterprises, Delhi.

Library of Congress Cataloging-in-Publication Data
Kapur, Ratna, 1959–
   Subversive sites: feminist engagements with law in India / Ratna Kapur and Brenda Cossman.
     p. cm.
   Includes bibliographical references and index.
   1. Women—Legal status, laws, etc.—India. 2. Feminist jurisprudence—India.
I. Cossman, Brenda, 1960– . II. Title.
KNS516.K36   1996   346.5401'34—dc20   96–7992
               [345.406134]

ISBN: 0–8039–9315–3 (US-hb)   81–7036–552–X (India-hb)

Sage Production Editors: Ritu Vajpeyi-Mohan and Evelyn George

The idea of neutral dialogue is an idea which denies history, denies structure, denies the positioning of subjects.

Gayatri Spivak
The Post Colonial Critic: Interviews, Strategies, Dialogues
editor, Sarah Haraysym
(Routledge: New York 1990)

Two or three things I know, two or three things I know for sure, and one of them is that to go on living I have to tell stories, that stories are the one sure way I know to touch the heart and change the world.

Dorothy Allison
Two or Three Things I Know for Sure
(Dutton: New York, 1995)

Contents

Acknowledgements

We are indebted to the enormous generosity of the law office of R. K. P. Shankardass, particularly to Kumar Shankardass, without whom our ability to communicate with each other across two continents would have been radically curtailed and who provided us with open access to the law library, to computer, fax and email facilities. We are also grateful for the endless patience and assistance of his staff, Baldev Sharma and Kasturi Lal Kapur.

We would like to thank Eliza Erskine for her commitment to the manuscript—we would never have finished it without her discerning eye. We are grateful to Kristen Elliot, Prabha Kotiswaran, Radhapyari, Ashraf Unissa, Leti Volpp, and Donna Young, who provided us with invaluable research assistance. We must also thank Jill Grant, whose assistance throughout the project was inestimable.

Special thanks to Annie Bunting, Shohini Ghosh, Marlee Kline, Janaki Nair, and Tanika Sarkar for their comments on various portions of the manuscript at various stages of its development. Chapter 4 benefited from its presentation at a conference organized by the South Asian Studies Centre at Cornell University, in April 1996.

We gratefully acknowledge that the book was supported in part by a grant from the International Development Research Council, Ottawa, Canada. We would like to thank the National Law School of India University for their support in this project, particularly the many engaging students whose excitement over these new perspectives to law has been an ongoing source of inspiration. We would also like to express our thanks to the Centre for Feminist Legal Research for providing a place to complete the final editing of the manuscript.

Ratna Kapur would like to thank Ramma Shankardass for her constant encouragement throughout this project and continuously nurturing her intellectual endeavours. A special thanks to Salbiah Ahmed and the Asia Pacific Forum on Women, Law and Development for providing her with the space to develop and share the ideas discussed in this book. She is also grateful to the International Centre for Law and Development, and

Dr. Clarence Dias for initially giving her the opportunity to begin thinking about law differently. She is indebted to the many activists who allowed her to develop a praxis of feminist legal engagement. Finally, she would like to thank her extended family for their support.

Brenda Cossman thanks Judy Fudge and Shelley Gavigan her colleagues at Osgoode Hall Law School, for their intellectual engagement, and whose influence on her work has been more profound than they may suspect. She is also indebted to the support of her colleagues Bruce Ryder and Mary Condon, whose encouragement was always appreciated. She thanks Osgoode Hall Law School, for its generous support, and particularly for awarding her the Osgoode Hall Research Fellowship in 1992–93 which provided her the precious gift of time to think, write, and travel to India. She also thanks the Faculty of Law at the University of Toronto, which kindly provided her with a peaceful atmosphere to write in the fall of 1992. She is indebted to Sarah Kraiser for her unique contribution in helping her meet the deadline for the manuscript.

We would both like to express our appreciation to our publishers Sage. We benefited enormously from the comments of the anonymous reviewer. And a special thanks to Ritu Vajpeyi-Mohan who edited our manuscript with such care and attention.

Finally, we both benefited from the endless pa(w)ndering through our manuscript by our companions, Sushi and Krid.

Introduction

Norms and ideals arise from the yearning that is an expression
of freedom: it does not have to be this way, it could be otherwise.

Iris Marion Young
*Justice and the Politics of Difference**

In *Subversive Sites: Feminist Engagements with Law in India*, we attempt
to engage with the question we pose to ourselves and our readers. Is law
a subversive site? Over the course of a century and a half, successive
women's movements have turned to law as a way of securing their
political goals. Social reformers and feminist activists have successfully
lobbied for law reform in both the public and private realms of women's
lives, in the hope that law would somehow transform these realities. Yet,
despite this intensive engagement, so little seems to have altered in
women's day-to-day lives. Is this because law is inherently conservative
and designed to resist the progressive agendas of feminist visionaries?
Is it because law is one of many discourses which operate to sustain and
naturalize unequal power relations? Has law been too central in our
struggles for social and political change? Has law outlived its usefulness
in our struggles, or have we not·yet fully exploited its potential? Are we
rightly disillusioned with law, or only with the unrealistic expectations
we have of it?

These are amongst the many searching questions that this book seeks
to explore. We offer no easy answers, but examine the contours of law
in feminist struggles for social change. We seek to strengthen feminist
engagements with law by revealing the complex and contradictory nature
of law. The theoretical framework that we seek to develop in *Subversive
Sites* is a feminist one. Feminist legal studies is emerging as a new, and
in our view, significant area of study, analysis and practice in India. It

* Princeton: Princeton University Press, 1990.

is an area of research that is providing important new insights into the ways in which law operates in the context of women's lives. In developing our feminist analysis of law, we draw heavily on the recent theoretical developments in poststructuralism and cultural studies. We will attempt to move beyond the understanding of law as a simple instrument of either oppression or social engineering which has informed much of the earlier work on women and law in India. Building on the work of more recent feminist studies, we argue that the role of law cannot be adequately captured by a dichotomous understanding of law as either an instrument of oppression or of liberation. We believe that the terrain of law is much more complex, in both the oppression of women, and in its promise for challenging that oppression.

Subversive Sites offers another way of reimagining the story of feminist engagement with law, and negotiating the dilemmas that this engagement has presented. We attempt to reveal and explain the contradictory nature of law. We examine the ways in which law has been implicated in the subordination of women. Many studies have been done reviewing the laws that impact on women's status, and highlighting those laws that continue to discriminate against women. Our study moves beyond these reviews, and examines at a deeper level the contradictory ways in which the law is implicated in the oppression of women. We explore the ideological assumptions that inform the legal regulation of women and the ways in which law subordinates women—the complex and subtle forms in which law reinforces deeply gendered assumptions, relations and roles. Legal discourse has constructed women as gendered subjects—it has constructed women as wives and mothers, as passive and weak, as subordinate and in need of protection. It is a discourse which has contributed to the subordinate position of women through its very construction of women's roles and identities. At the same time, law is a site where these roles and identities have been challenged. It is a site where social reformers and feminist activists have sought to displace previously dominant understandings of women's appropriate roles and identities, and sought to reconstruct women's roles and identities as more full and equal citizens. In place of an instrumentalist vision of law, we argue that law needs to be reconceptualized as a site of discursive struggle, where competing visions of the world, and of women's place therein, have been and continue to be fought out. We believe that such a reconceptualization of law can better capture both the possibilities and limitations of law, and law's contradictory nature in women's struggles for social change.

In *Subversive Sites*, we focus our analysis on the legal regulation of women in and through the family. We do not provide an overview of the various family laws in India, or of the various legal provisions that continue to discriminate against women. Rather, we examine the legal regulation of women in the family as a site of women's oppression, of contradiction and of struggle. Our focus is on the extent to which the legal regulation of women is informed by and serves to reinscribe familial ideology. By familial ideology, we are referring to a set of norms, values, and assumptions about the way in which family life is and should be organized; a set of ideas that have been so naturalized and universalized that they have come to dominate common sense thinking about the family. Although women in India live in an enormous diversity of family forms, we believe that it is nevertheless possible to identify a dominant ideology of family that informs the legal regulation of women. Familial ideology constructs the family as the basic and sacred unit in society, and women's roles as wives and mothers as natural and immutable. This vision of the family, and women's roles therein, appears throughout the law as self-evident, and beyond question. As we will illustrate, it is a vision of the family that has operated to undermine women's full and equal participation in society, and which continues to justify this inequality. It is a vision of the family that continues to limit law's ability to deliver on its promise of equality for women.

Our focus on the legal regulation of women in and through familial ideology is intended to highlight the complex and contradictory ways in which law reinforces women's subordination. There are many other ways in which law has historically contributed to women's inequality, and there are many other dimensions to the legal regulation and subordination of women that our analysis does not explore. We argue that the family is a major site of women's oppression; we do not suggest that it is the only site. Sexuality, for example, is another major site of women's oppression. Women are constituted in and through the discourses of sexuality in important ways. And it will be important for feminist legal analyses to consider the ways in which these discourses may be overlapping and mutually constituting.

We will explore the relationship between familial ideology and women's equality rights. The discourse of equality has been a cornerstone in the women's movement's challenge, past and present, to patriarchal social relations, and particularly, to laws that explicitly discriminate against women. It has been the powerful resonance of the liberal discourse of equality and equal rights that has legitimized the demands of the women's movement that women be granted the same basic legal rights as men. However, the realization of formal equality rights, although not yet complete in the Indian context, has not eliminated the subordination of women. As we will illustrate, formally equal laws can continue to produce substantially unequal results.

There are many reasons for this gap between formal equality rights and substantive inequality, including the underforcement of the law, and the inaccessibility of the legal system to the majority of Indian women. Beyond these significant factors, however, we believe that it is important to interrogate the ideological role that law plays in constituting and sustaining the subordination of women. It is within this context that we consider the relationship between equality and familial discourses. The realization of formal equality rights in the legal regulation of women inside and outside of the family has not displaced the familial ideology. We will illustrate the extent to which the legal regulation of women continues to be informed by familial ideology, long after equality rights have been attained.

Subversive Sites simultaneously argues that familial ideology must be resisted and deconstructed, while the importance of familial relationships and the roles that women play in their families neither be denied nor devalued. Feminists engaged with law must find ways to affirm these roles and relationships, without rigidly reinforcing them as women's natural destiny. We argue for a feminist legal revisioning which recognizes and challenges the hegemonic potential of law and familial ideology. We seek the subversive spaces that law might offer in reconstructing women's roles and identities in ways more conducive to their full and equal participation in social, political, economic, and cultural life.

Subversive Sites is the product of a collaborative endeavor. In collaboration, we draw on the insights offered by feminist legal scholars and activists in different parts of the world. Feminists outside of India have developed diverse approaches to feminism and law, which in our view, offer some potential for advancing the analysis of feminist legal struggles in India. We do not believe that this scholarship can be unproblematically applied to the Indian context. But we do believe that some of the insights that have emerged from this expansive and increasingly sophisticated literature may be of assistance in revisioning feminist engagement with law in India. We use the term 'we' throughout our text, in a manner that is not altogether consistent. It is primarily used in relation to our authorship, that is, referring to our arguments and opinions. But, we also use 'we' in a rather broader sense that is intended to engage the reader in the challenges and dilemmas presented. As Martha Minow writes 'My use of "we" ...represents an invitation to the reader to assent, to disagree, but above all, to engage with this focus. I use "we" moreover, to emphasize the human authorship of the problems and solutions at hand and to avoid locutions that eliminate human pronouns.'[1] We use 'we' in much the same way. We do not purport to be speaking on behalf of anyone other than ourselves. But, we are inviting the reader to engage in the dilemmas and problems we raise—to agree, to disagree, but as Minow notes, above all to engage. By using 'we', we attempt to avoid the false objectivism of the detached author, and to capture the sense of perspective, location and participation that is essential for scholarship and for the resolution of the dilemmas that confront all of us who endeavor to use law to advance progressive social movements.

In chapter 1, we set out our understanding of the role of law in feminist struggles for social change. We begin by reviewing some of the different approaches to law that have been developed in the literature on women and law in India which, in our view, do not yet capture the complex and contradictory nature of law. Drawing on the insights of feminist legal studies, we argue for a reconceptualization of the role of law, which can better capture both the limitations of law, and its possibilities in struggles for social change. We argue that feminist engagement with law should be revisioned as a discursive struggle, where feminists seek to displace previously dominant understandings of women's roles and identities. We then attempt to briefly review the history of the movements for women's rights, and attempt to reread this history of engaging with law as discursive struggle.

In chapter 2, we begin to explore familial ideology and the sexual division of labour in the legal regulation of women. The chapter begins with a review of the concepts of family, familial ideology and the sexual division of labour, as we deploy them in our analysis. We argue that despite the diversity of family forms and experiences in India, it is possible to identify a dominant familial ideology, based on the ideal of the joint family, and certain prescribed roles for women and men therein. We then examine some of the ways in which this dominant familial ideology shapes the legal regulation of women, both inside and outside of the family. Our discussion is organized around two different dimensions of familial ideology: moral regulation through which women are constituted as, and judged in accordance with the standards of, loyal wives and self-sacrificing wives; and economic regulation through which women are constituted as economically dependent. The way in which familial ideology is implicated in the oppression of women, and in reinforcing women's economic dependency extends far beyond the actual legal regulation of the family in personal laws. Familial ideology and the assumption of women's traditional roles as economically dependent wives and mothers extends into the legal regulation of women in the labour market, and even to the (de)regulation of women in the new economic policies. Chapter 2 explores the influence of this familial ideology in the areas of family law, criminal law, labour law, and the new economic policies. Rather than simply highlighting laws that explicitly discriminate against women, this chapter explores the extent to which assumptions about women's roles in the family are deeply embedded in the law, including many laws that have been designed for women's benefit. We consider the extent to which familial ideology informs judicial approaches to these formally equally laws, to produce considerably less than equal results for women.

Familial ideology not only continues to inform the legal regulation of women. It also operates to limit and undermine attempts to address women's subordination in and through law. In chapter 3, we further explore the relationship between the discourse of equality and familial ideology, in the context of constitutional sex discrimination challenges. In particular, this chapter will explore the extent to which familial ideology has informed and undermined efforts to challenge laws that explicitly discriminate against women. It examines some of the efforts to use fundamental rights to equality in Articles 14, 15 and 16 of the Constitution to challenge legal rules and provisions that discriminate against women. In so doing, attention is focused on the extent to which familial ideology has informed the judicial understanding of gender difference and thereby undermined efforts to use equality rights to advance women's claims.

As the chapter will demonstrate, judicial approaches to equality have been overwhelmingly influenced by a formal approach to equality, that is, an approach in which equality is equated with sameness, and in which only those who are the same are to be treated equally. This formal approach to equality stands in contrast to a substantive approach, which directs attention to the question of historic and systemic disadvantage. In considering these two models of equality in greater detail, we argue that feminists need to direct their attention to developing this substantive model, which holds greater promise for women's struggles. However, as we also illustrate in this chapter, the formal model of equality continues to dominate judicial thinking, and focuses attention on the question of the relevance of gender difference. We identify several approaches to gender difference—protectionist, sameness and compensatory. We argue that the judiciary more often than not seems to adopt a protectionist approach, in which women are assumed to be naturally different and weaker than men, and thus in need of protection. In adopting such a protectionist approach to gender difference, in which women are seen as different from men and in need of protection, the courts have been able to uphold virtually any legislative distinction on the basis of sex. We explore the ways in which familial ideology in particular has informed the judiciary's understanding of women's difference, that is, the ways in which women are constituted as different and as in need of protection in and through familial ideology. As a result, fundamental rights challenges have often operated to reinscribe the very familial and legal discourses that have constituted women as different and subordinate.

In chapter 4, we turn to examine some of the ways in which legal discourse is being used to advance the political agendas of the Hindu Right. In particular, we explore the ways in which the concepts of equality and secularism have been taken up, and redefined by the Hindu Right in accordance with their vision of the world. We further examine the ways in which the Hindu Right has appropriated specific legal issues relating to women, such as violence against women, obscenity, and the reform of discriminatory personal laws. We explore the role of familial ideology in the discursive strategies of the Hindu Right. We examine the ways in which the discourses of equality, secularism, and familialism have been deployed by the Hindu Right in an effort to rearticulate a traditional, yet thoroughly modern, identity for women in Indian society.

Through this chapter, we begin to see a rather different dimension of law's relationship to social change. Law and legal discourse is being used by conservative and communalist forces to subvert many of the advances that have been made by women. It is not only progressive forces that can resort to law and legal discourse to advance their political claims. The Hindu Right is also engaging with law as a site of discursive struggle, where it is seeking to promote its normative vision of the world. And in so doing, it is transforming the legal terrain, and further complicating the role that law can play in feminist struggles. As we argue, law must be seen as a site of ongoing struggle between competing claims and visions of the world. In the current context, feminist engagement with law must recognize the formidable challenges presented by the claims and visions of Hindutva.

Given the limitations of law reflected in the earlier chapters, in chapter 5 we turn to consider the role the law can play in women's struggles for empowerment. Notwithstanding the limits of law, we argue that law remains an important site of struggle. The chapter returns to the argument first set out in chapter 1 that the role of law should be reconceptualized. We continue to argue for a revisioning of law as a site of discursive struggle, where competing visions of the world are fought out. After briefly reviewing the debates on the role of law and rights discourse in struggles for social change, we suggest some concrete strategies for engaging with law. We do not provide a blueprint for engaging with law; rather, we propose different ways for thinking about such engagement that will help feminists develop more complex and, hopefully, more effective strategies. We consider the specific dilemmas that arise for feminists engaging with law in the areas of law reform, litigation and legal literacy. We argue that we must bring our understanding of the complex and contradictory nature of law to each of these strategic engagements. Feminists engaged with law must complicate the legal claims they make, as well as re-evaluate their expectations.

In the context of litigation, we address the professional and ethical dilemmas that feminist lawyers experience in conducting litigation for women litigants and suggest ways for resolving such dilemmas. We also suggest ways for complicating the legal arguments that feminists deploy. In the context of law reform, we address the need to unpack and challenge the assumptions on which law is based, and to ensure that feminists' recommendations for reform do not inadvertently reinforce the deeply gendered assumptions that have contributed to women's subordination in law. And finally, we look at how legal literacy strategies might play a significant role in women's empowerment strategies, in allowing women to determine if, when and how they should resort to law. In considering each of these strategic engagements, we are attentive to the potential limitations of law; and to the ways in which engaging with law may even be detrimental to the broader project of social change. We argue that strategies for engaging with law must be firmly grounded in an understanding of the limits of law.

Is law a subversive site? Our tentative answer is that it might be, but that this question can only ever be answered partially and contingently. We believe that laws' role must constantly be interrogated, rather than assumed, and that this interrogation must always begin with the limitations of law. It is only through a careful and considered analysis of law's limitations that we can begin to reconstruct a positive role for law. If law is to be a subversive site, we must constantly remain open to revisiting and reimagining our strategies and our analysis. It is our hope that others will continue to push this analysis of law's subversive potential further, finding other questions that need to be addressed, other limitations that need to be negotiated, and new ways of imagining these struggles.

NOTES

1. Martha Minow 'Foreward: Justice Engendered' (1987) 101 *Harvard Law Review* 10 at 15.

1

Feminist Legal Revisions: Women, Law and Social Change

It is my deep belief that theoretical legal understanding and social transformation need not be oxymoronic.

Patricia Williams
*The Alchemy of Race and Rights**

But do the stories of history really teach anything at all?... Maybe it's just a hobby, something to do on a dull day. Or else it's an act of defiance: these histories may be ragged and thread-bare, patched together from worthless leftovers, but to her they are also flags, hoisted with a certain jaunty insolence, waving bravely though inconsequentially, glimpsed here and there through the trees, on the mountain roads, among the ruins, on the long march into chaos.

Margaret Atwood
The Robber Bride†

The demand for legal rights has long been a cornerstone of the women's movement in India. Social reformers in the nineteenth century, women in the independence movement, and activists in the contemporary women's movement, have all fought for women's rights and law reform. These women's rights activists have challenged laws that discriminate against women and demanded laws to prohibit violent practices against

---

* Cambridge: Harvard University Press, 1991.
† New York: Bantam, 1993.

women. In many ways, it has been these demands for 'women's rights' and 'equal rights' that have given the women's movement its political character. Many of the political campaigns for women's rights have been successful, in so far as the state responded by enacting new legislation. Laws prohibiting sati, child marriage, dowry and rape, to name but a few, have all been passed, as have laws removing obstacles to women's right to own property, suffrage, and employment, following agitations spearheaded by women's rights activists. While the specific laws often fall short of the demands of the movements for women's rights, the law has nevertheless been reformed in response to these political demands for change. Further, women's equality rights were recognized in the Constitution. More recently, the Indian state has ratified the *Convention on the Elimination of All Forms of Discrimination Against Women,*[1] which further commits the state to the promotion of women's equality.

Despite the legal victories over the years, the social, political and economic status of women has shown remarkably little improvement. There is extensive evidence of the startling amount of sexual and physical violence against women—rape, dowry and domestic violence persist in the face of legislation designed to eliminate these practices.[2] Similarly, women's socio-economic inequality has persisted in the face of the broad range of legislation intended to improve women's status.[3] Women continue to be paid less than men notwithstanding legislation designed to eliminate discrimination in remuneration. Women continue to bear the economic costs of childbirth, notwithstanding legislation designed to provide maternity benefits.[4] And the list goes on. In fact, there is increasing evidence to suggest that the socio-economic status of women in India, like other developing countries, is deteriorating. As we discuss in the next chapter, the process of global economic restructuring, being brought to India through the new economic policies which seek to maximize exports and minimize government spending, is having a devastating impact on the already precarious social and economic position of women. The gap between women's formal rights and their socio-economic status is widening.

This gap between women's formal legal rights and their continuing substantive inequality has not gone unnoticed by those involved in campaigns for law reform. The question of the role of law in struggles to improve women's status has been a recurrent dilemma. Since the early nineteenth century, movements for social and political reform have returned time and again to law. In many ways, law and legal discourse has played a central role in the struggles, and given those movements their political and discursive character. Yet, at the same time, many within these movements have expressed at least some degree of ambivalence on whether legal rights and law reform will bring about social change for women. Nor has this gap gone unnoticed within the academic writing on women and law. Some legal commentators have suggested that the problem is one of enforcement and access. Others have suggested that law alone may be unable to eliminate women's inequality. Yet others have begun to suggest that the problems are more structural, that law is informed by and serves to reinforce patriarchy.

In this chapter, we explore the question of the role of law in women's struggles for social change. We begin with a brief review of the literature on women and law in India. Notwithstanding the important insights that much of this writing has brought to the question of the gap between women's formal equality rights and substantive inequality, we argue that this literature is characterized by an under-theorization of the role of law in social change. Law is assumed to be either an instrument of change, or an instrument of oppression. We argue that this question of the role of law must be the subject of further interrogation, and that a more sophisticated analysis must be developed that can better capture law's complex and contradictory role in struggles to improve women's social, economic, political and cultural position. The chapter then argues in favour of a revisioning of the role of law. Drawing on the insights of recent feminist legal scholarship, we argue that law should be revisioned as a site of discursive struggle, where competing visions of the world are fought out. In the third section, the chapter turns to consider the central role that law has played in movements for women's rights since the nineteenth century. In reviewing this role, we illustrate the extent to which these movements have viewed law's relationship to social change with some ambivalence. We argue that these various engagements with law can be seen as discursive struggles, wherein reformers and activists sought to challenge and displace dominant understandings of gender, tradition and culture.

Women, Law and Social Change

■ Perspectives on Women and Law

A considerable literature on women and law began to emerge in the 1980s in India. Books and articles began to appear, documenting women's legal status, some arguing for reform, others celebrating past achievements. In this section, we attempt to review and characterize this literature. We argue that three very distinct perspectives are discernible in this literature: (*a*) protectionism; (*b*) equality; and (*c*) patriarchy. In the discussion that follows, we will describe each of these perspectives, and illustrate how the literature on women and law can be seen to fit within these categories. We will examine the very different understandings of gender relations within each approach, as well as the very different conceptualizations of the role of law in these relations. And we will argue that despite the important insights of much of this literature, the question of the role of law in women's struggles for social change has not yet been rendered sufficiently complex.

While we believe that the three categories that we have identified—protectionist, equality and patriarchy—are useful in characterizing and conceptualizing the literature on women and law, we are at the same time aware of the dangers of such a process of categorization. Categories, when they become rigid and inflexible, can often obscure more than they illuminate. Efforts to fit things into categories can become a process whereby the bits and pieces that do not fit are ignored or cut off. Overly rigid and inflexible categories can obscure important similarities and interconnections, and can limit the way we think about the issues before us.[5] Yet without categories, we would be unable to theorize and conceptualize the world around us: indeed, without categories, we would be unable to communicate with one another. As Angela Harris has argued, it is not that we can abandon the process of categorization, but rather that we should endeavor to 'make our categories explicitly tentative, rational and unstable, and that to do so is all the more important in a discipline like law, where abstraction[6] and 'frozen' categories are the 'norm'.[7] To return then to our efforts to categorize the literature on women and law, it is our hope that the categories we offer here, as well as others throughout the volume, are useful in conceptualizing the question of feminist engagement with law. At the same time, we recognize the need of the categories to remain flexible, and to recognize that not all writing about women and law will fit neatly and unequivocally into a single category. Indeed, it may be that the same writer may at one point seem to be informed by one perspective yet at another point informed by a rather different one. Our effort, then, is not so much one of classifying particular writers into particular perspectives, as it is of thinking about and conceptualizing the debates at a more general level.

Protectionism

In the first, and in our view, most problematic approach, the relationship between women and law has been posited as one of protection. These writers have emphasized the need for law to protect women who are assumed to be 'naturally weaker' than men.[8] For example, J. P. Atray in a chapter entitled 'The Weaker Sex' writes:

> This position of helplessness is so much visible among women in general that it has ceased to be any longer of much significance even to themselves.[9]

This protectionist approach simply accepts traditional and patriarchal discourses that construct women as weak, biologically inferior, modest, and so on. These and other so-called 'feminine' characteristics are perceived as natural, and thus, as the appropriate starting place for legal regulation. Writers within this approach often wax eloquently of women's roles within the family—roles which are assumed to be natural and sacred. To quote again from Atray:

> A woman's position as a wife has been given the highest place over all other roles which she is required to play because it is here that she is required to perform the most arduous of duties and the most difficult of responsibilities.... As a wife, she is beyond everything else and sits on a pedestal as high and as glorious as the imagination can reach.[10]

Women's roles as mothers are similarly celebrated, and naturalized as an inevitable consequence of the biological differences between women and men.

In this literature, the role of law is unproblematically asserted as protecting women. Laws that continue to treat women differently than men are accepted as a necessary part of this protection. This protectionist approach is often reflected in judicial approaches to the question of the relevance of gender difference. Since women are seen as weak and subordinate—and thereby in need of protection—women must be treated differently in law. Women's ostensibly natural differences are deployed to justify any differential treatment in law, and in effect, operate to preclude any entitlement to equality.[11] This approach is firmly located within patriarchal discourses. It does not problematize the way in which law treats women, nor does it consider women's subordinate status. While it is concerned with women as the subject of law, and even as a subject of rights, this literature is not within a feminist theoretical tradition. At most, writers within this approach call for a greater enforcement of the laws designed to protect women. The assumptions that women are 'naturally' weak, 'naturally' different, and 'naturally' in need of law's protection, are never interrogated but rather so universalized and naturalized that they are simply taken for granted.

Equality

In the second, and perhaps most common approach in the literature, the relationship between women and law is seen as one of promoting equality. This literature has primarily focused on providing empirical reviews of laws that affect women. Writers within this approach have tended to provide comprehensive reviews of the range of legal provisions that affect women, from personal laws to criminal laws, to labour laws. This literature highlights both laws that continue to discriminate against women and successful challenges to such discriminatory laws.[12] Writers within the approach have also tended to emphasize problems in relation to the under-enforcement of existing legal provisions which govern women's equality rights.[13] Implicit in much of this work is the assumption that law can play an important role in advancing women's equality by removing the legal obstacles that have limited women's full and equal participation. While this work recognizes that there is still some distance to go before women's rights are adequately protected in law, there is a general optimism regarding the extent to which much of this road has already been traveled. Again, the positive role of law has more often been assumed than interrogated.

To the extent that the question of the role of law has been specifically addressed within this approach the dominant view that emerges is one of law as social engineering. This view is found in both academic writing and government reports. For example, the *Report of the Committee on the Status of Women in India* places considerable importance on the role of law: 'One of the main characteristics of modern society is a heavy reliance on law to bring about social change'.[14] This role is highlighted in post-colonial states:

> The tasks of social reconstruction, development and nation building all call for major changes in the social order, to achieve which legislation is one of the main instruments. It can act directly, as a norm setter, or indirectly, providing institutions which accelerate social change by making it more acceptable.[15]

While the Report includes recommendations for sweeping legal reforms, this emphasis on the role of law in social engineering is not unqualified. For example the Report also notes some of the limitations of law in this process. 'But legislation cannot by itself change society. To translate these rights into reality is the task of other agencies. Public opinion has to be molded to accept these rights'.[16] The Report, while noting the role of the judiciary and the executive levels of government in this process, further observes that neither level of government has fulfilled this role.

With regard to the courts, the Committee notes that legislation has often been narrowly interpreted, and that the courts have often 'failed to give effect to the principles underlying the legislation'.[17] The subsequent focus of the Report is on revealing the areas in which the implementation of the law falls short of the principles it articulates.

Other government reports have echoed this view of the limits of law. The *National Perspective Plan* has observed:

> It is...necessary to realize that there are limits to the extent to which changes can be effected by law. Attempts at bringing about changes in women's status through either legislation or judicial activism can achieve little success without a simultaneous movement to change the social and economic structures and the culture of society.[18]

The view that emerges from both the *Report of the Committee on the Status of Women* and the *National Perspective Plan* is that law is a necessary but insufficient part of a more general strategy of bringing about social change. These reports, along with other literature in which the role of law is qualified, go some distance in recognizing the limitations of law in bringing about social change. These reports, however, remain firmly located within the law as social engineering thesis. As such, this literature does not question law's commitment to social change, nor does it consider the role of law in the subordination of women, beyond the discriminatory character of some laws. It does not interrogate the ideological character of law in constituting and sustaining unequal power relations beyond the liberal understanding of explicitly discriminatory laws. Rather, its focus is on both law reform and law enforcement.

This literature and its emphasis on equality can be seen within the context of liberal feminism. Liberal feminism begins from the basic premises of liberal theory: individualism and equality. Accordingly, the focus of liberal feminism has been on women as individuals—in particular, the extent to which women have been denied the status of individuals, and denied the liberal goal of equality. Liberal feminism has placed considerable attention on law. According to this approach, law has contributed to women's oppression by exclusion. Women's oppression is understood largely as a result of discriminatory treatment. Thus, law can contribute to overcoming that oppression by the creation of a legal order that includes women on an equal footing. As Boyd and Sheehy observe, underlying this approach is the '...liberal assumption that women's status...could be elevated by fair and neutral laws applied equally to women and men'.[19] Liberal feminist perspectives focus on eliminating statutory provisions and language that explicitly discriminate on the basis of sex, and/or reinforced sexual stereotypes. According to this perspective, women should be treated the same as men, and gender difference should be irrelevant in law.

Liberal feminist perspectives typically advocate for reform of the discriminatory laws. Legislation that discriminates on its face between women and men must be made gender neutral. Alternatively, legislation that discriminates in its impact must be reformulated to correct this impact. Liberal feminist perspectives on law have also developed a concern with equal opportunity and equality of result. In order to create conditions of equality for women, liberal feminists may argue in favour of affirmative action, that is, for rules that treat women preferentially in order to create substantive equality. Liberal feminism provides some important insights into the legal regulation of women. It has focused on and identified the various forms of discrimination against women in law, and has provided some of the major impetus for waves of law reform establishing formal legal equality for women. However, it is also limited in some very significant respects. There is, for example, no analysis within liberal feminism of the underlying structures of oppression. The focus on the individual, and in particular, on the equal treatment of the individual in law leaves the economic, social, cultural and political institutions that produce and reinforce women's oppression uninterrogated. There is, accordingly, no consideration of the role of law in transcending this oppression—the role is simply assumed rather than problematized.

The literature on women and law in India that emphasizes equality can be seen to be characterized by the same insights and limitations as liberal feminism. The literature has focused on, and brought attention to laws that treat women differently, and the need to reform such discriminatory laws. The literature has directly challenged the assumptions of the protectionist approach that women and men are 'naturally' different, and that these differences justify any and all differential treatment in law. This literature has insisted that the assumption of the relevance of difference be challenged. Indeed, according to this approach, the starting assumption should be one of equality not difference. This literature, like liberal feminist perspectives to law, more generally, has been important in challenging prevailing assumptions about women, in revealing the extent to which women continue to be discriminated against in law, and in demanding that laws be reformed to better reflect and promote women's right to full and equal participation in the world around them.

At the same time, however, this literature can be seen to be characterized by the same limitations as liberal feminism. Within this literature, the role of law is assumed, and the underlying structures of oppression are given scant attention. Although some of this literature recognizes that law alone will not be able to bring about all the changes necessary for women's full and equal participation in society, there is nevertheless little question that law has an important and positive contribution to make to this change. There is no interrogation of the deeper ways in which law may be implicated in women's socio-economic inequality. There is no consideration of the ways in which law may operate to reinforce the very structures that produce and reproduce this inequality. In attempting to reveal the limitations of law, it is not enough to identify discrimination, and recommend reform. Such an approach, at least implicitly, assumes that equality for women can be achieved through the elimination of discriminatory laws. Equality, in this view, is equated with formally equal treatment. The history of the women's movement is itself evidence enough of the inadequacies of such an approach. Laws upon laws have been passed; yet women's socio-economic inequality persists. Equality rights may be of considerable symbolic importance, and are certainly a necessary part of the struggle to remove obstacles (legal and otherwise) to women's substantive participation. But, formal equality rights have not been able to secure this participation.

Similarly, it is also not enough to draw attention to the under-enforcement of law, and recommend ways to ensure more efficient enforcement. The emphasis of this approach, which looks to increasing women's access and enforcement through such means as sensitizing the judiciary to women's issues, legal aid, family courts, and increased legal awareness for women, similarly assumes that law, if it is effectively enforced, can remedy the social problems for which it is designed. This emphasis on enforcement, although important, presumes that law can be effectively enforced. There is serious reason to question the institutional capacity of the legal system in India to realize the rights for its population. Moreover, this emphasis on enforcement obscures the question of the role that law plays in women's subordination. Eliminating discrimination and improving enforcement are not insignificant reforms. But, without a deeper understanding of the role of law in women's subordination, these reforms may only lead to further disillusionment with the legal system.

Patriarchy

A third approach in the literature on women and law is one in which law is seen as an instrument of patriarchal oppression. Nandita Haksar's ground-breaking work *The Demystification of Law for Women* examined the way in which law has reflected patriarchal oppression.[20] Haksar not only pointed out the laws that continue to discriminate against women, but further connected these laws, and judicial interpretations of these laws, to patriarchal social relations in which women have been oppressed. A number of writers have since attempted to further develop this analysis of the patriarchal nature of law.[21]

Lina Gonsalves' more recent analysis in her study *Women and the Law* can be seen as an example of scholarship within this law as patriarchy framework.[22] Gonsalves focuses on the enforcement (and lack thereof) of laws that were intended to benefit women, and argues that 'law enforcers...discriminate between women and men and unconsciously tend to reflect traditional and rigid attitudes towards women'.[23] She attempts to highlight the extent to which 'the police, public prosecutors and the judges, who are products of patriarchal society, are by and large biased against women, and...help to perpetuate and preserve the oppression of women'.[24] Gonsalves examines a broad range of laws affecting women—succession, maintenance, custody, divorce, rape, dowry—and attempts to illustrate the patriarchal biases in the courts' interpretation of these laws. The study is important, in its effort to reveal the biases and unstated assumptions about women that inform the case law, and undermine women's rights. Gonsalves is careful in the introduction and conclusion in stating that she does not believe that law is unimportant in women's struggles. She argues for example that 'we cannot ignore the law because it affects our daily life,' and that it would be inaccurate to suggest that the history of feminist engagement with law has not brought about significant change. Her focus is on the need to eliminate the patriarchal biases affecting the implementation of laws. However, at times her analysis of specific laws seems to undermine this position. For example she concludes that not only have laws intending to address violence against women such as the *Dowry Prohibition Act*, 'achieved little in transforming the social order and uprooting dowry as a social evil,' but moreover that:

> The outcome of trials and the unwillingness of the police to probe violence against women at home and in society has led to a situation in which the law as a whole can easily be taken to be an instrument of patriarchal oppression.[25]

In this view, law is seen as an instrument of patriarchy. It can be seen to loosely correspond to radical feminist perspective on law.[26] Radical feminism attempts to provide a more structural analysis of women's oppression, based on the concept of patriarchy. As Supriya Akerkar succinctly describes 'the context of radical feminism is that gender inequalities are the outcome of an autonomous system of patriarchy and that gender inequalities are the primary form of social inequality'.[27] Boyd and Sheehy further describe:

> This analysis locates women's oppression in patriarchy, a systematic expression of male domination and control over women which permeates all social, political and economic institutions. The desire for supremacy, the psychological pleasure of power, and male fear of female sexual and reproductive capacity are identified as the motivating forces of patriarchy.[28]

Radical feminist perspectives of law tend to examine the ways in which it is informed by and serves to reinforce patriarchal social relationships.

> Radical feminists focus on revealing the patriarchal nature of law and its oppressive impact on all women. Central concerns include the ways in which the legal system reinforces male control over women's sexuality and lives, together with the exclusion or marginalization of women's values and priorities in legal structures and processes.

Law is seen to be based on male norms, male experience and male domination. The focus of analysis is often on the legal regulation of sexuality and of violence. As Boyd and Sheehy describe '[l]aws governing reproduction, sexual assault, and pornography are viewed as extensions of patriarchal control over female sexuality, with violence against women reinforcing this control'.[29] Radical feminism has been an important contribution in attempting to locate women's oppression within broader structures of gender oppression, as well as in revealing 'the ways in which even the most intimate and personal relationships are political'.[30] In the context of law, it has been important in revealing the importance of the legal regulation of sexuality and of violence in the oppression of women. However, it is a perspective that is also limited in some important respects. It has been criticized for its understanding of patriarchy as ahistorical and universalistic; for its construction of women only as victims, rather than as agents of resistance and change, as well as for its focus on gender oppression to the exclusion of other forms of oppression. The exclusive focus on sexuality as the site of women's oppression leaves out the various other sites that contribute in equally significant ways to women's oppression, such as the family, and the economy. The complex and specific nature of relations of oppression tends to be reduced to monolithic and highly general explanations.

Further, although radical feminism offers a more systemic analysis of the nature of women's oppression, including the ways in which this oppression is sustained in law, this systemic analysis often does not extend to the question of the role of law in social change. Radical feminists often turn to the law to address the oppression of women, without sufficiently problematizing the role that law can play in overcoming this oppression. For example, the analysis of sexual violence against women, including the ways in which the law has sustained and condoned that violence, is often countered by an appeal to strengthen the criminal sanctions against sexual violence against women. After critiquing the role of the law in the oppression of women, radical feminists often turn to the law. There is a tension in radical feminism between their understanding of the law and the state as patriarchal, and their understanding of the role of the law and the state in struggling against the oppression of women; a tension which is never adequately addressed. Radical feminist perspectives on law have been important in highlighting the negative and deeply problematic stereotypes of women that inform law and law enforcement. Further, such radical feminist perspectives are also an important contribution in directing attention to the deeper structures of law and legal discourse, and suggesting a connection between these structures and women's oppression. However, in our view this radical feminist framework does not go far enough in explaining the role of law in women's oppression nor in women's struggles. It is not sufficient to simply assert that law is patriarchal, or that the law makers are sexist. The vision of law as an instrument of patriarchy tells us very little about the precise workings of law, and even less about if and how women can use law.

■ Towards Feminist Legal Studies

To the limited extent that the question of the role of law in women's struggles for social change has been considered in legal scholarship, we have thus identified two different feminist positions: a dominant and liberal feminist view of law as social engineering, in which law is seen to have discriminated against women, but which with reform can operate as an instrument of liberation for women; and a dissenting, radical feminist view of law as an instrument of patriarchal oppression. Again, while it is important to recognize and applaud the contribution that this literature has made to the study of women and law and to the development of feminist approaches to law, it is at the same time important to recognize the limitations of this literature on theorizing the role of law and social change. In our view, neither of these approaches captures the ambivalence that has characterized successive movements for women's rights. The dichotomous views—of law as either an instrument of social change, or an instrument of patriarchal oppression—fail to adequately capture the complex and contradictory nature of law.

These two feminist perspectives on the role of law in social change do not exhaust the possible range of feminist perspectives on law, nor the actual writings of feminist scholars engaged in law. Feminist legal studies have begun to explore the question of the role of law in feminist struggles from a multiplicity of perspectives, many of which defy simple classification. More recent feminist scholarship has begun to specifically address these tensions and contradictions in women's relationship to law. In this section, we briefly review two perspectives in law that we believe are of increasing importance in understanding the complex and contradictory nature of law: socialist feminism and poststructuralist feminism. We then examine the recent writings of several feminist scholars in India whose work defies any simple classification and in our view, signifies the beginning of a far more sophisticated analysis of the role of law in feminist struggles.

Socialist Feminism
Socialist feminism is based on an analysis of both gender and class, that is, it understands the oppression of women as deeply rooted in both patriarchal and capitalist relations. Within law, this approach not only examines particular laws that discriminate against women, but further explores the role of this legal regulation in reinforcing women's oppression. The focus of the analysis is often on the ideological nature of law, that is, the way in which law operates to reinforce unequal power relations by naturalizing and universalizing these relations. As Susan Boyd describes: 'feminists working on law's ideological aspect have explored the ways in which law as privileged state discourse reproduces, often indirectly, economic or sexual power through complex ideological processes, often including non-state institutions such as "the family"'.[31] A socialist feminist perspective attempts to reveal the complex and often contradictory ways in which the law operates in particular circumstances to shape and reinforce relations of class and gender. For example, the analysis might attempt to reveal the assumption of women's economic dependency that informs the legal regulation of women within the labour market and the family, and thus operates to reinforce women's subordinate role within the family. At the same time, a socialist feminist approach would attempt to highlight the contradictions within the legal regulation of women. While some laws protect women, other laws, indeed even the same laws in different contexts, can be used against women.

Socialist feminism directly challenges the basic economic, political and social structures of society. As an approach to law, socialist feminism has attempted to reveal law's role within a capitalist and patriarchal state; particularly, its role in sustaining and legitimating unequal power relations within this state. Socialist feminist legal scholars have attempted to explore the relationship between law, state and society, and the way in which this relationship is implicated in women's oppression.[32] It is a theoretical approach that also focuses on women's agency and resistance. The emphasis on both the contradictory nature of law, and the importance of resistance is such that law remains an important site of struggle, although victories within the legal arena must be seen and evaluated within the broader context of economic, political and social relations. Thus, an analysis informed by a socialist feminist perspective might advocate particular law reforms, while at the same time recognizing the more general limitations of such individual victories. Such reforms, like campaigns for formal equality for women, are seen as necessary but individually insufficient in women's struggle for social change.

Socialist feminism has been important in providing a more structural analysis of women's oppression that is attentive to the importance of both gender and class relations, and to the contextually and historically specific forms of women's oppression. However, socialist feminist approaches have also been subject to criticism for not having adequately explored the diversity of the forms of women's oppression—particularly, for not adequately recognizing and theorizing the significance of race, culture and religion. In the context of India, some have argued that socialist feminism fails to adequately address or theorize the role of religion in women's lives.[33] While this is an important criticism, some scholars have argued that the historical materialist methodology of socialist feminism and its emphasis on not prioritizing oppressions provides a basis for integrating these factors into its analysis in a way that does not seem possible within either liberal or radical feminism.[34] In this vein, more recent socialist feminist analyses have begun to explore the complex ways in which law shapes and reinforces relations of gender, class and race. Akerkar argues that socialist feminism has expanded the focus of its analysis to include a multiplicity of differences between women, and in so doing, has 'displaced the unified concept of woman and included class, nation, race, etc., differences within the body of [its] analysis'.[35] Although socialist feminist perspectives *on law* have not yet included a consideration of religion in women's lives, there is no reason that its analysis of historically and materially specific structures cannot be similarly extended to include this important factor. Indeed, socialist feminism's attention to the relationship between law, state and society, and to the role of the family and ideology in the oppression of women suggests that it may be well suited to the task of analyzing religion in the Indian context.

Poststructuralist Feminism

More recently, yet another perspective on feminism and law has emerged: poststructuralist or postmodernist feminism. This perspective draws on poststructuralist theory more generally, which eludes any simple, or singular definition. The various strands, however, all share a common object of critique of the basic philosophical tenets of the Enlightenment—rationality, objectivity, subjectivity. Poststructuralism rejects the concepts of objectivity and neutrality, insisting instead that knowledge is a product of perspective and thus always partial. It similarly rejects the Enlightenment's understanding of subjectivity, that is, of an individual subject that exists prior to its interaction with the society around it; a stable, coherent, self-constituting subject.[36] Poststructuralism argues that the subject does not exist prior to language or discourse, but rather, is produced through discourse. As Chris Weedon writes, 'poststructuralism proposes a subjectivity which is precarious, contradictory and in process, constantly being reconstituted in discourse each time we think or speak'.[37]

The poststructuralist challenge to objectivity and universal knowledge has lead many feminists to reject it as politically disempowering and nihilistic. If all knowledge is partial and contingent, how can we make normative claims about the oppression of women? Others have suggested that the poststructuralist critique of the subject undermines the possibility of agency on the part of the feminist subject, an agency which is essential to politics of resistance and change.[38] Poststructuralist feminists have argued that the recognition of the contingency and partiality of knowledge does not undermine our ability to engage in normative debate. Nor does poststructuralism necessarily involve a repudiation of agency. Rather, many have argued that it is precisely the way in which subjects are constituted in and through multiple and contradictory discourses that creates space for agency. Our subjectivities are never fixed but always in the process of being reconstituted. We negotiate our way through a multiplicity of discourses exercising reflection, choice, and action, although this agency is constituted and limited by our particular position within intersecting discourses. Despite the arguments that poststructuralist theory undermines the feminist project,[39] poststructuralist feminists have attempted to illustrate the ways in which this theory can in fact further our understanding of the subordination of women.[40] Poststructuralist feminism does not reduce women's oppression to singular or universal factors, but rather examines the multiple and shifting dimensions of women's oppression.

Feminist legal scholars have begun to adopt the insights of poststructuralism in examining the way in which law has contributed to women's subordination, and in exploring the future of legal strategies to overcome this subordination. Some feminist legal scholars have adopted the insights of poststructuralism to deconstruct the debates that have been plaguing feminist legal theory, such as the sameness/difference debate.[41] Others have used these insights on the discursive construction of knowledge and subjectivity to develop more complex and nuanced analyses of feminism and law.[42] Angela Harris, for example, has argued for the need to develop an anti-essentialist feminist perspective as a way of addressing the limitations of radical feminism, which posits an abstract and universal essence to women and oppression, and which has thus obscured the important differences among women, particularly, differences of race.[43] The insights of poststructuralism have thus been useful in addressing and integrating the challenge of difference and diversity among women.

Further, the insights of poststructuralism have been useful in examining law as discourse, and the ways in which legal discourses constitute women and gender identity, including law itself. Mary Joe Frug has argued:

> The postmodern position locating human experience as inescapably within language suggests that feminists should not overlook the constructive function of legal language as a critical frontier for feminist reforms. To put this 'principle' more bluntly, legal discourse should be recognized as a site of political struggle over sex difference.[44]

Mary Joe Frug argues that legal rules 'encode the female body with meanings', and legal discourse

> then explains and rationalizes these meanings by an appeal to the 'natural' differences between the sexes, differences that the rules themselves help to produce. The formal reasons of legal neutrality conceals the way in which legal rules participate in the construction of these meanings.[45]

Feminist poststructuralist perspectives allow us to examine the competing and complex discourses that constitute women, including law itself.[46] It allows us to be attentive to the conflicts and contradictions within and among these discourses; that not all law constructs women in the same way. Some legal discourses have been liberating whereas others continue to be quite oppressive.

New Feminist Legal Studies in India

In reviewing these different feminist perspectives of law, we do not mean to suggest that either socialist feminism or poststructuralist feminism have provided all the answers to feminist inquiries into law. But, this scholarship shows that feminist legal studies have begun to develop increasingly complex and nuanced analyses of law's role in women's oppression, and its potential role in challenging the oppression. Feminist legal scholarship that has been developed outside of India cannot be unproblematically applied to the specificity of the struggles of the women's movement in India. As women of colour in North America and England, as well as in the so-called 'Third World' have argued, this scholarship has often obscured the multiplicity of differences that exist among women. The heterogeneity and specificity of women's experiences, oppressions and struggles have often been erased. Vasuki Nesiah, in her critique of American feminist legal theory, has argued that this scholarship has been largely oblivious of the question of global contradictions, and the impact of these contradictions on women located in developing countries. She further argues that to the extent that women in the 'Third World' have been addressed in this scholarship, they have tended to be constructed in universal and essential terms, and often 'as passive victims of male oppression'.[47] Nesiah argues that feminist legal theory must strive for a greater internationality, by paying closer attention to global contradictions, and to the specific socially constructed conditions in which women are located.[48]

Despite these limitations in the feminist legal scholarship, the theoretical debates that have emerged from the specific experiences of women engaging with law may still have resonance in India. The kinds of questions about the role of law that have begun to be asked by feminist theorists both inside and outside of India are strikingly similar, even though the specific experiences of oppression through and engagement with law may be worlds apart. Some of the most interesting and insightful work that has initially been written comes from disciplines other than law. Feminist historians have played a leading role in the articulation of a more complex understanding of the role of law in social change. Tanika Sarkar, Lata Mani, Janaki Nair and Prem Chowdhry are among the feminist historians who have critically examined the complex relationship between law in colonial India and women's subordination.[49] In addition to feminist historians, feminist work on law has begun to emerge within the social sciences and humanities more generally. In their ground-breaking discursive analysis of the Shah Bano case, Zakia Pathak and Rajeswari Sunder Rajan have examined law as discourse, and the way in which this discourse constitutes subjects.[50] More recently, economist Bina Agarwal's study of women and land rights in South Asia has explored the complex obstacles to women's land-ownership and control, and provided an insightful analysis of both the importance and limitations of law, and land rights in particular, for women.[51]

Recently, legal scholarship has begun to develop these feminist perspectives. Archana Parashar, in her study of family law reform, examines and evaluates some of the insights of debates within feminist legal studies.[52] She uses the insights of these debates to further her understanding of the role of law in social change, while rejecting those aspects of the debates that do not fit the Indian context. Parashar, in developing her analysis of the role of legislation and the promotion of gender equality, reformulates the theoretical insights of feminist legal studies to better fit the specificity of the legal regulation of women in India. While Parashar argues for the importance of law reform in women's struggles, her view of the nature of the role of law reform is informed by a consideration of the limits of law. She argues, for example, that 'instead of dismissing law reform as a means of achieving equality for women, it is more productive to realize the limitations of law and have appropriate expectations that law reform by itself will be insufficient to change society and end women's oppression'.[53] In her view, law can serve an important symbolic value: 'Symbolic legislation can be of liberating value as it can provide a focus around which forces of change can mobilize'.[54] In this respect, Parashar's work marks an important shift in feminist legal analysis, in its integration of rigorous and detailed legal analysis with a feminist perspective attentive to both the limitations and possibilities of law.

Other scholars have similarly begun to complicate feminist engagement with law.[55] Flavia Agnes' work has been an important contribution to the development of more complex and nuanced analyses of feminist engagement with law. Throughout her work, Agnes interrogates the impact of law reforms on women, and questions whether laws intended for women's benefit have lived up to their promise. Her work on violence against women, for example, has addressed the failure of law to adequately address the reality of violence.[56] Through a detailed examination of laws addressing rape, dowry, domestic violence, prostitution, indecent representation of women, sati, and sex determination tests, Agnes explores the broader questions of why law has had so little impact in women's lives, and whether law can bring about social change. In her analysis of rape laws, for example, Agnes reveals the ultimate failure of

the campaign for reform in the early 1980s to bring about a transformation in the definition of rape. She illustrates the extent to which 'the
same old notions of chastity, virginity, premium on marriage and fear of
female sexuality are reflected in the judgments of the post-amendment
law'.[57] Her analysis of the other legislative provisions intended to protect
women against violence similarly attempts to reveal the extent to which
the reforms did not fundamentally challenge and transform the underlying
assumptions about women's identities. Dowry laws, for example, failed
both to challenge attitudes about women and marriage including parental
pressure to 'marry off' their daughters, and to link the problem of dowry
with women's property rights in the parents' homes.[58] Agnes draws
attention to the fact that the Indian state has been all too willing to pass
new criminal laws to address these multiple forms of violence against
women and raises questions about the wisdom of conferring such powers
on the state.

> Each law vests more power with the state enforcement machinery.
> Each enactment stipulates more stringent punishment, which is con-
> trary to progressive legal reform theory of leniency to the accused.
> Can progressive legal changes for women's rights exist in a vacuum
> in direct contrast to other progressive legal theories of civil rights?[59]

Agnes is highly skeptical of this concentration of criminal law power in
the state in the name of protecting women. Her skepticism is heightened
by the fact that some of the laws 'which purport to protect women from
violence actually penalize the woman'.[60] As she observes, '[i]nstead of
empowering women, the laws strengthen the state'.[61]

Agnes' work on law has pushed feminist analyses well beyond the
either/or dichotomy of law as a mere instrument of social change, or an
instrument of patriarchy.[62] In going beneath the surface of legal discourse,
Agnes is attempting to reveal the assumptions embedded in this discourse, and the need to challenge these assumptions. And while she is
critical of protectionist legislation which vests increasing powers in the
state, she does not eschew the role of law in feminist struggles. Rather,
her work attempts to bring out some of the contradictions in the role of
law while at the same time making concrete suggestions for how law
might be made to better empower women.[63] Alongside her careful analyses of legal provisions and judicial interpretations of those provisions,
Agnes has begun to ask difficult questions about how law operates in
women's lives; questions which she does not presume to have simple or
straightforward answers.

Agnes' work has also been important in bringing attention to the issue of religious and communal differences among women. She has attempted to reveal the extent to which the contemporary women's movement has assumed the commonality of gender oppression. She argues that despite the movement's occasional attention to issues involving dalits, tribals, and landless labourers, and communal conflicts, it has

...overall worked from a presumption that gender lines can be drawn up clearly and sharply in a patriarchal society and within these parameters sexual assault and domestic violence affect women equally across class, culture and religious barriers.[64]

Agnes is critical of both the women's movement's failure to develop an explicitly secular agenda, and the resulting, though unstated, Hindu norm that has come to characterize the movement. She shows how the ideology of the women's movement adopted many of the symbols of the dominant Hindu culture, such as the 'mythical symbols of shakti and kali', along with a broad range of other 'Hindu iconography and Sanskrit idioms denoting women's power'.[65] Agnes further attempts to illustrate how this unstated Hindu norm has affected the legal strategies of the women's movement. In her view, it has resulted in insufficient attention being directed to discriminatory aspects of Hindu personal law, and inadvertently, supported the 'fiction popularised by the fundamentalists that the Hindu Code is the perfect family code which ought to be extended to other religious denominations in order to liberate women'.[66]

■ Revisioning Law

Feminist legal studies have begun to make important contributions in advancing the understanding of the role that law has played in women's oppression, and to the potential role that it can play in challenging that oppression. The new scholarship in India has begun to move beyond the instrumentalism and essentialism of earlier literature. Law is posited as neither a simple instrument of social engineering, nor of oppression, but rather, increasingly understood as a complex and contradictory force. This new scholarship has also begun to interrogate the assumptions about gender and the nature of women's oppression that characterized earlier work. It has begun to explore the diversity of oppression that women experience, across not only class lines, but also religion, ethnicity and culture, and the way in which the law has been implicated in that oppression.

We want to continue to push this analysis forward, and further reveal the complex and contradictory nature of law. By complex and contradictory, we mean to suggest that law's relationship to women's oppression is not always the same; law does not always operate in the same way, nor does it always produce consistent results. Carol Smart has described this contradictory role of the law in women's subordination as the 'uneven development of law'. As she argues, this concept

> ...allows for an analysis of the law that recognizes the distinctions between law-as-legislation and the effects of law, or law in practice. It rejects completely any concept of law as a unity which simply progresses, regresses, or reappears as a cycle of history to repeat itself. It perceives law as operating on a number of dimensions at the same time. Law is not identified as a simple tool of patriarchy or capitalism. To analyze law in this way creates the possibility of seeing law both as a means of liberation and, at the same time, as a means of the reproduction of an oppressive social order. Law both facilitates change and is an obstacle to change.[67]

Law reinforces relations of subordination, at the same time as it provides an important source of resistance and change.[68] It is this contradictory nature of law that we believe feminist legal studies must illuminate, and that we seek to reveal in this volume.

Our analysis relies heavily on the insights of poststructural feminism. We believe that it is helpful to understand law as discourse. Discourse analysis, developed primarily from the influence of Foucault's work, explores the relationship between knowledge, power and language, more specifically the way in which power is deployed and dispersed in and through multiple discursive fields. As Chris Weedon describes,

> Discursive fields consist of competing ways of giving meaning to the world, and of organizing social institutions and processes. They offer the individual a range of modes of subjectivity.[69]

It is in and through discourse that subjects are constituted, that is, that we become conscious and thinking subjects. We negotiate our way through complex and shifting discursive fields that constitute us in complex, contingent and often contradictory ways. Further, not all discourses are equal. Weedon describes:

> Within a discursive field, for instance, that of the law or the family, not all discourse will carry equal weight or power. Some will account

for and justify the appropriateness of the status quo. Others will give rise to challenges to existing practices from within or will contest the very basis of current organization and the selective interests which it represents.[70]

In our view, it is useful to understand law as discourse. A discursive analysis allows us to explore law as a particular way of giving meaning to the world. It allows us to understand the extent to which, in Lucinda Finley's words, '[l]aw is, among other things, a language, a form of discourse, and a system through which meanings are reflected and constructed and cultural practices organized'.[71] As Finley further argues, law is 'a particularly authoritative discourse':

> Law can pronounce definitively what something is or is not and how a situation or event is to be understood. The concepts, categories and terms that law uses, and the reasoning structure by which it expresses itself, organizes its practices, and constructs its meanings, has a particularly potent ability to shape popular and authoritative understandings of situations.[72]

A discursive analysis further allows us to connect law's power with this construction of meaning. Carol Smart, for example, has argued that law's power lies in its distinctive ability to define and pronounce authoritatively on the world around it.[73] She argues that law's distinctive claim to truth, in 'setting itself outside the social order' from where it can then 'reflect upon the world from which it is divorced' gives law a powerful ability to disqualify opposing discourses.[74] This authoritative nature of legal discourse has been particularly resistant to feminist challenges.[75] Feminist claims are defined as irrelevant, or are 'translated into another form in order to become legal issues'.[76] Other feminist scholars have similarly attempted to reveal the relationship between law's power and the construction of meaning. As Janine Brodie, Shelley Gavigan and Jane Jenson have succinctly argued, '[t]he power of law is to reflect and reinforce particular meaning system's over others'.[77]

Law as discourse can also assist in understanding the way in which it constitutes subjectivity. Legal discourse constitutes subjects as legal citizens; as individuals with rights and responsibilities vis-à-vis other citizens and the state. This discourse is both universalizing and naturalizing—all legal citizens are the same (they are *equal* before the law), and all legal citizens are natural subjects (they are equal *before* the law). Law is simply seen to protect the rights of individuals who are seen to exist prior to their constitution in and through legal discourse. As feminist scholars have attempted to illustrate, however, the discourse of law is not homogeneous. Legal discourse does not in fact constitute all legal citizens in the same way. Rather, legal discourse constitutes individuals as gendered subjects. Legal discourse is partially constitutive of women's identity. Legal discourse encodes women with meaning, and '...explains and rationalizes these meanings by an appeal to the 'natural' differences between the sexes, differences that the rules themselves help to produce'.[78] Feminist scholars have further argued, legal discourse does not constitute all women in the same way.[79] It is important to be attentive to the ways in which even the gendered discourse of law is not always homogenous. Legal discourse also partially constitutes women's racial, ethnic, religious and sexual identities. Sometimes these differences are explicitly inscribed in law, as we will see in the context of personal laws. At other times, these differences are obscured in law, as legal discourse assumes the homogeneity of all women, and attempts to universalize a common gender identity.

By understanding law as discourse we can recognize law's formidable power in constituting women's gendered identities, while at the same time, searching for ways to use this discourse to challenge those constructions. As an official, though relatively autonomous discourse of the state, law plays a role in legitimating unequal power relations. At the same time, it is the relative autonomy of law from other branches of the state that creates the possibility of it operating to challenge these unequal power relations. The legitimacy of law resides in its purported objectivity, neutrality and universality. While these values have been challenged and deconstructed in feminist scholarship, objectivity and universality are not entirely fictitious. In order to sustain its legitimacy, the rule of law must appear to be equally applicable to all of its subjects. The principles of equality before the law and of equal protection of the law must be accessible to all legal subjects, including those subjects who are members of socially disadvantaged groups. These values of legal liberalism create law's counter-hegemonic potential.[80] Women, colonized peoples, lower castes and other historically disenfranchised peoples have been able with some degree of success to appeal to legal discourse, to legitimize and realize their struggles for inclusion.

Law is then an important site of discursive struggle. It is a terrain on which competing visions of the world are fought out; on which contesting normative visions struggle for the power to define legal and political concepts that give meaning to our world. It is neither the only site of this discursive struggle, nor is it in any way the primary site. It is a site, among others, where this discursive struggle occurs. It is a place where contests over the meaning of equality, of secularism, of political liberty, are fought out and where dominant meanings come to inform not only judicial approaches, but also come to shape the way we understand the world that we live in. In this way, law is an important site of politics, if politics is similarly understood as a struggle over meaning; a place where we struggle for 'temporally bound and fully contestable visions of who we are and how we ought to live'.[81] We do not mean to suggest that law is simply reducible to politics: it has its own discourse, its own discursive claim to truth, and its own institutional structures in which this discourse is embedded. It is the distinctive nature of law and the distinctive way in which law operates as a terrain of political and discursive struggle that must be the focus of feminist legal studies.

We argue throughout this volume that feminist engagement with law should be seen in this context of discursive contestation. When feminists argue that women's rights to equality have been violated, they are engaged in a discursive struggle in which they are trying to transform the way in which people give meaning to the world around them. They are trying to denaturalize the way in which women are treated, by providing a different lens through which this treatment can be viewed. It is a contest over the meaning of equality, gender and gender difference. It is an effort to destabilize dominant meanings, and supplant these meanings with alternative visions about how we ought to live in the world.

In this revisioning of law, we are not suggesting that the insights of other feminist perspectives are not important or relevant. On the contrary, we believe that it is crucial for feminist legal studies to pay careful attention to broader social and economic structures, and the way in which legal discourse is mediated through these structures. In examining law as discourse, and as a site of discursive struggle, it is important not to lose sight of the institutions and structures within which discourses are embedded. Socialist feminism's attention to these social and economic structures is an important complement to poststructuralist feminism's attention to discourse. Socialist feminism's insistence on examining the relation between law, and state and economic institutions and structures can serve to 'remind us that some discourses become dominant inscribed in institutional practices, and "reinforce relations of domination"'.[82] Further, as we will discuss in the next chapter, socialist feminism's analysis of the family and of familial ideology provides in our view an insightful theoretical framework for an exploration of the contradictory role of law.[83] This analysis of familial ideology will in turn inform our analysis throughout the remaining chapters, as we will endeavour to illustrate the ways in which legal discourse continues to be shaped by this ideology. As we will argue, this familial ideology operates as a very real constraint in feminist efforts to engage with law, and redefine the meaning of gender and gender difference. Revisioning law as discursive struggle thus does not imply abandoning attention to material structures. Rather, the feminist theoretical framework that we seek to develop and deploy is one which borrows from the insights of both socialist feminism and poststructuralist feminism; it is one that is attentive to both discourse and the broader material structures within which discourse is embedded.[84] It is one that attempts to pay close attention to global contradictions and to the specific socially constructed conditions in which women in India are located.

Revisioning law as discursive struggle, and feminist engagement with law as an effort to challenge and redefine dominant meanings does not mean that anything is possible; it does not mean that we can redefine the meaning of gender at will. Feminist efforts to destabilize dominant meanings encounter very real opposition; opposition that is often firmly inscribed in dominant institutions and structures. Revisioning law as a site of discursive struggle can not simply wish such opposition away but rather requires that these powerful discourses be confronted and challenged head on. It requires careful attention to the ways in which these powerful and opposing discourses may be rooted in and shaped by dominant social and economic forces. And it requires attention to the ways in which these dominant structures and discourses may appropriate, and significantly alter feminist efforts to use law. Analysing feminist engagement with law must therefore include a careful consideration of the ways in which feminist claims may be transformed through the complex interplay with dominant social relations and competing discourses.

Revisioning Feminist Legal Histories: From Social Reform to the Contemporary Women's Movement

> ...if feminism is to be different, it must acknowledge the ideological and problematic significance of its own past....
>
> Kumkum Sangari and Sudesh Vaid
> *Recasting Women in India: Essays in Colonial History**

Law has long occupied an important position in organized efforts to improve women's status in India. Social reformers in the nineteenth century, women in the independence movement, and women in the

* New Jersey: Rutgers University Press, 1990.

contemporary women's movement have all sought legal reform. Although the focus and objectives of each wave of reform differed in important ways, each wave nevertheless turned to law as a vehicle for improving women's social, economic, political and cultural status and has thereby placed at least some hope in law's ability to deliver such social change. At the same time, each wave of reform had or came to have some reservations about the role that law could play in this social change. In this section, we briefly review these three waves of movements for women's rights to illustrate the important role that law has played in each one. In so doing, we attempt to highlight the ambivalence that the different movements exhibited towards law. Each successive movement for women's rights demonstrated at least some concern about the limitations of law in bringing about social change. Yet, each movement nevertheless chose to use law in their struggles. We argue that the tensions within the position and strategies of these social reformers and feminists activists cannot be adequately understood within instrumental understandings of law. We examine the complex role that law has played in movements for women's rights, and suggest that social reformers and feminist activists have sought in different ways to use law as a subversive site; to challenge and displace dominant understandings of gender, tradition and culture. They have sought to denaturalize assumptions about women's identities, roles and responsibilities; and to redefine dominant understandings of women and their role in the world.

At the same time, we will attempt to reveal some of the many important differences between these movements, particularly in terms of the particular legal strategies they pursued. In some ways, the three successive movements for women's rights can be seen to roughly correspond to the three approaches to women and law we identified in the previous section: the social reformers in the nineteenth century with a protectionist approach, in seeking protective legislation for women; the women in the independence movement with an equality approach, in seeking equality rights and the elimination of discrimination; and the contemporary women's movement with a patriarchy approach. The correspondence is far from exact, in that there were many dissident voices within each of these movements who sought to do things a little differently from others. Yet these three approaches may be helpful in conceptualizing some of the differences in the legal strategies pursued by each successive movement.

Our objective in this section, from the standpoint of feminist legal scholarship is *not* to provide a comprehensive history of women's rights since the nineteenth century, which has been well documented.[85] Our objective is rather more modest. We attempt to draw upon the work of some feminist and other historians who have documented and analyzed this history, and to bring into sharper relief the particular role that law played in these movements. In so doing, we are hoping to develop an understanding of the role of law in feminist struggles that can better capture the complexities and contradictions of law. We believe that feminist legal studies must be firmly grounded in an understanding of this history, and that an attempt to theorize feminist engagement with law without such a historical context would be seriously flawed. By the same token, the scope of our analysis allows us to do little more than very briefly, indeed, perhaps too briefly, review the official history (as opposed, for example, to a more subaltern approach) in an attempt to render more concrete our claim of the complex and contradictory nature of law. In our view more work will be need to be done within feminist legal scholarship to develop more complex and comprehensive feminist *legal* histories.

■ The First Wave: Social Reformers in the Nineteenth Century

Social reformers in the nineteenth century sought legal changes from the colonial administration to improve the status of Indian women. The women's question was raised as part of a broader agenda of social and political reform.[86] Social reformers sought to eliminate a host of social practices, from sati, to the prohibition on widow remarriage, to child marriage. The position of women within Hindu tradition was symbolically deployed by the British to legitimize colonial rule. Attention was directed at the most extreme of cultural practices as evidence of the 'barbarity' of Indian society and of its resulting need for foreign rule. Social reformers, in turn, sought to eliminate these cultural practices, and improve the position of women. In this section, we briefly examine two of the major campaigns for social reform during the nineteenth century—sati and child marriage.[87] Again, we emphasize that we do not purport to provide a comprehensive discussion of these campaigns, but simply attempt to highlight the role of law therein, and the efforts of social reformers to negotiate the contradictions of engaging in law reform through the colonial regime.

Sati

In the first half of the nineteenth century, social reformers such as Rammohun Roy campaigned for the elimination of sati. Rammohun Roy's arguments against sati were cast within the discourse of religion and scripture.[88] He argued that sati was not prescribed by shastric text, and that its resurgence corresponded to the degeneration of Hindu ethos. Rammohun's opponents similarly cast their arguments within this scriptural discourse, and attempted to undermine the credibility of Rammohun's interpretations.[89] A petition was submitted to the Governor General, signed by 800 persons opposing any instruction on sati, along with a statement signed by 120 pundits denouncing Rammohun's arguments, and arguing instead for the scriptural legitimacy of sati. Rammohun Roy was concerned, however, that any effort on the part of the colonial administration to abolish the practice of sati would not achieve the desired result. His views, as conveyed to William Bentinck, the Governor General at the time, are recorded in Bentinck's correspondence:

> It was [Roy's] opinion that the practice might be suppressed quietly and unobservedly by increasing the difficulties and by the indirect agency of the police. He apprehended that any public enactment would give rise to general apprehension, that the general reasoning would be, while the English were contending for power they deemed it politic to allow universal toleration and to respect our religion, but having attained supremacy their first act is a violation of their profession, and next will probably be, like the Muhammaden conquerors, to force upon us their own religion.[90]

While Rammohun Roy advocated the abolition of sati, he was not initially of the view that it should be done at the hands of the British government. He feared that intervention by the colonial administration in the religious practices of Hindu communities would lead to outrage and fierce opposition.[91] By legislatively prohibiting sati, the colonial state might only serve to provoke an orthodox backlash, by creating fear that the British were intent on interfering in religious affairs.[92] Rammohun seemed to suggest that other less public means should be deployed to make the commission of sati more difficult. His comments suggest an appreciation of the highly contentious terrain of law within the colonial regime, and the need to cautiously negotiate this terrain, lest the objectives of legal intervention be undermined by the very act of intervention.

Despite his apparent disagreement with the colonial strategy for abolishing sati, once the British administration enacted the regulation prohibiting sati in December 1829, Rammohun Roy openly supported it. In January 1830, along with 300 residents of Calcutta, Rammohun presented a petition to Bentinck supporting the prohibition.[93] The petition was intended to counter the mobilizing efforts of those who opposed any intervention in the practice of sati. Through the actions of the British and the reaction of the more orthodox forces who defended sati, law became a site within a broader discursive struggle about the scriptural legitimacy of sati. The enactment of the regulation prohibiting sati provoked a highly public controversy, in which the supporters and opponents of social reform, were engaged in a contest over tradition; over the power to define and redefine tradition. As Lata Mani has argued, the social reformers and orthodoxy were engaged in a struggle over the authenticity of Hindu tradition, a struggle in which scripture/religion/culture were all collapsed into an ubiquitous concept of 'tradition'.[94] As Mani has further argued, women were strikingly absent from the debates on sati.[95] Despite the British's alleged concerns with the 'barbarity' of the social practice, their position on sati was similarly cast within the discourse of religion. The central focus of the debate was whether sati was authorized within religious scripture. Women and the individual widow all but disappeared from the debate; they were 'neither subject, nor object' of debate, but rather as Mani has argued, 'women...became the site on which tradition was debated and reformulated'.[96] The discursive struggle in which the social reformers were engaged was over tradition and culture; women were simply the site of this contestation. Yet, the effect of this effort to redefine tradition was the introduction of legislation designed to protect women from the violence of sati. In redefining tradition, women's identities were partially reconstituted, and the public/private distinction renegotiated.

The effect of the sati campaign was contradictory. While the ordinance prohibiting sati was passed, the controversy had succeeded in mobilizing a resistant discourse that insisted on the cultural legitimacy of sati. The legislation condemned the practice of sati, but the outcome of the discursive struggle was somewhat more equivocal. In many ways, Rammohun Roy's fears were well founded, and his words of warning to Bentinck haunted the efforts of the social reformers throughout the nineteenth century. Campaigns to reform social practices through law were over and over again met with outcries of 'religion in danger', and threatened to upset the precarious legitimacy of colonial rule, premised in part on non-intervention in the customs and traditions of religious communities. Campaigns for law reform, rather than leading to the elimination of the violent or discriminatory practice in question often seemed to reinforce and rigidify the positions of those who defended these practices.

Child Marriage

The issue of child marriage was taken up in the latter half of the century, lead by reformers such as Behram Malabari and Ranade. The practice of child marriage came to be identified by social reformers as another social evil that needed to be eliminated. Hindu marriage had traditionally involved two components: (*a*) a wedding ceremony that took place anytime during a girl's childhood; and (*b*) the *garbhadaan*, or consummation ceremony, which took place within 16 days of the girl's first menstruation. In 1860 the *Criminal Law Amendment Act 10*, revised section 375 of the *Penal Code* to raise the age of consent to 10 years.[97] But in the 1880s, when the social reformer and journalist Malabari spearheaded another campaign to raise the age of consent yet again, a fierce political controversy erupted. The conflict between social reformers and political revivalists/nationalists reached a peak in the age of consent controversy at the end of the nineteenth century. Malabari's major political foe was Bal Gangadhar Tilak. Although Tilak's arguments against the Age of Consent Bill were multiple, his views on law and social reform could be seen as twofold. First, for Tilak, law was an ineffective means of changing behaviour and practices within the family. Although Tilak was in agreement that marriages should not be consummated below the age of puberty, he did not believe that legislation was the appropriate or effective method of eliminating child marriage. He was strongly of the view that 'reform which was imposed upon people through law could not be effective because it could neither ease family pressures upon the young couple, nor help the young couple to control its emotions; only education and knowledge could bring about this change'.[98] Second, and more significantly within the colonial context, law was seen as an instrument by which the British intended to legitimize their rule. Tilak and other revivalists/nationalists of this period rejected the legitimacy of the colonial regime, and thus flatly refused to engage in projects of law reform.[99]

> We would not like that Government should have anything to do with regulating our social customs or ways of living even supposing that the act of Government will be a very beneficial and suitable measure.

Tilak's call for 'education, not legislation' to diminish the evil was thus reinforced by his fierce opposition to asking the British to help bring about social reform.

The British government was initially quite hesitant to become embroiled in a controversy over Hindu marriage practices. In 1886, the colonial administration decided that no action should be taken, since the evil in question did not fall within the jurisdiction of existing civil or criminal law.[100] Malabari subsequently intensified his campaign, taking his message directly to England. And Gidumal, Malabari's chief propagandist, published a pamphlet focusing attention on amendments to the

Indian Penal Code. The Code had been reformed by the Age of Consent Act in 1860 without significant opposition. Gidumal proposed that another simple amendment be made, raising the age of consent again, this time to 12 years.[101] By 1891, when the Bill was considered by the Indian Legislative Council, the initial resistance to legislate in this area was overcome. The increased pressure on the London government to take action, coupled with the fact that the Bill was not a new foray into the legal regulation of Hindu custom, but simply on amendment to the existing criminal law, made the Bill more palatable to the colonial administration.[102] Despite intense opposition by the revivalists/nationalists, the Bill was passed.

Interestingly, the debates of the Legislative Council suggest that even the most avid supporters of the Bill recognized that the law was unlikely to bring about an end to the practice. Since the law was non-cognizable with respect to husbands and wives, there was some question as to whether it could ever be enforced. In response, Sir Andrew Scoble stated that he 'would settle for it as an "educative" measure, if it strengthens the hands of fathers of the families for protection of their daughters'.[103] According to historian Charles Heimsath, most supporters of the Age of Consent Bill 'realized that most social reform legislation had little more than educative effect'.[104] In at least one respect, then, the views of the supporters of this social reform legislation were not that different from the views of its most voracious opponents. Neither the supporters nor the opponents saw in law the ability to eliminate the practice. Neither side was possessed with an undying faith in the power of law to bring about social change. Even the supporters of the Bill held rather more modest views on law's potential, which was little more than educative. While the two sides of the debate held radically different views on the relative desirability of such educative measures, and, in particular, the appropriateness of such measures emanating from the colonial administration, neither side saw law as a simple instrument of social change.

In considering the role of law in this campaign, it is also important to note that two high profile legal cases were significant in the age of consent controversy. The first was the case of *Rukmabai*, who was married at a very young age, and who refused to live with her husband, on the basis of social, economic, and personal incompatibility.[105] Her husband brought a petition for restitution of conjugal rights. The court ordered that she return, and when she refused, the court threatened her with imprisonment. The threat was only removed after a vocal campaign by social reformers, and the personal intervention of Queen Victoria. As Tanika Sarkar observes '[t]he issue foregrounded very forcefully the problems of consent and indissolubility within Hindu marriage'.[106] But, it was the tragic and horrifying case of Phulmonee that galvanized public support for the Age of Consent Bill, and, in many ways, silenced the opposition. Phulmonee, a girl of about 10 or 11 years was raped by her 35 year old husband Hari Maiti, and died as a result of the injuries she sustained. Since the girl had been over the age of consent (10 years), the husband could not be found guilty of rape. He was charged with murder, but subsequently exonerated by the court. As Sarkar writes,

> Right after the Phulmanee episode, the revivalist-nationalists were maintaining a somewhat embarassed silence, which was broken only after the proposed bill came along. During this interval, it was the reformist voice alone that could be audible.[107]

As is often the case, it was the outcome within the judicial forum that gave impetus to the law reform campaign. The courts' decisions, along with the publicity given to these decisions, inadvertently helped highlight the inadequacy of the existing law and the corresponding need for reform.

The effect of the child marriage campaign was contradictory. While the legislation was ultimately passed, the controversy succeeded in mobilizing a resistant discourse that insisted on non-intervention in the realm of the private sphere. The legislation condemned the practice of child marriage by further raising the age of consent, but the outcome of the discursive struggle was to very effectively mobilize the political nationalists, and undermine the legitimacy of the efforts of the social reform movement in seeking legislative change from the colonial state. Further, Sarkar has argued that what was at stake in the age of consent controversy was no less than the definition of conjugality, which was in her view 'at the very heart of the formative movement for militant nationalism in Bengal'.[108] Political nationalists sought to redefine Hindu conjugality, and renegotiate the public/private, the domestic realm of the family, the home, as beyond the reach of colonial intervention. The family was reconstituted as a 'pure space' of Hindu culture and tradition, uncontaminated by colonial intervention. Women who occupied this space, in turn, came to represent all that was pure and untouched by colonialism. Social reformers, who were attempting to redefine Hindu tradition to exclude child marriage, were thereby trying to introduce change into the very sphere that in the eyes of the political nationalists was most representative of Hindu culture and tradition. The contest between the social reformers and the political nationalists was not simply over the legitimacy of engaging with the colonial state, but was also a contest over the power and authority to define Hindu culture and tradition.

Law and Social Reform

The social reformers of the nineteenth century were not possessed with an undying faith in the power of law to eliminate social practices. Rammohun Roy recognized that a prohibition on sati was unlikely to immediately bring this violent practice to an end, and was concerned with political implications of engaging with the colonial state. And the contradictions of engaging with the colonial state came to a head at the end of the century in the child marriage debate. Despite the recognized problems of seeking law reform from the British, law reform strategies were pursued. Social reformers were of the view that law had a role to play in bringing about the change in attitudes and customs that would be required to eliminate these social practices. At the same time, it is important to recognize that their focus was not exclusively on legislative reform. Social reformers placed considerable importance on the role of education in bringing about change and eliminating discriminatory social practices. Chandararkar once noted that education was 'accomplishing silently what no law could have accomplished—unsettling people's minds, raising controversies…and thus forwarding the cause of social progress'.[109] Indeed, the power of law in the process of social reform was often cast within this broader context of education. Law was not seen to bring about change through its direct enforcement as much as through its symbolic or educative effect, by contributing to a more general change in attitudes.

Law was a site on which competing visions of Hindu tradition and custom were fought out. Social reformers sought to reform this tradition and custom, while simultaneously seeking support for this reform in Hindu scriptures. The conservative and orthodox forces that opposed reform similarly sought to legitimate the authority of their very different vision of Hindu tradition and custom in Hindu scriptures. The contest was very much over who had the authority to define tradition and custom; a contest which was fought out on the terrain of law. In the last decades of the nineteenth century, the contradictions of engaging on this terrain came to the fore as political nationalists entered the fray and sought to undermine the very authority of this terrain. In these debates, law was again a site on which the much broader visions of the social reformers and the political nationalists were fought out. But this time, the legitimacy of law itself was of issue. While the social reformers were successful in so far as their demand to raise the age of consent was passed into law, the political nationalists were enormously successful in their efforts to rearticulate the domestic sphere as beyond the reach of the colonial intervention.

The strategies of the social reformers were informed by a form of protectionism. Women were not assumed to be equal to men; indeed, the discourse of equality was strikingly absent from the debates, as were the voices of women themselves.[110] Social reformers sought to eliminate customs and practices that they considered to be evils perpetrated on women. They sought protective forms of legislation, prohibiting these practices. The discourse within which these legal reforms were sought was heavily embedded with familialism. As Meera Kosambi has argued, '[t]he patriarchal image of the ideal woman, as the ideal wife and mother, was generally accepted and propagated even by progressive social reformers'.[111] Women were assumed to be wives and mothers by nature, and the social evils had to be eradicated in order to protect women in these roles. Even the campaigns for women's education, which gathered support from the mid-nineteenth century, and which would bring women out from the confines of the family, were justified in the name of the family. Educated women would be stronger in their roles as wives and mothers.

■ The Second Wave: Women's Rights in the Independence Struggle

By the end of the nineteenth century these issues of social reform began to be taken up by women, who came to the forefront of the movements for women's rights. The focus of early campaigns was largely on women's education and public participation, rather than legislative reform.[112] Although women continued to express the need to eliminate social practices such as child marriage, the fierce resistance and hostility generated by the Age of Consent Bill in the last decades of the nineteenth century lead many to shy away from further law reform efforts. The early part of the twentieth century witnessed the emergence of all-India women's organizations.[113] The Women's Indian Association was set up in 1917, the National Council of Women in 1925, and the All India Women's Conference in 1927. With the emergence of these all-India women's organizations came a new political and social agenda. By the 1920s, women's suffrage had become a central issue, and attention soon returned to the question of child marriage, as well as a more comprehensive reform of personal laws. This women's movement which although concerned with the question of women's emancipation, came to play an important role in the independence movement.[114] In this section, we will briefly examine two of the major issues of the women's movement: (a) the campaigns for political representation and constitutional equality and (b) the campaigns to reform personal law.

Political Representation

Beginning in 1917, the issue of women's suffrage and political representation came to occupy the centrestage of many women's organizations. The issue was initially conceptualized as a means of achieving further social reform.[115] Women leaders were of the view that 'the enfranchisement of women would mean additional support for reform legislation. The question of women's suffrage was first raised by the Women's Indian Association in 1917.[116] In 1919, the *Government of India Act* allowed the vote for only 3 per cent of Indian adults in the Provincial Assembly, and less than 1 per cent in the Central Assembly (based on property requirements). While women were not included, the Provincial Assemblies were empowered to eliminate the exclusion clause, and although many of the Assemblies did so, the property qualifications continued to operate to effectively disqualify the vast majority of women who had no independent access to property.[117] As the political movement for self rule continued, women's organizations continued to push for women's suffrage.

As the campaigns for political representation and legislative reform developed, a contest emerged over the discursive terrain of the movement, that is, whether the demands were to be articulated in the discourse of uplift or the discourse of equality. The early women's movement, based primarily in the middle and upper classes, drew heavily on revivalist ideals of gender difference and Indian womanhood in support of their efforts to improve women's position. The turn of the century was a 'time of resurgent Hinduism', and marked 'a clear ideological shift' from the social reform debates of the nineteenth century.[118] The 'western' and 'alien' ideas of the social reformers came into disrepute, as intellectual and spiritual leaders—from Vivekananda, and Aurobindo, Annie Besant and Sister Nivedita—sought to resurrect the ideals of the Hindu past. The glorification of women's roles as wives and mothers which emerged in the political nationalism and revivalism during the age of consent controversy—as a pure space uncontaminated by Western colonialism—came to infuse the very discourse of nationalism. 'Indian womanhood' became the very embodiment of nationalism, as the nation came to be constructed as divine mother, as mother India, and as women became 'the mothers of the realm'.[119]

The early women's movement drew on this reconstructed identity of women as mothers of the nation. More specifically, the discourse of 'women's uplift' was used to support demands for the reform of social practices. According to this discourse, women's roles as wives and mothers, and their distinctively feminine values such as sacrifice and loyalty, should be strengthened. The elimination of debilitating social practices, alongside education for women would allow women to 'perform their roles in a more enlightened manner', as well as allow for a greater influence of feminine values on society.[120] Annie Besant and Sarojini Naidu—two prominent leaders of the women's movement during this period—presented the goals of the movement in this discourse of women's uplift. Women's uplift was linked with national development, and a discourse emerged of Indian women as mothers of the nation.[121] In so doing, they relied heavily on revivalist and nationalist discourse insisting, for example, that 'India's greatest will not return until Indian womanhood obtains a larger, freer, fuller life, for largely in the hands of Indian women must be the redemption of India'.[122] The leaders of the women's movement deployed this discourse of women's uplift to argue not only for the elimination of debilitating social practices, but also to support a greater public role for women. It was argued that women's distinctive roles and values as self-sacrificing mothers and dutiful wives could make an important contribution to the public sphere. In this way, the early women's movement could be seen to have made a significant departure from the social reformers of the previous century, in advocating roles for women beyond the family.

But, as the women's movement developed, a new discourse began to infuse its campaigns. In the 1920s, instead of 'women's uplift', some voices began to speak of women's equality. As Jana Matson Everett has described, within this rather different ideological vision, the goal of the women's movement was equal rights for women and men.[123] Equal rights would involve eliminating the barriers that women faced 'in the form of legal and social inequalities—which prevented [them] from realising their full capacities'.[124] By the 1930s, this equal rights discourse, and its emphasis on achieving equality for women within economic, political and familial spheres, had displaced the discourse of women's uplift which had dominated the earlier movement.[125] Everett has suggested that this shift can be understood in terms of the intricate relationship between the women's movement and the national movement, particularly in so far as '[t]he concept of equal rights was more suited than the concept of women's uplift to the task of reforming the anglicised system of law'.[126] A split developed within the movement for women's political representation between the women's uplift faction, which supported enfranchisement through 'wifehood qualifications', that is, being the wife of a man of certain property qualifications and an equal rights faction, which supported universal adult suffrage and formally equal treatment of women.

By the 1930s, 'equal rights' came to dominate the discourse of the women's movement and the demands for political representation. Sex equality was accepted by the Indian National Congress in its 1928 Report which advocated the principle of sexual equality and universal adult suffrage. At the Karachi session in 1931, Congress adopted these principles.[127] In 1946, the Constituent Assembly was assigned the task of framing a constitution for the emerging independent nation. The Assembly appointed an Advisory Committee, which in turn appointed a Fundamental Rights Sub-committee, which was assigned the task of preparing a draft of the Fundamental Rights section of the Constitution. There was no opposition within sub-committee to the commitment to political and economic sex equality. The Constituent Assembly in turn recommended the adoption of equality rights. Article 15 of the Constitution included a prohibition on discrimination on the grounds of sex. Article 15(3) allowed for special measures for women and children. Article 16 guaranteed equality of opportunity in employment, and prohibited discrimination on the basis of sex in employment.

Hindu Personal Law Reform

The second major law reform issue taken up by the women's movement was in relation to personal laws. Women's organizations first turned to the reform of Hindu personal law in the 1920s as another dimension of achieving women's uplift. In the 1920s, legislative reform in the area of child marriage came back onto the political agenda. The Women's Indian Association advocated raising the age of consent and the first three sessions of the All India Women's Conference passed resolutions against child marriage. In 1927, Har Bilas Sarda introduced a Bill to restrain the solemnization of child marriage. In 1928, the government appointed the Age of Consent Committee to study the question of further reforms to the age of consent. In its Report, the committee recommended that the age of consent should be raised to 15 and 18 years, in marital and non-marital cases respectively. It also recommended that the minimum age for marriage of girls should be set at 14 years. The government partially accepted the recommendations of the committee, by agreeing to establish a minimum age of marriage, and the *Child Marriage Restraint Act* was passed.

By 1928, women's organizations had begun to broaden their demands to include legislative reform in inheritance and marriage.[128] The demand for a Hindu Code that would remove all legal disabilities of women in marriage and inheritance was first raised by the All India Women's Conference in 1934. These demands for the reform of Hindu law, and the elimination of legal disabilities was increasingly cast within the equal rights discourse which displaced the earlier women's uplift discourse.[129] By 1940, the campaign to reform Hindu personal laws began to receive some Congress support. At the same time, the demand for a Uniform Civil Code was introduced into national debate. The Report of the sub-committee on 'Women's Role in a Planned Economy' called for the enactment of a Uniform Civil Code, which would gradually replace all personal laws. In 1941 and 1944, a government committee was established to further consider the question of codification of Hindu law. In 1943, the issue of the Hindu Code came before the Legislative Assembly, who commissioned a draft code.

The efforts to reform personal laws proved to be rather more controversial than the demands for women's suffrage and political representation. Conservative and orthodox voices within Congress, as well as those in the Hindu Mahasabha strenuously opposed the Hindu Code Bill. The proposed reforms to Hindu laws were seen as leading to the destruction of the family. No less than 'the purity of family life, the great ideal of chastity and the great ideal of Indian womanhood' was considered to be at stake.[130] Inheritance rights for daughters, equal divorce rights, and the monogamy clause were among the most controversial, and most intensely debated of the proposed reforms. Property rights for women were, in the words of Pandit Thakur Das 'equality run mad'.[131] Granting equal property to women would lead to a breakdown of the joint Hindu family, which was seen as the most fundamental unit of society. Opponents feared litigation, fragmentation and increasing violence among family members. The Bill was seen by many as the 'demolition of the entire structure and fabric of Hindu society'.[132] Women's roles and identity were very much at issue in these debates. Supporters of the Bill argued within the discourse of equal rights, insisting that equality within the public sphere be extended to the family. They argued against women's economic dependency and in favour of independence and equality. Opponents of the Bill held very different views about women's roles and identities. As Jana Matson Everett describes:

> Opponents of the HCB asserted that men's and women's obligations were different, which made it unfair for men and women to have the same property rights. Some opponents claimed that women had equal rights under Hindu Law, but that the Hindu conception of sex equality involved dissimilarity, not identity. Other opponents claimed that women occupied a revered position in Hindu society, and the identical property rights would mean a decline in their status.[133]

The opponents of the Hindu Code Bill drew on many of the same assumptions about gender and gender difference that had informed the women's movement's earlier discourse of uplift. The idea of women as naturally different from men, with distinctive roles and values—largely abandoned by the women's movement—was very much a part of the discourse of those opposing the Bill. This understanding of gender difference, which had informed both the social reformers and the political nationalists in the nineteenth century, remained dominant. The women's movement, with its discourse of equality rights, now found itself in a position of challenging and attempting to displace this dominant discourse.

When the Hindu Code was put to the Indian Legislative Assembly in 1945, it was defeated. After independence, the Code was brought to the provisional parliament, and it again produced a storm of opposition. The Hindu Code Bill was defeated, resulting in the resignation of the law minister, Ambedkar. Further efforts at reforming Hindu personal law were delayed until 1955, when four separate pieces of legislation were enacted that significantly improved the legal status of women under Hindu personal law. The *Hindu Marriage Act*, the *Hindu Succession Act*, the *Hindu Minority and Guardianship Act*, and the *Hindu Adoption and Maintenance Act* were all enacted in 1955.

The legal regulation of the family, and of women's roles therein, was a site of intensive discursive struggle, as the women's movement sought to extend the promise of equality rights to the private sphere. The very same political actors who had agreed to those equality rights within the public sphere but a few years earlier, fiercely resisted this effort to renegotiate the boundaries between the public and private. The idea of women as full and equal participants in the political and economic sphere carried the day. But, the idea of women as full and equal participants in the domestic sphere was simply too radical. Maitrayee Chaudhuri suggests that this greater commitment to equality rights in political and economic life than in family life:

...perhaps had something to do with the increasingly sharp differentiation of the public and the private sphere. It was easier to accord to the state the right to intervene in secular matters of politics and economics. It was far more difficult to give the state a similar unquestioned legitimacy to social engineering in matters of marriage, family and inheritance.[134]

Despite the fact that the reforms were ultimately passed into law, there was no decisive discursive victory. The discourse of equality was not able to successfully challenge and displace the ideological construction of women as wives and mothers within the family.

Law, Equality and Women's Rights

Initially, and on the heels of the nineteenth century social reform, the early women's movement shied away from law. Not unlike the concerns expressed by Roy a century earlier, there was a concern that demands for legal reform would produce a defensive reaction, rather than advance women's position. Yet, as the movement developed, alongside the nationalist movement, greater reliance came to be placed on law, and strategies for law reform. The emphasis of the campaign for both constitutional rights and the Hindu Code Bill came to focus on formal equality. This tone of the campaign was captured by a comment made by Hannah Sen, a leading member of the All India Women's Conference, 'The conference...will continue to safeguard the rights of women, reasserting this unshaken faith in the complete equality of all citizens before the law'.[135] The language of these campaigns came to be expressed within the discourse of liberal feminism, that is, a focus on individual rights and formal equality. At least part of this reliance on law, and the discourse of liberal feminism, can be accounted for in terms of the discourse of the broader nationalist movement, as well as the legacy of legal regulation by the British within the colonial era. The adoption of this discourse of liberal feminism may thus speak less to the undying faith of women's rights leaders in law than to the political exigencies of the particular historical movement. Indeed, many of the women in the independence movement were self avowed socialists and communists, and their vision of women's roles in post-independence India went well beyond liberal feminism's focus on individual opportunity and equality. *The Report of the Sub-committee on Women's Role in a Planned Economy* illustrated just how far-reaching was the vision of women's liberation: no less than a fundamental transformation in economic, political and familial structures was seen to be required. Nevertheless, by the time of the post-war speeches, the leadership of the All-India Women's Conference increasingly focused almost exclusively on the liberal discourse of equality rights.[136] As Everett describes, the main strategy pursued 'was the passage of legislation guaranteeing sex equality and special provisions for women in the areas of employment, politics, education and personal law'.[137] The campaigns were part of a struggle for formal equality, that is, for the legal and political recognition of women as formally equal citizens in the emerging nation-state. The struggle to secure sex equality within the constitution was very much an aspirational struggle. Women sought to ensure that the principle was included as part of the political vision for a newly-emerging nation-state. Gone were the dilemmas of the earlier generation of social reformers of seeking reform from an alien regime.

Women in the independence movement struggled to ensure that the blueprint for an independent India included women's equality.

The efforts of this women's movement met with mixed results. The discursive struggle to construct a legitimate political subjectivity for women was successful. The leaders of the women's movement were able to carve out a space from within which women could enter into politics, and the public sphere. This political subjectivity was initially constructed within the discourse of Hindu revivalism, of women as mothers of the nation. As the movement developed, the discourse through which this position was constructed shifted to one of equality. The discourse of equality was successful in the public sphere: political representation and constitutional equality rights were achieved. But, the discourse of equality proved to be considerably less well suited to the discursive struggles within the private sphere of the family. The discourse of equality—of women as the same as men, and entitled to the same treatment—ran head on with the dominant ideological construction of women as wives and mothers, as fundamentally different from men. The inability of the discourse of equality to challenge and displace this ideological construction within the private sphere further cast a shadow back on the discursive struggles within the public sphere. While the discourse of equality prevailed in this sphere—women achieved formal political and economic equality—the outcome in the private sphere suggests that those achievements did not entirely displace the construction of women as wives and mothers. Women could be 'equal' in the public sphere, without being the same as men in the private sphere. Women could be equal in the public sphere at the same time as they were wives and mothers in the private sphere. The discourse of equality could gain hold in the public sphere, without fundamentally challenging or displacing the hold of familial ideology in the private sphere.

■ The Third Wave: The Contemporary Women's Movement

Law has again played a prominent role in the most recent wave of the women's movement. The women's movement has launched major campaigns to reform rape and dowry laws in the late 1970s, campaigns to reform personal laws and implement a Uniform Civil Code, to improve the legislation prohibiting sati, and to prohibit sex determination tests in the 1980s, and has continued to press for further amendments to sexual assault laws in the 1990s. Yet, during this period, the women's movement has increasingly questioned the role of law in their struggles to improve women's social, economic, political and cultural status. Notwithstanding its reliance on law and legal strategies, there is a strong sense of ambivalence, disillusionment and skepticism about law. In this section, we will examine this tension in the engagement with law. We try to illustrate once again the extent to which law has been a site for a broader discursive struggle over the identity and status of women, as feminists have endeavoured to challenge and change the subordinate position of women. We focus on two legal campaigns which raised very different issues and dilemmas for the contemporary women's movement: rape and the Uniform Civil Code.

Rape

The contemporary women's movement was galvanized at the end of the 1970s largely through two campaigns for law reform—rape and dowry.[138] The debate to reform the rape laws demonstrates the centrality of law in this movement. A national campaign emerged around the rape case of Mathura, a young tribal woman who was raped in police custody.[139] The lower court held that she was 'of loose morals', and acquitted the two police officers. The High Court overturned the decision. But, on appeal to the Supreme Court of India, the decision of the lower court was reinstated. The Supreme Court held that there was insufficient evidence that Mathura resisted the sexual intercourse. The Supreme Court decision led to a public outcry of the miscarriage of justice, and a national campaign to reform the rape laws. The protest was ignited by an open letter written by four Delhi University law professors to the Chief Justice of India, calling for a rehearing of the case. The Bombay Forum Against Rape wrote to women's organizations around the country, proposing that demonstrations be held on International Women's Day (8 March) to demand that the case be reopened. Women's groups across the country joined in the protest, organizing marches and demonstrations to denounce the decision, and to bring attention to the issue of sexual violence against women.

In the campaign that ensued, the women's movement was attempting to challenge the prevailing legal and social understanding of rape and consent—in which consent could be implied from the absence of injuries or passive submission, in which only the 'utmost resistance' could demonstrate that she did not consent, and in which a woman of 'loose morals' would simply be assumed to consent. Further, the discourse of the campaign was not one of equality, but rather, represented a significant shift to a discourse of patriarchy. The feminist campaign against rape was attempting to connect this violence against women with the idea of systemic oppression of women by men. In the words of one feminist organisation 'For us rape is an act of hatred and contempt—it is a denial of ourselves as women, as human beings—it is the ultimate assertion of male power'.[140] The feminist campaigns, and the issue of police rape was enthusiastically picked up by the media, and the protest spread well beyond the women's movement. The subsequent police rape of a young woman, Maya Tyagi in Baghpat, Haryana, intensified the protest, with mainstream political parties entering into the rape controversy. With the entry of mainstream politicians, the discourse of the rape campaign began to transform. Politicians spoke with outrage of the increasing attacks on women, and of the shame and dishonour brought on women and their families. The discourse was not one of patriarchy, but of one of protectionism, that is, of the need to protect women's honour and chastity from violation.

The central government appointed a Law Commission to study the issue. The Law Commission recommended comprehensive reforms to the rape law, echoing many of the demands of the women's movement. Recommendations included shifting the onus of proof regarding consent to the accused, and excluding the relevance of a woman's past sexual conduct from a rape trial. The Bill subsequently introduced by the government fell considerably short of these recommendations, and included some regressive provisions demanded neither by the women's movement nor the Law Commission.[141] The Bill was met with considerable criticism and was referred to a joint parliamentary committee for further debate. The committee did not report until in November 1982, and in 1983, amendments to the rape law were finally passed. The amendments included the recognition of custodial rape in which consent was not relevant; and the establishment of mandatory minimum sentences for rape.

While the feminist campaign was successful in so far as the issue of police rape was placed firmly on the public agenda, and legislation was passed to address it, the broader discursive struggle over the meaning of rape was somewhat less successful. As Flavia Agnes' evaluation of the case law following the amendments to the rape law has revealed, the reforms have had very little effect in challenging the traditional definition of rape, and many of the same assumptions about women's sexuality continue to inform the cases.[142] For example, ten years after the Mathura case, the Supreme Court reduced the mandatory minimum sentence of ten years imposed on two police officers found guilty of raping a young woman—Suman Rani—to a maximum of five years.[143] After noting the argument of the counsel for the accused that 'the victim Suman Rani was a woman of questionable character and easy virtue with lewd and lascivious behaviour', the court concluded that 'the peculiar facts and circumstances of this case coupled with the *conduct* of the victim girl in our view, do not call for the minimum sentence'[144] (emphasis added). The women's movement was not able to displace these assumptions about virginity, chastity and the unruly nature of women's sexuality. Rather, its demands for the reform of rape laws was taken up and supported by other, more conservative political voices, and cast within the more traditional discourse of shame and dishonour.

It is also important to note that although feminist activists were of a common view on the need to contest dominant understandings of rape and consent, not all were agreed on the particular strategies to be pursued. Some voiced concerns about strategies that relied too heavily on the state, and particularly, on criminal law. At the time that the Bill was introduced into parliament in 1980, many women's organizations had heated debates over whether the provision regarding the onus of proof for consent should be extended to all forms of rape. Some were concerned that such extensive criminal powers could be used against male activists, and would constitute an undue violation of civil liberties.[145] The amendments to the rape law did not go so far as to shift the burden of proving consent onto the accused, but introduced a presumption in favour of a victim who stated that she did not consent and restricted the application of this clause only to cases of custodial rape. Nevertheless, the question of the reliance of the women's movement on the state and more specifically, on the power of criminal law has remained controversial. While some within the women's movement have continued to lobby for criminal legislation to protect women against violence, others have grown increasingly concerned about the willingness of the state to enact such legislation and thereby extend its criminal powers.[146]

In the aftermath of the campaigns to amend the rape laws as well as a similar campaign to reform the dowry laws,[147] a sense of disillusionment seemed to take root in the women's movement regarding the role that law reform could play in improving women's lives.

> The discovery that there was no connection at all between the enactment of new laws and their implementation had left many feeling rather bitterly that the Government had, with the greatest of ease, side-tracked their demands, and this gave rise to further questions about the efficacy of basing campaigns around demands for changes in the law.[148]

Yet, the disillusionment experienced by many women's groups did not lead to a complete abandonment of law. Some women's organizations shifted their focus away from law reform, and towards taking up the individual cases of women in courts.[149] Litigating these cases became a more significant focus for some women's organizations, who sought to provide legal assistance, and other forms of support for women going through the judicial system. And at the same time, many feminists became concerned with the lack of institutional support for women, as a result of which many women's centres were set up in the early 1980s, designed to provide women with legal assistance, health services and counselling.[150]

The Shah Bano Controversy and the Uniform Civil Code

As events developed through the 1980s, women's organizations did not shy away from further demands for law reform. The Shah Bano controversy gave rise to a campaign for the reform of personal laws through a Uniform Civil Code. Shah Bano, a 73 year old Muslim woman, who was divorced by her husband of 40 years brought a petition for maintenance from her husband under section 125 of the *Criminal Procedure Code*. According to Muslim personal law, she would only have been entitled to maintenance for the period of *iddat*, that is, three months after the divorce. In April 1985, the Supreme Court held that she was entitled to maintenance under section 125.[151] Although this was not the first time that the court had made such an order, its comments on the Quran provoked enormous outcry. The court had held that allowing this maintenance would not violate the Quran. The court further called for the enactment of a Uniform Civil Code. Conservative and orthodox forces within the Muslim community responded with outrage, and cries of religion in danger. In their view, the Supreme Court had encroached on the authority of Muslim theologians who alone are permitted to interpret the Quran. And many within the Muslim community suspected that the judgement was intended to undermine Islamic law, in accordance with the agenda of the Hindu Right. An independent member of parliament introduced a Bill to save Muslim personal law. The women's movement, along with progressive Muslim organizations, campaigned against the Bill. The Hindu Right also campaigned vigorously against the Bill, which in its view, was simply another example of the Congress government 'pandering to minorities'. The government, initially supportive of the Supreme Court decision, reversed its position and supported the enactment of the *Muslim Women's (Protection of Rights on Divorce) Act* in May 1986, which provides that section 125 of the *Criminal Procedure Code* does not apply to divorced Muslim Women.[152]

The Shah Bano controversy reignited the debate over the Uniform Civil Code. The women's movement, which had been demanding a Uniform

Civil Code since the time of independence, intensified its campaign. Feminist activists pushed, again, for the adoption of an explicitly non-sexist, secular code. Support for a Uniform Civil Code did not, however, come from the women's movement alone. The Hindu Right—the Bharatiya Janata Party (BJP), the Rashtra Swayamsevak Sangh (RSS), and the Vishva Hindu Parishad (VHP)—also rallied around the Uniform Civil Code. The very same forces that had vehemently opposed the demands of women in the independence movement for a Hindu Code Bill were now echoing women's demands for a Uniform Civil Code.[153] Needless to say, the Hindu Right's support for the Uniform Civil Code was based on a very different agenda, that is, of attacking the rights of minorities and the Muslim community in particular.

The controversy over the Shah Bano case, the *Muslim Women's Act* and the Uniform Civil Code was cast in a dichotomous and highly polarized discourse: for or against the Supreme Court judgement; for or against the Act; for or against the Code.[154] It was this dichotomized discourse of the debate that inadvertently allied the women's movement with the Hindu Right, and its vicious attack on minority rights. Despite the efforts of some feminist activists and organizations to distinguish their position, within the broader popular discourse the positions were seen as one and the same. Feminist efforts to challenge the oppression of women within the private sphere of the family was appropriated, and transformed to support the communalist discourse of the Hindu Right.[155]

The sati controversy that arose shortly thereafter is an interesting contrast to the Shah Bano controversy. The sati of Roop Kanwar in Deorala, Rajasthan, in 1987, gave rise to a campaign against sati, and a demand for further legislation. Roop Kanwar's public sati was immediately followed by a glorification of sati campaign, as the site of immolation became a pilgrimage spot, orchestrated by the Sati Dharma Raksha Samiti and other pro-sati supporters.[156] The issue rapidly became integrally connected to Rajput community identity, and many within the Hindu Right stepped in to protect and uphold Rajput 'tradition'. Sati was defended, yet again, as a cultural tradition, sanctioned by religious scriptures. In opposition, the women's movement organized marches and demonstrations, denouncing sati and demanding that the government take action. The Rajasthan state government moved quickly and introduced the *Rajasthan Sati (Prevention) Ordinance* in October 1987, and the central government soon followed with the *Commission of Sati (Prevention) Act* in January 1988.[157]

Both the Shah Bano and the Roop Kanwar controversies raised and challenged issues of family, religion, tradition and gender.[158] Both cases encountered sharp resistance from conservative and orthodox voices within the Muslim and Hindu community, respectively. Both cases sought legal intervention in the private sphere of the family; a sphere considered by these conservative views to be governed by the dictates of religion and scripture, not secular law. In both cases, the effected communities responded with outcries of 'religion in danger'. The women's movement had to negotiate these intense forms of resistance in both its campaign against the *Muslim Women's Act* and in favour of the Uniform Civil Code, as well as its campaign in favour of new legislation prohibiting sati. But in the case of the Shah Bano controversy, the women's movement, along with other progressive voices, had to negotiate the additional dilemmas of proposing reform with a minority community. And in so doing, the women's movement found itself with a strange ally—the Hindu Right. The discursive strategy of challenging discrimination against women within the private sphere of the family was largely subsumed with the discursive strategy of the Hindu Right of challenging the legitimacy of minority rights.

Law, Gender, Patriarchy

Feminist activists within the contemporary women's movement have, like their predecessors, turned to law to advance their struggles to improve the conditions of women's lives.[159] The legal campaigns have met with mixed results. The rape laws were amended, though not as envisioned by the women's movement. The women's movement lost in its campaign for a Uniform Civil Code, but was successful in its lobbying efforts in relation to sati. But the campaigns cannot be evaluated in terms of legislative enactments alone. The broader, political struggle over meaning also met with contradictory results. The rape campaign did not transform the legal meaning of rape; it did not succeed in displacing the problematic constructions of consent, nor the assumptions about women's sexuality. But it did nevertheless have some effect in the struggle over the social and cultural meaning of rape. The campaign made an inroad in revealing the violence that women experienced, and in condemning that violence. Yet, the women's movement could not ultimately control the discourse within which this violence was condemned. Shame and dishonour continued to inform the popular and legal discourse.

The campaign against the *Muslim Women's Act* and in favour of a Uniform Civil Code produced a different set of contradictions. The effort to challenge and condemn the socio-economic discrimination against women in the family proved to be rather more complicated in the context of minority communities. Challenging the role and status of women within minority communities became a challenge to the very identity of those communities. Redefining tradition, which has proven to be difficult enough within the dominant Hindu community, proved to be even more treacherous within minority communities. Gender could not be singled out and redefined, without threatening the very integrity of the community to define its own cultural traditions. The effect of the campaign, although unsuccessful on the legislative front, was to inadvertently contribute to the Muslim community's sense of vulnerability and to give further legitimacy to the discursive strategies of the Hindu Right in attacking this community. In contrast, the sati campaign, although it raised similar issues in challenging religious and community traditions, did so within the context of the dominant Hindu community (albeit within a subset of this community). Here the discursive struggle was, as in the nineteenth century debates, over the authority to define tradition. The defenders of sati argued that opponents were alienated from their culture. But, in sharp contrast to the debates in the previous century, the opponents of sati cast their arguments in explicitly feminist terms: sati was violence against women; it was the most heinous violation of a women's right to life; it was murder.

The contemporary women's movement engagement with law has been highly contradictory. On the one hand, feminist activists have successfully campaigned for reforms to a broad range of criminal and civil law; on the other hand, the legislative enactments often fell short of the demands of the movement. While the law reform campaigns succeeded in raising public awareness on issues of violence and discrimination against women, the legislative enactments seemed unable to live up to the promise of stemming this violence and discrimination. And while disillusionment with law has grown within its ranks, few within the contemporary women's movement advocate relinquishing the terrain of law altogether. Some observers have been critical of what they believe to be the inconsistency of the women's movement's approach to law.[160] Nandita Gandhi and Nandita Shah in their study of the legal campaigns of the contemporary women's movement have argued that such criticism fails to appreciate both the political understanding of law that informs the women's movement, as well as the diversity of political strategies between and among women's organizations. They argue that '[t]here are practically no groups which have an undiluted faith in the legal system or which tend to jump into legal campaigns. Rather, there are some who make more use of the legal system than others'.[161] Gandhi and Shah's interviews with several organizations brings these different legal strategies to light. Some organizations provide women with legal services, through legal aid centres; others resort to law defensively; other groups adopt a 'law as catalyst' approach, in which individuals are advised 'not to go to court but vigorously campaign for legal reforms'. Another group described its approach to law as follows:

> ...we believe that law and protesting for changes in law are still important because one can justify one's position by it. People tend to believe that if it is a law it must be right, and if it is broken then there will be punishment. Secondly, it is easier to inform women of their 'rights'. A husband has no right to beat, a woman has the right to property therefore she should not forgo her share, etc....

The All India Democratic Women's Association explained its position that the demand for laws 'forms the backbone of any movement for progress...it is true that laws alone cannot fundamentally alter the legal status of women...cruelty against women cannot be arrested. It primarily depends on the success in raising the consciousness of the people against discrimination against women'.[162] Gandhi and Shah's review of these different views suggests that there is no uniform position on the role of law in the women's movement.[163] Some organizations are more willing to engage in campaigns for law reform or individual litigation than others. Some organizations are more reticent than others of the political utility of such campaigns. Yet, few organizations have relinquished law as a site of struggle. And conversely, it seems as if few organizations expect that law will actually deliver its promise of justice to women.[164] Activists in the women's movement express the extent to which they are caught between not being able to afford to ignore the law, and yet, not expecting the law to be able to bring about significant or effective change. Their experiences of struggle, victory and frustration have produced an understanding of the important yet limited role of law in their efforts to improve and transform the conditions of women's lives.

In our view, this seemingly contradictory engagement with law reflects the very real contradictory nature of law itself. The women's movement has gained considerable ground in its struggles to illuminate and condemn the reality of violence within women's lives. The campaigns against rape, as well as those against dowry, sati, female sex selection, have been important in the struggle over the social and cultural meaning of violence against women. These issues of violence against women have been brought into the public arena, where feminists have sought to redefine their meaning. Legal provisions may not have been able to stem the violence; nor have feminists been successful in displacing many of the assumptions that inform their legal definitions.[165] But legal discourse has been central in the very naming of these issues as social practices which need to be eliminated.

Law has been an important site on which feminist activists and lawyers have engaged in these contests over the meaning of gender and violence, as well as family, tradition and culture. And while these struggles have been important, they cannot be celebrated as unequivocal victories. Sometimes the feminist discourse has been appropriated by the state, to justify increasing state power in the name of protecting women. Often the legislative responses have failed to challenge the underlying assumptions about gender, violence and family. And sometimes, the struggles have given momentum to the resistant discourses of religious conservatives. The results of these discursive struggles have been contradictory. While succeeding in putting issues of violence and discrimination on the public agenda, the contemporary women's movement's engagement with law has not been able to control the meaning which is given to them.

■ Feminist Legal Histories and the Politics of Meaning

This brief review of the movements for women's rights since the nineteenth century suggest that law has played a central, though rather complex role. In many ways, it has been the demand for law reform that has given each movement its particular character, and that has mobilized support for (and against) these movements. Again and again, social reformers and feminist activists have returned to law, to articulate and embody their demands for change. Yet, within each movement the demand for law reform was part of a larger social and political project. Though law reform campaigns were often a central component in the overall strategy of promoting social and political change, law was not always seen as a panacea to the social problems that women faced. Without losing sight of the historical specificity of each movement for women's rights, nor the diversity of positions within each movement, the similarities between these movements cannot escape notice. Each movement, in its turn, pushed for reforms to the law. Yet, each movement held, or came to hold, at least some reservations as to what such legal reform could reasonably be expected to accomplish. As Radha Kumar has observed:

> ...doubts and fears about the nature of legislation and the role of the state have formed a kind of constant undercurrent to movements for women's rights, even while they have demanded this or that legislation.[166]

She describes the parallels between the campaigns for the prohibition of sati in the early nineteenth century, and in the late twentieth century as 'sufficiently close to be startling':[167]

Both Ram Mohan Roy and contemporary feminists voiced the unhappy feeling that they were being thrown back on demands for legislation at a time when violence against women, and the legitimisation of such violence, were mounting. Similarly, both expressed fears that legislation was not only inadequate as a solution, but might actually lead to a conservative backlash. The orthodox response to both Ram Mohan Roy and contemporary feminists, in fact, was that neither represented the 'true' desires of Indian women or Indian society, being de-racinated westernists.[168]

Kumar further observes parallels in the approaches of these activists in relation to questions of enforcement and under-enforcement of the law. After recognizing that legislation was being interpreted by the judiciary in ways that undermined its objective, social reformers in the nineteenth century and feminist activists in the late twentieth century have sought further reforms to the legislation to limit judicial discretion.[169] Similarly, the under-enforcement of the law became cause for concern for both social reformers and contemporary activists.[170]

We want to push this analysis of the similarities between the movements further, and suggest that each movement, in its own way, was engaged in a discursive struggle. Law has been a site on which each movement contested dominant understandings of gender, tradition and culture. In the nineteenth century, social reformers sought to redefine tradition, and in the process, reconstituted women's identity as in need of the protection of the law. In the early twentieth century, women activists challenged prevailing constructions, by attempting to introduce a political subjectivity for women—a role and voice through which women could enter into the political domain. Although initially framed within the discourse of Hindu revivalism—of women as mothers of the nation—by the 1930s, women in the independence movement sought a fundamental redefinition of gender through the discourse of equality. The contemporary women's movement has again sought a redefinition of tradition and gender, in revealing and challenging the violence and oppression that women have experienced in their lives.

The content of the legal strategies pursued by the successive movements for women's rights differed in significant ways. Social reformers in the nineteenth century sought largely protective legislation for women. The legislative reforms were all based on the underlying assumption that women were naturally different from men, and that these differences needed to be recognized in order to protect women. Women were seen to be, by nature, wives and mothers. They were located exclusively within the family—sati, the prohibition on widow remarriage, child marriage—against which women needed to be protected. There was no challenge to the construction of women's identities as wives and mothers, within the familial sphere. Nor was there any claim made to the equality of women. In stark contrast, the women in the independence movement in the twentieth century came to demand equality rights for women. The earlier discourse of women's uplift which relied heavily on revivalist ideals of women's natural roles as mothers of the nation, was displaced by an increasing reliance on the discourse of equality. The campaign for women's suffrage and for women's constitutional rights were premised on the demand for formal equality, that is, for the formally equal treatment of women and men. Women in the independence movement sought to not only improve women's position in the family, but also, to promote women's equality in the public sphere. Equality for women was sought in civil, political and economic life. And it was the effort to improve women's position within the family by extending this discourse of equality to the family that provoked the strongest reaction. Equality within the public sphere was easier to sell than was the introduction of the discourse of equality into the private realm of the family.

In the contemporary women's movement, yet another shift in the discourse and content of the legal campaigns is apparent. Although the women's movement has continued to campaign for equality rights where such rights have not yet been achieved (such as property rights within the family), law reform campaigns have focused on issues such as sexual and family violence which are particular to women. Rape, dowry, sati, the indecent representation of women are all issues which focus attention on women's differences. In some ways, the particular legal strategies are resonant of the campaigns for protective legislation in the nineteenth century. Demands were made to strengthen criminal and civil laws to protect women against violence. Yet, unlike the demands of the social reformers, the appeal was no longer to an underlying assumption of women's natural differences but rather, an appreciation of the way in which women's lived reality is different from men. The contemporary women's movement has been structured around the concept of patriarchy as women have sought to identify and understand ways in which they have been subordinated through violence, harassment, and other oppressive social practices.

Despite the differences in the content of the legal strategies, each movement, in its turn, sought legal intervention in the domestic realm, and a renegotiation of the public/private distinction. In the nineteenth century, social reformers sought to prohibit sati and child marriage; practices which occurred within the family, and which would thus require legal intervention in a sphere considered beyond the legitimate reach of colonial law. The campaigns to reform Hindu personal law in the independence movement, and to reform other personal laws in the 1980s again sought legal intervention in the domestic realm. Within each wave of reform, it has been these efforts to challenge and transform women's role and status within the family that has generated the greatest resistance.

The efforts of each movement to use law as a subversive site were resisted by powerful, opposing discourses, often cast in the rhetoric of 'religion in danger'. The campaigns of the social reformers against sati and child marriage encountered the powerful and opposing discourses of religious conservatives and political revivalists. In the case of sati, the discourse of religion was firmly inscribed in dominant structures and institutions, and set the discursive terrain within which the pros and cons of sati could be debated. In attempting to redefine 'tradition', the effect of the discursive strategies of the social reformers was to reinscribe the very primacy of religious discourse, particularly within the private realm of familial relations. In the case of child marriage, the discursive strategies of the social reformers to redefine 'tradition' by legislatively increasing the age of consent had the unintended consequence of strengthening the opposing discourses of political revivalism. While the social reformers won the age of consent issue in the narrow sense, the social and political meaning of the age of consent controversy which became increasingly dominant in popular discourse was that of the political revivalists. The campaigns to reform Hindu personal law at the time of independence similarly encountered the powerful, opposing discourse of both the religious orthodox and the Hindu revivalists. The discourse of equality that successfully carried the day in the political sphere was not able to displace the familial discourse that constructed women as wives and mothers in the private sphere. Paradoxically, the discourse of equality could not displace the discourse through which women's political subjectivity was initially constructed. Rather, this revivalist discourse of women as wives and mothers continued to haunt efforts to redefine women's roles within the family. Although Hindu law was ultimately reformed, the discursive struggle over the family and women's roles therein remained unresolved. The contemporary women's movement has continued to encounter these powerful resistant discourses. Any challenge to the traditional roles, identities and status of women within the family continues to be met with cries of religion in danger, and of the family under attack. Moreover, the contemporary women's movement has increasingly had to contend with its issues and strategies being appropriated by the Hindu Right.

Each movement for women's rights has seen the discourse of its demands reshaped through its encounter with these political forces. And the outcome of these campaigns were often quite contradictory. A legislative victory has often had the effect of strengthening a resistant discourse. The age of consent controversy, and the Hindu Code Bill both, inadvertently, strengthened the discursive strategies of Hindu nationalists. The legislative defeat in the Shah Bano controversy had a similar effect. Further, each movement has had to contend with the meaning and implications of engaging with law. At one level, the recurrent dilemmas was whether the effort to use law in the discursive strategies would only aggravate a conservative backlash. At another level, the movements had to contend with the contradictions of engaging with the very institutional structures that were identified as oppressive. Social reformers had to negotiate with the colonial state; feminist activists in the contemporary movement have had to negotiate with a state that they characterized as patriarchal. Both of these movements have faced the dilemmas of whether their campaigns for law reform—particularly in the nature of criminal law—would serve to strengthen both the power and legitimacy of the state. Only women in the independence movement were relatively free of this dilemma, in so far as they were participating in the very project of building a new, independent and socialist state.

While the content of these discursive struggles was quite different, each of the movements for women's rights can thus be seen to have resorted to law as part of their broader discursive struggle. Social reformers sought to challenge and displace the colonial construction of Hindu tradition as barbaric and uncivilized, by reforming and improving the treatment of women. Women in the independence movement first sought to challenge the exclusion of women from the public sphere, by reconstructing women's identities as mothers of the nation. Subsequently, they came to challenge the construction of women's difference, and to redefine women as equal to men, in the public and private spheres alike. The contemporary women's movement has once again sought to challenge and redefine prevailing constructions of gender identity, in revealing the multiple ways in which women have been the victims of male violence, harassment and discrimination, particularly in the private sphere of the family. And although these discursive struggles have produced contradictory results, social reformers and feminist activists have had a significant impact in these efforts to redefine the meaning of gender and tradition.

Conclusion

Our review of these successive movements for women's rights has attempted to highlight both the ambivalence that social reformers and feminist activists have expressed in their engagement with law, and the extent to which these engagements can be seen as efforts to contest dominant constructions of gender. We have also attempted to illustrate that the results of these engagements were often contradictory. While legislative reforms were realized, the unintended consequence was sometimes to mobilize resistant discourses. Legislative victories were thus at least partially undermined by the meaning given to these measures in popular discourse. Our reading of this history has attempted to give content to our argument of the complex and contradictory nature of law in struggles for social change. We believe that this history has much to teach us about law's potential and limitations in the struggles, and that efforts to further develop feminist legal studies must return again and again to this history. Feminist legal studies must take as its point of departure this experience of women's engagement with law. It should seek to explain and theorize that experience, with a view to developing ever more strategic engagements—past and present. As such, feminist legal studies in India takes the ambivalence towards law articulated by the women's movement not as something that can be explained away as the musings of those who do not understand law's mysteries, but rather, as reflecting the lived experience of legal and political struggle. This ambivalence may provide an important lens through which to study law. It may help us explore the nature of law, and its relationship to women's oppression. And it may help us discover new ways of engaging with law.

Efforts to theorize around the role of law in feminist struggles for social change must in our view continue to be more firmly grounded in the history of the women's movement's engagement with law. It is a history rich in struggles, victories, frustrations, and continuing struggle. It is a history that vividly demonstrates the complexities of legal strategies, and the contradictory nature of law. At the same time, it is important not to romanticize these struggles as having resolved all the difficult questions about law. For example, the women's movement has until recently largely assumed that women's oppression in and through patriarchy is uniform.[171] These assumptions have begun to be questioned, as the middle class, urban and Hindu bias of the movement has been revealed and critiqued.[172] Feminist activists and scholars are now beginning to further complicate their understanding of the heterogeneity and specificity of women's experiences of discrimination and oppression—a process that has not as yet been extended to legal campaigns. It is therefore important that we continue to push our understandings and analysis of these and other dilemmas forward. Feminist legal scholarship has an important role to play in continuing to complicate our understandings of law to better reflect the complex and contradictory nature of law, and thereby to assist in the continuing development of ever more sophisticated strategies for engaging with law. The relationship between feminist legal studies and the women's movement's engagement with law is a dialectic one, in which practice informs theory which informs practice. Elizabeth Schneider has emphasized this fundamental interaction between feminist theory and practice as a form of consciousness raising:

> The idea of consciousness raising as a method of analysis suggests an approach to social change which recognises dynamic tension, reflection, and sharing as essential aspects of growth. Feminist theory values this process which starts with experience, generalises through self-reflection and evaluation, and then returns to experience.[173]

This consciousness raising has been the method that the women's movement itself has used. Feminist legal studies attempts to broaden the circle, to include feminist legal academics, who may be able to bring particular theoretical and legal expertise to bear on the questions already under consideration within the women's movement.

It is important to emphasize that critical reflection on the limitations of law does not imply a rejection of law's role in social change. The history of the successive movements for women's rights demonstrates that law has played an important role in challenging dominant constructions of women's identity. At the same time, there are many ways in which law continues to shape and sustain unequal power relations. In revealing this contradictory nature of law, we remain committed to the idea that law can be a subversive site; that it can play a role in the struggles for social change by women and other disadvantaged groups. However, we believe that it is a mistake to begin with this role in feminist struggles for social change, without having first examined the extent to which law constitutes and sustains the subordination of women. We cannot, in other words, explore the possibilities of law without first, or at least simultaneously, engaging with the limitations of law. In the chapters that follow, we will examine these limitations in greater detail. The chapters that follow must also be seen as part of the effort to destabilize and subvert dominant meanings, of law, of women, of equality. We will provide a different lens through which law can be viewed—a lens that endeavours to illustrate and magnify the way in which law has operated to reinscribe women's subordinate position. We will try to reveal the extent to which law and legal discourse has not only not treated women equally, but has been deeply implicated in constituting women as naturally different and subordinate subjects. It is this contradictory nature of law that we will attempt to illustrate throughout the book. We will return to examine the question of the role of law in social change in chapter 5 where we will consider the debates on the role of rights discourse in feminist struggles for social change, and suggest ways to make our strategies for engaging with law more nuanced and complex.

NOTES

1. *The Convention on the Elimination of All Forms of Discrimination Against Women* was ratified by the Government of India on 9 July 1993.
2. Committee on the Status of Women in India, *Towards Equality: Report of the Committee on the Status of Women in India* (New Delhi: Ministry of Education and Social Welfare, 1975).
3. See generally, *Report of the National Commission on Self-Employed Women and Women in the Informal Sector* (New Delhi: National Commission on Self-Employed Women and Women in the Informal Sector, 1988).
4. *Ibid.*
5. Angela Harris, 'Race and Essentialism in Feminist Legal Theory' (1990) 42 *Stanford Law Review* 581.
6. *Ibid.*
7. *Ibid.* at 586.
8. See for example V. L. Deshpande, *Women and the New Law* (Chandigarh: R. K. Malhotra, Punjab University Publications, 1984); J. P. Atray, *Crimes Against Women* (New Delhi: Vikas, 1988); and M. J. Anthony, *Women's Rights* (New Delhi: Dialogue Publications, 1985).
9. Atray, *supra* note 8 at 17.
10. *Ibid.*
11. This protectionist approach is further explored in the analysis of constitutional case law in chapter 3.
12. See for example Rama Mehta, *The Socio-Legal Status of Women in India* (New Delhi: Mittal, 1987), particularly in her chapter 'Instrument of Social Engineering'; Justice E. S. Venkataramiah, 'Women and the Law', in B. K. Pal, ed., *Problems and Concerns of Indian Women* (New Delhi: ABC, 1987); Shyamala Pappu, Chandermani Chopra, and Mohini Giri, 'Women and the Law', in B. K. Pal, ed., *Problems and Concerns of Indian Women* (New Delhi: ABC, 1987); Kirti Singh, 'Increased Judicial Awareness to the Problems of Women', in B. K. Pal, ed., *Problems and Concerns of Indian Women* (New Delhi: ABC, 1987); R. K. Jani, 'Women and Legislative Measures', in R. K. Sapru, ed., *Women and Development* (New Delhi: Ashish, 1989); Rani Jethmalani, 'India: Law and Women', in Margaret Schuler, ed., *Empowerment and the Law: Strategies for Third World Women* (Washington, D.C.: OEF International, 1986) 60.
13. Lotika Sarkar, Rama Devi, Neera Sohoni, Justice V. R. Krishna Iyer, Madhava Menon, S. C. Bhatia, *Handbook on Women and Law, Volume One* (New Delhi: Department of Adult and Continuing Education and Extension, University of Delhi, 1990).
14. *Towards Equality, supra* note 2 at 102.

15. *Ibid.*
16. *Ibid.* at 103.
17. *Ibid.*
18. Government of India, *National Perspective Plan for Women, 1989–2000; Report of the Department of Women and Child Development* (New Delhi: Ministry of Human Resources, 1988) at 135.
19. Elizabeth A. Sheehy and Susan B. Boyd, 'Canadian Feminist Perspectives on Law: An Annotated Bibliography of Interdisciplinary Writings' (Special Publication of Resources for Feminist Research, December 1989).
20. N. Haksar and A. Singh, *The Demystification of Law for Women* (New Delhi: Lancer Press, 1986).
21. Upendra Baxi, in 'Patriarchy, Law and State: Some Preliminary Notes' (Paper presented at the Second National Conference on Women's Studies, Trivandrum, 9–12 April 1984), has argued that constitutional law is patriarchal: '...the Indian Constitution coolly contemplates a male dominated society...it does not see patriarchy as problematic, it perceives it as natural'.
22. Lina Gonsalves, *Women and the Law* (New Delhi: Lancer, 1993).
23. *Ibid.* at xiii.
24. *Ibid.* at xii.
25. *Ibid.* at 108.
26. In drawing this correspondence, we are not suggesting that all writers who speak of the patriarchal nature of law are radical feminists. Many in fact would identify themselves as socialist feminists, and would denounce radical feminism as an inappropriate theoretical framework. In fact, in the context of the Indian women's movement that label 'radical feminist' has often been used in a derogatory fashion. As Madhu Kishwar has observed in 'Why do I not Call Myself a Feminist', *Manushi* (November/December 1990) 2 at 4, labels such as radical feminism or bourgeois feminism have been used not 'as descriptions of positions taken by individuals or groups or the work done by them but as epithets to condemn people you don't like'. Our use of the term is not intended as such an epithet, but rather, to refer to a type of analysis *of law* that particular writers are deploying.
27. Supriya Akerkar, 'Theory and Practice of Women's Movement in India', *Economic Political Weekly* (29 April 1995) WS–2, at WS–6.
28. Sheehy and Boyd, *supra* note 19 at 2.
29. *Ibid.*
30. Akerkar, *supra* note 27 at WS–6.
31. Susan Boyd, '(Re)Placing the State: Family, Law and Oppression' (1994) 9 *Canadian Journal of Law and Society* 39, at 60. See also S. Gavigan, 'Law, Gender and Ideology', in A. Bayefsky, ed., *Legal Theory Meets Legal Practice* (Edmonton: Academic Printing and Publishing, 1988) 283.
32. Boyd *supra* note 31, Gavigan *supra* note 31. See also Gavigan 'Paradox Lost, Paradise Revisited: Feminist, Lesbian and Gay Engagement to Law' (1993) 31 *Osgoode Hall Law Journal* 589.
33. Archana Parashar in *Women and Family Law Reform in India: Uniform Civil Code and Gender Equality* (New Delhi: Sage, 1992) has argued that '...socialist feminist theory is inadequate in the Indian context because of the fact of emphasis on religion which has a significance in any definition of State and patriarchy. Religion occupies an important part in the lives of most Indians and is specially relevant for women because it has a bearing on personal matters through religious personal laws. These

laws are thus intimately linked to any analysis of the position of women and the role played by the State in maintaining or changing that position'.

34. Marlee Kline, 'Race, Racism and Feminist Legal Theory' (1989) 12 *Harvard Women's Law Journal* 115.

35. Akerkar, *supra* note 27 at WS–5. Akerkar, however, is highly critical of the 'notion of difference as experiential diversity' that has largely informed this work. She agrees with the critique of Amrita Chhachhi and Rene Pittin, 'Multiple Identities, Multiple Strategies: Confronting State, Capital and Patriarchy', *Confronting State, Capital and Patriarchy: Women Organising in the Process of Industrialisation* (MacMillan, forthcoming), as cited by Akerkar, 'that socialist feminists in trying to accomodate these differences, have a tendency to stress the primacy of one identity over the other, or simply to add together gender, ethnicity, and class as parallel identities based on parallel systems of domination, patriarchy, colonialism, racism and capitalism'.

36. There is no single poststructuralist critique of the subject. While various trajectories of poststructuralist thought share a common critique of the humanist, Cartesian, transcendent subject, as Susan Hekman, 'Reconstituting the Subject: Feminism, Modernism and Postmodernism' 6(2) *Hypatia* (Summer 1991) 44–63, writes, at 45:

   [t]here is no one 'postmodern' critique of the subject…Foucault's treatise on the 'death of man', Derrida's decentering of the subject, and the Lacanian-inspired discussions of the 'subject in process', despite their differences, have all called into question the major tenets of the subject-centred epistemology of modernity.

   It is, however, the Foucauldian critique of the subject that has been most influential in the feminist poststructuralism reviewed herein. See Chris Weedon, *Feminist Practice and Poststructuralist Theory* (Oxford: Basil Blackwell, 1987)

37. Weedon, *ibid.* at 3.

38. Nancy Hartsock, *Money, Sex and Power: Towards a Feminist Historical Materialism* (Boston: Northeastern University Press, 1983). For an excellent discussion of the dilemma presented by the poststructural deconstruction of the subject 'woman', see Akerkar, *supra* note 27.

39. Nancy Hartsock, for example, has argued 'Why is it that just at the moment when so many of us who have been silenced begin to demand the right to name ourselves, to act as subjects rather than objects of history, that just then the concept of subjecthood becomes problematic?' in 'Foucault on Power: A Theory for Theory', in Linda Nicolson, ed., *Feminism/Postmodernism* (New York: Routledge, 1990) at 163.

40. Susan Hekman *supra* note 36; Chris Weedon *supra* note 36; Judith Butler, *Gender Trouble: Feminism and the Subversion of Identity* (New York: Routledge, 1990). Akerkar *supra* note 27, for example, argues that the subject of woman can be used strategically in a way that retains the subject's agency by reconceptualizing the category as an imaginary one. See Akerkar, WS–8 to WS–10.

41. This sameness/difference debate involves the question of the relevance of gender, and whether gender difference should be taken into account in law. The sameness position argues that these differences should not be relevant. The law should treat women and men the same. In contrast, the difference position argues that there are many ways in which gender differences are very relevant, and must be taken into account in law. The debate is discussed in greater detail in chapter 3.

42. See Susan Williams, 'Feminist Legal Epistemologies' (1993) 8 *Berkeley Women's Law Journal* 63; Carol Smart, *Feminism and the Power of Law* (London: Routledge, 1989);

Carol Smart, 'Law's Power, the Sexed Body and Feminist Discourse' (1990) 17 *Journal of Law and Society* 194.

43. Harris, *supra* note 5.
44. Mary Joe Frug, 'A Postmodern Feminist Legal Manifesto' (1992) 105 *Harvard Law Review* 1045 at 1048. See also Mary Joe Frug, *Postmodern Legal Feminism* (New York: Routledge, 1992).
45. *Ibid.*
46. Brenda Cossman, 'A Matter of Difference: Domestic Contracts and Gender Equality' (1990) 28 *Osgoode Hall Law Journal* 303 at 352.
47. Vasuki Nesiah, 'Toward a Feminist Internationality: A Critique of U.S. Feminist Legal Scholarship' (1993) 16 *Harvard Women's Law Journal* 189 at 204. (Reprinted in Ratna Kapur, ed., *Feminist Terrains in Legal Domains: Interdisciplinary Essays on Women and Law in India* (New Delhi: Kali for Women, 1996).
48. *Ibid.*
49. See for example Tanika Sarkar, 'Rhetoric Against Age of Consent: Resisting Colonial Reason and Death of a Child-Wife', *Economic and Political Weekly* (4 September 1993); Lata Mani, 'Contentious Traditions: The Debate on Sati in Colonial India', in Kumkum Sangari and Sudesh Vaid, eds., *Recasting Women: Essays in Indian Colonial History* (New Delhi: Kali, 1989) 88; Janaki Nair, *Women and Law in Colonial India: A Social History* (New Delhi: Kali, 1996); Prem Chowdhry, 'Conjugality, Law and State: Inheritance Rights as Pivot of Control in Northern India' (1993) *National Law School Journal* 95; Chowdhry, *The Veiled Women: Shifting Gender Equations in Rural Haryana 1880-1990* (Delhi: Oxford University Press, 1994); and Chowdhry, 'Culture, Ideology and State: Subverting Female Inheritance (*Act of Succession*, 1956)' *Modern Asian Studies* (forthcoming).
50. Zakia Pathak and Rajeswari Sunder Rajan, 'Shah Bano' (1989) 12:3 *Signs: Journal of Women in Culture and Society* 558 at 573: 'Certainly, the Constitution of India, following Western constitutional models, did envisage this unity of the Indian subject within the legal system'. At 577: 'In the ideal, subjects in law are undifferentiated, nondescript, equal and singular. The Shah Bano case points to the contradictions inherent in such "ideal" subjectification'.
51. Bina Agarwal, *A Field of One's Own: Gender and Land Rights in South Asia* (Cambridge: Cambridge University Press, 1994).
52. Parashar, *supra* note 33.
53. *Ibid.* at 30.
54. *Ibid.* at 33.
55. Nivedita Menon, in 'Abortion and the Law: Questions for Feminism' (1993) 6 *Canadian Journal of Women and the Law* 103, has explored questions of the conceptualization of rights within the context of women's struggles around abortion, sex selection and reproductive choice. Menon's work can be seen as a discursive analysis of the women's movement's engagement with law around the issue of reproductive choice. In the context of abortion, the women's movement has demanded that women have a right to choose, and control over their bodies. Yet, within the context of sex selection, the same groups have argued for a limitation on the same right. Menon attempts to illustrate the contradictions within the liberal discourse of rights for feminism. She argues that rights are discursively constituted, that is, that rights only acquire meaning within specific contexts and specific discourses. 'Thus, the "right" over "one's body" is set in a particular matrix within feminist discourse, but once in the arena of law where diverse discourses of rights converge, its effects are not within the control of its originating discourses'. (at 117) While illustrating the difficulties

that feminists must confront in using rights discourse to express their political demands in relation to abortion and sex selection, Menon resists the conclusion that feminists necessarily need to reject the discourse altogether. Rather, she suggests that feminists 'must learn to talk of rights in a manner which is highly self-conscious and very cautious'. (*ibid.*). While Menon's work can be characterized as a discursive analysis, in many ways, her work defies any simple characterization. Her analysis is also attentive to material structures. She attempts to situate her analysis of abortion and law within the broader context of the political economy of development in India. Menon considers the development strategies pursued by the Indian state and the relationship of population control to the state strategies. Her work can thus be seen to be informed by both the materialism of socialist feminism and the discourse analysis of poststructural feminism.

56. Flavia Agnes, 'Protecting Women Against Violence?: Review of a Decade of Legislation, 1980–89,' *Economic and Political Weekly* (25 April 1992) WS–19.
57. *Ibid.* at WS–21.
58. *Ibid.* at WS 24–25.
59. *Ibid.* at WS–19.
60. *Ibid.*
61. *Ibid.*
62. Her work on maintenance has similarly examined the law within the broader context of women's economic dependency, and attempted to illustrate how the law has failed to adequately address this dependency. See Flavia Agnes, *Give Us this Day Our Daily Bread: Procedures and Case Law on Maintenance* (Bombay: Majlis, 1992).
63. See also Flavia Agnes, 'Triple Talaq Judgment: Do Women Really Benefit?' *Economic and Political Weekly* (14 May 1994) 1169; and Agnes, 'Fighting Rape—Has Amending the Law Helped?', *The Lawyers* (February 1990) 4.
64. Flavia Agnes, 'Women's Movement within a Secular Framework Redefining the Agenda', *Economic and Political Weekly* (7 May 1994) 1123 at 1123.
65. *Ibid.* at 1123–24.
66. *Ibid.* at 1126. The strategies of the Hindu Right in relation to minority personal law and their call for a Uniform Civil Code are discussed in greater detail in chapter 4.
67. Carol Smart, 'Feminism and Law: Some Problems of Analysis and Strategy' (1986) 14 *International Journal of the Sociology of Law* 109.
68. *Ibid.*
69. Weedon, *supra* note 36.
70. *Ibid.*
71. Lucinda Finley, 'Breaking Women's Silence in Law: The Dilemma of the Gendered Nature of Legal Reasoning' (1989) 64 *Notre Dame Law Review* 886 at 888.
72. *Ibid.*
73. Smart, *Feminism and the Power of Law*, *supra* note 42.
74. *Ibid.*
75. *Ibid.*
76. *Ibid.*
77. Janine Brodie, Shelley Gavigan and Jane Jenson, *The Politics of Abortion* (Toronto: Oxford University Press, 1992) at 13.
78. Frug, *supra* note 44, 'A Postmodern Feminist Legal Manifesto'.
79. See Harris, *supra* note 5; Agnes, *supra* note 56.
80. See Ernesto Laclau and Chantal Mouffe, *Hegemony and Socialist Strategy: Towards a Radical Democratic Politics* (London: Verso, 1985) on the democratic potential for new social movements created by the principles of equality and liberty. See also Alan

Hunt, 'Rights and Social Movements' (1991) 17 *Journal of Law and Society* 309; and Amy Bartholomew and Alan Hunt, 'What's Wrong with Rights?' (1990) 9 *Law & Inequality* 1 (arguing on the counterhegemonic potential of rights discourse). For a different view, which warns that both progressive and reactionary social movements can be mobilized through rights discourse, see Judy Fudge, 'What Do We Mean by Law and Social Transformation?' (1990) 5 *Canadian Journal of Law and Society* 48; and Fudge, 'The Public/Private Distinction: The Possibilities of and Limits to the Use of Charter Litigation to Further Feminist Struggles' (1987) 25 *Osgoode Hall Law Journal* 485. See also Smart, *Feminism, supra* note 42.

81. Wendy Brown, 'Feminist Hesitations, Postmodern Exposures' (Spring 1991) *Differences* 3 at 77. As Janine Brodie. Shelley Gavigan and Jane Jenson, *supra* note 77, at 7 have argued: 'In many ways…political struggle is a struggle about meaning. Although particular social understandings are inherent in the institutionalization of subordination, not all social actions necessarily accede to the dominant representation of themselves, their interests or political issues. New social voices with different understandings may arise to contest the power structure and to represent themselves and their interests differently. The result is conflict about collective identities—about who we are and who has the right to make claims—as much as it is about who get what, when and how'.

82. Brenda Cossman, 'Family Inside/Out' (1994) 44 *University of Toronto Law Journal* 1 at 28. Susan Boyd has argued in 'Some Postmodernist Challenges to Feminist Analyses of Law, Family and State: Ideology and Discourse in Child Custody Law' (1991) 10 *Canadian Journal of Family Law* 79 at 99, that discourse analysis cannot in itself explain 'how discourses are constituted and reproduced, nor how some discourses come to be more powerful and privileged than others'. She argues that the concept of ideology can assist in retaining 'a sense of the ways in which power flows from material (economic and social) circumstances in order to understand the hierarchy of discourses'.

83. We develop our analysis of familial ideology in chapter 2. For a general discussion, see Gavigan, *supra* note 32. On the relationship between discourse and ideology, see Boyd, *supra* note 82; Cossman, *supra* note 82; Marlee Kline, 'The Colour of Law: Ideological Representations in First Nations Legal Discourse' (1994) 3 *Social and Legal Studies* 451.

84. Rosemary Hennessy, in *Materialist Feminism and the Politics of Discourse* (New York: Routledge, 1993) describes materialist feminism as a distinctive feminist perspective which attempts to negotiate the insights of both socialist feminism and postmodernism. At 5, she writes 'Materialist feminism is distinguished from socialist feminism in part because it embraces postmodern conceptions of language and subjectivity. Materialist feminists have seen in postmodernism a powerful critical force for exposing the relationship between language, the subject, and the unequal distribution of social resources'.

85. For a more comprehensive discussion of the history of movements for women's rights in India, see Radha Kumar, *The History of Doing: An Illustrated Account of Movements for Women's Rights and Feminism in India, 1800–1990* (New Delhi: Kali for Women, 1993). See also the essays in the groundbreaking collection, Sangari and Vaid, eds., *Recasting Women, supra* note 49 and Janaki Nair, *supra* note 49.

86. There is a debate as to whether this social reform movement ought to be seen as a women's movement, since it was conducted on women's behalf primarily by men. The first wave of the women's movement is more often used to refer to the movement

that emerged in the early twentieth century. We are using 'first wave' to refer to the first waves of legal reform.

87. There were many other campaigns for social reform which involved women, and their legal rights, including widow remarriage and property rights. For a discussion of these campaigns, see Kumar, *supra* note 85; Charles Heimsath, *Indian Nationalism and Hindu Social Reform* (Princeton: Princeton University Press, 1964); Nair *supra* note 49.

88. See generally, Lata Mani, *supra* note 49.

89. *Ibid.*

90. Arvind Sharma, *Sati: Historical and Phenomenological Essays* (Delhi: Motilal Banarsidass, 1988) at 45, citing Upendra Nath Ball, *Rammohun Roy* (Calcutta: U. Ray and Sons, 1933) at 97–98.

91. Kumar, *supra* note 85 at 9. See also J. Liddle and R. Joshi, *Daughters of Independence: Gender, Caste and Class in India* (New Delhi: Kali, 1986); K. Sangari and S. Vaid, eds., *Recasting Women: supra* note 49.

92. Kumar, *supra* note 85 at 4.

93. See Mani, *supra* note 49 at 105, citing 'Address to Lord William Bentinck', *English Works* (16 January 1830) at 475–77.

94. Mani, *supra* note 49 at 109–18.

95. *Ibid.*

96. *Ibid.* at 118.

97. As a result of this amendment, the *garbhadaan* could not then be performed until after the girl reached 10 years of age, regardless of whether her menstruation started before that age. Despite this potential intervention with the *garbhadaan*, this amendment provoked little controversy.

98. Meera Kosambi 'Women, Emancipation and Equality: Pandita Ramabai's Contribution to Women', *Economic and Political Weekly* (29 October 1988) WS–38 at 1863, citing Editorial, *Kesari* (2 September 1890); reprinted in Tilak, *Samagra Lokamanya Tilak*, Vol. V (Samaj ra Sanskriti), (Pune: Kesari Prakashan, 1976).

99. Mahratta (29 May 1881) at 1 quoted by Stanley Wolpert, in *Tilak and Gokhale: Revolution and Reform in the Making of Modern India* (Berkeley: University of California Press, 1962), in Sharma, *supra* note 90 at 46.

100. Heimsath, *supra* note 87 at 158.

101. *Ibid.* at 161.

102. *Ibid.* at 170.

103. As quoted in Heimsath, *ibid.* at 173.

104. *Ibid.* at 173.

105. *Dadaji* v. *Rukhmabai*, [1886] 10 Bom 301.

106. Sarkar, *supra* note 49 at 1870.

107. *Ibid.* at 1874.

108. *Ibid.* at 1869. See also Engels, 'The Limits of Gender Ideology: Bengali Women, the Colonial State and the Private Sphere, 1890–1930', (1989) 12 *Women's Studies International Forum*.

109. As quoted in Heimsath, *supra* note 87 at 47.

110. Kosambi has argued, *supra* note 98 at WS–46, that the only notable exception to this absence of the discourse of equality was in the context of widow remarriage, where 'the inequality of treatment of widows and widowers...was too glaring to be ignored'.

111. *Ibid.* at WS–46.

112. As Jana Matson Everett, *Women and Social Change in India* (New Delhi: Heritage, 1979) argues at 68, 'the social hostility encountered by the reformers taught thoughtful

women's rights activists to downplay reforms and to focus instead on promoting women's public participation by associating it with patriotic and religious causes'.

113. For a discussion of the emergence of the women's movement in the early twentieth century, see Everett, *ibid.*

114. Geraldine Forbes, 'Caged Tigers: "First Wave" Feminists in India' (1982) 5:6 *Women's Studies International Forum* 525. Indeed, their understanding of the problems that women faced was intricately connected to the struggle for independence. See Liddle and Joshi, *supra* note 91 for a discussion of the connection made by the women's movement between women's oppression and foreign imperialism.

115. Everett, *supra* note 112 at 103.

116. The issue was raised in the context of Montagu's visit to discuss demands for political representation. It was not, however, mentioned in this report.

117. Liddle and Joshi, *supra* note 91 at 35.

118. Maitrayee Chaudhuri, *Indian Women's Movement: Reform and Revival* (Delhi: Radiant Publishers, 1993) at 75.

119. *Ibid.* at 78. See generally Kumar, *supra* note 85.

120. Chaudhuri, *supra* note 118 at 83.

121. Sister Nivedita stated for example in 1911: 'In India the sanctity and sweetness of Indian family life have been raised to the rank of a great culture. Wifehood is a religion; motherhood, a dream of perfection; and the pride and protectiveness of men are developed to a very high degree'. ('The Present Position of Women' (1911) *Modern Review* 196, as quoted in Everett, *supra* note 112 at 65–66.) Sarojini Naidu similarly spoke of Indian women as mothers of the nation. In 1916, she stated, for example: 'It is suitable that I who represent the other sex, that is the mothers of the men whom we wish to make men and not emasculated machines, should raise a voice on behalf of the future mothers of India'. (As quoted in Kumar, *supra* note 85 at 50.)

122. Everett, *supra* note 112 at 88, quoting Annie Besant, *Speeches and Writings of Annie Besant* (Madras: G. A. Natesan, 1921) at 73.

123. *Ibid.* at 82.

124. *Ibid.* at 83.

125. *Ibid.* at 82, 92–100.

126. *Ibid.* at 94.

127. For a detailed review of the campaign for political representation, see Everett, *supra* note 112 at 101–40.

128. *Ibid.* at 147–48. As Everett describes, these demands were also presented in terms of women's uplift, that is: 'to enable women to make a large contribution to society or to relieve women's suffering. The demands concerning inheritance did not call for equal inheritance rights for women but did call for increasing women's rights'. For an excellent discussion of the reform of Hindu personal law, see also Parashar, *supra* note 33 at 77–143.

129. Everett, *supra* note 112 at 96–97, 148–49.

130. N. C. Chatterjee, '26 April 1955 *Lok Sabha Debates*' 1955 Vol. IV Part II as cited in Reba Som 'Jawaharlal Nehru and the Hindu Code: A Victory of Symbol Substance?' *Occasional Papers on Perspectives in Indian Development*, Centre for Contemporary Studies, Nehru Memorial Museum and Library, New Delhi, April 1992.

131. *Constituent Assembly Debates* 1949 Part II, as cited in Som, *ibid.* at 23.

132. Chaudhuri, *supra* note 118 at 188.

133. Everett, *supra* note 112 at 176.

134. Chaudhuri, *supra* note 118 at 187.
135. As quoted in Everett, *supra* note 112 at 98.
136. Everett, *ibid.* at 98–99.
137. *Ibid.* at 99.
138. For a detailed review of these campaigns, see Agnes *supra* note 56, and Kumar *supra* note 85.
139. *Tukaram* v. *State of Maharashtra*, A 1979 SC 185. Mathura's case was preceded by Rameeza Bee's case, which was the first case to give rise to a concerted campaign against rape. Rameeza Bee was raped in police custody, and the failure of the state to take any action against the officers precipitated a mass demonstration. The case set the stage for a major campaign against rape in police custody.
140. From A Study by Stri Sangharsh, as quoted in Kumar, *supra* note 85 at 142.
141. As Flavia Agnes describes, *supra* note 56 at WS–20, the Bill included a provision making the publication of accounts of a rape trial a non-bailable offence. 'This meant a virtual censorship of press reports of rape trials. This was ironical because the public pressure during the campaign was built up mainly through media publicity and public protest'.
142. *Ibid.* at WS–21.
143. *Prem Chand* v. *State of Haryana*, A 1989 SC 937.
144. *Ibid.* The decision gave rise to an outcry that the courts were still taking past sexual conduct into account, along with all the other traditional assumptions about women's virginity and chastity. A subsequent petition for review of the order was dismissed by the court, but in so doing, the court took the opportunity to 'clarify' its reasoning, noting that the only relevant conduct had been the victim's delay in reporting the rape. For a further discussion of this case, see chapter 2.
145. The socialist feminist conference in Bombay in 1980 had a major debate over the proposal to extend this clause to all forms of rape. While some feminist organizations supported the extension, others were opposed on the ground that it would be giving the state too much power. Ultimately, the anti-extensionists carried the day, but the debate had been fierce and divisive. See Kumar, *supra* note 85.
146. For example, Agnes, *supra* note 56 has argued at WS–19 that '[i]nstead of empowering women, the law serves to strengthen the state. And a powerful state conversely means weaker citizens, which includes women'.
147. The anti-rape protests were followed by campaigns against dowry. Women's organizations across the country sought to bring public attention to this long hidden violence against young, newly-married women. (Mary Fainsod Katzenstein 'Getting Women's Issues onto the Public Agenda: Body Politics in India', *Samya Shakti*, Vol. VI 1991–92, 1 at 8–9.) The experience with the campaign to reform dowry laws was similar. While a new law was introduced in 1985, it too fell short of the demands of the women's movement. See generally Agnes, *supra* note 56.
148. Kumar, *supra* note 85 at 143.
149. *Ibid.*
150. *Ibid.*
151. *Mohammad Ahmed Khan* v. *Shah Bano Khan* A 1985 SC 945.
152. According to the Act, which effectively codifies Muslim personal law of maintenance, a divorced woman's husband is obliged to return her *mehr* (dower) and pay her maintenance during the period of *iddat*. If the divorced woman cannot support herself at the end of that period, her children, parents or relatives who would be entitled to inherit her property, are responsible for her support. If they cannot support her, the responsibility then falls to the state Wakf Boards.

153. For a more detailed discussion of the Hindu Right, its political ideology and strategies, see chapter 4.

154. Nasreen Fazalbhoy 'The Debate on Muslim Personal Law' (Paper presented at the Third National Conference on Women's Studies, Chandigarh, 1–4 October 1986) argues at 8 that the debate was 'reduced simply to a fight between those who were (for) and those who were against the judgment. Those who took a position (for) became the 'progressives' and those against, the 'fundamentalists'. This highly dichotomized discourse virtually displaced any progressive Muslim voice within the debate. At 9, she writes: 'Those who were against the judgment were the protectors of the Shariat, fighting against distortions in the Quran and those who supported the judgment were those who wanted to destroy Islam or use it for their own purposes. Muslims who supported the judgment were simply excluded from participating in the debate since they were considered to be outside the pale of Islam. The protagonists here were therefore muslims and nonmuslims'.

155. The role of the Uniform Civil Code in the agenda of the Hindu Right is discussed in greater detail in chapter 4.

156. For a more detailed account, see Kumar, *supra* note 85 at 175–81.

157. It is not clear that the passage of this Act represents an unequivocal feminist victory, or a feminist victory at all. As Lata Mani has written in 'Multiple Mediations: Feminist Scholarship in the Age of Multinational Reception' in Helen Crowley and Susan Himmelweit, eds., *Knowing Women: Feminism and Knowledge* (Cambridge, England: Polity Press in Association with the Open University, 1992), at 317 many 'feminists warned against the danger of demanding more stringent laws and greater state intervention.... They highlighted the appalling lack of will demonstrated by the state in prosecuting Roop's inlaws, and the possibility that the state would merely abuse the greater powers that would accrue to it'.
    And as Indira Jaising in 'The Murder of Roop Kanwar', *The Lawyers* (January 1987) has asked in relation to the passage of this Act: 'Is the Indian Penal Code dead when it comes to crimes against women?'. Flavia Agnes has similarly questioned whether the state's willingness to vest more power in quasi-criminal legislative, alongside the fact that the legislation punishes women who attempt to commit sati, can really be said to be a feminist victory. Agnes *supra* note 56.

158. Both the *Commission of Sati [Prevention] Act, 1987*, and the *Muslim Women's (Protection on Divorce) Act* have been challenged as violating women's fundamental rights. Both cases remain pending in the Supreme Court. In this respect, these cases are illustrative of the dynamic of the women's movement's engagement with law. Having lost their campaigns within the legislative arena, these campaigns have been reformulated in the judicial arena: law is again being used to challenge law.

159. The efforts to reform personal laws and sati laws were not the only campaigns for law reform during the 1980s. Throughout the decade, other important struggles for legal reform included the effort to ban the use of amniocentesis for sex determination. Women's organizations mobilized around individual cases, such as Mary Roy's challenge to the *Travancore Christian Succession Act, 1916*, as violating her right to equality. During this period, women's organizations have also focused on the question of women's access to the judicial system, and have organized around providing women with legal counsel, legal aid, as well as demanding reforms to the court system, such as family courts, alternative dispute resolution and mahila panchayats. Again in the 1990s, notwithstanding the skepticism about the role of law, many women's organizations continue to turn to law to advance their strategies for improving the conditions of women's lives. Campaigns for law reform continue which

reflect the increasing maturity and sophistication of the movements, in the way the reforms are formulated and the campaigns conducted. A recent example is the effort to further reform the law on sexual assault. Initially commissioned by the National Commission on the Status of Women to examine the problem of child rape, an ad-hoc committee has proposed wide ranging amendments to the rape law. These recom- mendations go further than the earlier reform proposals of the mid-eighties, in seeking to challenge the ideological assumptions on which the rape law is based. The new proposals suggest a broader definition of rape to include different forms of sexual assault and thereby include all forms of non-consensual activity between adults. The recommendations sought to challenge assumptions of female sexuality and ensure that it was available to women regardless of their marital and familial status. The Commission unfortunately refused to take up the bill despite the enthusiastic support it received from women's groups and institutions both within the country and abroad. Nevertheless, the draft recommendations have been used by women's organizations to initiate a national discussion on sexual assault and on the need for further reforms. *See* Shomona Khanna and Ratna Kapur, *Memorandum on Law Reform Relating to Sexual Offences*, Centre for Feminist Legal Research, 1996. The women's movement has also continued to resort to the judicial system, in supporting women in their individual cases. For example, in September 1992, Bhanwari Devi, a middle aged, informally educated rural woman, working for a government sponsored women's empowerment programme, was raped by several high-caste men from her village. The rape was an act of retaliation against her work with a campaign to stop the practice of child marriages which was prevalent in the community among the upper castes. The women's movement rallied to support Bhanwari in getting a criminal case registered against her rapists who were subsequently arrested. In November 1995, all of the accused were acquitted by the District and Sessions Court in Jaipur. The women's movement once again rallied to file an appeal in the High Court, and at the same time continuously generated publicity for the case through the visual and print media, and holding a public hearing.

160. Upendra Baxi, for example, after reviewing several different understandings of the role of law held by different women's organizations, concludes that 'the legal order remains a big puzzle for those committed to struggle and action for the emancipation of women'. Quoted in Nandita Gandhi and Nandita Shah, *Issues at Stake: Theory and Practice in the Contemporary Women's Movement in India* (New Delhi: Kali, 1992) at 269.

161. *Ibid.* at 270.

162. *Ibid.*

163. *Ibid.* at 213. In Gandhi and Shah's words: 'Undoubtedly, the law and legal reform are an integral part of the movement's campaigns and strategy. This has raised a number of reactions: one opinion is that legal reforms are a safe, status quo strategy, another that legal reform is a meaningless pursuit undertaken at the cost of concrete, grassroots level activities. And there is always that gnawing, recurring question about whether efforts at legal reform have any impact on the lives of women'.

164. *Ibid.* at 268. Gandhi and Shah conclude: 'Even the most liberal of those within the movement have little hope that laws can change social discrimination and customs or that the state will be an impartial dispenser of justice. Groups are aware that women are surrounded by a prevalent patriarchal ideology which permeates every part of their lives including the legal system, to deny them their rights, equality and freedom.... The majority of the women's groups see legal reform as a broad strategy for challenging the inferior position of women and the injustices heaped on them;

for legitimacy and social recognition of their issues; and for some short term legal redress'.

165. See Agnes, *supra* note 56 at WS 21–22.
166. Kumar, *supra* note 85 at 4.
167. *Ibid.*
168. *Ibid.*
169. *Ibid.*
170. *Ibid.* at 166. Kumar, *supra* note 84 observes, at 143–44, some of the important differences between the centres at the beginning of the twentieth century, and those established in the 1980s. She suggests that the 1980s centres were distinctive in their effort to provide services to address a broad range of issues, in their explicitly feminist, rather than social welfare, philosophy, and in adopting a more flexible and individualist approach to women's problems. Other interesting parallels included a similar shift in the focus of the social reformers at the end of the nineteenth century from law reform to social services and the shift of the contemporary women's movement in the 1980s. Just as the social reformers turned to providing services for widows following their recognition of the limited effect that the reform of the law was having on these widows' lives, so too did the contemporary women's movement shift to providing services for women following their disillusionment with the effect of law reform on bringing about meaningful change in women's lives.
171. In fact, each of the movements for women's rights have assumed the commonality of women's experience. Virtually no attention was given by the social reformers to the ways in the which the practices of sati and child marriage might affect women of different class, caste or religious backgrounds differently. The problems of predominantly middle class, upper caste, Hindu women were universalized as the problems of women. Women in the independence movement were largely drawn from a similar middle class, upper caste and Hindu background. Although some of these activists identified as socialists and communists, and were thus attentive to issues of class, little attention was given to the potential significance of other differences. This early women's movement has also been criticized for its elitist nature, and its failure to mobilize support among working class and rural women (see Everett, *supra* note 112 and Kumar, *supra* note 85). And the focus on the reform of Hindu personal law in the end left the problems faced by women from other religious communities off the political agenda. The contemporary women's movement has similarly focused on the commonality of women's oppression across class, cultural and religious differences.
172. Agnes, *supra* note 56, Akerkar, *supra* note 27.
173. Elizabeth Schneider, 'The Dialectics of Rights and Politics: Perspectives on the Women's Movement' (1986) 61 *New York University Law Review* 589 at 603.

2

Women, Legal Regulation and Familial Ideology

...at one and the same time the family is seen as naturally given
and as socially and morally desirable. The realms of the 'natural'
and the socio-moral are nowhere so constantly merged and
confused as in our feelings and thoughts about the family.

Michelle Barrett and Mary MacIntosh
*The Anti-Social Family**

I'm not frightened of the darkness outside. It's the darkness
inside houses that I don't like.

Shelagh Delaney
A Taste of Honey†

In this chapter, we will examine some of the ways in which familial
ideology shapes and informs the legal regulation of women, both inside
and outside of the family. We explore the influence of this familial
ideology in the area of family law, criminal law and labour law. Rather
than simply highlighting laws that explicitly discriminate against women,
this chapter examines the extent to which assumptions about women's
roles and identity in the family are deeply embedded in the law, including
those laws that have ostensibly been designed for women's benefit. We
begin with a discussion of the concepts of familial ideology and the
sexual division of labour. In the sections that follow, we attempt to

* London: Verso, 1982.
† New York: Grove Atlantic Monthly Press, 1989.

illustrate how this familial ideology and sexual division of labour shapes and informs the law. Our discussion is organized around two different dimensions of familial ideology: moral regulation through which women are constructed as, and judged in accordance with the standards of, good wives and sacrificing mothers; and economic regulation through which women are constructed as, and rendered into positions of, economic dependence. We will attempt to illustrate some of the different ways in which these assumptions about women inform the legal regulation of women, and how this legal regulation in turn operates to reinforce these assumptions of familial ideology.

The 'Family', Sexual Division of Labour and Familial Ideology

Family is a concept which is often taken for granted as representing a group of people related by ties of blood and marriage. Indeed, the family is asserted throughout national and international human rights documents as 'the basic and fundamental unit of society'.[1] It is a term the meaning and importance of which is more often assumed than examined. In this section, we argue that the concept of family is not simply descriptive of kinship and household structures, but rather, is a discourse through which these structures are given meaning. It is a way of giving meaning to a particular grouping of individuals who are related by blood and marriage. We further argue that 'family' is a dominant ideology, through which a particular set of household and gender relationships are universalized and naturalized. Although women in India live in diverse family forms, we argue that ideology of the joint family is the dominant form, which shapes and informs legal regulation.

The term 'family' has often been conflated with the term 'household'. In India, the terms family and household have often been used interchangeably in legal definitions. For example, in the Census of India from 1881 to 1941: 'The household or family consisted of those who lived together and ordinarily cooked at the same hearth including their servants and visitors'.[2] In 1951, the Census dropped the term 'family', and used only the term 'household'.[3] The National Sample Survey Organization and the Department of Labour use similar concepts of household in their data collection.[4] In both these legal and public policy definitions increasingly 'household' came to be used to refer to those persons with a common residence and with some degree of economic cooperation.[5] Academic work on the family has also called for a more precise distinction between the terms 'family' and 'household' to help eliminate some of the confusion around the use of the term 'family'. A. M. Shah's influential work on the family in India, for example, distinguished between household and family, defining household as a commensal and residential unit, composed of members sharing a single hearth and roof, and family as a wider kinship group whose members may live in more than one household.[6] Hilary Standing adds a further dimension to the distinction between family and household. She defines household as 'co-resident units in which the distribution and exchange of commodities and services such as wages and domestic work are organised primarily through relations of kinship'. Family, on the other hand, is defined as 'those kinship based relations that are located within co-residential groups and to the particular *ideological* forms taken by kinship structures within the [particular] context'[7] (emphasis added). Family, then, is not simply descriptive of these kinship and household structures, but rather is an ideological discourse through which these structures are given meaning. By ideological we are referring to a representational process whereby beliefs, norms, and explanations 'are constructed historically in conjunction with, and in relation to, material and cultural conditions and power relations, but are presented as natural, inevitable and necessary'.[8] In the context of the family, by ideological, we are referring to the way in which ideas about a particular set of household arrangements are constructed as natural and inevitable. As Barrett and MacIntosh have argued:

> ...the currently dominant model of the family is not timeless and culture free...This hegemonic family form is a powerful ideological force that mirrors in an idealised way the characteristics attributed to contemporary family life. It has only a tenuous relation to co-residence and the organisation of households as economic units.[9]

It is a representational process through which the family comes to be presented as 'a sacred, timeless and so natural institution that its definition is self-evident'.[10] Family, then, does not simply describe the empirical reality of kinship or household structures, but has an additional ideological dimension: it is a discourse through which certain relationships are given meaning; through which this meaning is naturalized and universalized, and through which unequal power relations are obscured and legitimated.

The concept of familial ideological has been an important focus of analysis within much socialist feminist scholarship, exploring the role of the family in the oppression of women. Socialist feminists have examined the ways in which this familial ideology operates to naturalize a particular set of kinship and household structures, namely, the patriarchal nuclear family, and the sexual division of labour therein. Through this ideology, women are constructed as wives and mothers, responsible for child rearing and domestic labour, whereas men are constructed as husbands and fathers, responsible for the financial welfare of the family. As this scholarship has emphasized, familial ideology is shaped by and rooted in material relations, particularly in the material relations of capitalism. The sexual division of labour was closely associated with the emergence of the 'family wage', and the idea that men should be able to earn a wage that was sufficient to support his family. Women could thus remain in the home, and tend to their responsibilities for child care and domestic labour.[11] This family wage was intended to release women from the double burden of household work and paid employment, but in the process created women's economic dependency on their husbands. Familial ideology was both shaped by and served to naturalize this family wage, and its allocation of gender roles. Women's roles within the domestic realm as wives and mothers was thus rendered a natural and self-evident product of their biological role in reproduction; simply a part of our collective common sense. This scholarship has further demonstrated the extent to which this dominant familial ideology has both shaped and reinforced the public/private distinction, and the construction of the family as private. This understanding of the family as private, and beyond state intervention has operated to both immunize the oppression of women within this domestic sphere, as well as to obscure the extent to which this private sphere is itself created and protected by state regulation.[12] These socialist feminist scholars have revealed the important role of familial ideology in the continuing naturalization of this idea of privacy, which despite the extensive regulation of the domestic sphere, continues its ideological hold.

The concept of familial ideology has made an important contribution to the understanding of women's oppression in industrial, capitalist societies. But, if it is to be of any explanatory value beyond this context, it must be rendered responsive to the historically and materially specific conditions of women's lives. As Chandra Mohanty has argued, if concepts such as familial ideology, the sexual division of labour and economic dependency are simply '...assumed to be universally applicable, the resultant homogenisation of class, race, religious, and daily material practices of women in the third world can create a false sense of the commonality of oppressions, interest and struggles between and among women globally'.[13] In her view, such concepts 'can be useful only if they are generated through local, contextual analyses'.[14]

It is therefore important to begin by recognizing that the analysis of familial ideology and the sexual division of labour within the family has been developed largely in relation to the nuclear family that has been the dominant household arrangement in industrial capitalist societies. In India, the nuclear family is *not* the dominant ideological form. Rather, any discussion of familial ideology must begin with the joint family—a household structure that is commonly believed to be the dominant form. As many sociologists have pointed out, however, there is no clear consensus as to the meaning and content of the joint family. Indeed, there has been considerable confusion in the way in which the term has been deployed.[15] It is sometimes used to refer to a specifically *legal* definition of family. Legally, the joint Hindu family is comprised of all males lineally descended from a common ancestor, who have an interest in joint or coparcenary property. According to this definition, which is based on classical Hindu law, the family unit is essentially concerned with property ownership, not with common residence. In contrast to this legal definition, the joint family is also used to refer to a *sociological* definition of the family, that is, to describe a particular household structure which is commonly believed to be the way in which most Indians live. This sociological definition of the joint family was heavily influenced by the writings of Indologists, particularly by the work of Sir Henry Maine (1863) 'who believed that he had discovered in India a living example of the patriarchal family in ancient times'.[16] Based on the texts of classical Hindu law, Maine described this joint family as a group of natural male descendants 'held together by subjection to the eldest living ascendant father, grandfather or great grandfather'.[17] Over the years, this conception of the joint family as representing the most prevalent type of Hindu family has come to be reflected in sociological definitions. Although there is no absolute consensus on its form, its features are commonly listed as two or more married couples, with a common residence and/or hearth.[18] The authority structure is commonly considered to be patriarchal; succession to be patrilineal; and living arrangements to be patrilocal.[19] In composition, it tends to consist of parents, sons, their wives and children, and unmarried daughters.[20]

Many sociologists of the Indian family have simply assumed this joint family to be the most prevalent family form in India. Irawati Karve, for example, in her influential early work on the sociology of the Indian family, argued that this joint family lay at the heart of Indian kinship, uniting the divergent traditions of the north, south and eastern kinship structures.[21] Other studies on Indian kinship have suggested that the essence lies elsewhere, although their work has largely assumed the prevalence of the joint family. In revealing some of the striking characteristics of

Indian kinship, these studies further reveal dimensions of what we believe to be part of the dominant ideology of the joint family. For example, Thomas Trautmann has argued that the principle of *kanyadana* (the gift of a virgin in marriage) was the true expression of the unique Indian culture of kinship.[22] Louis Dumont has argued that the unity lies in the importance ascribed to relations of affinity—that is, relationships established through marriage—and in the asymmetry of these relations.[23] Both Trautmann's and Dumont's work have contributed to the understanding of the family in India as a complex set of unequal relations between intermarrying families, wherein 'wife givers' are ritually inferior to 'wife takers'.[24] According to the practice of *kanyadana*, marriage is seen as gift of a woman from her birth family to her marital family, wherein she not only goes to live with her husband's family (according to the patrilocal nature of the joint family), but moreover, is considered to sever her connection with her natal family, and to become the responsibility of her husband's family.

The empirical realities of Indian society diverge rather considerably from the normative ideal of the joint family. A. M. Shah's studies on the family in India have suggested that this joint family was not in fact the most prevalent form of household structure in the past, particularly in rural areas.[25] He has argued that the joint family may have been more prevalent in traditional urban areas.[26] Pauline Kolenda's studies on the family have revealed the vast regional differences in family and household structure in India.[27] Kolenda has illustrated the inadequacy of the two categories of 'nuclear' and 'joint' in the context of Indian household types. She developed a widely used typology of family forms, which distinguishes between eleven different family types, from joint family to supplemental nuclear family to single parent family.[28] Kolenda's studies reveal that the majority of Indians do not live in joint families, but rather, in either joint or supplemental nuclear families, that is, nuclear families with at least one additional adult member such as an elderly parent or an unmarried daughter.[29] Some studies suggest that this supplemental nuclear family is increasingly becoming the typical family form among the urban middle and upper classes in India.[30] Other studies point out the single person or sub-nuclear household arrangements which are increasingly common in India.[31] There has been an enormous increase in female headed households, in which a woman and her children (and possibly other relatives) live apart from the husband and father, due to employment, abandonment or widowhood.[32] Women headed households now constitute 30–35 per cent of rural households, either through male migration or abandonment.[33]

Similarly, the idea of the sexual division of labour does not accurately describe the empirical realities of Indian women's lives. For instance, poor, rural women have long been involved in subsistence farming within the family. Their unpaid work on the family farm has been and continues to be essential for the subsistence food production. Further, many poor and working class women—urban and rural alike—are employed in wage labour outside of the home. Many women may in fact be the sole wage earner within the household. Recent studies have found that over 50 per cent of rural women work as agricultural wage labourers. In urban areas, poor women are likely to be employed in domestic service. Further, the last decades have seen a tremendous increase in middle class women's participation in the labour market, a process that is only intensifying with the new economic policies.[34]

The concept of the sexual division of labour has been extended beyond a description of sex roles within the family to also explain the nature of women's increasing participation in the labour force, that is, to the gender segregation of the labour market and the relegation of women to low paying, low skilled jobs.[35] Women's participation in the labour market has been structured around the assumption that women are economically dependent on men, and thus do not need a family wage. Women's work was often assumed to be temporary—as young, unmarried women would only work until such time as they married—or supplemental to the incomes of male family members. Women's participation in the labour market has been further shaped by the idea that women's skills are analogous to the skills they perform—without financial compensation—in the family. Yet, even here, the concept cannot be unproblematically deployed to describe the empirical realities of Indian women's work. Recent feminist research has begun to reveal the ways in which the nature of women's work and the sexual division of labour is mediated through class and caste.[36] For example, the withdrawal of women from work outside of the home can operate as an important marker of class and caste status. While the nature of women's work changes, a sexual division of labour within the family is maintained.[37] Other research has similarly illustrated the extent to which the sexual division of labour applies in differing degrees to women's lives across socio-economic class.[38] Among the poor and working class, women are likely to be engaged in low paying wage labour in the unorganized sector. Within the family, these women are likely to remain responsible for child care and domestic labour, creating a significant double burden. Among the upper classes, women are more likely to participate in higher paid employment, including professional employment, and to delegate their responsibility for child care and domestic labour to domestic servants employed within the household. However, even these women do not escape from the sexual division of labour altogether in so far as they remain responsible for supervising the labour of the domestic servants. Even at the upper income levels, in which women may participate in professional occupations, their roles and responsibilities within the family continue to be informed by the sexual division of labour, although their relationship with it is mediated in significant respects through their class position. It is not possible, then, to generalize on the 'double burden' facing women who work outside of the home, but rather, as Bardhan observes, 'domestic work and the double burden is class divided not class neutral'.[39]

Familial ideology and the sexual division of labour are thus not concepts that can be unproblematically applied to describe the way in which all Indian women live in and are subordinated in families. Many women live in nuclear, supplemental nuclear or single parent families, *not* in joint families. And many women work as wage labour outside of the family, and as unpaid but productive labour inside the family, wherein they make important—often essential—contributions to the financial provision of the family. And the nature of women's work both inside and outside of the family is mediated by relationships of class, caste and other materially specific contexts.[40] But, this diversity and complexity does not mean that familial ideology and the sexual division of labour are not useful analytical concepts. Despite these divergences between the empirical realities of family forms and women's roles therein, and the normative ideals of the joint family and the sexual division of labour, these normative ideals have not been displaced. Notwithstanding the important demographic variations in the ways in which people live in families, the joint family continues to be the dominant conception of family, and the dominant way in which people define their family, regardless of its lack of correlation to their own domestic arrangements. The subjective attitude towards family bonds and responsibilities continues to be informed by the dominant discourse of the joint family. Sylvia Vatuk suggests:

> If circumstances dictate that some members [of family] must live apart—as long as they do not do so in rejection of family bonds, but in furtherance of them—the family may continue to be regarded as an undivided unit and to operate in most respects much the same way as if all occupied a common residence.[41]

Promilla Kapur similarly comments on the adherence to the idea of a joint family:

> Indeed, even where the traditional joint family system breaks into nuclear units, it has given rise to a modified or new type of joint family

system. It merely breaks structurally, whereas functionally and senti-
mentally, individual units continue to form part of the joint family.[42]

This disjuncture between household and family further underscores the
argument that family is not simply descriptive of kinship and household
structures, but is a discourse through which these structures are given
meaning.

Similarly, the increasingly complex and diverse nature of women's
participation in the labour force does not mean that the concept of the
sexual division of labour is without explanatory force. Within dominant
normative visions, child care and domestic labour continues to be seen
as primarily women's responsibility, regardless of the nature of their
participation in the labour force. And as we will attempt to demonstrate,
the sexual division of labour does continue to provide insights into the
nature of women's participation in a highly segregated labour market and
the legal regulation of this work.

In considering this discrepancy between the normative ideal of family
and the empirical realities of family life in India, it is useful to keep in
mind that familial ideology has never accurately described the way in
which women live in families, even within industrial capitalist societies.
A debate has recently emerged within feminist scholarship that has begun
to highlight the discrepancy between lived experiences of family and
dominant familial ideology within these industrial societies. Socialist
feminists have been criticized for failing to recognize the diversity of
family forms. Some women of colour have argued that the concept of
familial ideology obscures the racial diversity among women and the
way in which the family may be an important source of support and
sustenance in a racially hostile world.[43] Socialist feminist scholars have
argued in response to this critique that the concept of familial ideology
is more normative than descriptive: it is not intended as a descriptively
accurate picture of how people live in families, but rather, as a norm
embedded in state policies and legal regulation about how people ought
to live in families. Both Susan Boyd and Shelley Gavigan have argued
that although experiences of family may differ, these different familial
experiences continue to be shaped and regulated by the dominant ideological form. Gavigan argues that despite 'the dissonance between many
people's lived experience and the dominant ideology of family...the
ideology of the patriarchal nuclear family provides the prism through
which relationships are examined, and the measure against which they
are judged, notwithstanding a shifting demography which indicated that
the idealised nuclear family household may be becoming increasingly
less typical'.[44]

In our view, this debate has resonance for the discussion of familial ideology in the Indian context. There is no question of the enormous and profound differences in familial forms and experiences in India. Yet, it may still be important to speak of an ideologically dominant family. This familial ideology gives meaning to the grouping of individuals within household and kinship structures—meaning that is universalized and naturalized. This ideology of the joint family may not accurately represent the diversity in the material reality of actual households in India, nor the diversity of positions that women occupy in those households. Nevertheless, as Patricia Uberoi has observed that the joint family 'remains a veritable article of faith among most educated Indians', despite the challenges to the simplistic formulation that has come from much recent empirical work.[45] The joint family does continue to dominate the way in which people think about family; it continues to be 'a prism through which relationships are examined...and judged',[46] particularly within the context of law. As Roland Lardinois has argued '...the Hindu Joint Family is a familial group and at the same time, *a category of thought, a way of seeing the world and of organising it so to give it meaning*'[47] (emphasis added). As such, familial ideology is not entirely fictitious or illusory. In order to be effective, ideologies must have resonance with individuals' experience of the world.[48] Lardinois argues that an understanding of the family in India requires 'a break with the spurious alternative between the representations and actual reality, and it must be shown that the representations, made by the agents of family structures in which they live, have as much reality as the structures themselves'.[49] These representations of family, which we refer to as dominant familial ideology, are partially constitutive of the family structure itself. Familial ideology continues to have resonance because it is partially constitutive of individuals' identities within their families. It is in and through this familial ideology that women's and men's gendered identities within the family are constructed. It is through this ideology that women, despite their differences, are constituted as mothers and wives. Familial ideology operates to obscure women's differences of class, caste and ethnicity, and to constitute women as homogeneous. It is in and through this dominant familial ideology that the complex and unequal relationships between intermarrying families is constituted and reproduced—that women are transferred by way of gift from their birth families to their marital families. And within this process, women are not only constituted as economic dependents to be transferred from one family to another, but this dependency is presented as a 'natural' consequence of the 'natural' roles. It is thus through this familial ideology that unequal gender relations are constituted and sustained, naturalized and obscured.

While it is important to examine the particular way in which the sexual division of labour operates in particular women's lives, familial ideology resists such historically and materially specific analysis. Law, which simply assumes the homogeneity of women's experience, is particularly resistant to such historically and material specific analysis. We will attempt to illustrate the extent to which familial ideology and the sexual division of labour inform the legal regulation of women, both inside and outside the family. The law has been based on the assumption of women's traditional roles in the family, and their economic dependency on men. There is rarely any acknowledgement of the variation in familial forms across class, caste or ethnicity, nor of the different roles/status of women within these different forms. The sexual division of labour is not only assumed in the legal regulation of women, but it is universalized and naturalized. As we will reveal, it is in this respect that the law plays an important ideological role, in shaping and sustaining the understanding of women as possessing certain natural attributes that makes them suitable for a life of domesticity as mothers and wives. In so doing, the law legitimates and reinforces patriarchal social relations. The law is based on and serves to reinforce the discursively constituted homogeneity of familial ideology.

Our analysis will examine two different manifestations of familial ideology: moral and economic regulation. By moral regulation, we are referring to the ways in which women's identities as wives and mothers are constituted—self-sacrificing mothers, loyal and chaste wives, dutiful and virginal daughters—to name but a few of the more central features. Familial ideology, which constitutes these identities for women, shapes and informs the legal regulation of women in the family. We will argue that divorce law, the restitution of conjugal rights, as well as many aspects of criminal intervention in the family, are all informed by this moral regulation, and in turn, operate to reinforce the identities ascribed for women therein. Women who live up to the ideals of motherhood and womanhood are accorded some protection; those who fail to measure up are penalized. By economic regulation, we are referring to the ways in which the assumption of economic dependency contained within familial ideology and the sexual division of labour operates in women's lives. Many aspects of legal regulation are shaped by assumptions of women's economic dependency within a patrilineal and patrilocal joint family. Within this structure, women are assumed to be economically dependent on male members of their families—fathers, husbands, adult sons. We will attempt to reveal the extent to which both maintenance and property laws, as well as the legal regulation of women's work, are shaped by and serve to reinscribe women's economic dependency.

By distinguishing between these two aspects of familial ideology, we are not suggesting that moral and economic regulation are entirely conceptually distinct. These two aspects of regulation are overlapping and mutually constituting; they are in effect two sides of the coin of familial ideology. There are many ways in which the assumptions underlying these two aspects of regulation are mutually reinforcing. The relationship between economic and moral regulation is particularly evident in the context of maintenance law, where we will illustrate that the assumptions about women's economic dependency and women's roles as ideal wives converge. As we will demonstrate, although economic dependency forms the basis of the law, women's entitlement to maintenance is made conditional on their adherence to norms and standards of ideal wifehood.

Throughout the chapter, we examine some of the ways in which familial ideology, the public/private distinction, and the sexual division of labour shapes and informs the legal regulation of women. In so doing, we will be attentive to the uneven and often contradictory ways in which these constructs inform different laws. The construction of women as wives and mothers, as economically dependent on their families, has been partially constitutive of women's subordinated position. The legal regulation of women in and through this familial ideology sustains this subordination. At the same time, familial ideology sometimes operates to protect women. When women have been good wives and mothers, when they have lived up to the expectations that this ideology imposes on them, a decision often goes in their favour. But, by the same token, a woman whose life has deviated from the roles allocated to her by this familial ideology may often find herself on the losing side of the law. Similar contradictions can be seen in the way in which the public/private distinction shapes and informs the law. Sometimes, the public/private distinction is deployed to immunize the private, familial sphere from legal scrutiny; at other times, the privacy of the family is deployed to justify legal regulation to protect the family from third party intervention.

It should be further noted that feminist research and criticism on the family has often been understood as attacking the family. Indeed, this understanding of the feminist approach to the family has frequently been deployed to delegitimize and reject feminism, and as will be further illustrated in chapter 4, to foster support for right wing and reactionary social movements that want to 'save' the traditional family from these attacks. This understanding of feminist research on the family, however, is far too simplistic. The critical analysis and deconstruction of the role of the family and familial ideology in the subordination of women does not necessarily imply that the family must be rejected or destroyed. Rather, feminist criticism has attempted to highlight the extent to which the family has operated as a site of contradiction for women. Feminist research has attempted to illustrate, for example, that the family is essential to women's socio-economic survival at the same time as it is the site of women's socio-economic oppression. The family may be an important source of emotional support for women at the same time as it may be a site of emotional destruction and violent relationships. While some feminist perspectives and research on the family have concluded that the family should be rejected, others have argued for a more complicated understanding of the role of the family in women's lives. Those aspects of the family that are most oppressive must be rejected and restructured, while those aspects of the family that are most important must be supported. For example, we might develop policies that attempt to eradicate women's powerlessness and enforced dependency within the family, while at the same time supporting women's role in the provision of child rearing and child care, health care, food production and nutrition in the family. Similarly, it is possible to argue that the legal regulation of women needs to be defamilialized in some respects without necessarily arguing that the family must be rejected.

The arguments that we put forward cannot be captured as pro-family or anti-family. We believe that the role of the family in the oppression of women, and particularly, the role of legal regulation in this oppression, is subtle and complex, and cannot be adequately described by such dichotomous positions. We will attempt to reveal and deconstruct the ways in which women are oppressed in the family. At the same time, we will argue that women's roles and responsibilities within the family must be recognized and affirmed, without being naturalized or universalized. We may in certain contexts then argue in favour of the defamilialization of the legal regulation of women, that is, argue in favour of treating women as individuals and not as family members. Yet, in other contexts, it may be necessary to argue that it is important to take into account the role that women play within their families. The family is a site of diverse and often contradictory experiences for women. It is a site of oppression and a site of resistance for women. It is a concept the meaning of which must be constantly interrogated and deconstructed. Yet, it is a concept that remains central to our analysis of the oppression of women.

Moral Regulation of Women in and through the Family

The ways in which familial ideology shapes and informs the legal regulation of women is most readily apparent in the laws that directly intervene in the family. The legal regulation of the family has been a highly contested site since the nineteenth century. The efforts of social reformers and feminist activists to prohibit violent and oppressive practices within the family, from sati to child marriage to dowry, as well as their efforts to reform personal laws, from widow remarriage to property and succession rights, have time and again been resisted as an undue intervention into the 'private' sphere of the family. Despite this resistance, and the continuing hold of the vision of the family as private and beyond legitimate state intervention, the family is the subject of extensive legal regulation. Few aspects of family life are exempt from some form of regulation, with laws addressing the entry into, subsistence of and exit from marriage. In this section, we examine a number of different personal and criminal laws that directly intervene in and regulate the family. We focus our discussion on the law of divorce and restitution of conjugal rights, and the criminal law of adultery and dowry. Our objective in this discussion is not to provide a comprehensive review of the statutory provisions and case law in these areas. Rather, we attempt to reveal the ideological dimensions of this legal regulation, and the contradictory impact for women. Many family laws continue to be characterized by formal inequality for women—women are not guaranteed the same rights and responsibilities as men, but are discriminated against on the basis of sex. At a deeper level, many family laws are informed by assumptions about women's sexuality and roles in the family—as daughters, wives, and mothers. In this section, we consider the way in which this familial ideology both operates to justify the formal inequality of the law, and informs the judicial approaches to formally equal laws in a way that produces less than equal results. Laws that apply equally to women and men are often interpreted in and through the lens of familial ideology, with the effect of reinscribing women's identities within the family as wives and mothers, with less than equal rights. By examining selected examples of statutory provisions and decided cases, we will explore the specific ways in which familial ideology operates to naturalize and universalize the construction of women, their roles inside the family, and the conduct that is expected of them in carrying out these roles.

■ Loyal Wives and Self-Sacrificing Mothers: The Regulation of Women in Family Law

By way of introduction, it is necessary to add a word of caution about our discussion of family laws. Different religious communities continue to be regulated by their own personal laws, rendering this area of legal regulation enormously complex and detailed. Although we attempt to draw examples from different personal laws, the discussion focuses, perhaps disproportionately, on Hindu personal law. This focus is intended to correct the often disproportionate focus and critique on minority personal laws. We believe that it is important to highlight the ways in which it is not only these minority laws that discriminate against and oppress women. At the same time, our discussion in this section, and in the subsequent discussion of property and maintenance, attempts to highlight some of the similarities in the assumptions that inform these different personal laws and constitute women's identities. We attempt to reveal the extent to which there is a certain similarity in the way in which familial ideology informs these laws and the construction of women in and through these laws. Familial ideology naturalizes and universalizes the construction of women as wives and mothers, as economically dependent, as passive, dutiful and self-sacrificing, across a broad range of personal laws. It is an example of the often homogenizing nature of legal discourse, which obscures the multiplicity of differences between and among women, and the very different ways in which women live in and experience their families.

Divorce

Divorce is governed by the different personal laws of each community. Hindus, including Buddhists, Sikhs and Jains, are governed by the *Hindu Marriage Act, 1955*; Christians by the *Indian Divorce Act, 1869*; Parsis by the *Parsi Marriage and Divorce Act, 1936*; and Muslims by the *Dissolution of Muslim Marriages Act, 1939*, which provides the grounds on which women can obtain a divorce, and the uncodified customary law. Civil marriages and inter-community marriages and divorces are governed by the *Special Marriage Act, 1956*. The grounds for divorce in each of the laws is primarily fault based, although the Hindu law and *Special Marriage Act* provide for mutual consent divorce. Under Muslim law, a husband has a right to extrajudicial divorce without stipulating any grounds. In contrast, a wife has a more limited right to judicial divorce on the grounds stated within the provisions of the *Dissolution of Muslim Marriages Act, 1939*. Our discussion focuses on two grounds for divorce: adultery and cruelty. In discussing these grounds for divorce, we briefly outline the statutory provisions, and then examine some of the ways in which these provisions have been interpreted and applied by the courts. We will illustrate the extent to which these judicial approaches have been heavily informed by familial ideology, and demonstrate the contradictory outcomes of these cases for women.

ADULTERY: Adultery is a ground for divorce under all personal laws, except Muslim law.[50] The particular provisions vary amongst different personal laws, but at the ideological level, the assumptions on which the adultery provisions are based are very similar. Adultery is understood as a fundamental violation and repudiation of the marital relationship. Yet, the implications of adultery have long been considered to be quite different for women and men. Women's adultery has been judged more harshly, and considered a more fundamental repudiation of the relationship. This double standard has been based largely on property notions within familial ideology: of women as the property of their husbands, and of ensuring that property is only inherited by the legitimate heirs of the husband.[51] In this section, we illustrate the way in which these property based notions within familial ideology and their implications for women's sexual conduct inform both the statutory provisions, and the judicial interpretation of these provisions. Our discussion focuses on Christian and Hindu law; the former being an example of law that explicitly embraces a double standard, and the latter an example of where the double standard can be found by scratching beneath the surface of a formally equal law.

Divorce amongst Christians is governed by the provisions of the *Indian Divorce Act, 1869*. Section 10 provides that a husband can secure a divorce on the grounds of his wife's adultery, but a woman must establish an additional ground, namely, cruelty, rape, incest, bigamy, or desertion in order to secure a divorce.[52] The double standard of divorce is thus explicitly contained within the statutory provisions. A woman who commits adultery is considered to be a disloyal wife, and to have repudiated the marital relationship. But, a man who commits adultery is not considered to have repudiated the relationship, unless he also commits some additional misconduct. Disloyalty, in and of itself, is not sufficient for a husband's conduct to be judged as violating the relationship. As a result of this formal inequality, Christian women seeking a divorce must be able to prove that their husbands are both adulterous and particularly odious. Most commonly, divorce is sought on the basis of adultery and cruelty. If one element is missing, or cannot be proven to the satisfaction of the court, the petition will be dismissed. In *Dawn Henderson* v. *D. Henderson*,[53] for example, a wife brought a petition for divorce against her husband under section 10. She alleged that her husband had tried to force her to become a prostitute, and that he was leading 'an adulterous immoral life, visiting brothels and being friendly with prostitutes'.[54] In the court's view, the wife had established cruelty: 'There cannot be a greater degree of cruelty than to compel a chaste wife to submit to the overtures of other persons, out of an ignoble desire to make gain by prostituting the wife'.[55] But, she was not able to provide the evidence required to establish her husband's adultery. As a result of section 10, her petition for divorce was rejected by the court. Even though she was able to demonstrate that she was a good and chaste wife, and that he was a bad and cruel husband, she was unable to marshal the evidence to prove that he had also committed adultery.[56]

The *Indian Divorce Act, 1869*, provides for damages to be claimed against the third party in adultery, that is, a husband can claim damages from his wife's lover. Section 34 states that the right is available only to the husband and not the wife.[57] Once again, the double standard of adultery is expressly contained within the law. Further, this provision for damages demonstrates the underlying property notions informing the law of adultery. A wife's adultery is not only more serious than a husband's adultery, but a wife's adultery is further seen as a harm to the husband. The wife is constructed as the property of her husband, which has been damaged by a third party, and the husband can thereby claim damages against this third party. As the courts have expressly observed, the provision is justified as a form of compensation to the 'aggrieved husband for the loss or injury suffered due to provisional withdrawal from the society of his wife which is absolutely given to him to the exclusion of any other in the world'.[58] Marriage is understood to involve a husband's exclusive right to his wife's sexuality, as a form of property right. And any violation of this right to exclusive sexual access by a third party thereby entitles the husband to appropriate compensation.

The principles for determining appropriate compensation are also of interest in the way in which a wife's 'value' to her husband is to be established. These principles were set out by the courts in the early part of this century and have remained unchallenged.[59] The Bombay High Court stated that in assessing damages on the ground of adultery: '...the Court should consider whether the wife was in the past a good wife and took good care of her husband's house and children, or whether she was a worthless wife, always out of the house and not attending to her duties'.[60] The amount of compensation is determined according to the actual value of the wife to the husband; the injury to the husband's feelings, his marital honour and his matrimonial and family life.[61] A wife is thus judged according to an ideal standard of good wife and good mother. A woman who deviates from the roles accorded to her within this familial ideology will thus not be as valuable to her husband, and the compensation to which he will be entitled will be reduced. It is important to recognize that although this provision for damages has rarely been used in post-independence India, its continued existence on the face of the law is significant, and speaks volumes of the assumptions that underlie the Christian law of divorce more generally. And although it may not be used often, it is still used from time to time.[62]

Under the *Hindu Marriage Act, 1955*, women and men have an equal right to divorce on the basis of adultery.[63] Although the ground is equally available to both parties, there is much to suggest that women and men are judged differently—more specifically, that women are judged against a norm of a 'good wife': chastity, loyalty and self-sacrifice. It is interesting to note that much of reported case law involves petitions brought by husbands rather than wives, on this ground. And although the ground is equally available, the impact of committing adultery is different for women and men. If adultery is established against the wife, she will forfeit her rights to maintenance, as well as be subjected to social and familial ostracism.

Much of the case law on adultery deals with the standard of proof required to establish that it has occurred, and whether on the facts, this burden of proof has been met. The Supreme Court has held that the standard of proof required in cases of adultery is based on the preponderance of probabilities as in other civil cases and not on proof beyond a reasonable doubt as in criminal cases.[64] While this burden of proof applies equally to women and men, women who are alleged to have committed adultery seem to be judged by a particular set of norms. Women who step outside the norms established for good wives, which include mere association with a man other than her husband, seem to be quite vulnerable to a charge of adultery. For example, in *Thimmappa* v. *Tgunnava*,[65] the court held that the wife's absence from her house some time and her association with a stranger to her husband's family without reasonable explanation or any explanation, was sufficient to constitute adultery and grounds for granting a divorce to her husband. In *Ganta Nagamani* v. *Ganta Lakshmana Rao*,[66] the fact that the wife had been seen in the company of a man who was not her husband was sufficient to uphold the husband's petition for divorce on grounds of his wife's adultery. Similarly, in *Sanjukta Padhan* v. *Laxminarayan Padhan*,[67] the trial judge held that evidence of a wife and stranger emerging from a deserted house during the night was sufficient to prove that the wife had committed adultery. The wife argued that her husband had fabricated the case to secure a divorce as he wanted to marry a second time because she had not delivered a male child; had criminally assaulted her when she refused to let him marry again; and forced her to leave the matrimonial home and live with her father. These arguments were dismissed, and the husband's petition for divorce was granted on the basis of her adultery.

The cases dealing with the evidentiary requirement where the wife is alleged to have committed adultery are not consistent. For example, in *Rajendra Agarwal* v. *Sharda Devi*,[68] the court held that the fact that the respondent-wife's clothes were disorderly when her husband entered the house and there was an impression of a kiss on her cheek was sufficient evidence to draw an inference that the wife had sexual intercourse with the man who was also present in the house at the time the husband returned. In contrast, in *P.* v. *P.*,[69] the presence of the respondent wife in a restaurant cabin with her blouse and brassiere unhooked and the co-respondent holding her breast in his hands was held by itself not sufficient to permit any inference of adultery. The apparent inconsistencies between these two cases might be partially explained by the class status of the parties in different cases. The court in *P.* v. *P.* stated that the social condition of the parties and the manner in which they were accustomed to live would influence the finding of adultery.

> What can be said to be natural mingling of the opposite sexes in a jet set world will be alien to a person belonging to ordinary middle class and the unusual mingling of two persons of opposite sex in seclusion for any length of time amongst that class can justifiably lead to an inference of adultery.[70]

The inconsistencies within the cases also reveal the contradictory impact of familial ideology on women. The pervasive interest of the state in preserving the institution of marriage and the normative family at times operates to protect women from allegations of 'sexual impropriety' and deviation from the norm of a good wife. In the *Sharda Devi* case, for example, the court stated that in a Hindu marriage, if there is any chance of reconciliation the court should be slow in granting divorce.[71] In this case, the husband and wife had been living separately for such a long period of time that the possibility of reconciliation seemed highly unlikely. However, in *P.* v. *P.*, as the court found some possibility of reconciliation, the case was decided so as to preserve the marriage tie.

CRUELTY: Cruelty is a common ground for divorce under Hindu, Muslim, Parsi and civil law, and a partial ground of divorce under Christian law.[72] Yet, like adultery, the definition of the type of behaviour that constitutes cruelty varies according to the gender of the petitioner. Despite the fact that cruelty is often equally available to husbands and wives, the way in which the law is interpreted and applied suggests that women and men are evaluated by rather different standards. In this section, we examine some of the ways in which familial ideology, and its moral regulation of women, shapes the judicial interpretations of cruelty. The discussion focuses primarily on Hindu personal law, although some examples are drawn from other personal laws.

Under Hindu law, cruelty is a ground available to both men and women in divorce proceedings. Prior to 1976, cruelty was a ground for judicial separation under section 10 of the *Hindu Marriage Act*. The Act required the petitioner to show that the respondent had treated him or her with such cruelty as to cause a reasonable apprehension in his or her mind that it would be harmful or injurious for the petitioner to live with the respondent. In 1976, the *Hindu Marriage Laws (Amendment) Act* introduced cruelty as a ground for divorce.[73] The phrase 'as to cause a reasonable apprehension in the mind of the petitioner that it will be harmful or injurious for the petitioner to live with the other party' was omitted in section 13(1)(i)(a), which seemed to then broaden the definition of cruelty. The Supreme Court has held that cruelty includes both mental and physical cruelty. Mental cruelty has been defined as 'conduct of such a nature that the wronged party cannot be reasonably asked...to continue to live with the party'.[74] The court must take into account:

> ...the social status, educational level of the parties, the society they move in, the possibility or otherwise of the parties ever living together in case they are already living apart and all other relevant facts and circumstances which it is neither possible nor desirable to set out exhaustively. What is cruelty in one case may not amount to cruelty in another case. It is a matter to be determined in each case having regard to the facts and circumstances of that case.[75]

The courts have defined cruelty as necessarily involving a subjective element of how the conduct in question affects the particular parties in question, and insisted that any determination of cruelty will thus necessarily revolve around the facts and circumstances of the particular case.[76] This subjective nature of cruelty as well as the fact that the courts have expressly recognized that what constitutes cruelty in one case may not be cruelty in another, has created considerable inconsistency and unpredictability in the law. Further, the subjective nature of the test has created considerable space within which the courts can take into account their assumptions about the nature of family, and of men's and women's different roles therein. As the following discussion will attempt to reveal, familial ideology can be seen to inform the ways in which the cruelty provision has been interpreted by the courts.

Petitions brought by a husband for divorce on grounds of cruelty are often successful if he is able to establish that his wife has not conformed with her traditional role as a Hindu wife. A recent decision of the Andhra Pradesh High Court held that the wife's removal of her mangal sutram, a symbol of marriage worn as a necklace at all times in the hope that a husband be given a long life, was an act 'not expected from an educated Hindu Brahmin woman'. Her act was held to constitute cruelty against the husband whose petition for divorce was allowed.[77] The cruelty consisted of the wife's removal of her necklace, considered an act of disrespect and disobedience in the context of a Hindu brahmin woman. Indeed such a woman is required to attend to her husband's wants and needs and pray for his health and longevity. All of these actions are to be done without reward, a wife finding her fulfillment in her husband's fulfillment. Thus the cruelty in this instance consisted of the wife's defiance of her normative role and her lack of complete subservience to her husband.

A wife often responds to an allegation of cruelty with arguments that she has conformed to the norms of a 'good wife'.[78] In *Deepak Natkar* v. *Deepali Natkar*, for example, the wife was working at a place at some distance from the matrimonial home. The husband accused her of refusing to cohabit with him and filed a petition for divorce on grounds of cruelty based, in part, on this allegation. The lower court refused to grant a decree of dissolution of marriage, and the husband appealed. On appeal, the wife refuted the allegation of cruelty by stating that she 'performed all the duties as a faithful Hindu wife to the best of her ability'.[79] The court held that on the evidence, the wife 'always remained ready and willing to perform her duties and obligations as a faithful wife'.[80] In the court's view, the petitioner's work was not sufficient to constitute cruelty even though it meant living away from her husband for periods of time. The correspondence between the parties demonstrated that the husband was pleased that she was providing financial assistance to his family and thus did not object to her working. She remained ready and willing to be with her husband when he wanted her to come. As a result, the husband's appeal was dismissed.

In *Vimlesh* v. *Prakash Chand Sharma*,[81] the petitioner husband alleged cruelty on the grounds that his wife did not discharge her marital obligations. This failure to discharge her obligations allegedly included the non-consummation of the marriage, her refusal to do household work and her desire to renounce the world as a nun. The wife denied these allegations and stated that she had been 'a good serviceable wife' and had been 'discharging her marital obligations'.[82] She was able to demonstrate that she had 'all the love and respect for her husband'.[83] The court held that it was evident from her letters to her husband that she was a 'totally devoted Hindu wife'.[84] In her letters, she addressed her husband as 'master or God of her heart'.[85] In the court's view, her letters clearly implied that 'even if some difficulties are created and she continuously faces separation from her husband,…she would maintain her chastity and would remain alive for her husband'.[86] In light of these statements, coupled with the overriding view that it is the 'law of nature to keep husband and wife together and to maintain their union', the court dismissed the husband's petition. In this case, the wife was able to defeat an allegation of cruelty by demonstrating her complete and utter subservience to her husband. She was able to convince the court that she behaved in a way that conformed to the norms of a good Hindu wife, which involved fidelity, self-sacrifice and devotion to her husband. As in the case of *Natkar*, allegations of cruelty were measured against the norm of the good wife. The women's conduct in both of these cases was measured according to the norms of familial ideology, and the extent to which they conformed to roles and identities accorded to women therein. In both cases, the women were able to defeat the claims by proving that they did in fact measure up to the ideal of the good wife.[87]

In contrast, the wife in the case of *Santana Banerjee* v. *Sachindra Nath Banerjee*,[88] was unable to defeat her husband's petition for divorce on the basis of cruelty because she could not demonstrate that she had lived up to these ideals. The basis of the husband's complaint was that his wife did not want to live as a housewife and that she concealed the fact that she was radio artist and also worked as a teacher. He also alleged that his wife was conscious of her class status and family background and continuously accused him and his family of being rustic and uncultured. He accused her of associating with other men and refusing to consummate the marriage on the ground that she was 'not prepared to become a mother at the cost of her youth'.[89] In her examination at trial, the wife stated that she was not indifferent to domestic matters and denied that she was not willing to lead the life of a traditional Bengali married wife. Despite her plea, the court held that she had caused mental cruelty to her husband by making disparaging remarks against him and his family. The High Court upheld the husband's petition and concurred with the view of the trial court that the wife never conducted herself in a manner befitting a Bengali housewife. In this case, the wife was unable to live up to the norms of the good wife against which allegations of cruelty are judged. She was unable to persuade the court that her behaviour was consistent with that of a good Bengali housewife.

Women's roles as good mothers have also been continuously scrutinized through the cruelty provisions. The refusal to have children has frequently been held to constitute cruelty. In *Satya* v. *Siri Ram*,[90] the husband petitioned for divorce on the grounds that his wife had an abortion without his consent. The court held:

> [the husband, his sister, and his parents were] always crazy to have a child in the family but the appellant [wife] dashed their hopes by resorting to termination of pregnancy. This conduct of the appellant, to my mind, undoubtedly amounts to cruelty if not physical, mental at least and the respondent is well within his right to claim the decree of divorce on that ground.... Now the wife deliberately and consistently refuses to satisfy a husbands natural and legitimate craving to have a child, the deprivation reduces him to despair and it naturally affects his mental health. This is more so in the case in hand where the parties to the litigation are Hindus. In this sort of case the Court has to attach due weight to the general principle underlying the Hindu law of marriage and sonship and the principle of spiritual benefit of having a son who can offer a funeral cake and libation of water to the manes of his ancestors.[91]

The refusal to have children was held to be an act of cruelty as it thwarted the 'natural instinct' of a woman and also deprived the husband and his parents of a male progeny which is essential to perform the last rites.[92]

These assumptions about the good wife and mother sometimes operate to support a woman's petition for divorce on the basis of her husband's cruelty. For example, a wife's allegations of cruelty against her husband have been upheld where he has attacked her 'moral character'. In *Patul Devi* v. *Gopal Mandal*,[93] the wife went to her father's house because her husband beat her frequently. The husband filed a criminal complaint against the father alleging that he had enticed his daughter away for immoral purposes. This complaint was subsequently dismissed. The husband filed for restitution of conjugal rights, but his petition was rejected on the grounds that the allegation he made against the father in the criminal complaint had caused his wife mental distress and was therefore a just cause for leaving the matrimonial home. With regard to the husband's cruelty, the court stated:

> Having regard to the conditions obtaining in India and the importance attached to the purity of matrimonial relations, I cannot conceive of a case of greater mental distress and real apprehension of harm and injury for a wife than her husband's suspicion of faithlessness and unchastity on her part.[94]

It was thus the husband's allegation of unchastity, rather than physical violence against his wife that constituted the husband's cruelty. It was the offence by the husband to a 'good' wife: because she had established that she was a good wife—chaste, faithful, dutiful—there could be no greater cruelty than attacking her good character. Where a woman lives up to the ideals of familial ideology, she can sometimes deploy these ideals to her advantage.[95]

The impact of this familial ideology informing the judicial approach to cruelty can thus be seen to be contradictory. On the one hand, a woman who has lived up to the ideals can deploy this familial ideology to defeat her husband's petition, or even succeed in her own petition for divorce. On the other hand, a woman who in any way deviates from the traditional roles allocated to women risk loosing to their husband's petitions. Familial ideology operates to protect the interests of some women whose lives most closely reflect its ideals, while penalizing those whose lives deviate from these ideals. Yet, even where a woman 'wins', the effect of the decision is to reinscribe the assumptions of familial ideology.

Cases decided under the *Special Marriage Act, 1956*, which governs civil marriages and inter-community marriages, show some similar trends. Under this Act, the husband and wife are both entitled to file for divorce on grounds of cruelty. In spite of the formal equality, the interpretation given to this provision by the courts reproduces the ideological construction of women as good wives. For example, in *Iris Paintal* v. *Autar Singh Paintal*,[96] the husband complained that his wife had been harassing him ever since his promotion required that he spend greater time in the office. He also accused her of humiliating him in front of friends. The wife's defence was that she had 'always taken pleasure and felt happy about the progress and promotion of the petitioner'.[97] In the court's view, the wife had not complied with the norms of a good wife, especially as she wanted the husband to live away from his relatives. The court held:

[i]n spite of living in the Indian Society, [the wife] has attempted to have a marriage in which the relatives have nothing to do with the married couple. This was practically an impossibility and any attempt to achieve such an objective—of having nothing to do with the relatives of the husband—cannot but amount to cruelty of the husband—as marriage is not merely a promise to live with one individual, but in reality, in the social circumstances prevalent in India hithertofore means coming into, and becoming a part of another family, a family other than the family of one's birth, i.e. the family of the husband.[98]

The recognition of cruelty as a grounds for divorce was significant as it expanded the grounds on which women and men could exit from a difficult marriage. However, the courts have interpreted this ground against the norm of familial ideology. When applied to women, this amounts to a moral evaluation of her conduct, and whether it conforms to the norm of a good mother and wife. A wife who fails to perform her marital obligations, which are primarily concerned with caring for and obliging her husband, is vulnerable to a charge of cruelty. Similarly, a woman who attempts to exercise her reproductive choice is considered to have transgressed the norms of a good mother who will have children to satisfy the desires and hopes of her husband and his family.

Cruelty is not equally available to women and men in all personal laws. In Muslim law, for example, a man can divorce his wife without stipulating any grounds through the practice of *talaq*. A Muslim woman, however, can only secure a divorce on the grounds stipulated in the *Dissolution of Muslim Marriages Act, 1939*.[99] Cruelty is included within the Act as a ground on which a woman can obtain a divorce. Cruelty is defined in section 2(viii) as:

> (a) habitually assaults her or makes her life miserable by cruelty of conduct even if such conduct does not amount to physical ill-treatment, or
> (b) associates with women of evil repute or leads an infamous life, or
> (c) attempts to force her to lead an immoral life, or
> (d) disposes of her property or prevents her exercising her legal rights over it, or
> (e) obstructs her in the observance of her religious profession or practice, or
> (f) if he has more wives than one, does not treat her equitably in accordance with the injunctions of the Quran

This definition of cruelty includes elements which are explicitly based on the moral regulation of the husband's conduct. A husband who associates with 'women of evil repute' or who attempts to force his wife 'to lead an immoral life' will be considered to have treated his wife with cruelty. Interestingly, a husband's conduct is defined against a norm of women's sexual conduct: a husband will be considered to have acted badly where he associates with a 'bad woman' or where he tries to force a 'good woman' to act badly. At the same time, there are aspects of this definition of cruelty that are considerably more progressive than other personal laws. For example, it is the only personal law which enables a woman to divorce if her husband attempts to dispose of her legal property or prevent her from exercising rights over her property. It also expressly recognizes physical violence as cruelty, and as a ground for divorce.

In Christian law, cruelty is not in itself a ground for divorce, but rather, is a ground which if coupled with adultery, allows a woman to obtain a divorce. Since a husband can obtain a divorce on the basis of his wife's adultery alone, he does not need to resort to the cruelty ground. The Christian law of divorce thus sets up an asymmetry in the cruelty ground.

Restitution of Conjugal Rights

The restitution of conjugal rights enables one spouse to seek the intervention of the court in directing his or her partner, who leaves the matrimonial home without good cause, to return. It has long been a controversial legal remedy. In the past, the remedy was exclusively available to men to ensure and protect their control over their wives. Where a wife refused to remain with her husband, or where a woman's father refused to send her to live with her husband, the husband could petition for the restitution of conjugal rights. And a woman who refused to comply with an order for restitution of conjugal rights could be imprisoned. It was precisely such a case in the late nineteenth century—the high profile case of Rukmabai—that mobilized supported for the Age of Consent Bill.[100] In the 1920s, the restitution of conjugal rights again came under scrutiny, particularly its penalty of imprisonment. A Bombay High Court refused to uphold an order committing a woman to jail for failing to follow an order for restitution of conjugal rights, noting that 'the days are passed when a wife is considered as a mere slave or chattel of husband'.[101] In 1922, a Bill was introduced into the Legislative Assembly to abolish the penalty of imprisonment in these cases. The *Report of the Sub-committee on Women's Role in Planned Economy* in 1940 recommended the abolition of the remedy in both Hindu and Muslim personal law. But, the *Hindu Marriage Act, 1955*, did not implement the recommendation. Instead, the restitution of conjugal rights was made equally available to women and men. The *Report of the Committee on the Status of Women* in 1975 again recommended its abolition, but no action has yet been taken. As we discuss in the next chapter, the provision has been subjected to repeated though ultimately unsuccessful constitutional challenges. In the courts' view, the fact that the remedy is equally available to women and men is sufficient to dismiss any allegations of sex discrimination. But, the early history of the remedy made the discriminatory assumptions informing the restitution of conjugal rights quite explicit. It was a remedy through which a husband could literally enforce his property rights to his wife's company. Despite efforts to make the law more equal, those assumptions continue to inform the law. As we will reveal, despite the formal equality of the law, women continue to be judged by the norms and values of familial ideology.

The remedy of restitution of conjugal rights continues to be available under the *Hindu Marriage Act*, the *Indian Divorce Act*, the *Parsi Marriage and Divorce Act*, and the *Special Marriage Act*.[102] It is a tool for preserving the marital unit, and is, in principle, equally available to both spouses. However, the case law indicates that the remedy has been used overwhelmingly by men, in an effort to have their wives return to the matrimonial home. And despite the formal equality of this remedy, the norms against which women and men are judged in petitions for the restitution of conjugal rights is anything but equal. The case law illustrates the extent to which this remedy is informed by and serves to reinforce dominant familial ideology, and its construction of women as wives and mothers. In petitions for the restitution of conjugal rights, the courts are called upon to judge the conduct of the spouse—usually the woman—who has left the matrimonial home. The legal issue is whether the spouse has left without good reason. But for a woman who has left the matrimonial home, the question of the reasonableness of her conduct is judged against the norms and standards of an ideal wife. In this section, we examine some of the cases decided under the *Hindu Marriage Act, 1956*, and attempt to reveal that the courts time and again evaluate the reasonableness of the wife's withdrawal from the matrimonial home and the company of her husband against the ideal of a good and dutiful Hindu wife.

A number of the decisions on the restitution of conjugal rights deal with the issue of a wife taking up employment at a place which is at some distance from the matrimonial home, requiring her to live away from her husband. In *Tirath Kaur* v. *Kirpal Singh*,[103] a husband petitioned for restitution of conjugal rights arguing that his wife had left the matrimonial home to take up a job at a distant place and that she refused to resign her job and join him despite his repeated requests. The wife stated that she took up a job because of her husband's financial stringency. Despite the distance, the parties would meet one another frequently, especially during holidays. She also sent a portion of her salary to her husband and father-in-law. She alleged that ultimately she was unable to meet the increasing demands of her husband for more money. He demanded that she resign her job and she refused. However, at no time did she want the marriage to end. The trial court allowed the husband's petition holding that:

> the husband was justified in asking the wife to live with him even if she had to give up service but as she was not prepared to do so on any condition whatsoever and the conjugal duties could not be performed

by living at such a long distance, the husband was entitled to the restitution claim.[104]

The wife appealed the decision, but the High Court rejected her appeal.

[A] wife's first duty to her husband is to submit herself obediently to his authority, and to remain under his roof and protection. She is not, therefore, entitled to separate residence or maintenance, unless she proves that, by reason of his misconduct or by his refusal to maintain her in his own place of residence or for other justifying cause, she is compelled to live apart from him.[105]

The fact that a wife wanted to work was not sufficient justification for her to withdraw from the conjugal company of her husband and the matrimonial home. A distinction was made between a wife who is compelled to leave the matrimonial home as a result of her husband's misconduct and a wife who chooses to leave the home to fulfill her own aspirations. A wife who chooses to leave is seen to have violated a Hindu wife's duty to place her husband's needs and interests before hers. The requirements of cohabitation and conjugality are constructed in relation to needs of the husband and obligations of the wife to fulfill those needs.

In *Gaya Prasad* v. *Bhagwati*,[106] the wife decided to work at a place away from the matrimonial home as a result of her husband's adverse financial circumstances. She asked the husband to live with her, but he refused and tried to coerce her to give up her job. She alleged that her husband and his father threatened her if she refused to give up her job. The husband filed a petition for restitution of conjugal rights which was dismissed by the lower court. However, on appeal, the High Court held that the wife had withdrawn from her husband's company without reasonable excuse. The court stated:

According to the ordinary notions of Hindu society, the wife is expected to perform the marital obligations at her husband's residence. She can accept service at a different place but not so as to clash with the husband's marital rights which she is duty-bound to render. It is, therefore, plain that there could only be an arrangement for her staying separately for continuing her service by mutual consent and concurrence of both the parties but she could not impose her unilateral decision on the husband by merely stating that she had no objection to allow the husband to live with her at the place where she has accepted service. The instant case amounts in our opinion, to a virtual withdrawal from the society of the husband and, therefore, the fact of

separation which is established in this case amounts...to the matrimonial offence of desertion [by the wife].[107]

In the court's view, the wife was not entitled to reject her husband's
'offer to bring her to their matrimonial home'.[108] As in *Tirath Kaur*, the
court was firmly of the view that a Hindu wife could not freely choose
to live apart from her husband for the purpose of employment. According
to the court, although a wife could take a job away from the matrimonial
home, she could only do so with the permission of her husband. Any
conflict between her employment outside of the home and her marital
obligations must be resolved in favour of her marital obligations.

In a similar case, *Surinder Kaur* v. *Gurdeep Singh*,[109] a wife took up
a job at a place where the parties resided, but subsequently resigned and
took up a job 100 miles away from the matrimonial home. The husband
filed a petition for the restitution of conjugal rights which was subsequently settled. When the wife failed to abide by the terms of the
compromise, a second petition was filed by the husband for the restitution
of conjugal rights. He stated that his wife resigned her first job and took
up employment elsewhere without his consent. The wife alleged that she
had been beaten by her husband and turned out of the house twice during
the time she was employed in her first job. She was not willing to return
to the matrimonial home as she apprehended that she would be in danger.
The court dismissed her appeal on the grounds that the acts of cruelty
had not been proved so as to justify the wife's withdrawal from her
husband's company. Relying on the decision in *Tirath Kaur* the court
held that where a wife accepted a job at a place different from where
the husband resided and without his consent, it was reasonable to infer
that she had left without reasonable excuse. The court stipulated the
rights and obligations of the parties to a marriage:

> According to Hindu law, marriage is a holy union. The relationship
> between a husband and wife imposes upon each of them certain marital
> duties and gives each of them certain legal marital rights. The marriage
> imposes a duty on the husband to protect his wife, to give her a home
> to provide her with comforts and necessities of life within his means
> and to treat her nicely. It enjoins on the wife the duty of attendance,
> obedience to and veneration for the husband and to live with him
> wherever he may choose to reside.[110]

In *Surinder Kaur* the wife's conduct was quite explicitly judged against
the norm of a good Hindu wife who must follow her husband and obey
his wishes in return for his protection. There was no recognition or
acceptance of a wife's right to work, at least not within the context of a

matrimonial relationship. In fact, the courts rarely seem to consider this issue in the restitution of conjugal rights cases, but rather focus on whether the woman had a compelling reason to leave the 'comfort and protection' of the matrimonial home and her husband's company.

The courts do not always order that a wife return to the matrimonial home. For example, when a woman has taken a job away from the matrimonial home with her husband's consent, and where he has access to her, a wife will not generally be held to have withdrawn from her husband's company.[111] In considering whether a wife had withdrawn from the home with good reason, the courts are also called upon to consider the conduct of the husband. Where a husband has been found to have violated his marital obligations, the courts may find that the woman did indeed have good reason to leave. In *Swaraj Garg* v. *K. M. Garg*, where the husband and wife worked in different places, the husband filed for restitution of conjugal rights on the grounds that the wife should reside in her matrimonial home.[112] The husband's petition was dismissed by the trial court, but was allowed by the single bench of the Delhi High Court. The wife's subsequent appeal succeeded. However, on the issue of who had the right to determine the matrimonial home, the court stated, 'Normally, the husband would be earning more than the wife and therefore, as a rule the wife may have to resign her lesser job and be with the husband, who would be expected to set up the matrimonial home'.[113] Although the court accepted that an exclusive right to the husband to decide the matrimonial home would be contrary to the provisions of Article 14, it nevertheless held that:

> When the husband and wife did not agree where they should stay, the husband must have a casting vote. With respect, a casting vote is only a tiebreaker and is useful when a stalemate is to be broken because the matter has to be decided one way or the other. Between the husband and the wife, the decision as to the matrimonial home has to be taken on the balance of circumstances. If the circumstances are equally balanced in favour of the wife and the husband, then there would have been a stalemate and neither of them would be able to sue for restitution of conjugal rights.[114]

On the facts, the court held that the wife had a reasonable excuse for not resigning her job. The wife was already working at the time of the marriage and had some prospect of a promotion in her job. This situation together with the financial adversity of the couple, justified the wife's withdrawal from her husband's company.[115]

In considering whether a wife had withdrawn from the home with good reason, the courts are also called upon to consider the conduct of the husband. Where a husband has been found to have violated his marital obligations, the courts may find that the woman did indeed have good reason to leave. For example, in *Tulsa* v. *Pannalal*, a husband filed for restitution of conjugal rights.[116] The wife had left the matrimonial home on the grounds that her husband had treated her with cruelty and had also deserted her. The husband admitted that he beat his wife because she did not get up at 6:00 a.m. but at 7:00 a.m. and did not wear the clothes he wanted her to. The court held:

> As a devoted wife, it was no doubt [the wife's] duty to get up before her husband was to leave for his work, but if she did not, the husband was not entitled to beat her. Likewise, as the dutiful wife, she should have respected the wishes of her husband as to the particular clothes to be put on a particular occasion, but if she did not again, the husband had no right to beat her.[117]

The court dismissed the application for restitution of conjugal rights, but only after admonishing the wife for dereliction of her duty towards the husband, which, nevertheless did not confer a right on the husband to beat her. The court found that the husband's treatment of his wife—in having beaten her, left her at her father's home, and not made sufficient amends—justified the wife in living separately from her husband. The petition for restitution of conjugal rights was dismissed.

In both *Garg* and *Tulsa*, the court refused to grant the husband's petition. The duty of the wife to remain in the matrimonial home and with her husband was countered by the illegal conduct of the husband. In the first case, the illegal conduct consisted of the husband's demand for dowry and in the latter, the beatings. As long as the wife was able to demonstrate her compliance to the norm of a good wife, the law protected her from any abuse or exploitation. Again, we can see the contradictory nature of familial ideology for women. In these cases, because women were able to live up to the expectations of them as good wives, the law protected them. At the same time, the reasoning in these cases serves to reinforce the deeply gendered assumptions about women's roles in the family.[118]

■ Protecting Good Women and Private Families: Criminal Law Interventions in the Family

Since the nineteenth century, social reformers and women's rights activists have sought to extend the legal intervention of the law, particularly the criminal law, into the realm of the family. As we discussed in chapter 1, the engagements with law have sought a renegotiation of the public and private spheres, through an incremental encroachment of the 'public'—the state sanctioned criminal law—into the 'private' sphere of the family. Despite these repeated challenges to the public/private distinction, and the steady expansion of the scope of criminal intervention into previously 'private' spheres, the distinction has not been eliminated. Rather, the public/private distinction continues to shape the way in which the *Indian Penal Code* intervenes in the family. The criminalization of some activity, and the non-criminalization of other, remains distinctively marked by the idea of family as private, and as the legitimate arena of containing, in the name of protecting, women's sexuality. Similarly, the enforcement of laws specifically enacted for the express purpose of protecting women also continue to be shaped by the public/private distinction, and the idea of the family as private. Despite provisions within the *Indian Penal Code, 1860*, condemning various forms of violence within the family such as dowry harassment and murder, the public/private distinction and the familial ideology which sustains it, operates to undermine the enforcement of the provisions. The family continues to be constructed as a private sphere, sometimes beyond the legitimate intervention of the law, sometimes requiring the law to protect its privacy. Efforts to challenge the public/private distinction are resisted in and through the very familial ideology on which the distinction is based and reinforced. Familial ideology, which continues to constitute the family as a private sphere, operates to undermine the effective enforcement of laws designed to intervene within this private realm. In this section, we will examine several issues where the criminal law intersects with the family, that is, where the criminal law has been called upon to intervene and proscribe certain practices within the family. We examine the contradictory ways in which the public/private distinction continues to inform the criminal law and its interpretation, and the way in which familial ideology continues to shape even those laws that were designed to benefit women.

Criminal Interventions in Marital and Non-Marital Sex

In this section, we briefly examine a number of provisions of the criminal law dealing with marital and non-marital sex: adultery, marital and non-marital rape, homosexuality and prostitution. We argue that these legal interventions are shaped by the public/private distinction. But, we further argue that this distinction works in highly particular, and seemingly contradictory ways. Sometimes, these legal interventions construct the family as private and beyond legitimate intervention; other times these interventions can be seen to protecting private families and good women therein from any third party intervention. Sometimes, the public/private distinction informs the nature of the sexuality in question: if it is private and within the family, the law will protect it; if it is public, it will not. And sometimes, even private sexuality is constructed as public, that is, as within the legitimate intervention in the law. As we will attempt to argue, running through these shifting uses of the public/private distinction lies the assumptions of familial ideology, wherein the privacy of the family and the honour of good women—chaste wives, virgin daughters—is held sacred.

In addition to being a ground for divorce, adultery continues to be also a criminal offence recognized by the *Indian Penal Code, 1860*. Section 497 provides:

> Whoever has sexual intercourse with a person who is and whom he knows or has reason to believe to be the wife of another man, without the consent or connivance of that man, such sexual intercourse not amounting to the offence of rape, is guilty of the offense of adultery.

The penalty for adultery is imprisonment up to five years. The section further provides that in 'in such cases, the wife shall not be punishable as an abettor'. Section 497 thus makes adultery committed by a man an offence. Adultery committed by a woman is not an offence under section 497. Further, section 198 of the *Code of Criminal Procedure, 1973*, allows the husband of the 'adulteress' to prosecute the man with whom she committed adultery. It does not allow the wife of the adulterer to prosecute him or the adulteress. This criminal law of adultery is based on a host of problematic assumptions about women, sexuality and the family. To begin with, the law formally distinguishes between the adulterous conduct of women and men.[119] Only a man can be prosecuted, and thus according to the law of adultery, criminal responsibility is placed only on men. Within this legal regulation, adulterous women are seen to have virtually no agency; or at least, not enough agency to make them criminally responsible for their behaviour. Women are constructed as victims, and are thereby to be protected by being exempted from criminal sanctions.

Further, only the husband of an adulterous wife can prosecute the third party with whom she committed adultery. The wife of an adulterous husband cannot similarly initiate a prosecution against her adulterous husband, nor against the woman with whom he had the adulterous relationship. Within this legal regulation, women are not only denied any sexual agency, but are also not seen to be harmed by the commission of the offence. The criminal law of adultery is not simply protecting the sanctity of the marital relationship, but rather, much like adultery within the context of divorce, it is protecting a husband's interest in his exclusive access to his wife's sexuality.[120] In many ways, the adultery provisions reflect the same assumptions that underlie the divorce laws. Wives are constructed as the property of their husbands and any violation of a husband's exclusive sexual access to his wife is seen as a harm to the husband. But, the fact that adultery continues to be recognized as a criminal offence within the *Indian Penal Code, 1860*, is significant in its own right. Adultery is not seen as simply a private matter between spouses, but rather, as a public matter in which the state can legitimately intervene to protect a man's property rights over his wife. The criminal law is called upon to protect the marital relationship from intervention by a third party, and to protect women's moral character. The protection of the private relationship between husband and wife is seen to be in the broader public good. The public/private distinction is deployed rather differently. The private realm of the family is seen to require the public intervention of the criminal law, to protect the sanctity of the marital relationship by in effect policing the boundaries of this relationship and ensuring that third parties do not violate it. The criminal law of adultery is an example of the extent to which the law itself constructs the private realm. The law constructs the marital relationship as private by prohibiting any third party intervention in it. The criminal law is called upon to reinforce the construction of the marital relationship as private, and the construction of the family as based on sexual exclusivity.

The public/private distinction operates rather differently within the context of rape. The extent to which the rape laws continue to reflect traditional assumptions about women's sexuality—chastity, virginity, honour—has been well documented.[121] Despite the reforms to the rape laws, judicial decisions continue to be informed by these assumptions and protect only those women who have adhered to these norms. In our view, this legal regulation can further be viewed through the lens of familial ideology and the public/private distinction. Unlike the criminal law of adultery which zealously guards the privacy of sex within the marital relationship from third party intervention, the legal regulation of rape is concerned only with sex within the public realm, that is, with rape that occurs outside of the realm of the family. And even when the rape has occurred in the public sphere, the legal regulation can be seen to be further shaped by whether the women's sexuality is of a public or private nature. Where woman's sexuality is considered private, that is, guarded within the confines of the family, as a virgin daughter or a loyal wife, the criminal law may protect her. When women adhere to the norms of the good Hindu wife and/or daughter, she may receive some protection from third party intervention. But when a woman deviates from these norms—by having consensual sex outside of marriage—the law considers her sexuality to have become public, and thus, not to come within the purview of the protection of the criminal law.

For example, section 155(4) of the *Indian Evidence Act, 1872*, provides that the defence may introduce evidence to demonstrate that the prosecutrix is of 'a generally immoral character'. The purpose of the section is to provide the defence with a means to discredit the testimony of the witness. It is based on the assumption that 'unchaste' women cannot be believed, at least not when it comes to matters of sex. As soon as it is demonstrated by the defence that the woman is sexually promiscuous, her sexuality belongs to the public sphere and is no longer entitled to the protection of the criminal law. Instead it is penalized. The case law is filled with similar examples of this distinction between women's private and public sexuality. The Mathura rape case, in which the Supreme Court overturned the conviction of two police officers on the basis that the young woman had not demonstrated utmost resistance and thus must have consented, can also be seen in light of the fact that Mathura had run off with her lover.[122] She was no longer a good woman (neither virgin daughter nor chaste wife) within the confines of the family. Ten years late, in the equally controversial Suma Rani rape case, the Supreme Court reduced the mandatory minimum sentence of two police officers, partially on the basis that Suman Rani was 'a woman of questionable character and easy virtue with lewd and lascivious behaviour'.[123] Again, in this case, Suma Rani had eloped with her lover; as a woman who was 'used to having frequent sexual intercourse', she was no longer a good woman with the private confines of the family.[124] By way of contrast are those cases where women were considered to be virgin daughters or chaste wives. Here, the same assumptions of chastity and virginity operate, but with different results. In the courts' view, the dishonour and shame brought about by rape to the innocence of virgin daughters and the loyalty of chaste of wives is such that these women would be unlikely to make false allegations,[125] be predisposed to delaying reporting rape, and/or unlikely to be able to resist rape.[126]

Good women in private families may thus be protected by the law—unless of course they are raped within their families. Marital rape is not recognized under current legal definitions of rape. Section 375 of the *Indian Penal Code* states that 'Sexual intercourse by a man with his own wife, the wife not being under fifteen years of age, is not rape'. The origin of the exclusion of marital rape from the purview of the criminal law is based on a compilation of law prepared by Sir Matthew Hale C. J., in 1736, entitled *Pleas of the Crown:*

> The husband cannot be guilty of a rape committed by himself upon his lawful wife, for by their mutual matrimonial consent and contract the wife hath given up herself this kind unto her husband which she cannot retract.[127]

In other words, a woman surrenders her right to consent to sexual relations at the time of entering into a marriage and the husband is given an unconditional, unqualified right of sexual access to her. Every act of sexual intercourse is deemed to be consensual as such consent is considered to be given at the time of marriage. The continuing exemption of marital rape from the purview of the criminal law sustains the assumption of the wife as exclusive property of the husband. As stated by Katherine O'Donnovan:

> Its immunity from the purview of the criminal law is explained on the grounds that the female victim is a wife. This justification can be understood in the context of the dominant familial ideology and female sexuality which treats a wife as property and as having no sexual agency or decision making in sexual activity within the marital context.[128]

Marital rape was one of the issues taken up during the campaigns to reform the rape law in the early 1980s. The Law Commission recommended that the marital exemption to rape be removed, and that the criminal law recognize marital rape. This recommendation was not taken up by the government, and thus not included in the *Criminal Law Amendment Act, 1983*. But, the Act did narrow the marital exemption somewhat. Section 376A of the *Indian Penal Code* provides that the rape of a woman by her husband from whom she was judicially separated constitutes rape, and is punishable by up to two years imprisonment. While section 376A can be seen to begin to challenge the exemption of the marital relationship from the purview of the criminal law of rape, the challenge is a fairly minimal one. A husband is only to be held criminally responsible where there has already been a judicially recognized rupture in the marital relationship. Presumably, it is this judicially sanctioned rupture in the marital relationship that revokes a wife's assumed consent to sexual intercourse with her husband. Section 376A thus does not challenge the assumption that the act of marriage gives rise to an unqualified and unconditional consent on the part of the wife to sexual intercourse with her husband. Rather, it simply recognizes that the act of judicial separation revokes this consent. Further, a conviction under section 376A carries a significantly lower penalty than other forms of rape. The mandatory minimum sentence in non-custodial rape cases is seven years and ten in the case of custodial rapes.[129] The relatively low sentence accorded to judicially separated men convicted of raping their wives—two years—creates a hierarchy of the crime. Once again, it is a man's status as a husband that is the explanation for reducing the harshness of the criminal law.

By way of contrast yet again, not all sexuality that is located within the private sphere is considered by the criminal law to be private. Homosexual sexual activity has long been penalized under the provisions of the *Indian Penal Code, 1860*. Section 377 provides:

> Whoever voluntarily has carnal intercourse against the order of nature with any man, woman or animal, shall be punished with imprisonment for life, or with imprisonment of either description for a term which may extend to ten years, and shall also be liable to fine.
>
> Explanation—Penetration is sufficient to constitute the carnal intercourse necessary to the offence described in this section.

When it comes to particular kinds of sexuality, which in the law's view is 'against the order of man', the location of that sexuality is irrelevant.[130] Rather, the so-called 'perverse' nature of this sex is such that it becomes public and thus the legitimate subject for state intervention. Unlike marital rape, where the private nature of the sex immunizes it from any criminal intervention, in the case of homosexuality, the fact that it may be conducted in private is irrelevant, since it cannot, by definition, be conducted with the *right* kind of privacy, that is, with the heterosexual family, between husband and wife. Private sex is thus only immunized if it is legitimate private sex, that is, sex within marriage.

The shifting nature of the public/private distinction is again apparent in the legal regulation of prostitution. The *Immoral Trafficking Prevention Act, 1956*, prohibits trafficking, as well as solicitation. And in so doing, the law casts is net very widely. Section 7 prohibits women from carrying on prostitution in or near a public place, such as a hospital, a place of public religious worship, and an educational institution. Section 8 prohibits women from soliciting or seducing 'by words, gestures or willful exposure of her person' which includes simply sitting by a window, or on the balcony of a building. But, the prohibitions are not limited to the public sphere. Section 3 prohibits the keeping of brothels. And under section 20, a woman can be brought before a magistrate to show cause that she is not a prostitute. If she cannot, then the magistrate can order that she be removed from the jurisdiction. This section not only allows 'suspicious' looking (unaccompanied by a husband) women to be picked up from a public place, but also extends into the private sphere. The mere suspicion of prostitution in a residential home is sufficient for a magistrate to demand that a woman show cause as to why she should not be removed.[131]

The legal regulation of prostitution under the *Immoral Traffic Prevention Act, 1956*, is, on the one hand, concerned with restricting the space in which sex work can occur, that is, away from public view. But, it is also concerned with the mere fact of prostitution itself, such that, even sex work or sex workers in a private home can fall within the scope of the Act. Similar to the regulation of homosexuality, it is the very nature of the sexuality in question, in this case, sex for sale, that makes it public, and therefore, within the legitimate reach of the criminal law. Sex work, even within the privacy of a sex worker's home, can never really be private. Its very nature, for sale and outside of marriage, places it firmly outside of the protected realm of familial privacy, and renders it public.

We can thus see the extent to which the public/private distinction is a rather shifting one. Sometimes the criminal law constructs the family as private, and in need of protection (adultery); other times, as private, and thus beyond its reach (marital rape). Yet, running through both the regulation of adultery and marital rape is an understanding of the marital relationship as the exclusive site of legitimate sexuality. By way of contrast, the regulation of homosexuality and prostitution are both unconcerned with the location of the sexuality in question, since the nature of the sexuality renders it public. And the legal regulation of non-marital rape can be seen to vacillate between the public realm of illegitimate sex, and the private realm of legally sanctioned sex. The legal regulation of rape remains concerned with the location of a woman's sexuality. If her sexuality has been contained within the confines of the family, it is private and protected. If not, it is public and subject to considerably less protection. Despite the shifting nature of the public/private distinction, running throughout these various areas of criminal intervention is a dominant familial ideology, which constructs good women as chaste wives and virgin daughters, and with protecting these women, within the privacy of their families.

Dowry Violence

The *Dowry Prohibition Act, 1961*, prohibited the giving or taking of dowry, defined as any property or valuable security given in consideration of marriage and as a condition of the marriage taking place.[132] The maximum punishment for the offence was six months and or a fine of Rs.5,000.[133] In order to prosecute a husband for demanding dowry, the prior permission of the government had to be sought and the complaint had to be filed within one year by the person aggrieved.[134] There were few prosecutions under the Act and even fewer convictions. In the late 1970s and early 1980s, women's groups in India brought attention to a particular kind of violence that women—particularly young, recently married women—were experiencing in their families: women were being harassed and in some cases, ultimately murdered by their husbands and in-laws in an effort to extort money and/or property from the women's natal family. The campaign to bring this practice to light, and to attempt to put an end to it, came to focus on strengthening the legal prohibitions on dowry. Activists lobbied for amendments to the *Dowry Prohibition Act, 1961*, and the introduction of new provisions into the *Indian Penal Code* to deal with the offence.

In 1983, a series of amendments were introduced to the legal regulation of dowry and dowry violence. The *Dowry Prohibition Act, 1961*, was amended, expanding the definition of dowry[135] and increasing the punishment.[136] The one year limitation was removed and it was possible for someone other than the woman to file a complaint. The *Indian Penal Code* was also amended to add new offence of cruelty by a husband or relative of a husband towards his wife. According to the new provision, cruelty to a married woman, which includes willful conduct which drives her to suicide or attempt to commit suicide, was made punishable for a term up to three years and a fine. The section defines cruelty as harassment of the married woman which coerces her or her parents or relations to meet the unlawful demands of dowry by her husband and in-laws.[137] In 1986, a second series of amendments were introduced to the legal regulation of dowry and dowry violence. The *Dowry Prohibition Act* was again amended to further increase the punishment.[138] A ban was imposed on advertisements for dowry and if a woman died an unnatural death her property was to devolve on her children or to her parents in case she had no children. Section 304B was introduced to the *Indian Penal Code*, which provides that where the death of a woman is caused by burns, bodily injury or otherwise than under normal circumstances within seven years of marriage, and evidence reveals that she was subjected to cruelty or harassment by her husband or his relatives prior to her death in connection with any demand for dowry, her death is to be considered a dowry death.[139]

The new statutory provisions were intended to protect women from being harassed or killed for purposes of dowry. The amendments to the *Dowry Prohibition Act*, the *Indian Penal Code*, as well as other minor criminal acts, attempted to provide mechanisms for the intervention in, and proscription of, violent practices against women within the family. While these reforms came largely in response to the campaigns of the

women's movement, a debate emerged from within the women's movement as to the efficacy of these new legal provisions. Some feminists
have argued that the reforms recognized the existence of dowry demands
and harassment, but sought to resolve it by dealing with the symptom
rather than the cause of the problem.[140] The law reforms dealing with
dowry and dowry violence were not connected to the structural inequality
of women within the family, and thus did little to address a young wife's
lack of power within her marital family, and her total economic dependency on her husband and his family. Parents continue to be frequently
willing to meet the dowry demands of a son-in-law and his family, in
order to ensure that the wife remains in the matrimonial home. A
woman's economic dependency and the lack of equal property rights or
the recognition of matrimonial property, compel her to remain in the
matrimonial home and meet the unreasonable demands of her husband
and in-laws, in order to preserve the marital unit, her only security. The
law reform continues to operate within the framework of this arrangement
and the familial ideology that sustains it.

The failure of the legal regulation of dowry to challenge the assumption
of women's economic dependency and to transform their status of dependency has lead some feminists to argue for rethinking of the question
of dowry. Madhu Kishwar has argued that until such time as the laws
and practices of inheritance are transformed, enabling women to claim
their rightful entitlement to property, women should not be deprived of
their dowries.[141] Although her position created a flurry of debate, within
which many feminists stressed the need to continue to condemn the
practice of dowry,[142] Kishwar's controversial position on dowry has
highlighted the importance of inheritance rights for women, and has
brought into sharper relief the failure of dowry laws to in any way address
the structural problem of women's economic dependency. As Bina Agarwal has argued, both sides of the debate over dowry have been concerned
with the general issue of how to best improve women's position within
their household, and have differed only on the question of whether the
prohibition on dowry is a good way to accomplish this objective.[143] This
debate has thus begun to bring to light the extent to which the problems
such as dowry facing women within the family cannot only be cast as
'social evils' or 'domestic violence' that need to be eliminated, but must
also be viewed through the lens of economic dependency.

We are substantially in agreement with the need to address women's
economic dependency, and to reform the legal regulation of property to
which we turn in the next section of the chapter. However, we propose
for the moment to bracket this question of economic dependency and the
reform of other laws, and focus our inquiry on the dowry laws in their

own right. In our view, even the more limited promise of criminal intervention in the family as a means of punishing those who commit dowry violence and sending a strong message of condemnation of these practices, has been highly contradictory. On the one hand, this legal regulation of dowry was a clear challenge to the construction of the family as private, and a recognition of the difficulties involved in prosecuting crimes that occur within the family. The message has not gone unnoticed by the courts. In *State of Punjab* v. *Iqbal Singh*, for example, the Supreme Court, after reviewing the various amendments to the legal regulation of dowry, stated:

> The legislative intent is clear to curb the menace of dowry deaths with a firm hand. It must be remembered that since such crimes are generally committed in privacy of residential homes and in secrecy, independent and direct evidence is not easy to get.[144]

Similarly, in *Om Parkash* v. *State of Punjab* where the Supreme Court commented that in considering evidence in dowry deaths 'the Court has to be conscious of the fact that a death connected with dowry takes place inside the house, where outsiders who can be said to be independent witnesses in the traditional sense, are not expected to be present'.[145]

Yet, on the other hand, this legal regulation of dowry has not displaced the public/private distinction nor the familial ideology that sustains it. Rather, as we will attempt to reveal, the dowry laws have often been interpreted by the courts within the discursive framework of familial ideology and have operated to reinforce the construction of women therein. A classic statement of this familial ideology can be seen in the case of *State (Delhi Administration)* v. *Laxman Kumar*, where the husband, mother-in-law, and brother-in-law were charged with dowry murder.[146] The Supreme Court overturned the High Court's acquittal, and found the husband and mother-in-law guilty. In its concluding remarks, however, the court revealed the assumptions about the nature of marriage, and of women's role therein. Although observing that there may be some truth in the High Court's view of the need to promote women's economic independence, the court was more concerned with its disagreement with the High Court regarding the history of dowry. According to Ranganath Misra J.

> In the olden days, in the Hindu community, dowry in the modern sense was totally unknown. Man and woman enjoyed equality of status, and society looked upon women as living goddesses. Where ladies lived in peace, harmony and with dignity and status, Gods were believed to

be roaming about in human form. When a bride was brought into the family, it was considered to be great event and it was looked upon bringing fortune into the family not by way of dowry but on account of the grace the young lady carried with and around her.[147]

The court went on to comment on its views about the nature of marriage:

The religious rites performed at the marriage alter clearly indicate that the man accepts the woman as his better-half by assuring her protection as guardian, ensuring food and necessaries of life as the provider, guaranteeing companionship as the mate and by resolving that the pleasures and sorrows in the pursuit of life shall be shared with her and Dharma shall be observed. If this be the concept of marriage, there would be no scope for worldly considerations, particularly dowry.[148]

The court's idealized notion of marriage naturalizes the role of men as financial providers, and of women as in need of men's protection. The court further elaborates on its idealized vision of marriage:

Every marriage ordinarily involves a transplant. A girl born and brought up in her natural family when given in marriage, has to leave the natural setting and come into a new family. When a tender plant is shifted from the place of origin to a new setting, great care is taken to ensure that the new soil is suitable and not far different from the soil where the plant had hitherto been growing; care is taken to ensure that there is not much of variation of the temperature, watering facility is assured and congeniality is attempted to be provided. When a girl is transplanted from her natural setting into an alien family, the care expected is bound to be more than in the case of a plant. Plant has life but the girl has a more developed one.[149]

The court then discusses how a young bride will have to learn to adapt to her new setting, and how this process of adaptation must be two sided:

Give and take, live and let live, are the ways of life and when the bride is received in the new family she must have feeling of welcome and by the fond bonds of love and affection, grace and generosity, attachment and consideration that she may receive in the family of the husband, she will get into [a] new mould; which would last her for life.... The process has to be a natural one and there has to be exhibition of co-operation and willingness from every side. Otherwise how would the transplant succeed.[150]

In this case, the husband was found guilty of dowry death. But, the court's comments begin to illustrate the contradictory nature of the dowry laws, and of convictions thereunder. Although the court condemns the practice of dowry, its approach merely accepts the patrilocal assumptions of dominant familial ideology whereby brides are seen to be transferred from their natal families to their marital families. This idea of transfer is so strongly embedded in the judicial reasoning that women are literally analogized to plants, transplanted from one family to another. Young wives are constructed as fragile property, in need of protection and tender care.[151] Despite its willingness to intervene in the private sphere of the family to condemn the dowry violence, the *Laxman* case does little to challenge the dominant familial ideology. Rather, the court seems to call for a return to a mythical golden age when the normative ideal of the family and of women's cherished roles therein was untarnished by such violent practices.

The plant analogy is again seen in *Paniben* v. *State of Gujarat* in which a mother-in-law was charged with murdering her daughter-in-law. In its opening comments, the Supreme Court remarked:

> Everytime a case relating to dowry death comes up, it causes ripples in the pool of the conscience of this Court. Nothing could be more barbarous, nothing could be more heinous than this sort of crime. ...Sympathy to the fairer sex, the minimum sympathy is not even shown. *The seedling which is uprooted from its original soil and is to be planted in another soil to grow and bear fruits is crushed*[152] (emphasis added).

Once again, women and young wives are protected in the name of sympathy to the fairer sex (and plants). This discourse both reflects and reinscribes not only the construction of women as weak, and in need of protection, but moreover, the dominant familial ideology within which young brides are constructed as little more than property, transferred from one family to another.

Assumptions about women's moral character, particularly as good self-sacrificing mothers, can also be seen to inform judicial approaches to dowry deaths. For example, in *Harbans Lal* v. *State of Haryana*[153] the husband and mother-in-law were accused of murdering the wife and her nine month old baby. In the court's view, the fact that the baby was also killed ruled out the possibility of suicide:

> If the deceased Santosh Rani was committing suicide, she as a mother, would be the last person not to save her daughter of tender age. The

fact that the child also received burns and died would positively go to show that both of them were burnt to death at the hands of others who can be none else than the two accused.[154]

In the court's view, the norms of motherhood were such as to make it literally unthinkable that a young mother could kill her child. Similar norms of the self-sacrificing mother were brought to bear in the case of *Brij Lal* v. *Prem Chand*.[155] In this case, a young woman had committed suicide, and her husband was charged with abetment. In the court's view, the fact that the young woman had a baby son was an important factor in concluding that she had not committed suicide of her own volition:

> Veena Rani would not have easily reconciled herself to forsaking her one and a half year old son and commit suicide. No mother, however, distressed and frustrated would easily make up her mind to leave her young child in the lurch and commit suicide unless she had been goaded to do so by someone close to her.[156]

In this case, it was inconceivable to the court that a young mother could kill herself, and thereby abandon her child. The ideal of the self-sacrificing mother shaped the court's view that a mother's commitment to her child would invariably take precedence over her own misery. Yet again, in *Goverdhan Raoji Ghyare* v. *State of Maharashtra*, in which a husband was charged with the dowry murder of his pregnant wife, the possibility of suicide was rejected on the basis that 'the deceased was in an advanced state of pregnancy and according to us it was rather unlikely that a would-be mother would commit suicide at that stage for not only killing herself but also the child in her womb'.[157] In each of these cases, these norms of motherhood discredited the theory of suicide and resulted in the accused being convicted, since in the courts' view a good mother could neither kill her child (or foetus), nor could she decide to kill herself of her own volition, and thereby abandon her child.[158]

By way of contrast, in *Paniben*, where the mother-in-law was charged with and found guilty of dowry murder, the Supreme Court stated:

> It is strange that the mother-in-law who herself is a woman should resort to killing another woman. It is hard to fathom as to why even 'the mother' in her did not make her feel. It is tragic deep rancour should envelop her reason and drown her finer feelings.[159]

The court was thus of the view that no leniency should be shown in the question of sentencing: 'The language of deterrence must speak in that it may be conscious reminder to the society. Undue sympathy would be harmful to the case of justice'.[160] While deterrence is undoubtedly an important objective of the criminal regulation of dowry, it is noteworthy that the court attaches particular importance to the fact that it is a woman who has committed this crime. The mother-in-law had violated the very essence of good motherhood, and thus, a strong message of condemnation was required. Like the cases of *Harbans Lal*, *Brij Lal* and *Goverdhan*, the theory of suicide was rejected because, in the court's view 'a tender lass after only five years of married life with an affectionate husband and a young daughter to foster could not have resorted to that rash act merely because there were quarrels between her and her mother-in-law'.[161] But unlike these other cases, in *Paniben* it was also the mother-in-law's violation of these norms of motherhood that necessitated such harsh condemnation. Similarly, in the case of *Kundula Bala Subrahmanyam* v. *State of Andhra Pradesh*, where a mother-in-law was again charged with dowry murder, the Supreme Court, after commenting on the increasing incidence of dowry deaths, stated:

It is more disturbing and sad that in most of such reported cases it is the woman who plays a pivotal role in this crime against the younger woman, as in this case, with the husband either acting as a mute spectator or even an active participant in the crime, in utter disregard of his matrimonial obligations. In many cases, it has been noticed that the husband, even after marriage, continues to be 'Mamma's baby' and the umbilical cord appears not to have been cut even at that stage.[162]

Without in any way condoning the violence that women, as mothers-in-law, have inflicted on other women, it is nevertheless important to point out that it is this dimension of the violence that seems to most trouble the courts. In their view, these women are not simply committing crimes, but they are violating their roles as mothers within the family. Further, in this passage from *Kundula*, it is apparent that the court was also concerned that the husband was violating his role within the family—that of guardian and protector of his young bride. In all of these cases, the accused were ultimately found guilty. But the assumptions underlying the court's decisions can be seen to be shaped by the very familial ideology that creates and sustains women's subordinate position in the family.

The legal regulation of dowry can thus be seen to be highly contradictory. On the one hand, the legal provisions have resulted in the successful prosecution of many husbands and in-laws who have murdered young women. The veil of privacy which once immunized violence within the family from virtually any criminal prosecution has thus been at least partially lifted. But, this legal regulation has not succeeded in displacing the familial ideology that creates and sustains the subordinate position of women within the family. Rather, the practice of dowry violence is measured against the norms of the traditional family, and the roles accorded to each member of the family. Husbands are seen to be failing in their duty to act as their wives' guardians and protectors. Mothers-in-law are seen to be failing in their special duty to assist the young bride adjust to her new setting. The patrilocal nature of dominant familial ideology, whereby women are seen to sever all ties with their natal families, and to become the responsibility of their marital families, is in no way questioned, but merely naturalized. Women are analogized to seedlings, as precious and fragile, in need of care and protection in their new families. And time and again, theories of suicide are rejected, not because of the legal provisions which create a presumption of guilt on the part of the husband and his family, but because a good self-sacrificing mother would not be so selfish as to abandon her child. Within this discourse, not only is dowry violence rarely connected to the structural inequality of women within the family,[163] but the familial ideology which creates and sustains this structural inequality is virtually eulogized. Not only is there no critique of the familial arrangements, whereby daughters are transferred from their birth families to their marital families, but the courts literally call for a return to a mythical golden age when these transfers of young women were celebrated. The problem with the dowry laws thus does not only reside in its failure to address women's economic dependency within the family, but also, in its failure to displace the dominant familial ideology which creates and sustains this dependency. Its challenge to the public/private distinction is at best a partial one, in which the criminal law has been allowed to enter into the terrain of the family, but only on the terms set out by familial ideology.

Privacy, Familial Ideology and the Power of the Criminal Law

The efforts of the women's movement to resort to the criminal law to intervene in the family, and protect women against the abuses perpetrated against them within this private realm has produced contradictory results. As we discussed in chapter 1, the women's movement has been successful in pushing back the boundaries of privacy, and naming rape and dowry, along with other forms of violence, as criminal offences in which the state can legitimately intervene. But the various legislative enactments and amendments have not succeeded in displacing the public/private distinction altogether, nor the familial ideology that helps to sustain it. The idea of the family as private, and the construction of women as wives and mothers, and as weak, passive and in need of protection, are still very much apparent in the judicial interpretations of the laws intended to benefit women. Indeed, the idea of the family as private and the familial ideology that creates and sustains this public/private distinction operates in many cases to undermine the effectiveness of these legal provisions. And even when the courts do convict an accused under one of these criminal provisions, the grounds on which they do so is often shaped by and sustains the familial ideology that has constituted women as weak, passive and in need of protection. The intervention of the criminal law into the private sphere of the family can thus be seen to be informed by and to reinforce the moral regulation of women in and through familial ideology.

Women, Familial Ideology and Economic Regulation

> Her father protects her in childhood, her husband in her youth, her son in her old age. A woman is never fit for independence.
>
> Manu
> *Manusmritis*

The legal regulation of women in and through the family is not based exclusively on this moral regulation, but also has important economic dimensions. In this section, we begin by briefly examining two aspects of economic regulation within the family—maintenance and property—which illustrate the important role of family laws in reinforcing women's economic dependency. In the second section, we examine the legal regulation of women in the labour market. We will illustrate the extent to which this legal regulation in both the family and the labour market is shaped by and helps to reinforce familial ideology and the sexual division of labour. And we will argue that many of these problems are only being intensified under the new economic policies.

■ Property

The law of property is one area of legal regulation where formal equality has not yet been guaranteed. The law of succession, across virtually all personal laws, continues to discriminate against women as daughters and as wives. The law of succession continues to be heavily shaped by the assumptions of patrilineal and patrilocal joint family. And even where some of the legal obstacles have been removed, these assumptions continue to operate to undermine women's ability to claim their property rights. The law of succession is both shaped by, and operates to reinforce, women's economic dependency on their husbands. Further, as we will attempt to argue, the failure of the law to recognize marital property only further contributes to this economic dependency.

Succession

Under the rules of intestate succession, women in most communities are granted fewer rights than men. Although different personal laws discriminate against women differently, there is nevertheless a common presumption underlying most rules of intestacy that women are economically dependent on men. In this section, we focus primarily on the law governing Hindus, and comment only briefly on the laws from other communities in an attempt to illustrate the similarities of the assumptions underlying the law.

The *Hindu Succession Act, 1956*, reformed Hindu personal law to give women greater property rights. Prior to the enactment, women had few inheritance rights. A widow could only inherit a life interest in the property of her deceased husband, and a daughter had virtually no inheritance rights at all.[164] The *Hindu Succession Act, 1956*, changed these inheritance rights, and allowed women full ownership rights in the property they inherited from their husbands.[165] Further, daughters were granted property rights in their fathers' estate. If a Hindu male died intestate, all of his separate or self-acquired property would now devolve in equal shares to his sons, daughters, widow and mother.[166]

Despite these property rights granted to women as wives/widows and daughters, many discriminatory aspects remained in the law. First, there is a continuing discrimination in relation to ancestral property. Ancestral property has traditionally been held within and regulated according to the joint Hindu family. The joint Hindu family consists of only male members descended lineally from a common male ancestor. These members of the joint Hindu family have an interest by birth in the joint or coparcenary property. Since women cannot be coparcenaries, they are not entitled to a share in the ancestral property by birth. The amendments to the *Hindu Succession Act, 1956*, did not affect the right to inheritance of coparcenars—males only—at birth. Thus, a son's share in the property of his intestate father will be in addition to the share they acquire at the time of birth. Thus, ancestral property continues to be governed by a wholly patrilineal regime, whereby property descends only through the male line.

Second, females heirs are treated differently than male heirs in relation to a dwelling house. If the intestate's property includes a dwelling house, then none of the female heirs have the right to partition such a house until the male heirs choose to divide their respective shares,[167] or if there is only one male heir present.[168] If the female heir is a daughter, however, she shall only be entitled to residence if she is unmarried, deserted, separated,[169] or widowed.[170] The rules governing the inheritance of the dwelling house can thus be seen to be governed by an assumption of a patrilocal household structure. The dwelling house is assumed to be needed as the residence of the son's joint families, a residence which will only be partitioned when the sons decide to do so. Moreover, a daughter will only be entitled to reside in the house if she is unmarried. Married daughters are assumed to be residing with their husbands, in their husband's homes, and thus, not in need of, nor entitled to reside in their deceased father's home.

By way of contrast, assumptions of economic dependency can also be seen to shape the law in the way the law treats female heirs as mothers preferentially to male heirs as fathers. A mother of a Hindu male who dies intestate is treated as a Class I heir, and entitled to an equal share along with the widow and children. But a father is treated as a Class II heir, and only entitled to inherit if there are no Class I heirs. The law, which treats women advantageously in this case, can be seen to be informed by assumptions of economic dependency within dominant familial ideology. A widowed mother is considered to be the responsibility of her adult son. In the event that the son should predecease his mother, the law thus provides in advance for his mother, whether she is yet widowed or not.

The patrilineal assumptions of dominant familial ideology is also reflected in the laws governing a Hindu female who dies intestate; laws that are markedly different from those governing Hindu males who die intestate. The property is to devolve first, to her children and husband; secondly, to her husband's heirs; thirdly, to her father's heirs, and lastly, to her mother's heirs. The priority is thus given first to keeping her property within her husband's lien—first to him and their children, and then to his heirs. Further, section 15(2) provides that any property that she inherited from her father or mother should devolve, in the absence of any children, to her father's heirs. Similarly, any property that she inherited from her husband or father-in-law should devolve to her husband's heirs. The provisions of section 15(2) attempt to guarantee that property continues to be inherited through the male line from which it came—either back to her father's family, or back to her husband's family.

Finally, it should be noted that the *Hindu Succession Act, 1956*, allows a person full testamentary power over his or her property, that is, a person can will away all of their property as they wish. As Bina Agarwal has observed '[i]n principle the provision is gender neutral, but in practice it can be and often is used to disinherit females'.[171] It is in light of this testamentary power that section 22 of the *Hindu Adoptions and Maintenance Act* must be read, which provides that the heirs of a deceased Hindu are obliged to maintain the dependents of the deceased out of the estate inherited by them from the deceased.[172] The law thus does not forsake dependents—but it does operate to keep them in a state of dependency. Moreover, this right of maintenance for a widow, unlike her right to intestate succession, is dependent on her not remarrying.[173]

The rules of inheritance continue to be shaped by patrilineal assumptions, of property descending through the male line; and of women's economic dependency on some male member in the family, either a father, husband or son. These assumptions were once more explicit in succession law, with women's virtual exclusion from any inheritance rights. But the reforms have not completely displaced these patrilineal assumptions nor the corresponding assumptions of women's economic dependency. And these unequal property rights operate to reinforce dependency in women's lives. Women are not simply *assumed* to be economically dependent, but rather, the assumptions that inform the law continue to constitute women as economically dependent.

Very similar assumptions about women's economic dependency can be seen to inform other personal laws. Under Muslim law, succession is governed by the personal law of each sect. The majority of Indian Muslims belong to the Sunni sect and are governed by the laws of the Hanafi School.[174] Although the rules of succession are complicated, the general principle is that the female heir will take half the share of the male.[175] A Muslim under the Hanafi law is only entitled to bequeath one third of his estate, while the remainder of the estate is governed by the rules of intestate succession. A testator cannot bequeath anything to an heir without the permission of the other heirs, and therefore the possibility of redressing some of the formal discrimination against women under the rules of intestacy are restricted.[176] At the same time, the rules do afford some protection to the widow and daughter's right to inherit absolutely. Unlike the traditional Hindu law, Muslim law recognized the right of females to inherit at a time when women enjoyed few, if any, legal rights. These personal laws of succession were thus a progressive measure at a time when women within other communities had no similar rights. Yet these laws have not kept pace with developments in equality and women's rights in so far as they continue to discriminate between males and females at the formal level. The inheritance law assumes that women do not need as much property as men. It can be seen to reflect an underlying assumption of women's economic dependency; that women will be economically dependent on a male relative—father, husband, adult son—and thus, will not be in need of the same amount of property as males, who will have others economically dependent on them.

Christian personal law is also informed by similar assumptions of economic dependency. According to the *Indian Succession Act, 1925*, a widow is entitled to a one-third share in her husband's property.[177] In contrast to both Hindu and Muslim law, the remaining two-thirds go to her husband's lineal descendants when they exist.[178] If there are no lineal descendants, the widow is entitled to one-half of the property and her father succeeds to the rest of the property. If the father is not alive, her mother, brother and sisters share in the remainder equally. If there is no father, mother, brother or sister, nor children of brothers or sisters, the property is distributed amongst those relatives who are in the nearest degree of kindred.[179] Sons and daughters are entitled to inherit equally.[180] Although women are entitled to inherit equally as daughters, the assumptions of economic dependency continue to inform a wife's inheritance. A widow is assumed to be at least partially economically dependent on her adult children. And if she has no children, then she is assumed to be once again the responsibility of her father, who is entitled to a significant portion of her husband's property.[181]

Notwithstanding the significant differences among personal laws governing property, familial ideology can be seen to continue to shape these different laws. With the exception of Parsi personal law which provides equal inheritance rights to women and men,[182] the legal regulation of succession discriminates against women, to different degrees, in all personal laws. As wives, and sometimes as daughters, women are not entitled to the same inheritance as husbands and sons. The law continues to be shaped by the patrilineal and patrilocal nature of the ideologically dominant family, and its assumptions of women's economic dependency. The assumption that property should descend primarily through the male line has not been completely displaced. Nor has the assumption that married daughters become the economic responsibility of their husbands families. Despite reforms to these laws, the rules of inheritance continue at some level to both assume and inscribe women's economic dependency on some male member in the family—unmarried daughter on her father, wife on her husband and widow on her adult son(s). These laws of succession continue, in different degrees, to discursively and materially constitute economic dependency in women's lives. Finally, it should be noted that even the granting of formal equality rights to inheritance has in practice failed to displace the dominant familial ideology, whereby women as daughters and sisters continue to voluntarily give up their property claims to their brothers.[183] As Bina Agarwal has demonstrated, a woman's natal home continues to be constructed as her brothers' rightful home, and a 'good sister' is one who recognizes her brothers' entitlement to it. Further, even a woman who may want to assert her property rights has to weigh the risks of alienating her brothers who may be her only source of socio-economic security should her marriage breakdown.[184] The patrilineal and patrilocal assumptions of dominant familial ideology continue to inform not only the law, but moreover, the social relations within the family, which only further contribute to the discursive and material construction of women's economic dependency.

Marital Property

The legal regulation of property during marriage across all personal laws is based on a regime of separate property.[185] According to the regime of separate property, each spouse is considered to own the property to which he or she has legal title. Each spouse is free to acquire, maintain and dispose of their separate property. And on marital breakdown, each spouse keeps his or her own property. A spouse is entitled to possession of whatever she or he brings into the marital relationship,[186] and to property owned in their own name. There is no recognition of marital property, whereby spouses would share the property acquired during the marriage. The regime of separate property is an important step forward from the older regime which precluded married women from owning property in their own names. It is based on a formal model of equality, whereby each spouse is equally free to acquire and dispose of their property. However, in the context of the sexual division of labour and unequal rules of inheritance, this formal equality of property ownership does not produce equal results. The sexual division of labour, which allocates different roles to women and men within the family, puts women and men in very different positions vis-à-vis property acquisition. Men, who are assumed to be the financial providers for their families, will have greater opportunity to acquire and hold property than women, who are assumed to be responsible for child care and domestic labour within the family. And the continuing legacy of patrilineal inheritance, whereby property is passed on disproportionately to male heirs further ensures that any property acquired during a marriage is more likely than not to be in a husband and/or his joint families' name. When a marriage ends, most property acquired during the marriage will likely have been acquired by the husband and his family, and in his name. According to the regime of separate property the husband will simply be entitled to retain this property. The contribution that the woman may have made to the marital relationship in terms of domestic labour and child care is not recognized as a contribution to property. Even where women work outside of the home during the marriage, and contribute to the finances of the family, intra-familial resources often remain controlled by the male head of the household. If a woman's earnings are used towards the purchase of a home, she will be able to make a claim to that property, even if it is registered in her husband's name. But, if a woman's earnings are used towards household expenses, as they often are, while her husband's earnings are thereby freed to allow him to acquire property, a women will not be able to claim any beneficial interest in that property. Thus, even where women do work outside of the home, the unequal implications of separate property for women and men are not entirely overcome. This regime of separate property negates the value of women's work within the family. At the time of exit from the marriage, neither her contribution to the rearing of children and domestic work, nor the loss of educational and employment opportunities are recognized or compensated. Women's work within the home is not seen as contributing to the acquisition of property. Familial ideology defines these activities as the 'natural' concern and obligation of women in their capacities as wives and mothers and not as the basis for any property entitlement.[187]

■ Maintenance

The provisions governing maintenance like those governing property and inheritance are based on assumptions of the sexual division of labour and women's roles as good wives, mothers and daughters. There are several forms of maintenance available to women. Every personal law makes some provision for women to be maintained while proceedings for judicial separation and divorce are pending in court, as well as at the time of divorce. In addition, there is some provision for maintenance of a wife under each personal law during the course of a marriage.[188] The *Code of Civil Procedure* imposes a further obligation on husbands to maintain their wives following marital breakdown. While these laws differ in significant ways, the legal regulation of maintenance is shaped by both the moral and economic assumptions of familial ideology. The laws are based on the assumption that women are economically dependent and that they are entitled to maintenance on the condition that they conform to their designated roles, that is, as good mothers, supplicant wives, and dutiful daughters.

Women are entitled to financial support on the assumption that they are economically dependent on men in marital relationships. But, the entitlement to maintenance is not an unfettered right. Rather, a woman's right to maintenance is made conditional on her conduct—particularly, her sexual conduct. Under Hindu law a wife will lose her entitlement to maintenance during the course of the marriage if she is unchaste or ceases to be a Hindu.[189] Similarly, an order for permanent maintenance can be modified or rescinded if the applicant remarries, or if the wife is unchaste or if the husband has had sexual intercourse with any woman outside of wedlock.[190] Under Christian law, women have a right to permanent alimony, but this right only arises in very limited circumstances in light of the restricted grounds on which she can secure a divorce.[191] Under Parsi law, an order to pay permanent alimony will only be granted to the wife on condition that she remains chaste and unmarried.[192] Under the *Special Marriage Act*, a wife is not entitled to permanent maintenance if she is unchaste or remarries.[193] According to the Principles of Muslim Law, a husband is bound to maintain his wife unless she 'refuses herself to him or is disobedient. Such refusal or disobedience can be justified by non-payment of prompt dower or the husband's cruelty'.[194] Underlying these limitations is the assumption that women who are not chaste, or who remarry, can look elsewhere, that is, to another man for support. Sexual conduct and exclusivity in a marital relationship even after breakdown thus determines a women's entitlement to maintenance. Women's rights are contingent on the courts' moral evaluation of her behaviour. Those who most closely conformed to the ideal wife and mother are regarded as deserving. Those who deviate from these ideals are cut off. If years after the breakdown of the marriage, a woman has a relationship or commits adultery while separated from her husband, she forfeits her right to maintenance. Morality rather than economic need becomes the governing criteria.

The assumption underlying all of these laws is that women will always be dependent—the legal issue is simply determining who ought to bear the responsibility for that dependency. This assumption of economic dependency reflects a certain material reality in women's lives. The roles allocated to women through the sexual division of labour within the family coupled with a property regime that does not recognize marital property within the family operate to make many women economically dependent on their husbands, and their husband's family. As a result, on marital breakdown, women may not have access to property or to an independent source of income. Women's lives continue to be structured in such a way as to make economic dependency a material reality in their lives, and to make maintenance necessary on marital breakdown.

Maintenance law both assumes and reinscribes this economic dependency. The entitlement to support is based on the fact of marriage and its breakdown. There is little analysis or consideration of economic need, but simply an assumption of dependency. This absence of any consideration of women's actual economic needs on marital breakdown is evident in both the grossly inadequate sums of maintenance ordered by the courts, as well as in the way in which maintenance is cut off if a woman has a sexual relationship with another man. It is the mere sexual relationship, rather than any actual analysis of whether the woman has become financially dependent on the man, that terminates the support. The fact of a sexual relationship may not significantly alter a woman's need for financial support. Further, support is seen to address financial dependency, rather than as a form of compensation for work in, and contribution to the marriage. Women get support not because they are entitled to it by virtue of the contribution they have made to the marriage, but rather, simply because they have no alternative source of income. In this way, support law operates to reinforce the prevailing idea of marriage as a relationship of dependency—of women dependent on men—rather than as a relationship of interdependency—in which men are equally dependent on women for their contribution to the relationship. In this regard, it is important to see the law of maintenance within the broader context of the legal regulation of the financial implications of marital breakdown. As we have discussed, none of the family laws recognize any entitlement to marital property. Neither the law of maintenance nor the law of property recognize or compensate the work and contribution of women to the marital relationship. We can again see the way in which the identities constituted for women in and through familial ideology operate to naturalize women's economic dependency. Women, as loyal wives and self-sacrificing mothers, are simply performing their 'natural' roles. Women's work within the home is transformed into an act of loyalty and duty; it becomes the defining moment of women's identities as wives and mothers. To even suggest that women should be compensated for this work thereby becomes 'an insult to Indian womanhood'.[195] Within this discursive construction, marital property is a conceptual impossibility. And maintenance is only justified if a woman has lived up to her wifely duties.

This critique of the assumption of economic dependency should not be taken to mean that women should not receive financial compensation on marital breakdown. Rather, the critique is directed at the way in which this compensation is conceptualized and justified. It is quite possible to imagine a legal regime which could address women's financial needs on marital breakdown without negating their contribution to the marriage.

Maintenance could be based on financial need, rather than assumed dependency and sexual conduct. Or, maintenance could be based on the principle of compensation, that is, that women should be compensated for the real and valuable work that they contributed to the family. The legal regulation of both property and maintenance, however, continue to be informed by familial ideology, within which men are assumed to be responsible for the financial provision of their families, and in which women are not seen to contribute to the acquisition of property or the economic well-being of family. Indeed, within this discursive framework, it remains virtually impossible to speak of 'compensation' since women are not seen to make contributions that can be compensated. Reforming maintenance law would thus require a conceptual shift in the way in which women's work in the home is understood; a shift which the dominant familial ideology continues to powerfully oppose. This familial ideology continues to quite successfully constitute women's 'natural' identities as wives and mothers, and shape their limited entitlement to maintenance on the (reluctant) recognition that some male family member will have to support them.

■ The Legal Regulation of Women's Work

In this section, we shift our analysis to the legal regulation of women in the labour market. The Directive Principles of State Policy of the Indian Constitution provide for the protection of women workers.[196] Special provisions are made in various labour laws protecting and promoting the rights of women.[197] These legislative provisions have been widely criticized as failing to adequately protect women's rights.[198] Women workers suffer from the under-enforcement of labour legislation in general, as well as from the under-enforcement of legislation specifically designed to protect and promote the interests of women workers. The problem with these legislative provisions, however, does not lie in their inadequacy of the enforcement mechanisms alone. In this section, we examine the extent to which the sexual division of labour within the labour market operates to undermine the potential efficacy of these laws. Women continue to be disproportionately represented in occupations that are semi or unskilled, low paying, and more often than not, within the unorganized section.[199] This labour market segregation has produced significant wage differentials between women and men. It has also had the effect of placing women workers outside the purview of much labour legislation as well as outside the realm of trade union organizations. We focus our discussion on two of the most significant labour laws enacted to protect and promote the particular interests of women workers: the *Equal Remuneration Act, 1976*, and the *Maternity Benefits Act, 1961*. We will illustrate the ways in which these legislative provisions designed to address discrimination against women continue to be undermined by the gender segregation of labour market.

The Equal Remuneration Act, 1976

The *Equal Remuneration Act, 1976*, provides for equal pay for equal or similar work.[200] 'Same work or work of a similar nature' is defined in the Act as: '...work in respect of which the skill, effort and responsibility required are the same, when performed under similar working conditions, by a man and a woman'.[201] The definition further provides that work will be considered to be the same or of a similar nature if any differences in skill, effort and responsibility between women and men 'are not of practical importance in relation to the terms and conditions of employment'.[202] The Act also prohibits discrimination in the recruitment of workers, and since its amendment in 1987, further prohibits discrimination in promotions, transfers and training.[203]

However, the practice of paying women lower wages for equal or similar work persists. First, the Act does not impose a duty on employers to evaluate whether the work of women and men is of a similar nature, nor does it establish any institutional procedure by which such evaluations would be made. Rather, the responsibility for initiating complaints rests entirely with individual employees. The Act does provide for the appointment of inspectors, who are empowered to review whether employers are in compliance with the law. But, in the absence of a duty on employers to examine whether the work of women and men is in fact of a similar nature, enforcement through individual complaints and/or government supervision will be, at best, uneven.

Second, and in our view, more significantly, women and men, more often than not, do not perform the same work. Rather, labour market segregation continues to concentrate women in lower paying sectors and occupations.[204] Yet, because women and men are not performing 'equal or similar work', the wage differentials are not in violation of the Act. This problem in the scope of 'equal or similar work' is illustrated in the decision of the Supreme Court in one of the few cases dealing with wage differentials between women and men to reach the apex court. In *Mackinnon, Mackenzie & Co* v. *Audrey D'Costa*, a claim was brought by a woman who had worked as a stenographer, alleging that she was paid less than male stenographers employed by the same company, and that the company was thus in violation of the *Equal Remuneration Act*.[205] The Supreme Court held that the women and men stenographers in question did the same work, and that the female petitioner was thus entitled to equal pay. However, in its general comments on the principle of equal pay for equal work, the court qualified, and in some important respects, limited the scope of the principle. The court first noted that in approaching the question of whether work is the same or of a similar nature, the authority should take a broad view, and not allow differences in detail to defeat a claim for equality.[206] In its view, the authority 'should look at the duties generally performed by men and women'.[207] By way of example, the court considered differences in the working times of women and men, and was of the view that women who work during the day could not claim equal pay with men who work at night, if women were also working nights at the same pay as men. But the court then stated:

> We do not suggest that there can be no discrimination at all between men and women in the matter of remuneration. There are some kinds of work which women may not be able to undertake. Men do work like loading, unloading, carrying and lifting heavier things which women cannot do. In such cases there cannot be any discrimination on the ground of sex.[208]

The statutory requirement of equal pay for equal or similar work was thus not seen to require an interrogation of the differential value attached to women and men's labour. Rather, the court implicitly accepted that the work 'men do...like loading, unloading, carrying and lifting heavier things' was worth more than the kind of work that women perform. This focus on substantially similar work thus narrowed the potential applicability of the Act. Instead of being able to address the wage discrimination created and sustained by the sexual division of labour, this approach is limited by the very structures that have created the discrimination. Rather than challenging the sexual division of labour, this approach allows this sexual division of labour to undermine the statutory objective of narrowing the wage gap between women and men.

The principle of equal pay for equal or similar work adopted in the Act can be contrasted to the broader principles of comparable work, or equal pay for work of equal value. These approaches recognize the reality of the gender segregation of the labour market, and the fact that women are thus often employed in job ghettos, where there are no male employees performing 'equal or similar work'. Thus, these approaches broaden the nature of the inquiry to include work of equal value. In this way, the gender segregation of the labour market does not operate as a bar to a claim for equal pay. And as a result, such an approach can begin to address the wage discrimination that has resulted from this gender seg-regation. The principle of equal pay for equal work, however, is unable to support such substantive interrogations and thus remains limited by the very structure of the labour market.

Women's position in the labour market is further reinforced by their position in the family. Women are relegated to the unorganized sector of the labour market, in part because they do not have the opportunity to acquire the skills and training that could help them to improve their employment situation.[209] Women continue to work in the home and bear the burden of domestic work, which is time consuming, particularly in poor households. Family obligations keep women out of the paid labour force for considerable periods of time and consequently their skills atrophy. Their domestic chores do not afford them the time to develop their skills and train for better jobs, and thus restrict the opportunities and incomes available to women when they enter the paid labour force. Further, as the Committee on the Status of Women observed, 'the practice of identifying a workday as equivalent of seven to nine work hours' also contributes to the wage differentials between women and men. As the Report stated: 'Many women are unable to report to duty on time because of household responsibilities and do not get the full rates. It was reported to us that half an hour delay could lead to a loss of half day's wage'.[210] Familial obligations and the sexual division of labour work together in reinforcing women's unequal position in the labour market. There is a link between the fact of the female wage labour being advantageous as a cheap and flexible source of labour power to capital with the presup-position of a particular form of the family. Women's wages need not cover the costs of their reproduction because of the assumption of a position within the family of financial dependence on their husbands or cohabitants. Wages lower than the value of labour power are thereby considered to be justified.[211] This wage discrimination is related to women's economic dependency within the family, not only in terms of reflecting the assumption of this dependency, but also in reinscribing the material conditions of dependency. Even those women who do work outside of the home, and have access to independent income, may not achieve a substantial level of economic independence. A woman's stand-ard of living even at the subsistence level may be dependent on her husband's income, despite the fact that she works outside of the home.

The Maternity Benefits Act, 1961

The *Maternity Benefits Act, 1961*, provides for 12 weeks maternity leave and benefits.[212] Women are prohibited from working for a six week period immediately following childbirth. Pregnant women are also entitled to take up to 6 weeks paid leave of absence prior to their expected date of delivering, entitling women to a total of 12 weeks paid maternity leave.[213] The Act further provides for nursing breaks, twice a day, when the woman returns to work, until the child is fifteen months old. In order to qualify, women must have worked a minimum of 30 days within the 12 months prior to child birth. The *Maternity Benefits Act* prohibits the employer from discharging a woman during her maternity leave, or otherwise changing her conditions of employment.[214] As the Supreme Court stated in *B. Shah* v. *Labour Court, Coimbatore*, the *Maternity Benefits Act* 'is intended to achieve the object of doing social justice to women workers'.[215] It is an example of a legislative provision specifically designed to take women's reproductive roles into account, and ensure that women are not discriminated against in employment as a result of these roles. But, the *Maternity Benefits Act* does not apply to all women workers. The Act specifies that it applies to women who work in factories, mines and plantations.[216] The Act thus excludes the vast number of women who are concentrated in the unorganized sector, particular in the agriculture sector outside of plantations. Further, the nature of women's labour market participation operates to undermine the efficacy of the rights accorded women under the Act. Even women who officially fall within the scope of the Act are often in practice denied any benefits under it. Women are often unable to work at the same place of employment for the required qualifying period. Employers often manipulate women's working conditions to ensure that they do not qualify.[217] Even within the organized sector, many of the same labour practices are found, which operate to undermine women's access to benefits.

Further, the Act is unable to address the various discriminatory practices of employers towards their women employees during and after their pregnancies. For example, there is evidence to suggest that '[i]t is a common practice among employers to refuse to hire pregnant women, to demote or terminate women if they become pregnant, and to deny them promotion and pay raises'.[218] The *Maternity Benefits Act* 'provides only minimal protection against these practices'. Some studies say that the Act has resulted in employers tending not to hire women. Faith Herndon's study of the *Maternity Benefits Act* concludes that 'by requiring employers to pay maternity benefits without extending extra protection to women, the Act actually encourages employers to discriminate against them'.[219] Although penalties have been raised under the recent amendments to the Act, the penalties are 'still not high enough to deter many employers from the temptation of trying to evade the Act'.[220] Other studies have questioned the extent to which the *Maternity Benefits Act* can be seen to be responsible for employers not hiring women. For example, the *Report of the Committee on the Status of Women* stated that '[t]he theory that maternity benefits has proved to be a deterrent to women's employment cannot be substantiated as the total expenditure on maternity benefits under the Maternity Benefits Act between 1961 and 1970 is negligible'.[221] Moreover, in light of the increasing number of women workers being integrated into the labour market in the last decades—a process that is only being accelerated under the new economic policies—it would seem that the *Maternity Benefits Act* is not so much discouraging employers from hiring women as it is simply not an effective law. The inefficacy of the Act seems to lie more in the ability of employers to evade its scope, and thus, to avoid paying any benefits. Women in the unorganized sector simply continue to fall outside the effective purview of the Act. Employers continue to manipulate the conditions of women's employment, such that they are unable to qualify for benefits. And as Herndon pointed out, the Act provides little to no protection against these practices.

Further, the nursing provisions of the Act are in many respects contingent upon the availability of on site child care facilities. Labour laws specifically provide for crèches for children of working mothers in factories, and plantations.[222] But these laws are rarely enforced and in many work sites, particularly in the unorganized sector, women are actively discouraged by their employers from bringing their children.[223] When women do bring their children, they are often prohibited by their supervisors from tending to and even nursing them. Further, where crèche facilities are available, these facilities are well below the prescribed standards and level of supervision.

The sexual division of labour and familial ideology can be seen to affect the legal regulation of women's labour in complex ways. The sexual division of labour underlies labour market segmentation, according to which women are relegated into sex segregated, low paying, unorganized sectors of the economy. This labour market segmentation in turn operates to undermine the substantive rights set out in the *Equal Remuneration Act*, and the *Maternity Benefits Act*. Women's location in sex segregated occupations effectively precludes the operation of any rights under the *Equal Remuneration Act, 1976*. Similarly, their location in the unorganized sector operates to preclude the enforcement of their rights under the *Maternity Benefits Act*. The result is that the very problem that these laws were intended to address—namely, discrimination against women in the labour market—continues.

Women and the New Economic Policies: Intensifying the Contradictions

Many of the problems that women workers have faced are being intensified as a result of the new economic policies being pursued by the

Indian government since 1991. These new economic policies, which have taken the form of liberalization of trade, deregulation of investment, privatization of industry, and devaluation of the currency have begun to fundamentally transform the Indian economy, with a view to increasing export oriented production, and decreasing state spending. Research on these new economic policies is beginning to reveal the gendered impact of this process of restructuring and deregulation.[224] The reduction of government expenditures on food and public transit subsides, as well as on social services such as health, education, rural employment and anti-poverty programmes is increasing the demands on women within their households, who are considered to be responsible for the welfare of children, the elderly, and other family members.[225] These decreasing subsidies, coupled with devaluation of the rupee and an increase in indirect taxation has resulted in a substantial increase in the cost of basic necessities, and forcing women who did not already do so to work outside of the home to finance the costs of the household.

The increasing need for women to work is coupled with a restructuring of the labour market, and an increasing demand for women workers. Some writers have suggested that the increase in women's labour market participation as a result of these new economic policies is a positive feature.[226] Others have contested this view, arguing that statistics indicating an increase in women's employment is not necessarily indicative of economic empowerment for women. Jayati Ghosh, for example, argues that:

> ...the feminisation of work that is sometimes noticed consequent upon such liberalising policies need not provide much cause for celebration, since they are often associated not only with exploitative work conditions and increased aggregate burden of women's work within and outside the household, but also with declining levels of total family or household income as male members lose gainful employment.[227]

Moreover, the feminization of the labour force must be seen within the context of the simultaneous casualization of the labour force. The emphasis on increasing international competitiveness through cost reduction is resulting in the casualization of the labour market, that is, a decreased reliance on a permanent workforce, and a greater reliance on a casual workforce that works for lower wages and no benefits. The manufacturing sector, once characterized by higher degrees of trade union organization and thus, higher wages, is increasingly shifting to a casual labour force. The process of restructuring can be seen to be intensifying the problems that women workers already faced in the labour market.

Deregulation and centralisation are likely to make the emerging labour market more segmented then in the past. With greater casualisation, feminisation and use of contract labour wage differentials between regular and other type of workers would increase.[228]

Restructuring is further reinscribing sex segregation as well as the low wages and poor working conditions already associated with women's work. Gender segmentation is increasing and the conditions of employment are further deteriorating. Casualization of the labour force means that more and more women are working in the manufacturing sector, at the same time as this sector is coming to be characterized as 'unorganized', that is, outside the purview of protective legislation and trade union organization.[229] As a result of the reduction in the size of the public sector and the consequent loss of jobs, as well as the shift in the manufacturing sector to increasingly casual labour, fewer working women are getting access to maternity benefits and other laws passed for their protection. As a result of this restructuring, the protective legislation is becoming even more elusive to the mass number of women who are increasingly participating in the labour market on a casual basis. The protections of the *Maternity Benefits Act* and the *Equal Remuneration Act, 1976*, which were already largely ineffective as a result of the gender segmentation of the labour force, are being further eroded by the gendered impact of restructuring. Labour market segregation, which was already undermining the efficacy of the *Equal Remuneration Act*, is being intensified. Similarly, the concentration of women in the unorganized sector, which was already undermining the efficacy of the *Maternity Benefit Act*, is also being accentuated. The gendered impact of the new economic policies is being shaped by and mediated through the gender segregation of the labour market, and is having the effect of further inscribing this sexual division of labour. Furthermore, there is increasing talk of expressly rolling back some of these legislative protections. Export promotion zones are being set up, where industries are granted ad hoc exemptions from certain protective labour legislation. Moreover, one measure that has been proposed is the restriction of maternity benefits to the first two children. The dual impact of such a measure reduces the cost to the employer who in any case tries to avoid complying with the provisions of the *Maternity Benefits Act*.[230]

The new economic policies are accentuating the conditions of labour market segmentation that have constituted women's economic vulnerability, and in turn reinforcing the effects of the sexual division of labour on women. But the impact of these policies on women will not be measurable in economic terms alone. The profound socio-economic transformation being brought about through these policies is likely to also effect the moral regulation of women, in and through familial ideology. The new economic policies are resulting in the renegotiation of the public and private distinction. This restructuring is seeking to 'shrink the public—the realm of political negotiation—and, at the same time, expand and reassert the autonomy of the private sector and the private sphere'.[231] Services once provided by the state are being reprivatized. The public sphere is being contracted, as the private sphere is expanding. Janine Brodie has argued that this renegotiation of the public and private and the process of privatization is resulting in the reconstitution of the domestic, in which the normative family and women's roles within it are being reaffirmed as the fundamental building block in society.[232]

> This emphasis on the family is particularly stark in new right rhetoric which blames both the welfare state and feminism for the breakdown of the family and the social fabric. More broadly, however, there is a growing consensus that families should look after their own and state policies should make sure that they do.[233]

Although Brodie is examining the impact of this restructuring discourse in western capitalist societies, her observations on the reconstitution of the domestic and the revalorization of the family have resonance well beyond.[234] This reconstitution of the domestic sphere is facilitating the retraction of the public sphere. The state can justify its reduction in social services by redefining 'the family' as the place where these services ought to be provided. As the state increasingly withdraws from the provision of health care, education, and child care, the responsibility for these basic needs is transferred to the private sphere of the family and the market. The reconstitution of the domestic and the revalorization of the family helps to renaturalize the idea that there are the sites where these basic needs ought to be provided. This revalorization of the family seeks to deploy and reinscribe familial ideology, and its naturalized and universalized roles for women as wives and mothers. At the same moment that women are being called upon to assume more responsibility within the labour market, women's roles as wives and mothers are being intensified. These contradictory pulls on women's labour and identities are being negotiated through the powerful discourse of familial ideology. As we will examine in greater detail in chapter 4, it is in and through this dominant familial ideology that the Hindu Right is attempting to contain the potential challenge to the patriarchal family presented by women's increasing integration into the economy. It is similarly in and through this familial ideology that mass media and advertising are reconstituting a new, but 'traditional', identity for women that contains the radical potential of their new roles within their roles as wives and mothers. The new Indian woman is one who can take on the challenges of modernization, without forsaking her primary role as wife and mother. The revalorization of the family thus operates to both naturalize the privatization of state services, and contain the increasingly contradictory demands on women. Rather than displacing assumptions about women as good and dutiful wives, and self-sacrificing mothers, the new economic policies are drawing upon and reinscribing the same set of norms and values of women's gendered identities. And the effect is that the moral and economic dimensions of familial ideology will continue to operate in tandem. The naturalization of women's roles as wives and mothers creates the conditions for, and serves to reinscribe the assumptions of, women's dependency within the family, and of the lower value of work in a highly segregated labour market.

Conclusion

In this chapter, we have attempted to reveal some of the ways in which familial ideology, the public/private distinction, and the sexual division of labour shapes and informs the legal regulation of women. We have attempted to reveal the contradictory nature of this familial ideology in the legal regulation of women. Women's roles and identities are constituted in and through familial ideology, and individual women are then judged according to their adherence to these norms and standards. Women who demonstrate obedience, self-sacrifice, and loyalty to their husbands are often protected in divorce or restitution of conjugal rights petitions. Women who deviate from these roles, however, are judged as bad wives and are thereby accorded less protection. Assumptions about women's roles within the family—as loyal wives and self-sacrificing mothers, as passive and submissive, devoid of agency—similarly inform the intervention of the criminal law within the family. Laws regulating criminal intervention into marital and non-marital sex are informed by a shifting public/private distinction, which operates to protect and promote women's traditional roles as good wives and mothers, and to condemn those women who deviate from these traditional norms. The legal regulation of dowry violence was similarly shown to be informed by the norms of the joint family, and the subordinate role of women therein. Criminal laws may have begun to pierce the veil of privacy that once immunized the family from any intervention, but it has not displaced the dominant familial ideology that created and sustains this public/private distinction. In the context of economic regulation, we have attempted to reveal the ways in which economic dependency is both assumed and reinscribed by maintenance and property laws within the family. Similarly, within the context of protective laws for women in the labour market, we have attempted to reveal the extent to which these laws are undermined by the very sexual division of labour that creates and sustains women's precarious labour market participation—a problem that is only being intensified with the new economic policies.

Our objective in this chapter has been to look beneath the surface of the law, to examine the ways in which the legal regulation of women is shaped and informed by problematic assumptions about women's roles and identities within the family. In attempting to provide a broad range of examples of both the moral and economic regulation of women, the chapter is perhaps too ambitious. Again, it is important to emphasize that our objective has not been to provide a comprehensive review of the legal regulation of women in these areas, but rather, to illustrate the kind of analysis that we believe must be brought to the study of the legal regulation of women—an analysis that attempts to reveal the ideological assumptions that are deeply embedded within legal discourse. We believe that it will be important for feminist legal studies to continue to push this kind of analysis forward, taking closer and more detailed looks at a broad range of legal provisions and judicial interpretations.

NOTES

1. For example, Article 23 of the *International Covenant on Civil and Political Rights* states 'The family is the natural and fundamental group unit of society and is entitled to protection by society and the state'.
2. N. J. Usha Rao, 'Gaps in Definition and Analysis: A Sociological Perspective', in K. Saradamoni, ed., *Finding the Household: Conceptual and Methodological Issues* (New Delhi: Sage, 1992) 49 at 58–59. Rao is quoting from the *Census of India*, 1872.
3. *Ibid.* at 61. In the 1961 survey, the household was treated as an economic unit separate from the individuals within it. In 1971, 'household' was defined in greater detail: 'there may be one-member households, two-member households, or multimember households' (*ibid.* at 63; quoting from *Census of India*, 1971). It further made a distinction between the household of blood relations and unrelated persons or 'institutional households' (*ibid.* at 63).
4. *Ibid.* at 66–69.
5. Devaki Jain and Nirmala Banerjee, eds., *Tyranny of the Household: Investigative Essays on Women's Work* (New Delhi: Shakti Books, 1985), define economic household as 'the

entire group of persons who commonly live together and take their meals from a common means'.

6. A. M. Shah, *The Household Dimension of the Family in India* (New Delhi: Orient Longman, 1973).
7. Hilary Standing, *Dependence and Autonomy: Women's Employment and the Family in Calcutta* (London: Routledge and Kegan Paul, 1991) at 3.
8. Marlee Kline, 'The Colour of Law: Ideological Representations of First Nations in Legal Discourse' (1994) 3 *Social and Legal Studies* 451. In the context of law, see Alan Hunt, 'The Ideology of Law: Advances and Problems in Recent Applications of the Concept of Ideology to the Analysis of Law' (1985) 19 *Law and Society Review* 11. On ideology more generally, see Terry Eagleton, *Ideology: An Introduction* (London: Verso, 1991).
9. Michelle Barrett and Mary MacIntosh, *The Anti-Social Family* (London: Verso, 1982) at 3–4. See also Carol Smart, *The Ties That Bind: Law, Marriage and the Reproduction of Patriarchal Relations* (London: Routledge and Kegan Paul, 1984).
10. Shelley Gavigan, 'Law, Gender and Ideology' in Anne F. Bayefsky, ed., *Legal Theory Meets Legal Practice* (Edmonton: Academic Publishers, 1988) at 293. See also Gavigan, 'Paradise Lost, Paradox Revisited: The Implications of Familial Ideology for Feminist, Lesbian and Gay Engagement To Law' (1993) 31 *Osgoode Hall Law Journal* 589.
11. Shelley Gavigan, 'Paradise Lost', *ibid.* See also Jane Lewis, 'The Working-Class Wife and Mother and State Intervention, 1870–1918,' in J. Lewis, ed., *Labour and Love: Women's Experience of Home and Family, 1850–1940* (London: Basil Blackwell, 1986), and Joan Acker, 'Class, Gender and the Relations of Distribution' (1988) 13 *Signs* 473.
12. See generally Katherine O'Donovan, *Sexual Divisions in Law* (London: Weidenfeld and Nicholson, 1985); Fran Olsen, 'The Myth of State Intervention' (1985) 18 *Michigan Law Review* 835; Judy Fudge, 'The Public/Private Distinction: The Possibilities of and the Limits to the Use of Charter Litigation to further Feminist Struggles' (1987) 25 *Osgoode Hall Law Journal* 485; Nicholas Rose, 'Beyond the Public/Private Division: Law, Power and the Family' (1987) 14 *Journal of Law and Society* 1.
13. Chandra Mohanty, 'Under Western Eyes: Feminist Scholarship and Colonial Discourses', in Chandra Mohanty, Ann Russo, and Lourdes Torres, eds., *Third World Women and the Politics of Feminism* (Bloomington: Indiana University Press, 1991) at 68, writes: '...the existence of a sexual division of labour in most contexts cannot be sufficient explanation for the universal subjugation of women in the work force. That the sexual division of labour does indicate a devaluation of women's work must be shown through analysis of particular local contexts'. See also Hilary Standing, *supra* note 7 at 6.
14. Mohanty, *ibid.* at 68.
15. See Patricia Uberoi, *Family, Kinship and Marriage in India* (Delhi: Oxford University Press, 1993) at 383–86; Shah, *supra* note 6.
16. Uberoi, *ibid.* at 35.
17. Rao, *supra* note 2 at 56. As Rao further describes at 56: 'Due to Maine's position as the Law Member of the Government of India, between 1862–1869, this view of joint family came to be accepted by the Government as the most prevalent type of Hindu family which is reflected in the analysis of the Census Surveys, which began around that time. Thus, the Indological views regarding the concept of the Hindu family were popularized by the British administrators and are reflected in many of the definitions

of "joint family". formulated by anthropologists and sociologists'. See also Uberoi, *supra* note 15, at 31–33.

18. Shah, *supra* note 6 defines this sociological joint family as a household composed of two or more married couples. Pauline Kolenda's working definition in her influential work *Regional Differences in Family Structures in India* (Jaipur: Rawat Publications, 1987), is 'a commensal unit composed of 2 or more related married couples plus their unmarried children'. There is thus some divergence in the criteria according to which the jointness of the family is to be measured, that is, whether by common residence or by common hearth. Another common definition of the joint family can be seen to parallel the legal definition, that is, as three or more generations, related through the male line, living in a common dwelling or in close proximity, sharing property, income and various rights and obligations: See P. D. Devanandan and M. M. Thomas, 'Introduction', in Devanandan and Thomas, eds., *Changing Patterns of Family Life in India* (Bangalore: Christian Institute for the Study of Religion and Society, 1966) at 3.

19. In terms of cross-cultural familial forms, it has been identified as 'the asymmetrical community family', characterized by equality between brothers laid down by inheritance rules, and cohabitation of married sons and their parents. See Emmanuel Todd, *The Explanation of Ideology: Family Structures and Social Systems*, trans. David Garrioch (Oxford: Basil Blackwell, 1985) at 155.

20. Vanaja Dhruvarajan, *Hindu Women and the Power of Ideology* (Granby, Mass.: Bergin and Garvey Publishers, 1989 also New Delhi: Vistaar, 1989) at 36.

21. Irawati Karve, *Kinship Organization in India* (1st ed., 1953), as cited by Uberoi, *supra* note 15.

22. Thomas Trautmann, 'The Study of Dravidian Kinship', in Madhev M. Deshpande and Peter Edwin Hook, eds., *Aryan and Non-Aryan in India* (Ann Arbor: University of Michigan Center for South and Southeast Asian Studies, 1979).

23. See Louis Dumont, *Affinity as Value: Marriage Alliance in South India, with Comparative Essays on Australia* (Chicago: University of Chicago, 1983), 'Marriage Alliance' (1968) 10 *International Encyclopedia of the Social Sciences* 19, and 'Marriage in India: The Present State of the Question, III, North India in Relation to South India' (1966) 9 *Contributions to Indian Sociology* 90. Dumont, applying Levi Straus's theory of marriage alliance to the Indian context, focused on gift-giving rituals in marriage and kinship. As Patricia Uberoi describes, *supra* note 15, at 228, Dumont showed '(i) how kanyadana marriage creates asymmetrical gift-giving obligations—unidirectional from the wife-givers to the wife-takers, (ii) how these affinal rights and duties are transmitted from one generation to the next when a man's obligation to his married daughter's conjugal family is reproduced in his son's ritual and gift-giving relation to his sister's children and (iii) how the fit relation in India expresses and maintains an asymmetry of status between wife-givers and wife-takers'.

24. Both Trautmann and Dumont emphasize the unequal relationship between wife givers and wife takers, which begins with the gift of the virgin, and which is sustained through an asymmetrical flow of gifts and deference from the wife givers to the wife takers. As Trautman describes in detail, for a gift to remain a religious rather than a material gift, must not be given for any personal gain. Thus, no gifts must ever flow from the wife taker's family back to the wife givers, lest it be seen to corrupt the nature of the gift of the virgin, and reduce it to a mere commercial transaction.

25. Shah, *supra* note 6.

26. Shah, 'Changes in the Indian Family: An Examination of Some Assumptions', *Economic and Political Weekly* (1968) 127. See also Shah, *supra* note 6.

27. Kolenda, *supra* note 18.

28. Kolenda's eleven family forms are: nuclear, supplemental nuclear, sub-nuclear, single parent, supplemental single parent, collateral joint, supplemental collateral joint, lineal joint, supplemental lineal joint, lineal-collateral joint, and supplemental lineal collateral.

29. Kolenda, *supra* note 18.

30. See Promilla Kapur, 'Women in Modern India', in Man Singh Das and Panos B. Bordis, eds., *The Family in Asia* (New Delhi: Vikas Publishing House, 1978) 108 at 139; Patricia Caplan, *Class and Gender in India: Women and their Organizations in a South Indian City* (London: Tavistock Publications, 1985) at 62. But this suggestion should be distinguished from the theories of Indologists dating back to Maine that the transition from joint to nuclear families would accompany the process of industrialization and modernization. Shah, *supra* note 6, and Kolenda, *supra* note 18, among others have refuted the claim that the joint family was and is the most prevalent family form. Shah has suggested that the joint family may have been more prevalent in urban, rather than rural areas. Sylvia Vatuk's study of urban families in northern India, *Kinship and Urbanization: White Collar Migrants in North India* (Berkeley: University of California Press, 1972) concluded that the claims of a radical transformation in the Indian household structure due to urbanization are greatly exaggerated. Although she did find that nuclear and supplemental nuclear households were increasingly the common household form, she also found that much of the 'structural closeness' of joint families was maintained despite their being spatially separated: 'The persistence of interdependent relationships, of mutual rights and obligations for urban households and agnates living elsewhere, sustains close ties between kin despite occupational or geographical mobility' (at 194). In her view, the change in household structure was not caused by urbanization per se, but rather, in 'an underlying chain of forces which begins with education and permits occupational mobility, consequent geographic mobility and neolocal residence patterns. Urban residence is intermediate in the causal chain leading toward changed kinship organization. The changes I have described are intimately connected to the recent rise in India of a substantial white collar middle class from the peasantry' (at 191).

31. Ursula Sharma, *Women's Work, Class and the Urban Household: A Study of Shimla, North India* (London: Tavistock Publications, 1990).

32. Rao, *supra* note 2 at 62–66.

33. Government of India, *The National Perspective Plan for Women, 1989–2000 A.D.: Report of the Department of Women and Child Development (1988)* (New Delhi: Ministry of Human Resource Development) at xi–xii.

34. See discussion *infra* at notes 224–30.

35. *National Perspective Plan, supra* note 33 at 28. The World Bank, in *India: Poverty, Employment and Social Services: A World Bank Country Study* (Washington: The World Bank, 1989) similarly observes: 'In the sexual division of labour which prevails in many regions, women are primarily involved in specific operations like weeding, transplanting, and headloading; men specialize in digging and ploughing while also performing most other operations. Women are also involved in domestic work, gathering and processing of food and fuel and handicrafts. Women generally work 10–30% more hours than men per day. Male daily wage earnings exceed female earnings by 20–40%'. In the *National Perspective Plan*, the Government of India observes that '[i]n the economy, women are concentrated in occupations which are usually at the lowest rung of the ladder. In most occupations, they are involved in the more arduous and less skilled areas of work'.

36. Joanna Liddle and Rama Joshi, *Daughters of Independence: Gender, Caste and Class in India* (New Delhi: Kali, 1986) have explored the changing nature of women's work across caste. Liddle and Joshi, for example, have explored the changing nature of women's work across caste. 'The sexual division of labour is maintained throughout the caste hierarchy, but in different forms.... Amongst the higher castes, the men supervise the work of servants, hired labourers, and tenants, whilst the women are responsible for domestic work. Neither sex labours in the fields, but amongst all the castes, domestic work is performed exclusively by women. For upper-caste women, then, withdrawal from work outside the home (paid or unpaid) marks a release from arduous physical labour and a significant reduction in the amount of labour required of them' (*ibid.* at 90).

37. This withdrawal from work thesis, while useful in highlighting the status enhancing nature of the withdrawal of women from the public sphere of work, has been further complicated. Some writers have observed that the withdrawal from work thesis was developed primarily in the context of middle and upper castes in rural India, and cannot be unproblematically applied to the urban context. Papanek, for example has argued that status production work may more appropriately describe the reality of middle and upper class women in urban India. She argues that low levels of female participation in the labour market do not represent 'enforced idleness but a productive reoccupation of wives into family status-improving activities, such as the beautification of the home or the supervision of children's schoolwork in an increasingly competitive educational environment' (Papanek as quoted in Standing, *supra* note 7 at 11.) Standing has further argued that it is important not to treat this status production work as homogeneous, but rather, that it is important to disaggregate 'status enhancing or maintaining activities and time-filling and income substituting domestic activities'. She argues that this status enhancing work must be 'linked to the strategies of social reproduction of households in different classes. It is necessary to contextualise 'status' and to relate it to changing material conditions in rural and urban India' (Standing, *supra* note 7 at 11.)

38. Kalpana Bardhan, 'Women: Work, Welfare and Status: Forces of Tradition and Change in India' (1986) 6: 1 *South Asia Bulletin* at 4, for example, has illustrated that the nature of women's participation in the workforce is determined in important ways by women's class position. She describes the pattern of variation of women's participation in the workforce across class: '...very high rates of participation in wage labour and "unskilled" petty production at the bottom; withdrawal into domestic work and home based earning as poverty decreases; and at the higher income levels, women become employers and supervisors of servants and, with the greater incidence of education, move towards high participation in salaried jobs and the professions'. She notes that this is a variation in women's participation in the workforce at the national level, notwithstanding important regional differences, and that the rural pattern is beginning to closely approximate the urban pattern in this respect. Bardhan further argues: 'In a context of class stratification superimposed on traditional social hierarchy, one must be wary of generalising about women's double workload, about its severity and its implications.... The low paid maid servants produce time for more affluent women to study, learn marketable skills, pursue higher income jobs and the professions, engage in politics and social work, and, with growing demand for educated brides, to prepare for status enhancing or upwardly mobile marriages'.

39. *Ibid.*

40. There are many other material specific contexts which may affect women's position within their families, and the ways in which they are affected and constituted in

relation to familial ideology. As mentioned, age is another important factor in women's experience of family—a factor which will change for women within their lifetimes. A woman will acquire more power and status within a family with age. A daughter-in-law will have considerably less power than her mother-in-law within the family. Indeed, mothers-in-law may exert considerable control over daughters-in-law within the household, although both will have less power relative to the male heads of the household.

41. Sylvia Vatuk, 'Urbanization and the Indian Family', in Carla Border, ed., *Contemporary India: Essay on the Uses of Tradition* (Delhi: Oxford University Press, 1989). See also Vatuk, *supra* note 30 at 49–50 who notes that in her study she found that 'there is no specific colloquial term for the group commonly referred to in sociological and anthropological writing on India as the "joint family"—an agnatic extended family of 3 or more generations depth which shares a common household and forms a single productive and consumptive unit.... Yet, the concept of such a large, co-residential kin group, "joint" rather than separated into its constituent nuclear family units, exists nevertheless and is important in the normative aspect of family organization'.

42. Kapur, *supra* note 30 at 140.

43. Hazel Carby, 'White Women Listen! Black feminism and the boundaries of sisterhood', in Centre for Contemporary Cultural Studies, ed., *The Empire Strikes Back: Race and Racism in 70s Britain* (London: Hutchinson in association with the Centre for Contemporary Cultural Studies, University of Birmingham, 1982).

44. Gavigan, 'Paradise Lost, Paradox Revisited', *supra* note 10 at 605.

45. Uberoi, *supra* note 15 at 31.

46. Gavigan, *supra* note 10.

47. Roland Lardinois, 'Family and Household as Practical Groups: Preliminary Reflections', in K. Saradamoni, ed., *Finding the Household: Conceptual and Methodological Issues* (New Delhi: Sage, 1992) at 43.

48. Gavigan, *supra* note 10; Eagleton, *supra* note 8 at 15.

49. Lardinois, *supra* note 47 at 35.

50. See section 13(1) of the *Hindu Marriage Act, 1955*, section 27(1) of the *Special Marriage Act, 1954*, section 10 of the *Indian Divorce Act, 1869*, and section 32(3)(d) of the *Parsi Marriage and Divorce Act, 1936*. Adultery is not a ground for divorce for a Muslim woman, whose rights to divorce are governed by the *Dissolution of Muslim Marriage Act, 1939*, which consolidates and classifies the provisions of Muslim law relating to divorce by a woman married under Muslim law. However, if a Muslim woman is found to be 'living in adultery', she will forfeit her rights to maintenance under section 125(4) of the *Code of Civil Procedure*. This provision is similar to the older provision under the *Hindu Marriage Act, 1955*, which requires that the wife be 'living in adultery' and that one act of sexual intercourse is not sufficient to prove that she is living in adultery. However, this provision is related to a woman's right to maintenance rather than divorce, as Muslim law provides that a man can divorce his wife without stating any grounds.

51. Ursula Vogel, 'Whose Property? The Double Standard of Adultery in Nineteenth Century Law', in Carol Smart, ed., *Regulating Womanhood: Historical Essays on Marriage, Motherhood and Sexuality* (London: Routledge, 1992) 147–65.

52. Section 10, *Indian Divorce Act, 1869*. Several constitutional challenges have been brought to this provision (*Dwarka Bai* v. *Professor N. Mathews*, A 1953 Mad 792; and *Swapna Ghosh* v. *Sadananda Ghosh*, A 1989 Cal 1) which are discussed in considerable detail in chapter 3. Although section 10 has been upheld by the courts, usually on the basis of the 'natural' differences between women and men, a recent

decision of the Kerala High Court found the provision to be unconstitutional. The court held that this distinction in section 10 is violative of women's right to life and liberty under Article 21 of the Constitution, and that women can petition for divorce on grounds of cruelty, desertion or bigamy without having to prove adultery (*Times of India*, 25 February 1995).

53. A 1970 Mad 104.

54. *Ibid.* at para. 2.

55. *Ibid.* at para. 4.

56. The court was, however, able to provide some relief to the petitioner by granting her a judicial separation, and noted that it may be possible for the woman to bring an application for divorce in the future, should she acquire sufficient proof of adultery.

57. See *Robert Sebastian* v. *Linet Suba*, A 1992 Ker 412, where the lover was ordered to pay damages and the wife also lost custody of her child to her husband when she expressed her preference to live with her lover.

58. H. K. Saharay, *Laws of Marriage and Divorce* (New Delhi: Eastern Law House, 1992) at 293.

59. *Premchand Hira* v. *Bai Galal*, A 1927 Bom 594 at 597 (SB). See also *D'Cruz* v. *Mrs. D'Cruz*, A 1927 Oudh 34 at 35; *W. H. Thomas* v. *Mrs. Thomas*, A 1925 Cal 585 at 586 (SB); and (1947) 49 *Punjab Law Report* 321 at 326 (Lah).

60. *Premchand Hira* v. *Bai Galal, supra* note 59.

61. *Dr. Niranjan Das Mohan* v. *Ena Mohan*, A 1943 Cal 146 (DB). See also Saharay, *supra* note 58.

62. See *Sebastian* v. *Suba, supra* note 57, where an order was made for damages as recently as 1992.

63. Section 13(1)(i) of the *Hindu Marriage Act, 1955*. Adultery was the main ground for divorce used by parties seeking a divorce, up until the law was amended in 1976. A husband or wife could obtain a divorce if they established that their spouse was 'living in adultery'. The *Marriage Laws (Amendment) Act, 1976*, expanded the grounds on which divorce could be granted, as well as broadened the scope of the adultery provisions. The phrase 'living in adultery' was replaced with the phrase 'voluntary sexual intercourse with any person other than his or her spouse'. Section 13(1)(i). See for example *Rajendra Agarwal* v. *Sharda Devi*, A 1993 MP 142. As a result of this amendment it was no longer necessary to prove that a person was 'living in adultery' with someone other than his or her spouse, but only that sexual intercourse had taken place, even if it was only on one occasion.

64. See *Dr. N. G. Dastane* v. *S. Dastane*, A 1975 SC 1534, which held that the standard of proof required to determine adultery is on the balance of probabilities. Followed in *Mani Shankar* v. *Radha Devi*, A 1992 Raj 33, and *Rajendra Agarwal* v. *Sharda Devi*, A 1993 MP 142.

65. A 1972 Mys 234.

66. A 1992 AP 76. The case also involved a question of whether an earlier act of adultery by the wife had been condoned by the husband. The wife had admitted to the adultery in a letter, which she subsequently alleged had been written under duress. In the court's view, this earlier act of adultery may have been condoned by the husband. The court then focused its attention on whether a subsequent act of adultery—clearly not condoned—had been established.

67. A 1991 Ori 39.

68. A 1993 MP 142.

69. A 1982 Bom 498.

70. *Ibid.* at 501, paras. 17 and 18.

71. *Supra* note 73 at 144, para. 17.
72. See section 13(i)(a) of the *Hindu Marriage Act, 1955*, section 27(d) of the *Special Marriage Act, 1954*, section 10 of the *Indian Divorce Act, 1869*, section 32(3)(dd) of the *Parsi Marriage and Divorce Act, 1936*. See also section 2(viii) of the *Dissolution of Muslim Marriage Act, 1939*.
73. Section 13(1)(i)(a).
74. *Bhagat* v. *Bhagat*, A 1994 SC 710 at para. 17.
75. *Ibid.*
76. *Dastane* v. *Dastane, supra* note 64. In deciding whether a particular situation amounts to cruelty, the background of the parties, their social status and education, and their customs and manners need to be taken into account.
77. *Parimi Mehar Seshu* v. *Parimi Nageswara Sastry*, A 1994 AP 92 at 96.
78. See *Rajinder Bhardwaj* v. *Anita Sharma*, A 1993 Del 135 at 140, where the wife stated that she had been a 'most submissive, respectful and well behaving person'.
79. A 1992 MP 278 at 280.
80. *Ibid.* at 281.
81. A 1992 All 260.
82. *Ibid.* at 262.
83. *Ibid.* at 266.
84. *Ibid.*
85. *Ibid.*
86. *Ibid.*
87. The wife in *Gangadharan* v. *T. K. Thankam*, A 1988 Ker 245 was similarly able to defeat her husband's petition for divorce on the basis of cruelty. In this case, the husband complained of mental cruelty which included his wife's refusal to 'cook food for him, to wash his clothes and also to talk with the appellant for several days' (at 245). In response, the wife stated that after her marriage, 'she loved the appellant and acted always in accordance with his desire and dictates' (at 245). The court rejected the petition partly on the grounds that the wife's letters to her husband indicated that she was affectionate and 'concerned for her husband's health; prays for his health and expresses great desire to see him' (at 246).
88. A 1990 Cal 367.
89. *Ibid.* at 371.
90. A 1983 P&H 252.
91. *Ibid.* at 253, para. 3.
92. Similarly, in *Sushil Kumar Verma* v. *Usha*, A 1987 Del 87 a husband brought a petition for divorce on the basis of his wife's cruelty, on the basis that she had obtained an abortion, without the knowledge or consent of her husband. In the court's view '[i]n this country everyone wants to have at least one child, if not more, and in fact one of the primary ends of the marriage...is to have progeny' (para. 21). The court held that 'aborting the foetus in the very first pregnancy by a deliberate act, without the consent of the husband, would amount to cruelty' (at para. 22).
93. A 1963 Pat 93 (FB).
94. *Ibid.* at 97.
95. The contradictory role of law is also evident in cases where women have succeeded in securing a divorce on grounds of her husband's cruelty. In several cases dealing with a husband's impotency, the courts have recognized women's sexual needs within marriage. For example, in *Rita Nijhawan* v. *Balakrishan Nijhawan*, A 1973 Del 200, the Delhi High Court stated, at 209: 'Marriage without sex is an anathema. Sex is the foundation of marriage and without a vigorous and harmonious sexual activity, it

would be impossible for any marriage to continue for long. It cannot be denied that sexual activity in marriage has an extremely favourable influence on a woman's mind and body. The result being that if she does not get proper sexual attention, it will lead to depression and frustration'. In *Sirajmohmed Khan* v. *Hafizunnisa Yasinkhan*, A 1981 SC 1972 the Supreme Court stated, at 1976: 'Here is a wife who is forced or compelled to live a life of celibacy while staying with her husband who is unable to have a sexual relationship with her. Such a life is one of perpetual torture which is not only mentally and psychologically injurious, but even from the medical point of view is detrimental to the health of the woman'. Again, in *Srikant Rangachary Adya* v. *Anuradha*, A 1980 Kant 8 the High Court stated at 13: 'In these days it would be an unthinkable proposition to suggest that the wife is not an active participant in the sexual life and therefore, the sexual weakness of the husband which denied normal sexual pleasure to the wife is of no consequence and therefore cannot amount to cruelty.... It has been said that the sexual relations when happy and harmonious vivifies woman's brain, develops her character and trebles her vitality. It must be recognised that [there is] nothing more fatal to marriage than disappoint-ments in sexual intercourse'. The court further stated held: 'In the context of the changing status of women in society such a proposition (that the wife cannot refuse to stay with her impotent husband) would seem outdated and obsolete.... In other words, the court cannot compel the wife to stay with the husband on the ground that the husband though he is forcing her in a situation where her physical and mental well being might be adversely affected, as there is no intention on the part of the husband to inflict that cruelty, she should suffer that predicament without demur and be satisfied with a grab to bite and some rags to clothe her and a roof over her head'.

At the same time, mere allegations about a husbands impotency without further proof have also been regarded as a act of cruelty against the husband. In *Shanti Devi* v. *Raghav Prakash*, A 1986 Raj 13, the court held at 16, that a wife's allegation that her husband was impotent should not 'be lightly ignored as in a matrimonial matter it is [a] serious stigma on the manhood and is bound to cause grave mental agony and pain resulting in cruelty to the husband'. The decisions can be seen as somewhat contradictory. On the one hand, they constitute a recognition of women's sexual needs and agency within marriage. But, on the other hand, the decisions can also be seen within the more traditional framework that recognizes the need to restrict women's sexual needs to within the confines of marriage to ensure her sexual fidelity. If such needs are not met, she will become unruly and threaten the basis of the marital relationship.

96. A 1988 Del 121.
97. *Ibid.* at 125.
98. *Ibid.* at 128.
99. The Act was passed as an increasing number of Muslim women were apostatizing or leaving Islam and embracing another religion in order to get out of difficult marriages. Apostacy was regarded as dissolving a marriage according to Hanafi law. For a more detailed discussion see Archana Parashar, *Women and Family Law Reform in India: Uniform Civil Code and Gender Equality* (New Delhi: Sage Publications, 1992) at 151.
100. See discussion in chapter 1.
101. Radha Krishna Sharma, *Nationalism, Social Reform and Indian Women* (Patna: Janaki Prakashan, 1981) at 246.
102. Section 9, *Hindu Marriage Act, 1955*; section 22, *Special Marriage Act, 1954*; sections 32 and 33, *Indian Divorce Act, 1869*; section 36 *Parsi Marriage and Divorce Act, 1936*.
103. A 1964 Punj 28.

104. *Ibid.* at 29, para. 4.
105. *Ibid.*
106. A 1966 MP 212.
107. *Ibid.* at 214, para. 10.
108. *Ibid.*
109. A 1978 P&H 134. See also *Deepa Suyal* v. *Dinesh Chandra Suyal*, A 1993 All 244, where the court dismissed an appeal by the wife against the decision of a lower court granting her husband's petition for the restitution of conjugal rights. The wife left the matrimonial home as a result of the dowry demands made on her by her husband and his family. She also took up a job with the Central Reserve Police Force which the husband opposed. He stated that it was not necessary for his wife to take up a job as he was ready to maintain her and give her all the comforts she needed. The court directed its attention to the dowry demands which it held the wife had not been able to substantiate. As for her job, the court was of the view that she had a right to serve in the force and that this should be a matter of pride for the husband.
110. *Ibid.* at 136, para. 3.
111. In *Pravinaben* v. *Sureshbhai Tribhovan Arya*, A 1975 Guj 69, the fact that the husband was able to live with the wife in the place where she was first posted and as a result of which a daughter was born to them was held not to constitute a case in which there was a withdrawal by the wife from the 'society' of the husband. The issue was not whether the wife had withdrawn from the husband without reasonable cause, but whether she had in fact withdrawn from him. The birth of the daughter was sufficient evidence to disprove withdrawal and prove that there was enforced separation as a result of the requirements of the wife's job. There was no conscious choice on her part to remain separate from the husband, and she was able to demonstrate that she continuously invited the husband to be with her and enjoy a sexual relationship with her.
112. *Garg* v. *Garg* A 1978 Del 296.
113. *Ibid.* at 299.
114. *Ibid.* at 302. The general rule appears to be that a wife has a duty to live with her husband: see *Ramakrishna Pillai* v. *Vijaykumari Amma*, A 1990 Ker 55.
115. Similarly, in *Radhakrishnan* v. *N. Dhanalakshmi* A 1975 Madras 331, a husband sought a transfer in his job to a place other than where the parties resided. He subsequently filed a petition for restitution. The court refused to allow the petition on the grounds that it would require the wife to resign her job which helped to sustain both her and her child as the husband's earnings were very meagre. Moreover, the wife had no intention of denying her company to her husband.
116. A 1963 MP 5.
117. *Ibid.* at para. 10.
118. The courts are frequently aware that the restitution of conjugal rights is often used as a strategy for securing a quick divorce. If a wife does not comply with an order for restitution of conjugal rights, a husband can file for divorce on this ground which becomes effective within one year. This raises a dilemma for women who do not want to resign their jobs or return to abusive situations, yet want the marriage to continue. The cases demonstrate that the courts are inclined to find reasonable cause for withdrawal when it is demonstrated that the husband's conduct was such that it was not possible for the wife to remain in the matrimonial home, or if her decision to leave was taken with his consent. There is no corresponding right of the wife to choose to set up the matrimonial home elsewhere or to choose a career over her

obligation to reside in the matrimonial home. A wife's priority must be the matrimonial home and compliance with her husband's wishes and desires.

119. The constitutionality of these provisions were challenged, but upheld by the court in *Abdul Aziz* v. *Bombay* A 1954 SC 321, and again in *Sowmithri Vishnu* v. *Union of India* A 1985 SC 1618. These constitutional challenges are discussed in considerable detail in chapter 3.

120. In *Alamgir* v. *State of Bihar* A 1959 SC 436, the court considered section 498 of the *Indian Penal Code, 1860*, dealing with the enticement of a married woman for the purposes of having illicit intercourse. In the court's view, this section was similar in purpose to section 497 on adultery, and the court's comments thus shed light on the purpose and justification of these adultery provisions: 'The provisions of section 498, like those of section 497, are intended to protect the rights of the husband and not those of the wife. The gist of the offence under section 498 appears to be the deprivation of the husband of his custody and his proper control over his wife with the object of having illicit intercourse with her.... [T]he prima facie consent of the wife to deprive her husband of his proper control over her would not be material. It is the infringement of the rights of the husband coupled with the intention of illicit intercourse that is the essential ingredient of the offence'. (at 439).

121. See Flavia Agnes, 'Protecting Women Against Violence? Review of a Decade of Legislation, 1980–89', *Economic and Political Weekly* (25 April 1992) WS–19.

122. *Tukaram* v. *State of Maharashtra* A 1979 SC 185.

123. *Premchand* v. *State of Haryana* A 1989 SC 937. In a subsequent review petition, the court held that in referring to the 'conduct' of Suman Rani, they were neither characterizing her as 'a woman of questionable character and easy virtue nor made any reference to her character or reputation'. Rather, the court tried to argue that in fact it had been referring to her conduct 'in not telling anyone for about 5 days about the sexual assault perpetrated on her...' *State of Haryana* v. *Prem Chand* A 1990 SC 538. The court's effort at backtracking in the wake of considerable public controversy was difficult to sustain on the face of the express reasoning in the decision. Moreover, the Supreme Court has since held that any delay in reporting a rape should not be held against a rape victim, since there are many reasons that women, particularly rural women, may be unable to report the rape right away. It is difficult to read the Suman Rani case outside of the traditional assumptions about women's sexuality, and the distinctions between illegitimate (public) and legitimate (private) sexuality.

124. See also *Pratap Misra* v. *State of Haryana* A 1977 SC 1307, where the convictions of three men from the National Cadet Corp for raping a 23 year old pregnant woman, were reversed. The victim, who had miscarried five days after the rape, was the second wife of her husband, Bata Krishna. Because her husband had not divorced his first wife, the second marriage was not valid, and in the court's view, their relationship was not one sanctioned by marriage, but rather, one of 'illicit intimacy', in which the woman was described as a 'concubine'. One of the grounds on which the convictions were overturned was that the accused may 'have entertained some suspicion that [the prosecutrix] was not a good character and was merely a concubine of [Bata Krishna]. In this case, the fact that the victim was the second wife of her husband was sufficient to strip her of the protection of familial ideology—she was not a chaste and loyal wife, because in the court's view, she was not a wife.

125. For example, in *Krishnan Lal* v. *State of Haryana* A 1980 SC 1252 involving the rape of a minor, the court upheld the conviction of the accused. Krishna Iyer J., as he then was, rejected the argument that women lie about rape on the grounds that:

'[I]n rape cases, courts must bear in mind human psychology and behavioural probability when assessing the testimonial potency of the victim's version. The inherent bashfulness, the innocent naivete and the feminine tendency to conceal the outrage of masculine sexual aggression are factors which are relevant to improbabilise the hypothesis of false implications'. Similarly, in *Bharwada Bhoginbai Hirjibhai* v. *State of Gujarat* A 1983 SC 753, the court stated: 'A girl or a woman in the tradition bound non-permissive society of India would be extremely reluctant even to admit that any incident which is likely to reflect on her chastity had ever occured. She would be conscious of the danger of being ostracized by the society or being looked down by the society including by her own family members, relatives, friends, and neighbours. She would face the risk of losing the love and respect of her own husband and near relatives, and of her matrimonial home and happiness being shattered. If she is unmarried she would apprehend that it would be difficult to secure an alliance with a suitable match from a respectable or an acceptable family. In view of these and similar factors the victims and their relatives are not too keen to bring the culprit to book. And when in the face of these factors the crime is brought to light there is a built-in assurance that the charge is genuine rather than fabricated'. See also *State of Maharashtra* v. *Chandraprakash Kewalchand Jain*, A 1990 SC 658, at 665 para 27 where the court stated, 'Courts must also realise that ordinarily a woman, more so a young girl, will not stake her reputation by leveling a false charge concerning her chastity'.

126. In *Balwant Singh* v. *State of Punjab* A 1987 SC 1080, a woman aged 19/20 was gang raped by four men. The court rejected the argument that as she had not resisted, she must have consented, and held that a woman of such an age was not expected to offer resistance as would cause injuries to her body. The court was influenced by the medical evidence which indicated that she had been a virgin.

127. Vol. 1 at 629.

128. See Katherine O'Donnovan, *Family Law Matters* (London: Pluto Press, 1993) at 1.

129. Sections 376(1) and 376(2) of the *Indian Penal Code, 1860*.

130. See generally *G. D. Ghadge*, 1980 Cr. LJ. Bom 1380; *Chitranjan Dass* v. *State of U.P.* A 1974 SC 2352; *Fazal Rab Choudhary* v. *State of Bihar* A 1983 SC 323.

131. Section 20 of the *Immoral Traffic Prevention Act, 1956*, was challenged in *Shama Bai and another* v. *State of U.P.* A 1959 All 57, and in *State of U.P.* v. *Kaushiliya* A SC 1964 416 as violating constitutional guarantees. In both cases, section 20 was upheld. In Kaushiliya, the respondents, a group of 'prostitutes' working in the city of Kanpur, argued that section 20 conferred 'uncanalized and uncontrolled' power on the magistrate and enabled him to 'discriminate between prostitute and prostitute in the matter of restricting their movements and deporting them to places outside his jurisdiction, and that it also enables him on flimsy and untested evidence to interfere with the lives of respectable women by holding them to be prostitutes'. Although the High Court allowed the petition of the women, the Supreme Court set aside the decision stating at 421 that 'The differences between a woman who is a prostitute and one who is not certainly justify their being placed in different classes. So too, there are obvious differences between a prostitute who is a public nuisance and one who is not. A prostitute who carries on her trade on the sly or in the unfrequented part of the town or in a town with a sparse population may not be so dangerous to public health or morals as a prostitute who lives in a busy locality or in an over-crowded town or in a place within the easy reach of public institutions like religious and educational institutions. Though both sell their bodies, the latter is *far more dangerous to the public*, particularly to the younger generation during

the emotional stage of their life. Their freedom of uncontrolled movement in a crowded locality or in the vicinity of public institutions not only helps to demoralise the public morals, but what is worse, to spread diseases not only affecting the present generation, but also the future ones. Such trade in public may also lead to scandals and unseemly broils'. It further held that: 'The object of the Act is not only to suppress immoral traffic in women and girls, but also to improve public morals by removing prostitutes from busy public places in the vicinity of religious and educational institutions. The differences between these two classes of prostitutes have a rational relation to the object sought to be achieved by the Act. Section 20, in order to prevent moral decadence in a busy locality, seeks to restrict the movements of the second category of prostitutes and to deport such of them as the peculiar methods of their operation in an area may demand'. As a result, the court concluded that the differences between prostitutes constituted a reasonable classification on the grounds that one was clearly more dangerous than the other.

132. Dowry refers to, and in some ways mislabels, property and gifts given to a daughter by her parents at the time of marriage, traditionally known as her *stridhan*. The *stridhan* is intended to provide material security to a woman who is otherwise denied equal property rights under the Hindu personal law. Dowry, in its contemporary meaning, however, refers to a more recent practice involving the extraction or extortion of property from the wife and her parents by her husband and in-laws. There is no legal nor traditional basis for this practice. See discussion in chapter 10 of Paras Diwan and Peeyushi Diwan, *Women and Legal Protection* (Delhi: Deep and Deep Publications, 1994) at 158–60.

133. The offence was made non-cognizable and bailable, suggesting that it was not regarded as a serious offence at the time of the enactment of the law.

134. See the *Dowry Prohibition Act, 1961*.

135. The definition of dowry was extended to include any property or valuable security given or agreed to be given in 'connection with a marriage' rather than 'in consideration of a marriage'. Section 2(a), *Dowry Prohibition Act, 1961*, introduced by the *Dowry Prohibition (Amendment) Act, 1984*. The explanation to the section which provided that presents made at the time of the marriage to either party would not be deemed to be dowry was deleted as it was seen to have significantly diminished the strength of the dowry law. Explanation to section 2, *Dowry Prohibition Act, 1961*, omitted by the *Dowry Prohibition (Amendment) Act, 1984*.

136. The amendment raised the punishment to five years and a fine of Rs. 10,000 or the value of the dowry whichever was more. Dowry was made into a cognizable offence and the permission of the government to pursue a case was no longer required. The Act was not made to apply to presents given to the bride or groom.

137. Section 498(a), Chapter XX-A, *Indian Penal Code, 1860*, introduced by the *Criminal Law (Second Amendment) Act, 1983*. The *Code of Criminal Procedure, 1973*, was also amended to empower a magistrate to inquire into cases of suspicious death where a married woman dies within seven years of her marriage. Section 174 of the *Code of Criminal Procedure, 1973*, as amended by the *Criminal Law (Second Amendment) Act, 1983*.

138. The fine was increased to Rs. 15,000 and the offence was made non-bailable.

139. Section 302(b) of the *Indian Penal Code, 1860*, introduced by the *Dowry Prohibition (Amendment) Act, 1986*. The *Indian Evidence Act, 1872*, was also amended, with the introduction of section 113B which similarly raises a presumption of dowry death if the death has taken place within seven years of marriage, and there is evidence of the woman having been subject to cruelty.

140. See Flavia Agnes, *supra* note 121 at WS 24–27; and Madhu Kishwar, 'Rethinking Dowry Boycott', *Manushi* (September–October 1988) at 10.

141. See Kishwar, *ibid.*; Kishwar, 'Dowry and Inheritance Rights', *Economic and Political Weekly* (18 March 1989) 587; 'Continuing the Dowry Debate', *Economic and Political Weekly* (9 December 1989) 2738. For opposing views, see Palriwala, 'Reaffirming the Anti-Dowry Struggle', *Economic and Political Weekly* (29 April 1989) 942; and Laxmi, 'Family as an Area of Power Struggle', *Economic and Political Weekly* (13 May 1989) 1065.

142. See Palriwala and Laxmi, *ibid.*

143. Bina Agarwal, *A Field of One's Own: Gender and Law Rights in South Asia* (Cambridge: Cambridge University Press, 1994), at 480–83. Agarwal agrees that realizing inheritance rights for women is crucially important. But she disagrees that taking dowry can be an empowering strategy for women. In her view, the coercive elements of dowry are unlikely to be curbed, and dowry is not likely to be a particularly effective way to increase women's bargaining position within the family. Rather, property given as dowry rarely goes to the young woman, but rather is given directly to her in-laws. At 483, she writes: 'In my view, for the inheritance demand to gather strength will necessitate a refusal by large numbers of women to accept dowry as a substitute, even in the interim. Of course whether or not individual women should take such a stand, and sacrifice possible immediate interests for an uncertain future gain, is not something that others can decide on their behalf'.

144. A 1991 SC 1532, at 1537.

145. A 1993 SC 138, at 141. Similarly, *State of W.B.* v. *Orilal Jaiswal* A 1994 SC 1418, in considering whether the young woman had been subject to harassment and cruelty prior to her death, the Supreme Court stated, at 1429 'The abuse and insult hurled on the daughter-in-law usually are not expected to be made public so that the neighbours may have occasions to criticise the improper conduct of the accused'.

146. A 1986 SC 250.

147. *Ibid.* at 267.

148. *Ibid.* at 267–68.

149. *Ibid.* at 268.

150. *Ibid.* at 268.

151. These passages from *Laxman* have been quoted frequently with approval—most recently by the Supreme Court in *Kundula Bala Subrahmanyam* v. *State of A.P.* (1993) 2 SCC 684, at 701.

152. *Paniben* v. *State of Gujarat*, A 1992 SC 1817 at 1818.

153. A 1993 SC 819.

154. *Ibid.* at 825.

155. A 1989 SC 1661. Although the case was not strictly speaking one of dowry death, the court did comment on the provisions under the *Indian Penal Code*, and *Evidence Act* that would allow it to infer that a young woman's suicide was a dowry death, but held that it was unnecessary to resort to such provisions since there was adequate evidence to convict the husband under section 306 of the *Penal Code* of instigating her suicide.

156. *Ibid.* at 1666.

157. 1993 Supp (4) SCC 316, at 325–26.

158. In attempting to reveal and critique the norms of the self-sacrificing mother which have informed these decisions, we are *not* suggesting that the women in question did in fact commit suicide. In our view, there is little question that the court was quite correct in rejecting these arguments made on behalf of the accused. Rather, we

are simply attempting to highlight the *assumptions* that influenced the court in rejecting the theory of suicide—assumptions which we believe are informed by dominant familial ideology.

159. *Supra* note 152 at 1822.

160. *Ibid.*

161. *Ibid.*

162. *Supra* note 151 at 700.

163. There have been some references within judicial decisions to the need to promote women's economic dependency, but these comments remain framed within the discourse of familial ideology. For example, in *Laxman Kumar* v. *State of Delhi*, the Supreme Court cited with approval the comments of the High Court that 'once education and economic independence for women is achieved, the evil of dowry would meet a natural death. There seems to be force in what the High Court has said'. Yet, the Supreme Court then went on to elaborate its traditional view of marriage, and of women's roles therein as quoted before. More recently, the Supreme Court has again mentioned the importance of economic independence for women in relation to dowry in the case of *Kundula Bala Subrahmanyam* v. *State of Andhra Pradesh* (1993) 2 SCC 684. At 700, the court stated 'Lack of education and economic dependence of women have encouraged the greedy perpetrators of the crime'. At 701, the court further stated: 'Change of heart and attitude is what is needed. If man were to regain his harmony with others and replace hatred, greed, selfishness and anger by mutual love, trust and understanding and if women were to receive education and become economically independent, the possibility of this pernicious social evil dying a natural death may not remain a dream only'. However, it is important to emphasize that these comments by the court on the importance of achieving economic dependence came *after* the court had cited with approval and at length, the passage from *Laxman Kumar* on the nature of marriage, and the transfer of a woman as a plant from her natal family to her marital family. Our point here is that any recognition of the need for women's economic independence has been recognized within the limiting framework of familial ideology and its traditional roles for women—the very framework that has created women's structural inequality within the family.

164. Hindu customary law was significantly revised with the *Hindu Women's Rights to Property Act, 1937*, in which the Hindu widow was granted a right to intestate succession equivalent to a son's share in separate property among those governed by Mitakshara, and in all property among those governed by Dayabhaga. The widow also acquired a life interest in her husband's undivided coparcenary. The inheritance rights of daughters, however, remained unchanged. For an excellent and concise discussion of customary Hindu rights to inheritance prior to colonial rule, as well as its reformulation during colonialism, see Bina Agarwal, *supra* note 143, at 82–98, 198–211.

165. Section 14, *Hindu Succession Act, 1956*.

166. If there is a predeceased son, his wife and children would inherit the share that he would be entitled to if he were alive. The children of a predeceased daughter would similarly inherit the share that she would have been entitled to if she were alive. These Class I heirs also include the wife and children of a predeceased son of a predeceased son (but not those of predeceased daughter of a predeceased daughter). In the absence of Class I heirs, the property would devolve to Class II heirs, which includes nine entries: (1) a father; (2) a son's daughter's son, a son's daughter's daughter, a brother, a sister (3) a daughter's son's son; a daughter's son's daughter, a daughter's daughter's son, a daughter's daughter's daughter; (4) a brother's son, a

sister's son, a brother's daughter, a sister's daughter; (5) a father's father; a father's mother; (6) a father's widow, a brother's widow (7) father's brother, father's sister; (8) mother's father, mother's mother; (9) mother's brother, mother's sister. The heirs in an entry exclude the heirs in subsequent entries. If there are no heirs in Entry I then those in Entry II take, and so on. In the absence of any Class II heirs, the property devolves on agnates, that is, a person related by blood or adoption wholly through the males, and then, to cognates, that is, a person related by blood or adoption not wholly through males. See generally, *Mayne's Hindu Law and Usage, 12th edition* (New Delhi: Bharat Law House, 1986) at 948–50.

167. Section 23, *Hindu Succession Act, 1956.*
168. See *Mahanti Matyalu* v. *Oluru Appanama*, A 1993 Ori 36 (FB), and *Nalla Venkateshwarlu* v. *Porise Pullamma* A 1994 AP 87.
169. *Sripatinath Neogi* v. *Sm. Ira Rani Sur*, A 1992 Cal 60.
170. Section 23, *Hindu Succession Act, 1956.*
171. Agarwal, *supra* note 143 at 215.
172. Dependents are defined to include the parents, the widow, the minor sons, and the unmarried or widowed daughters.
173. Section 21(iii) *Hindu Adoptions and Maintenance Act, 1956.*
174. Under Hanafi law, the heirs are divided into three categories: 1. sharers, 2. residuaries, 3. uterine relations. The sharers have the first right to the estate and thereafter the residuaries and uterine relations take respectively.
175. Thus, if an intestate leaves a widow, son, and daughter, the widow will be entitled to inherit one-eighth of the estate, the son to 7/12ths (or 2/3 of 7/8ths), and the daughter to 7/24ths (or 1/3 of 7/8ths) respectively.
176. See M. Hidayatullah and Arshad Hidayatullah, eds., *Mulla's Principles of Mohammedan Law*, 19th ed. (Bombay: Tripathi, 1990) at 104.
177. The provisions of the Act are not applicable to Hindus, Muslims, Buddhists, Sikhs or Jains, but do include Jews, Armenians, Europeans and Indian Christians. A separate chapter governs the rules of succession as they apply to Parsis.
178. Section 33, *Indian Succession Act, 1925.*
179. *Ibid.*, section 48.
180. *Ibid.*, section 37.
181. A significant challenge in the area of property law was in the context of the Christian personal law. In 1986, Mary Roy challenged the *Indian Cochin Christian Succession Act* as being discriminatory. Although the case was decided on a technical ground, as a consequence, the *Indian Succession Act, 1925*, came to apply to Christians in Travancore, which slightly improved women's situation *Mary Roy* v. *State of Kerala*, A 1986 SC 1011. Although this did not eradicate the formal discrimination against women with regard to inheritance, nevertheless the Christian community has sought to limit the impact of *Mary Roy*, in particular, its retrospective application. More recently, the Christian community in Kerala is lobbying the state legislature to negate the retrospective application of *Mary Roy*. Thus even the small efforts to secure women some rights to property remains a contentious issue. In 1991, in a case concerning the distribution of property, the plaintiff, a Christian male tried to argue that the daughter of the deceased was not entitled to her one-third share in the property as she was given *stridhan*, that is, ornaments and household articles, at the time of her marriage. See *E. V. George* v. *Annie Thoman*, A 1991 Ker 402 (DB). The court held that there was no law in the light of *Mary Roy* that disqualified a daughter to inherit her parents property. The court stated that the challenge was an

attempt to resurrect the provisions of the *Cochin Christian Succession Act*, which were superseded by the *Indian Succession Act, 1925*.

182. The 1925 Act also governs succession regarding Parsis. Prior to 1991, a number of discriminations against females existed, ensuring that property remained substantially in the hands of male heirs. For example, prior to the amendment, the Act provided that a son was entitled to inherit a share that was double that of each daughter. Other provisions included one which stipulated that where a Parsi male died leaving one or both parents, the father was to receive a share equal to half the share of a son and the mother was to receive a share equal to half the share of a daughter (see section 57, *Indian Succession Act, 1925*). If the intestate was a female Parsi, then her property was distributed to the widower and her children in equal shares: see section 52. In case the child of an intestate died during his/her lifetime, the succession was dependent on whether the child was a son of a daughter. If a son died, then his widow and children would be entitled to share in the property. However, if a daughter died, the widower would be excluded and her children alone would share. The earlier position reflected the assumptions of economic dependency of a widow on a deceased in comparison to the position of a widower. These provisions have been amended. The children are now entitled to an equal share in the property of an intestate—that is, sons and daughters shall inherit equally (see sections 3, 4 and 5 of *Act 51* of 1991, which amends sections 51, 54 and 55 of the *Indian Succession Act, 1925*). Similarly, the previous discrimination between parents has been removed and they are now entitled to a share which is equal to half of the share of each child: section 51 of the *Indian Succession Act, 1925* as amended by section 3 of *Act 51* of 1991.

183. Agarwal, *supra* note 143 at 260–68.

184. *Ibid.* Agarwal discusses a host of obstacles to women asserting their property claims against their brothers. She also reveals the obstacles that her natal family may impose to real control over land that a woman may lawfully inherit. See *ibid.* at 292–315.

185. The regime of separate property was introduced through the *Indian Succession Act, 1865*, section 4, which provided that no person by marriage would acquire any interest in the property of the person he or she marries, and that married women were to be the absolute owners of all property vested in, or acquired by them. The *Married Women's Property Act, 1874 (Act No. 3 of 1874)* further provided, inter alia, that a married women was entitled to hold wages, earnings, money or other property acquired through her employment as her separate property.

186. Under the *Hindu Marriage Act, 1955*, a court is entitled to make such orders as are necessary with respect to property that was presented to the parties jointly at or about the time of the marriage: section 27, *Hindu Marriage Act, 1955*. This provision does not deal with any property acquired subsequent to the marriage and is only concerned with such property or articles that belong jointly to the parties or were given to them individually at the time of the marriage but have come to be used or dealt with jointly (*Pratibha Rani* v. *Suraj Kumar*, A 1985 SC 628 and *Suresh Kumar* v. *Smt. Saroj Bala*, A 1988 P&H 217; see also *Nandini Sanjiv Ahuja* v. *Sanjiv Birsen Ahuja*, A 1988 Bom 239). However, the Act does not allow a divorced woman an equal share of property, income and assets, unless these are in joint names or were gifts before or at the time of her wedding: *Subash Lata* v. *V. N. Khanna*, A 1992 Del 14. Thus, the work that women contribute, both directly and indirectly, to the acquisition and maintenance of property during the marital relationship goes unrewarded on marital breakdown.

187. The failure to recognize marital property has been extensively criticized. The *Report of the Sub-committee on Women's Role in a Planned Economy* in 1940 recommended

that 'the income and acquisition from any sources whatever made or acquired during the coverture will be owned by the husband and wife jointly'. Recommendation 68, *Report of the Sub-committee on Women's Role in a Planned Economy*. The reforms to Hindu personal law did not address these recommendations. In 1975, the government's *Report of the Committee on the Status of Women* again recommended that a wife should be able to claim to be part owner of property acquired during the marital relationship. See Government of India, *Towards Equality: Report on the Status of Women in India* (New Delhi: Ministry of Education and Social Welfare, 1975) at 140. Despite these recommendations and the continuing demands of the women's movement, no such reforms have yet been introduced to Hindu or any other personal law in relation to marital property. As these reports have recognized, the failure to recognize marital property has the effect of reinforcing women's economic dependency within the family. On marital breakdown, women are left with no independent source of financial security, but are instead forced to continue to rely on their ex-husbands through maintenance. For an argument in favour of recognizing marital property, see Poojitha, 'Community of Property Regime: A Call for Matrimonial Property Rights' in (1993) 1 *National Law School Journal* (Special Edition—Feminism and Law) 155.

188. See section 18 of the *Hindu Adoption and Maintenance Act, 1956* under which a wife is entitled to be maintained by her husband during her lifetime; section 24 of the *Hindu Marriage Act, 1955*, under which either spouse can claim interim maintenance which is generally one-fifth of the net income of the respondent, who is generally the husband; section 36 of the *Special Marriage Act, 1956*, applicable to interreligious marriages, which provides that interim maintenance can be paid to the wife after having regard to the husband's income, in order to ensure that she can support herself and bear the cost of proceedings; by a Muslim man to his wife during the course of the marriage (see *Mulla's Principles of Mohammedan Law, supra* note 128 at section 278), although she is only entitled to support on divorce during the period of *iddat*, that is for three menstrual cycles following the divorce; under the *Indian Divorce Act, 1869*, a woman is entitled to interim maintenance from her husband, during the matrimonial proceedings for nullity, judicial separation, divorce and restitution of conjugal rights, and the amount cannot exceed more than one-fifth of the husband's income (see section 36, *Indian Divorce Act, 1869*); there is no such limit on permanent maintenance awarded at the time of a divorce or judicial separation (see section 37, of the *Indian Divorce Act, 1869*); and under section 39 of the *Parsi Marriage and Divorce Act, 1936*, interim maintenance is payable to a wife up to one-fifth of the husband's net income, and permanent alimony is also available to the wife under section 40 of the same Act.

189. Section 18, *Hindu Adoption and Maintenance Act, 1956*.

190. Section 25 of the *Hindu Marriage Act, 1955*.

191. Section 10, *Indian Divorce Act, 1869*.

192. Sections 39 and 40 of the *Parsi Marriage and Divorce Act, 1936*.

193. Section 37 of the *Special Marriage Act, 1956*.

194. Section 278, *Mulla's Principles of Mohammedan Law, supra* note 176. A further limitation to a Muslim woman's rights was introduced by the *Protection of Muslim Women's Rights on Divorce Act, 1986*, which restricted a Muslim woman's right to maintenance on divorce to three menstrual cycles (section 3).

195. Statement of the Mahila Morcha, the women's wing of the BJP, discussed in greater detail in chapter 4.

196. Constitution of India, Articles 39 and 42.

197. See for example, the *Factories Act, 1948*, the *Plantations Act, 1951*, the *Mines Act, 1966*, and the *Bidi and Cigar Workers Act, 1966*.

198. *Shramshakti: Report of the National Commission on Self-Employed Women and Women in the Informal Sector* (New Delhi: National Commission on Self-Employed Women and Women in the Informal Sector, 1988).

199. Government of India, *Towards Equality, supra* note 187 at 63. The Report found that 94 per cent of women workers were in the unorganized sector. See also the *National Perspective Plan, supra* note 33. *Ibid.* at 28 which reported that 'approximately 90 per cent of women workers are engaged in the unorganized sector. Of these over 80 per cent are in agriculture and allied occupations. In the organized section, women constitute only 13.3 per cent of all employees'. As the *National Perspective Plan for Women* has further observed 'women are concentrated in occupations which are usually at the lowest rung of the ladder'. At 142–43, the Plan observes that in the agricultural sector, there is a provision for fixing minimum wages, but invariably the work that women do is classified as semi-skilled, or unskilled, and they are paid less, often much less, than minimum wage. See also *World Bank Country Study, supra* note 35.

200. *Equal Remuneration Act, 1976*, as amended, section 5.

201. *Ibid.*, section 2(h).

202. *Ibid.*

203. *Ibid.* section 5.

204. *National Perspective Plan, supra* note 33. *Towards Equality, supra* note 187, at 167 similarly observed 'Apart from the differentials in wages for the same jobs, discrimination against women is strengthened by having lower rates for the jobs of women'. At 231, the Report further stated that: '…old prejudices regarding women's efficiency, productivity, capacity for skills and suitability…debar them from employment in many areas. Wage discrimination is the result of this restrictive confinement of women to limited types of work'.

205. *Mackinnon, Mackenzie and Co.* v. *Audrey D'Costa*, A 1987 SC 1281.

206. *Ibid.* at 1286.

207. *Ibid.* at 1286.

208. *Ibid.* at 1286.

209. *National Perspective Plan, supra* note 33, at 25–26. See also Nalani Rajan, *Within the Fragments: A Non-holistic Approach to Indian Culture* (New Delhi: Affiliated East West Press, 1990) at 127.

210. *Towards Equality, supra* note 187 at 167.

211. *National Perspective Plan, supra* note 33.

212. *Maternity Benefits Act, 1961*, section 5.

213. *Ibid.*, section 4.

214. *Ibid.*, section 12.

215. A 1978 SC 12, at 16.

216. *Maternity Benefits Act*, section 2(1) provides that the Act applies to 'every establishment being a factory, mine or plantation including any such establishment belonging to government and to every establishment wherein persons are employed for the exhibition of equestrian, acrobatic and other performances'. Factory is defined as per the *Factories Act, 1948*, mine according to the *Mines Act, 1952*, and plantation according to *Plantations Labour Act, 1951*.

217. A. B. Saran and A. N. Sandhwar, *Problems of Women Workers in the Unorganized Sectors: Brick Kilns, Quarries and Mines of Bihar and West Bengal* (New Delhi: Northern Book Centre, 1990) at 193–94. See also *Neera Mathur* v. *L.I.C.* A 1992

SC 392, as an example of other ways in which employers try to avoid their obligations under the Act. Although the Supreme Court in this case upheld the rights of the female employee, and that the practice was a violation of her rights to privacy, many such employment practices nevertheless go undetected.

218. Faith Herndon, 'The Maternity Benefits Act, 1961', *The Lawyers Collective* (February 1989) 13 at 15.

219. *Ibid.* She further observes that: 'According to an Assistant Commissioner of Labour for Maharashtra, employers are responding to the MBA by hiring men over women in the desire to avoid shouldering payment of benefits. As long as the MBA is not combined with strict government oversight of recruitment, this paradoxical situation will remain'.

220. *Ibid.*

221. *Towards Equality, supra* note 187 at 191.

222. For example, the *Factories Act, 1948*, provides that every factory in which more than 30 women workers are ordinarily employed must provide suitable rooms for the care of children under 6 years of age.

223. K. Chandru, 'Women's Rights in Labour Laws', *Legal Perspectives* (no date). See also Saran and Sandhwar, *supra* note 216 at 176.

224. On the new economic policies in India and their gendered impact, see generally Indian Association of Women's Studies, ed., *The New Economic Policy and Women: A Collection of Background Papers to the Sixth National Conference* (Bombay: Tata Institute of Social Science, 1993); Jayati Ghosh, 'Gender Concerns in Macroeconomic Policy' (Keynote Address, Sixth National Conference on Indian Association for Women's Studies, 1993). On the gendered impact of structural adjustment policies more generally, see Diane Elson, 'The Impact of Structural Adjustment on Women', in Bade Onimode, ed., *The IMF, the World Bank and the African Debt: The Social and Political Impact*, Vol. 2 (London: Zed Books, 1989) 56; Isabella Bakker, *The Strategic Silence: Gender and Economic Policy* (London: Zed Books, 1994); Haleh Afshar and Carolyne Dennis, eds., *Women and Adjustment in the Third World* (London: MacMillan, 1992); Commonwealth Secretariat Expert Group on Women and Structural Adjustment, *Engendering Adjustment for the 1990s* (London: Commonwealth Secretariat, 1989).

225. The cutbacks in government funding to these social programmes which are dramatically increasing women's responsibilities within the household, as producers, consumers, household managers, and child rearers, remains largely unacknowledged in macroeconomic policy, where the prevailing assumption continues to be one of the elasticity of women's labour in the household. The cost of their unpaid time, and the increases in the time expenditures, have remained invisible. See generally, Elson, *supra* note 224.

226. Sudha Deshpande, 'Feminization through Flexible Labour in India: Evidence and Future Prospects', in *The New Economic Policy and Women, supra* note 173, 72–87 for example argues: '...to the extent that it [NEP] is likely to increase the demand for labour in general and that for female labour faster than in the past; offer wider choice of occupation to women entering the labour market in the near future; and reduce the extent of poverty among families of these working women, the change to NEP should be regarded as a positive change. We must remember for the present that to be exploited in the labour market is bad, but not to be exploited is worse'.

227. Jayati Ghosh, *supra* note 224.

228. Sudha Deshpande, 'Structural Adjustment and Feminization' (1992) 35:4 *Indian Journal of Labour Economics* 349 at 355.

229. The trend towards casualization of the work of urban women is becoming a feature not just in the informal sectors of cities in developing countries, but also in developed capitalist economies. At the same time the distinction between the formal sector and the informal sector is also being eroded: 'Women's jobs in the formal sector are being made more 'flexible'—which frequently means loss of security, loss of fringe benefits such as sick pay, pensions and maternity leave as well as increasing intensity of work. Export processing zones are one example of this trend. The contracting out of some public sector activities in some countries is another. The contracting out of health service ancillary services, such as cleaning, in the UK has led in some cases to women losing their sick pay entitlements and pension rights, suffering cuts in their wages, and facing new work quotas which give them more wards to clean, and less time to do it in. Increasing 'efficiency' in the public sector may be bought at the cost of deteriorating working conditions of women' (Elson, *supra* note 224 at 70).

230. It is also important to recognize that the new economic policies will not affect women as a monolithic category, but rather, the gendered impact will vary according to their socio-economic status. Sudha Deshpande has suggested that the NEP will result in an increase in wage differentials based on education. At 356: 'The highly educated women and men would be employed in high paid and highly protected core jobs while large masses of less educated would be competing for low paid jobs in the informal sector' (*supra*, note 228). While women are disproportionately represented at the lower end of the occupational ladder, it is nevertheless important to note that some women, namely, educated, upper middle class women, may benefit or at least not hurt from these programmes. Further there is some indication that the rising wealth and consumerism of the estimated 10 per cent of the population who will benefit from these programmes may intensify pressure on women to withdraw from work.

231. Janine Brodie, 'Shifting Boundaries: Gender and the Politics of Restructuring', in Bakker, *supra* note 172, at 47. See also Janine Brodie, *Politics on the Margins: Restructuring and the Canadian Women's Movement* (Halifax: Fernwood, 1995).

232. *Ibid.*

233. *Ibid.* at 53.

234. At the international level, the United Nation's International Year of the Family can be seen within this discursive framework. The International Year of the Family called upon governments to: 'i) increase awareness among government as well as the private sector on the importance of families, their functioning and associated problems; ii) strengthen national institutions to formulate, implement and monitor 'family sensitive' policies; iii) and improve the collaboration among national and international non-governmental organisations in support of multisectoral activities to strengthen families; iv) and build upon the results of international activities concerning women, children, youth, the aged and the disabled as well as other major events of concern to the family or its individual members'. See generally Ranjani K. Murthy, 'A Question of Perception: The United Nations and the Family', in *Voices: Journal on Communication for Development, Special Issue, Family Ties: Bond or Bondage?* (Volume II, No.2, 1994) 2 at 8; Ratna Kapur, 'Where Does Their Strength Come From?' *The Hindu* (12 September 1993); '1994 International Year of the Family: Building the Smallest Democracy at the Heart of Society', United Nations, Vienna, 1991.

3

Constitutional Challenges and Contesting Discourses: Equality and Family

I think that we must think seriously about difference. Otherwise, its meanings—embedded in unstated norms, institutional practices, and unspoken prejudices—will operate without examination or justification.

Martha Minow
Making All the Difference*

In this chapter, we turn to examine efforts at using law, and particularly, constitutional equality rights to challenge laws that discriminate on the basis of sex. We review some of the efforts to use Fundamental Rights to equality as guaranteed by Articles 14, 15 and 16 of the Constitution to challenge legal rules and provisions that are alleged to discriminate against women. We attempt to reveal the extent to which judicial approaches to equality, sex discrimination and gender difference have limited the role that constitutional rights have played in the promotion of women's substantive equality. The chapter begins by reviewing competing approaches to equality, and to gender difference. We argue that the judicial approach has been overwhelmingly influenced by a formal approach to equality, and a protectionist approach to gender difference. The formal approach, in which equality is equated with sameness, and the protectionist approach to gender difference, in which women are

* Ithaca: Cornell University Press, 1990.

understood as weak and in need of protection, have operated to limit the efficacy of these constitutional challenges.

The chapter focuses particular attention on the extent to which familial ideology has informed the judiciary's approach to gender difference, and the ways in which this ideology has operated to limit the attempts to use constitutional equality rights to challenge laws that discriminate against women. The chapter argues that the discourses through which women are seen as mothers and wives with particular social roles and responsibilities are important in constituting women as 'different'. Treating women differently in law is not seen as discrimination, but as protecting and promoting women's natural roles in the family. The chapter attempts to reveal the complex relationship between the discourses of equality and family, and the extent to which equality rights have as a result been ineffective in challenging familial ideology, and the roles allocated to women therein. Rather, Fundamental Rights challenges have often operated to reinscribe the very familial and legal discourses that have constituted women as different, and as subordinate. While this familial ideology is most evident in constitutional challenges to various personal laws, it is not limited to these challenges. Rather, assumptions regarding the sexual division of labour and the public/private distinction can also be found in decisions dealing with sex discrimination challenges to employment law, criminal law, and civil and political rights.

As we will attempt to illustrate, the role of equality rights litigation in challenging laws that allegedly discriminate on the basis of sex is contradictory. The judicial approaches have operated to limit the extent to which differential treatment of women is seen to be discrimination. And even where such differential treatment is seen to constitute discrimination, the results are not always unequivocally positive. For example, while some cases have struck down laws that have created legal obstacles to women's equality, the reasoning on which the results are based often reinforce assumptions about women as the weaker sex. Conversely, cases in which courts uphold laws that are designed to address women's substantive inequality may be done on the basis of similarly problematic reasoning. In evaluating the cases, we will thus pay close attention not simply to the results, but also to the court's reasoning, and in particular to the assumptions about women within this reasoning.

Further, it is difficult to evaluate the relative success of these constitutional challenges without considering the particular context in which each of these challenges have arisen. As this chapter will reveal, challenges are more often than not brought by individuals within the context of private litigation, and motivated by the individual agenda of the litigant to avoid the legal consequences of a particular law. As such, the challenge may or may not have anything to do with advancing a political agenda concerned with promoting women's substantive equality. These challenges have as often as not been brought by men, rather than women. The sex discrimination cases thus cannot simply be measured in terms of the willingness of the courts to strike down provisions that are alleged to discriminate on the basis of sex. Rather, as we will argue, it is essential to consider who has challenged the law, and for what purpose. For example, a case in which a court upholds a law that is alleged to discriminate on the basis of sex may be a failure from the point of view of the individual litigant. But, if that law was intended to promote women's equality, then the failure of the court to strike it down might be a success from the vantage point of women's substantive equality.

This chapter does not include a comprehensive review of all sex discrimination cases, but rather, focuses on those cases in which dominant familial discourses have operated and interacted with equality discourses.[1] As such, we are not suggesting that familial ideology will always operate to preclude effective constitutional challenges on the basis of sex discrimination. Our claim is much more modest—that in examining the legal legacy of challenges on the basis of sex discrimination, familial ideology has informed and constrained many decisions. We are not suggesting that it is the only factor nor even the most important factor in these decisions, but simply that it is *a* factor that needs to be taken into account. In other words, in evaluating the potential for equality rights strategies to challenge rules, regulations, and practices that discriminate against women, familial ideology needs to be considered.

Equality: Formal, Substantive, and the Relevance of Gender

■ Formal versus Substantive Equality

Equality rights are formally guaranteed in Articles 14, 15 and 16 of the Indian Constitution. But the Constitution tells us very little about the specific content of equality rights. The general principle of equality and non-discrimination is nowhere defined in the Constitution. Nor has there been any general agreement within political and legal theory as to the meaning of equality. While particular understandings of equality have been dominant at different times, equality has always eluded any simple or uniform definition. In this section, we begin by identifying two different approaches to equality through which the constitutional guarantees can be understood: a formal approach to equality, and a substantive approach to equality. While the formal approach to equality has been dominant within Indian constitutional law, fragments of the substantive approach have from time to time been identifiable. We will then examine the question of the relevance of gender difference within these models of equality.

In the formal approach, equality is seen to require equal treatment; that is to say that all those who are the same must be treated the same. It is based on treating likes alike. The constitutional expression of this approach to equality, in American and subsequently Indian equal protection doctrine is in terms of the similarly situated test, that is, the requirement that 'those [who are] similarly situated be treated similarly'.[2] Within this approach, equality is equated with sameness. Only individuals who are the same are entitled to be treated equally. Any differential treatment as between individuals or groups who are the same is seen to constitutes discrimination.[3] The similarly situated test requires that the court begin by defining the relevant groups or classes for comparison. This initial definitional step can preclude any further equality analysis. If the individuals or groups in question are seen as different, then no further analysis is required; difference justifies the differential treatment.[4] Accordingly, when groups are not similarly situated, then they do not qualify for equality, even if the differences among them are the product of historic or systemic discrimination.[5]

In contrast, the focus of a substantive equality approach is not simply with the equal treatment of the law, but rather with the actual impact of the law.[6] The objective of substantive equality is the elimination of the substantive inequality of disadvantaged groups in society. As Parmanand Singh notes, it 'takes into account inequalities of social, economic and educational background of the people and seeks the elimination of existing inequalities by positive measures'.[7] The focus of the analysis is not with sameness or difference, but rather with disadvantage. Substantive equality is directed at eliminating individual, institutional and systemic discrimination against disadvantaged groups which effectively undermines their full and equal social, economic, political, and cultural participation in society.[8] It is intended to 'promote a society in which the hitherto powerless, excluded, and disadvantaged enjoy the valued social interests (such as dignity, respect, access to resources, physical security, membership in community and power) available to the powerful and advantaged'.[9] The central inquiry of this approach is whether the rule or practice in question contributes to the subordination of the disadvantaged group. Within this approach, discrimination consists of treatment that disadvantages or further oppresses a group that has historically experienced institutional and systemic oppression.

The shift in focus from sameness and difference to disadvantage significantly broadens equality analysis. For example, within a formal equality model, the difference between persons with physical disabilities, and persons without disabilities could preclude an equality challenge. Because disabled persons are different, they do not have to be treated equally. Within a substantive equality model, however, the focus is not on whether disabled persons are different, but rather, on whether their treatment in law contributes to their historic and systemic disadvantage. Differences do not preclude an entitlement to equality, but rather, are embraced within the concept of equality. Within this model of equality, differential treatment may be required 'not to perpetuate the existing inequalities, but to achieve and maintain a real state of effective equality'.[10] Thus, the failure of a rule or practice to take into account the particular needs of disabled persons, and thus perpetuate the historic disadvantage of this group, would constitute discrimination, and violate their equality rights.

The debate over competing visions of equality was the subject of political controversy with the Mandal Commission, and reservations for scheduled and backward castes. Debates over the meaning of equality raged in the media. On one side, it was argued that reservations violated equality—that equality required that everyone be treated equally. On the other side, it was argued that reservations were fundamental to equality—that equality required that disadvantaged groups be treated differently. These debates highlighted the difference between the two models of equality, as well the extent to which the concept of equality is a site of contested meanings within Indian law and politics.

■ Formal Equality in Indian Constitutional Law

Indian constitutional law has been overwhelmingly informed by a formal approach to equality. The reasonable classification doctrine developed under Article 14 of the Constitution exemplifies this formal approach. Article 14 guarantees equality before the law and equal protection under the law. It has been interpreted as a prohibition against unreasonable classification. The Supreme Court of India has held that the equality guarantees do not require that the law treat all individuals the same, but rather, that any classifications made between individuals be reasonable. According to the Supreme Court, the classification must meet two conditions in order to be found reasonable.

(i)...the classification must be founded on an intelligible differentiation which distinguishes persons or things that are grouped together from others left out of the group (ii)...that differentia must have a rational relation to the object sought to be achieved by the statute in question.[11]

According to the doctrine of reasonable classification, only those individuals who are similarly situated must be treated the same in law.[12] Within this doctrine, equality does not require that all individuals are treated the same, but only those individuals who are the same. Equality is thus equated with sameness—and sameness is the prerequisite for equality. Only those persons who are the same are entitled to be treated the same.

This formal approach to equality spills over into the judicial approaches to Articles 15 and 16 of the Constitution, and the particular doctrinal tests which have been developed in relation to these rights to non-discrimination.[13] Article 15 prohibits discrimination on the grounds of religion, race, caste, sex, and place of birth. Article 15(3) allows the state to make special provisions for women. Article 15(3) has largely been interpreted as an exception to the principle of non-discrimination guaranteed by Article 15(1).[14] Non-discrimination is understood through the lens of formal equality, and its insistence on sameness. Special treatment, such as is authorized by Article 15(3) must therefore be seen as an exception to equality, rather than as a necessary dimension of it. In a second approach, Article 15(3) has been interpreted as part of the equality provisions as a whole, so that the differential treatment authorized by this article is not an exception to, but a part of, equality.[15] This second approach goes some distance towards a substantive model of equality, in so far as difference and special treatment do not preclude equality, but rather are embraced within it.

This modest shift towards substantial equality is limited, however, by the extent to which the principle of non-discrimination remains overwhelming influenced by formal equality. Discrimination has primarily been interpreted as any classification or distinction on the grounds prohibited by Article 15(1). Again, we can see the extent to which the approach is based on a formal model of equality, in which any distinction or differential treatment is seen as a violation of equality. Article 15(3) is thereby interpreted as authorizing the state to discriminate in favour of women.[16] In contrast, a substantive approach to equality would interpret discrimination in terms of whether the treatment of a particular group of persons contributed to their historic and systemic subordination, or to overcoming this subordination. Again, the emphasis of substantive equality is not on sameness or difference, but on disadvantage.

Some inroads have been made towards a substantive model of equality, most notably in relation to the equality of opportunity guarantees contained in Article 16. While a formal interpretation of equality of opportunity pervaded the early Article 16 case law with an emphasis on reasonable classification,[17] more recently, the courts' approach can be seen to have shifted away from this formal equality. In *Kerala* v. *N. M. Thomas*,[18] the Supreme Court addressed the question of the appropriate relationship between Articles 16(1) and 16(4).[19] The court held that Article 16(4) was not an exception to Article 16(1), and held that Articles 15 and 16 must be seen as facets of Article 14. Further, in *Thomas*, the Supreme Court began to articulate a substantive model of equality.[20] The clearest statement of this doctrinal shift is found in the judgment of Mathew, J. which explicitly rejects the formal model equality.[21]

> Though complete identity of equality of opportunity is impossible in this world, measures compensatory in character and which are calculated to mitigate surmountable obstacles to ensure equality of opportunity can never incur the wrath of Article 16(1).[22]

In *Thomas*, the Supreme Court began to articulate a substantive model of equality. While some courts have recognized the doctrinal shift in *Thomas*,[23] other courts and commentators have argued strenuously against it.[24] Not surprisingly, the *Thomas* case has been most severely criticized by those commentators who remain firmly committed to equality as formal equality. Their criticisms, however, are rarely articulated in such terms, but rather, remain focused on the narrow, doctrinal aspects of the case. Indeed, the failure of the court to go far enough in articulating its substantive model of equality can be seen to have contributed to this critical reaction.[25]

The Supreme Court has continued to approach Article 16 in a manner that is critical of formal equality, and appears to be more informed by a substantive approach. In *Roop Chand Adlakha* v. *Delhi Development Authority*,[26] the court was critical of the doctrine of classification within formal equality, observing that the process of classification could obscure the question of inequality.[27] In *Marri Chandra Shekhar Rao* v. *Dean Seth G. S. M.*,[28] the Supreme Court recognized that disadvantaged persons may have to be treated differently in order to be treated equally.

> Those who are unequal, in fact, cannot be treated by identical standards; that may be equality in law but it would certainly not be real equality.... The State must, therefore, resort to compensatory State action for the purpose of making people who are formally unequal in their wealth, education or social environment, equal in specified areas.[29]

In *Indra Sawhney* v. *Union of India*,[30] the Supreme Court again emphasized that equality of opportunity may require treating persons differently
in order to treat them equally. Although the continued use of the language
of formal equality—of the similarly situated test, and of classification—in
some ways limits the development in the majority decision, the minority
decision of Sawant J. went considerably further in articulating a more
substantive vision of equality. According to Sawant J., 'equality postu-
lates not merely legal equality but also real equality'. In his view, equality
'is a positive right, and the State is under an obligation to undertake
measures to make it real and effectual.... To enable all to compete with
each other on an equal plane, it is necessary to take positive measures
to equip the disadvantaged and the handicapped to bring them to the
level of the fortunate advantaged'.[31]

Notwithstanding these important developments in the Supreme Court
jurisprudence of equality as including compensatory state action for
historically and socially disadvantaged groups, formal equality continues
to dominate much judicial thinking on constitutional equality rights. As
we will demonstrate in subsequent sections, the courts' approach to
equality has been and remains overwhelming formal, with its focus on
sameness, and equal treatment.

■ Equality and Gender Difference

The debate over the meaning of equality is further complicated in the
context of women, and gender equality. The prevailing conception of
equality as sameness has led to a focus on the relevance of gender
difference. If women and men are different, then how can they be treated
equally? But if they are treated differently, then what becomes of the
principle of non-discrimination on the basis of sex? Do the constitutional
guarantees require that women and men be treated the same? Those are
but a few of the questions that have arisen in relation to the relevance
of gender difference. Three very different approaches to the question of
gender difference have been developed: protectionist, sameness, and
corrective. In the first approach, women are understood as different from
men—more specifically, as weaker, subordinate, and in need of protection. In this approach, any legislation or practices that treats women
differently than men can be justified on the basis that women and men
are different, and that women need to be protected. Any differential
treatment of women is virtually deemed to be intended to protect and
thus benefit women. This approach tends to essentialize difference, that
is to say, to take the existence of gender difference as the natural and

inevitable. There is no interrogation of the basis of the difference, nor consideration of the impact of the differential treatment on women. In the name of protecting women, this approach often serves to reinforce their subordinate status.

The second approach is an equal treatment or sameness approach. In this approach, women are understood as the same as men; that is to say, for the purposes of law they are the same, and must be treated the same.[32] In this approach, any legislation or practice that treats women differently than men is seen to violate the equality guarantees. This sameness approach has been used to strike down provisions that treat women and men differently. It has, however, also been used to preclude any analysis of the potentially disparate impact of gender neutral legislation. According to the sameness approach, it is sufficient that women and men be treated formally equally. Any recognition of gender difference in the past has been perceived as a tool for justifying discrimination against women.

Some feminist approaches have endorsed this conception of equality according to which gender difference ought to be irrelevant, and women ought to be treated exactly the same as men.[33] These feminists argue that any recognition of gender difference in the past has simply been a justification for discriminating against women. Advocates of this approach argue that so-called 'special treatment' has historically been a double-edged sword, that is, under the guise of protection, it has been used to discriminate against women. Any recognition of difference between women and men, and any attempt to accommodate those differences, is seen to provide a justification for continued unequal and discriminatory treatment.[34] They point to the use of gender difference in the past in prohibiting women to vote, to be elected to government, to be admitted to the legal profession, and other such participation in the economic, political and cultural dimensions of society.

In the third approach, women are understood as a historically disadvantaged group, and as such, in need of compensatory or corrective treatment. Within this approach, gender difference is often seen as relevant and as requiring recognition in law.[35] It is argued that a failure to take difference into account will only serve to reinforce and perpetuate the difference and the underlying inequalities. In this approach, rules or practices that treat women differently from men can be upheld, if such rules or practices are designed to improve the position of women. If, however, the legislation or practice is based on a stereotype or assumption that women are different, weaker or in need of protection, it would not be upheld.

Proponents of this corrective or compensatory approach attempt to illustrate how the ostensibly gender neutral rules of the formal equality approach are not gender neutral at all; but rather, they are based on male standards and values. As Nadine Taub has argued 'rules formulated in a male-oriented society reflect male needs, male concerns and male experience'.[36] In such a model, women will only qualify for equality to the extent that they can conform to these male values and standards. Thus, the corrective approach argues that gender differences must be taken into account in order to produce substantive equality for women.

There is no clear or unequivocal meaning to the concept of equality, nor in turn to the relevance of gender difference, but rather, a number of competing normative versions of these contested concepts. To identify these competing conceptions of equality is not, however, to suggest that each conception has equal ideological significance. The multiplicity of discursive visions of equality does not mean that each of those discourses carry equal weight, in terms of political and social meaning. Rather, some understandings of equality become dominant in ways that others do not. As we will illustrate in this chapter, some discourses of equality are inscribed in law in ways that others are not. In the sections that follow, we will attempt to illustrate the extent to which the ideologically dominant discourse of equality has been one in which equality is equated with sameness. Conversely, the dominant discourse of gender has been one of difference. The judicial approach to sex discrimination is overwhelming influenced by a formal approach to equality, and often, a protectionist approach to gender difference, which has operated to preclude any entitlement to equality. We will further attempt to illustrate that this problematic approach to gender is often informed by familial ideology, and an understanding of women's gender difference in terms of the sexual division of labour within the family. Familial ideology has been important in constituting women as 'different' from men. And accordingly, treating women differently is not tantamount to discrimination, but simply, the legal protection of women's natural differences. The dominant discourses of familialism and equality will be shown to interact in a way that thereby often preclude women's entitlement to equality.[37]

At the same time, it is important to recognize that the judicial approaches to equality and gender difference are not homogeneous. To argue that particular approaches have been dominant is not to argue that these approaches have been without exception or contradiction. Rather, we will illustrate the extent to which the judicial approaches to equality are a site of contest, in which competing visions of equality and gender difference compete. While a particular approach to equality has been and continues to be dominant—and in so doing, operating to reinforce and reinscribe the discursive constitution of women as different and subordinate—the presence of alternative visions of equality within the law creates space within which discursive struggles over the meaning of equality and gender difference can take place.

■ Deconstructing Difference

Our focus on two competing models of equality, and three competing models of gender is not intended to suggest that these approaches are exhaustive of the ways in which equality and gender can or should be theorized. Those approaches are, we believe, helpful in analyzing the Indian constitutional case law on sex discrimination. However, these approaches—particularly the approaches to gender—have been the subject of considerable debate. Feminist legal scholarship has, more recently, come to criticize the sameness/difference debate in which feminist equality theory and practice has become trapped.[38] Feminist legal scholars have attempted to take a step back from the sameness/difference debate and reconsider the very terms of the debate. Joan Scott, for example, has examined the way in which this sameness/difference debate has lead feminists into a dichotomous pairing of equality and difference.

> When equality and difference are paired dichotomously, they structure an impossible choice. If one opts for equality, one is forced to accept the notion that difference is antithetical to it. If one opts for difference, one admits that equality is unattainable.[39]

Scott argues that feminist scholarship must attempt to move beyond this either/or framework of debate, by deconstructing these binary pairs. She argues that our response must be to move beyond accepting this binary pairing as 'timeless and true' and 'start asking how the dichotomous pairing of equality and difference itself works'.[40] This would involve:

> ...the unmasking of the power relationship constructed by posing equality as the antithesis of difference, and the refusal of its consequent dichotomous construction of political choices.[41]

Martha Minow's work has similarly explored the ways in which difference has been constructed in law.[42] Her attempt to deconstruct difference is of considerable assistance in examining how this dichotomous pairing of equality and difference works. Minow begins from an understanding of difference as a comparative concept:

> 'Difference' is only meaningful as a comparison. I am no more different from you than you are from me. A short person is different only

in relation to a tall one. Legal treatment of difference tends to take for granted an assumed point of comparison.[43]

As she argues, this has not been the way in which difference has traditionally been understood, particularly in law. She argues that there are many unstated assumptions that inform the assignment of difference, including: (a) the assumption that differences are intrinsic, not relational; (b) the assumption of an unstated point of reference when describing someone as different; (c) the assumption that the perspective of the person seeing or judging is assumed to be objective; (d) the assumption that the perspective of others, particularly the perspective of those being judged is irrelevant; and (e) the assumption that existing social and economic arrangements are natural and neutral.[44] Difference does not, and cannot exist in isolation; it is always and necessarily in relation to something else that it is not. Differences only acquire meaning within a complex web of social relationships within which certain reference points become dominant. Women are as different from men as men are different from women. But men are not ascribed with the label of difference. Rather, men are the reference point from which others who are not men are thereby ascribed to be different.

Recognizing that differences are relational opens the possibility for recognizing that differences are a product of social relations—that difference is not a natural characteristic, but rather, a social construct. To recognize that particular differences are socially constructed is not to suggest that they are any less real in the lives of individuals who have been so constructed. It is not to suggest that we can make the difference go away by pretending that it is no longer there, or that it is no longer relevant. For example, familial ideology has constructed women as wives and mothers, and thus, as different from men, who are husbands and fathers. This difference, although socially constructed, has important material implications in the lives of women. As wives and mothers, they have been allocated certain roles and responsibilities, and denied others. As wives and mothers, they have, through both legal and social process, been rendered economically dependent on men. This economic dependency, although socially constructed, is very real in the lives of large numbers of women—they have no independent source of income or financial support. We cannot simply pretend that women ought to be the same as men, or that this gender difference ought not to exist. Ignoring the very real (albeit social) difference of economic dependency will not create substantive equality in women's lives, but rather, will only worsen their already precarious economic position. On the other hand, recognizing this difference risks reinforcing the unequal social relations that have created it, as well as the understanding of this difference as natural. Minow has referred to this problem as the 'dilemma of difference,' which she describes as the risk of both recreating and devaluing difference by either recognizing it or ignoring it.[45]

The sameness and difference approaches to gender can be seen to correspond to the two sides of this dilemma. The sameness approach, in denying the legal relevance of gender difference, both devalues difference and risks reinforcing the underlying social inequalities by judging women according to norms and standards based on men's experience. Conversely, an approach which affirms the legal relevance of gender difference, risks reinscribing this difference, and the underlying social relations which have produced it.[46] The protectionist approach, in accepting gender difference as natural and inevitable, simply reinforces the essentialist construction of difference, and the social relations of inequality that have produced the difference. The compensatory approach, on the other hand, although affirming the legal relevance of gender difference, attempts to reveal the relationships between the difference, and the social relations that have produced it. The compensatory approach attempts to denaturalize the difference, by illustrating the extent to which the difference is a social construct. Pregnancy and childrearing exemplify the dilemmas of gender difference in women's lives. The social and legal arrangements of child care are such that women's lives are very different from that of men's. Women not only bear children, but are responsible for raising them as well. The difference is not one that can simply be ignored. Yet, the legal recognition of this difference—usually within a protectionist approach—tends to both reflect and reinforce the common sense understanding of this difference as natural and inevitable. This difference, both produced and understood through familial ideology, which in universalizing and naturalizing the construction of women as mothers, places the socially and legally constructed arrangements of child care beyond consideration.

According to these insights of feminist legal scholarship, it is important that feminism not advocate an approach that unreflectively recognizes gender difference, nor one that unequivocally denies its relevance. First, it is not always the case that gender difference is relevant to a particular legislative rule or practice. Second, it is important that gender differences not simply be accepted at face value, but rather, that these differences always be interrogated and deconstructed. We need to ask about the 'nature' of difference in question. And we need to ask about who is different from whom? Where did the difference come from? Why is the difference relevant?

In the sections that follow, we will reveal many of these unstated assumptions that have informed the judicial approach to gender. We will pay particular attention to the role of familial ideology in constituting, universalizing and naturalizing gender difference. We will examine the extent to which gender difference acquires meaning in and through this familial ideology. By revealing the extent to which this familial ideology has operated to naturalize difference, we hope to begin to destabilize the essentialist construction of difference. We begin with a discussion of the constitutional challenges in the area of personal laws, as it is in this area that the influence of familial ideology is most readily apparent. We subsequently examine sex discrimination challenges in other areas including criminal law, employment law, civil and political rights, where the influence of familial ideology can also be seen to extend.

It is important to restate that it is not always easy to evaluate the results of constitutional challenges. Often the challenges have not been brought by women attempting to vindicate their rights to non-discrimination, but rather, by men who are attempting to avoid the legal implications of particular provisions. Often, women are found in the position of defending laws that are alleged to discriminate on the basis of sex. It is thus not possible to simply assume that a particular constitutional challenge can be evaluated on the basis of whether or not the court struck down the law in question. First, a particular law could be struck down (or upheld) on grounds that are extremely problematic, when measured in terms of competing visions of equality and gender difference. Second, even if a particular law is struck down (or upheld), on the basis of what may appear to be a normatively preferable vision of equality and/or gender difference, it is important to consider where the individual woman was located in the case. Thus, in evaluating constitutional challenges, it is important to recognize that the results in particular cases may be contradictory—a law may be found to be discriminatory and the individual woman may lose her case. Or a law may be upheld, as not violating equality rights, on the basis of a very problematic approach to gender difference and the individual woman may win her case. Constitutional challenges, like engagements with law more generally, are contradictory, and we will thus attempt to reveal these contradictions in our review of the case law, and our assessment of the relative success of these particular engagements.

Sex Discrimination and the Legal Regulation of the Family

Our review of the sex discrimination case law begins with equality challenges that have been brought against various family laws. It is within this case law that familial ideology is most readily apparent, and that we can begin to reveal the interaction between the discourses of family and equality. There are some cases in which the courts have held that laws that treat women differently than men are discriminatory and thus, in violation of the equality guarantees. Indeed, some cases recognize that the discriminatory treatment is based on sexist attitudes and practices that reinforce women's subordination. The approach adopted by those courts is one of formal equality and sameness—women and men are the same, and thus ought to be treated the same in law. However, other cases have rejected the challenges to family laws. These cases, though also adopting a formal model of equality emphasize the differences between women and men. Gender differences within the family are seen as natural and legitimate grounds on which to treat women and men differently. These gender differences operate to immunize the law from any serious interrogation of substantive inequalities.

■ Divorce

Section 10 of the *Indian Divorce Act , 1869*, provides that a husband may petition for divorce on the basis of his wife's adultery alone, but that a wife may only petition for divorce on the basis of her husband's adultery coupled with desertion, cruelty, rape, incest or bigamy. The provision has been challenged as violating Articles 14 and 15 on several occasions. In an early case, *Dwaraka Bai* v. *Professor N. Mathews*,[47] the court considered the constitutionality of section 10. The wife had petitioned for divorce, on the basis of her husband's adultery coupled with cruelty, and/or desertion pursuant to section 10. She further contended that section 10 discriminated on the basis of sex, in so far as she was not entitled to a divorce on the basis of her husband's adultery alone. The court rejected the wife's application for divorce on the ground that the alleged adultery had not been proved. The court concluded by briefly considering the constitutional challenge, although noting that any final determination of the issue was not necessary in light of its finding of fact. In the court's view, section 10 was based on differences in adultery committed by women and men, and thus constituted a sensible classification.

A husband commits an adultery somewhere but he does not bear a child as a result of such adultery, and make it the legitimate child of his wife's to be maintained by the wife. He cannot bear a child nor is his wife bound to maintain the child. But if the wife commits adultery, she may bear a child as a result of such adultery and the husband will have to treat it as his legitimate child and will be liable to maintain that child under s. 488, Criminal P.C.[48]

According to the court, these differences justified the different grounds for divorce, and section 10 was upheld.

Almost 40 years later, the constitutionality of section 10 was again considered in *Swapna Ghosh* v. *Sadananda Ghosh*.[49] In this case, the wife sought a divorce on the basis of her husband's adultery coupled with cruelty, desertion and/or bigamy. The High Court began by observing that several provisions of the Divorce Act were 'not only manifestly anachronistic, but have rendered themselves patently open to Constitutional Challenge'.[50] After reviewing the justification for this provision, namely, that a husband would not bear a child to be maintained by his wife, but a wife might bear a child to be maintained by her husband,[51] the court held:

> I would like to think that even assuming that the liability to conceive as a result of adulterous inter-course may otherwise be a reasonable ground for classification between a husband and a wife permissible under Article 14, since a wife conceives and the husband does not only because of the peculiarities of their respective sex, any discrimination on such ground would be a discrimination on the ground of sex alone against the mandatory prohibition of Article 15.[52]

The court, however, concluded that the case could be decided without a determination of these issues:

> My only endeavour is to draw the attention of our concerned legislature to this anachronistic incongruities [sic] and the provisions of Article 15 of the Constitution forbidding all discrimination on the ground of Religion or Sex and also to Article 44 staring at our face four decades with its solemn directive to frame a UCC.[53]

On the facts the court confirmed the divorce decree in favour of the wife on the grounds of the husband's adultery, coupled with both cruelty and desertion.[54]

The courts in *Dwaraka Bai* and *Swapna Ghosh* reached different conclusions on the constitutionality of section 10. In *Dwaraka Bai*, the provision was considered to be a reasonable classification, and thereby, upheld as constitutional. In *Swapna Ghosh*, the provision was considered to violate the prohibition on any classification on the basis of sex, and thus, in principle, unconstitutional, although the court stopped short of striking the provision down. It is also important to note that unlike in *Dwaraka Bai*, the question of the constitutionality of section 10 did not appear to have been raised by the petitioner in *Swapna Ghosh*. Despite these different conclusions, there are similarities in the approach of the court to the question of equality and gender difference. First, both decisions are located within a discourse of formal equality. In *Dwaraka Bai*, women and men were seen as different, and therefore as not qualifying for equal treatment. In *Swapna Ghosh*, the court similarly accepted that the differences between women and men might be the basis for a reasonable classification for the purposes of Article 14. The decision in *Swapna Ghosh*, however, turned on the court's approach to Article 15. The court was of the view that Article 15 prohibited any classification based only on the ground of sex.[55] In the court's opinion, differential treatment on the basis of the reproductive differences between women and men would constitute discrimination 'only on the ground of sex'. Sex was an absolutely prohibited ground for classification, and thus, section 10 of the Divorce Act which did not treat women and men the same, was in violation of Article 15(1).[56]

Second, there are interesting parallels in the courts' understanding of gender difference. In *Dwaraka Bai*, the differences between women and men justified the different grounds for divorce. In *Ghosh*, the differences between women and men did not justify the different grounds for divorce—women and men had to be treated the same despite these differences. Both decisions focus on the same biological differences of reproduction, which are seen as natural and as the only possible justification for the differential treatment. Both decisions collapse the biological differences of reproduction with the gender differences that have been socially constructed—differences that have also come to be viewed as natural and inevitable. Familial ideology and women's role in the family picks up from where biological difference leave off. Not only do women bear children, but as mothers, women are responsible for rearing the children they bear. Men, on the other hand, neither bear nor rear children. Rather, as fathers, they are responsible for financially maintaining children—and only those children who are the legitimate offspring of their wives. The sexual division of labour allocates to women and men very different responsibilities in relation to children—responsibilities which go well beyond mere biological differences. Yet, these socially allocated differences are similarly constituted as natural differences. The biological fact that women bear children is conflated with the socially constituted 'fact' that women are wives and mothers, and as such, the social differences are naturalized and essentialized. Women's roles as wives and mothers are thereby placed beyond the realm of legitimate differences. While both *Dwaraka Bai* and *Swapna Ghosh* can be seen to be informed by a formal approach to equality, and by a similar understanding of the gender differences between women and men, the decisions part company on the legal relevance to be attached to this gender difference. The court in *Dwaraka Bai* adopts a protectionist approach, within which the legislative distinction that treats women differently is justified on the basis that it protects women. By way of contrast, the court in *Swapna Ghosh* adopts a sameness approach, within which any differences between women and men must be ignored for the purposes of the law.

Both section 497 of the *Indian Penal Code, 1860*, which makes only adultery committed by a man an offence, and section 198 of the *Code of Criminal Procedure, 1973*, which allows only the husband of the 'adulteress' to prosecute the man with whom she committed adultery, but does not allow the wife of that man to prosecute him, have also been the subject of constitutional challenges on the ground of sex discrimination. In *Abdul Aziz* v. *Bombay*,[57] the accused, charged with committing adultery under section 497, challenged the section as discriminating on the basis of sex, and in violation of Articles 14 and 15. The High Court concluded that the difference of treatment was not based on sex but rather, on the social position of women in India. On appeal, the Supreme Court held that any challenge under 15(1) was met by 15(3). In a very brief decision, the court rejected the argument that 15(3) 'should be confined to provisions which are beneficial to women and cannot be used to give them a licence to commit and abet crimes'. The court held

> Article 14 is general and must be read with the other provisions which set out the ambit of fundamental rights. Sex is a sound classification and although there can be no discrimination in general on that ground, the Constitution itself provides for special provisions in the case of women and children.[58]

The sex discrimination challenge, brought by a man who had been charged with adultery, was thus rejected. In the court's view, the adultery laws fell within this exemption, that is, section 497 conferred a benefit on women, and thus, was allowed within Article 15(3).

The court's approach to equality rights can be seen to be informed by a formal model. Articles 14 and 15 of the Constitution require that no distinction be made on the basis of sex, that is, that women and men be treated the same. Article 15(3), however, is seen as an exception to this general rule, in providing that special provisions for women and children do not violate this injunction on differential treatment. The sex discrimination challenge, brought by a man who had been charged with adultery, was rejected. On further analysis, however, it is not clear that the adultery laws do in fact treat women preferentially. On one level, there is an obvious benefit to not being subject to criminal prosecution. Yet, at another level, the adultery laws are based on problematic assumptions about women, women's sexuality and the sexual relationships between women and men. Women are seen as the passive victims of aggressive male sexuality, incapable of agency in sexual relations, and therefore, must be protected. Within this understanding, adultery is seen as the fault of the man; a woman is simply his hapless victim; and therefore, not to be blamed. The failure to interrogate the law of adultery at a deeper level leaves these assumptions in place. The nature of the constitutional challenge leaves unchallenged the underlying assumption that adultery is conduct that ought to be criminalized. The court's approach, wherein any differential in treatment can be seen to be beneficial, and thus within Article 15(3), fails to adequately consider the questions of inequality and subordination.

In *Sowmithri Vishnu* v. *Union of India*,[59] section 497 was challenged as unconstitutional by a woman whose husband had prosecuted her lover for adultery. She argued that the section was discriminatory because the husband had a right to prosecute the adulterer, but the wife had no right to prosecute either her adulterous husband nor the woman with whom the husband had committed adultery. She further argued that the section was discriminatory in so far as it did not take into account situations where the husband had sexual relations with an unmarried woman. In dismissing the petition, the court held that confining the definition of adultery to men was not discriminatory as '[i]t is commonly accepted that it is the man who is the seducer and not the woman'.[60] Again, in the court's view, a wife who is involved in an adulterous relationship is the victim rather than the author of the crime. The offence is committed against the sanctity of the matrimonial home and it is the man who defiles that sanctity.[61]

The court's decision is firmly located within a formal equality approach, and a protectionist approach to difference. The court rejects the challenge on the grounds that in the context of adultery, women and men are different. The man is regarded as the seducer and the author of the crime. The approach essentializes women as passive, as incapable of agency in sexual relations, as victims. In the court's view, these differences are seen as natural.

Yet, even within this view, it is not clear why the wife of the adulterer cannot prosecute him. This question is more directly addressed by the court in *Revathi* v. *Union of India*,[62] when section 497 of the *Indian Penal Code, 1860*, and section 198(2) of the *Code of Criminal Procedure, 1973*, were again upheld. According to the court, these provisions

...go hand in hand and constitute a legislative packet to deal with the offence committed by an outsider to the matrimonial unit and poisons the relationship between the two partners constituting the matrimonial unit and the community punishes the 'outsider' who breaks into the matrimonial home and occasions the violation of sanctity of the matrimonial tie by developing an illicit relationship with one of the spouses...[63]

The fact that the wife of the adulterer is expressly prohibited from prosecuting her husband is the only exception to the general rule that anyone can set the criminal law in motion. This exception is based on an understanding of the very nature of the harm caused by adultery. Adultery is seen as a violation of a husband's property rights over his wife; more specifically, of a husband's exclusive access to his wife's sexuality. It is not a violation of a wife's rights since she does not possess the same claim to her husband. It is only the husband who can prosecute the adulterer since he is the only one who is seen to have suffered a harm. This basic difference in the understanding of adultery, a difference that is seen as natural, is used to justify the differential treatment, and thereby uphold the law.

The underlying and historical justifications for the criminalization of adultery remain unstated. The violation of the 'sanctity of the matrimonial tie' is the potential violation of a husband's right to ensure that the children his wife bears are his biological offspring. Historically, the provisions were based quite explicitly on the need to protect a husband's property—both his property in his wife and his children, and his real property; it was intended to ensure that his property was passed on to his rightful heirs.[64] Adultery has historically been understood as an offense against a husband's property. The law is deeply rooted in a familial ideology according to which only men were entitled to own and inherit property and in which men have the right to ensure that their property is to be inherited only by their biological offspring. This justification has never been hidden in the law, but rather, explicitly articulated and enshrined within the law.[65] Since women were not entitled to inherit property but rather, as wives, mothers and daughters simply entitled to be supported by the men on whom they are dependent, there could not be, by definition, any offense committed against the wife.

The failure to reveal these once historically explicit assumptions creates a tension in the law. Property laws have since been reformed to allow women to hold and inherit property. However, the social practice and attitudes of passing property down through the male line remains prevalent. Moreover, the idea of the violation of the sanctity of marriage has become so naturalized and so closely associated with the religious significance of marriage as a sacrament that the disjuncture between property laws and the criminal law of adultery remain invisible. The constitutional challenges to the adultery laws on the basis of sex discrimination have been unable to challenge these underlying assumptions about the nature of adultery. Familial ideology, which continues to constitute women and men as different (in this case, in terms of sexuality inside and outside of marriage) immunizes the legal provisions from judicial scrutiny. Equality, which in its formal manifestation, is simply about treating likes alike, is unable to probe beneath the discursive construction of women and men as different. The deeply gendered assumptions embedded in the criminalization of adultery and the differential discursive significance of the adulterous conduct of women and men remains well beyond the reach of constitutional challenge.

The cases on adultery raise the difficult question of what relevance, if any, should be given to gender differences that have themselves been constituted in and through unequal social relations. Women have not historically been accorded the same agency in sexual relationships as men. Women have historically and continue to be subject to sexual relations without their express consent, that nevertheless, in the law's view, falls considerably short of rape. The biological and social repercussions of sexual relations has historically and continues to be very different for women, than for men. Women not only bear children, but the social and legal arrangements of child care are such that women are responsible for rearing children, whether born inside or outside of marriage. The legal arrangements prevent women from securing the financial support of their children's biological fathers, if these children were born outside of marriage. Women who become pregnant as a result of an adulterous sexual relationship are thus in a very different social position from the men with whom they had the relationship. These sexual, familial, and moral discourses continue to constitute women in very different subject positions from men, with very different material implications. A failure to recognize this discursively constituted subject position of women thus fails to recognize the discursive and material reality of women's lives. Yet, the unproblematized recognition of this 'difference' risks reinforcing the very discursive relations that have constituted this subject position as natural and biological.

■ Restitution of Conjugal Rights

Section 9 of the *Hindu Marriage Act, 1955*, which provides for the remedy of restitution of conjugal rights, has repeatedly been challenged as violating Article 14.[66] In *Sareetha* v. *Venkata Subbaiah*,[67] the court held that section 9 did not meet the traditional classification test, and was thus unconstitutional. The court noted that section 9 did not discriminate between husband and wife on its face, in so far as 'the remedy of restitution of conjugal rights' is 'equally available to both wife and husband,' and it thus 'apparently satisfies the equality test'. Notwithstanding this formal equality, the court then turned its attention to the operation of the remedy.

> In our social reality, this matrimonial remedy is found used almost exclusively by the husband and is rarely resorted to by the wife.... The reason for this mainly lies in *the fact of the differences between the men and the women.* By enforcing a decree for restitution of conjugal rights the life pattern of the wife is likely to be altered irretrievably whereas the husband's can remain almost as it was before. This is so because it is the wife who has to beget and bear a child. This is practical, but the inevitable consequence of the enforcement of this remedy cripples the wife's future plans of life and prevents her from using this self destructive remedy. Thus the use of the remedy of restitution of conjugal rights in reality becomes partial and one-sided and available only to the husband....[68] [emphasis added]

The court thus held:

> As a result, this remedy works in practice only as an engine of oppression to be operated by the husband for the benefit of the husband against the wife. By treating the wife and husband who are inherently unequal as equals, Section 9 of the Act offends the rule of equal protection of the law. For that reason the formal equality that Section 9 of the Act ensures cannot be accepted as constitutional.[69]

The court in *Sareetha* concluded that notwithstanding the gender neutrality of the provisions regarding the restitution of conjugal rights, the law had a disparate impact on women. The law is used primarily by husbands against their wives; not by wives against their husbands. Accordingly, the court concluded that the law operated 'as an engine of oppression' against women. The court thus moved beyond a formal equality approach to consider the substantive inequalities which are produced by the operation of the law.

The approach adopted by the court in *Sareetha*, however, is not unproblematic, particularly in the approach to gender difference. In the court's view, the inequalities produced by the law are a result of the differences between women and men. The court focuses on the biological differences of reproduction, and, presents the differences between women and men as natural and inevitable. Yet, there is much more at stake than biological differences. The oppression to which the court refers is not merely the product of biological difference. It is a product of particular social relations which have allocated the responsibility of child care to women. The very strength of the dominant familial discourse is in the extent to which these social differences have been so effectively naturalized through the construction of women as wives and mothers.

In *Sareetha*, however, these social and biological differences are collapsed, and women's role in child care is constituted as a natural product of biological difference. The approach of the court to equality is commendable, in so far as it recognizes the impact of child rearing on women. And in this respect, the court demonstrates a willingness to look beyond the formal equality of the impugned law, and consider the actual impact of this law on women. In the court's view, the differences between women and men in relation to children results in a differential impact of the law. The approach to difference, however, is problematic in so far as it reduces this difference to a natural one.

The decision in *Sareetha* exemplifies some of the dilemmas presented by gender difference. If difference exists, and matters in the lives of individuals, then it must be recognized. Yet, in recognizing difference, we risk reinforcing the underlying social inequalities that produce these differences. In the context of the restitution of conjugal rights, there is a disparate impact of the law on women. This disparate impact needs to be taken into account if the substantive inequality is to be eliminated. In taking this disparate impact of the law into account, however, the court has essentialized what it perceives to be the reason for the disparate impact, that is, biological differences. In so doing, the recognition of difference has reinforced the social construction of difference, rather than in any way challenging it. In the context of *Sareetha*, the dilemma is how to recognize the impact of child rearing on women, without reinforcing the social inequalities that have produced this sexual division of labour. At a minimum, it is important that differences that are recognized are not naturalized, but rather, revealed as the products of particular social relations. Differences may need to be recognized. But at the same time, these differences must be deconstructed.

In *Harvinder Kaur* v. *Harmander Singh Choudhry*,[70] the constitutionality of the provision for the restitution of conjugal rights was again considered. In this case, the husband petitioned for the restitution of conjugal rights, and the wife opposed. The district court granted the decree to the husband. The wife appealed the decree and brought a constitutional challenge to section 9 of the *Hindu Marriage Act, 1955*.

The Delhi High Court rejected the challenge and declined to follow the case of *Sareetha*. In the court's view, Choudhery J.'s characterization of the restitution of conjugal rights as forced or coerced sex, and thus, in violation of sexual autonomy, was mistaken. First, this characterization gave undue emphasis on the sexual dimension of marriage. According to the court, the objective of section 9 is to restore cohabitation and consortium, of which sexual relations is but one element.

> To say that restitution decree 'subjects a person by the long arm of the law to a positive sex act' is to take the grossest view of the marriage institution. The restitution decree does not enforce sexual relations.[71]

Second, in the court's view, the restitution decree can be seen as the first step in the path toward divorce. If the decree is not obeyed for one year, the parties can then apply under section 13(1-A) of the *Hindu Marriage Act* for a divorce. In the court's view, the decree operates to encourage reconciliation and as a cooling off period before the parties proceed for divorce.

In considering the constitutionality of section 9, the court made two points. First, it noted that while *Sareetha* was based on the assertion that 'a suit for restitution by the wife is rare,' this was only true prior to the enactment of the *Hindu Marriage Act* in 1955. The Act was amended in 1964 allowing either party of the marriage to petition under section 13. Thus, in the court's view, '[t]here is complete equality of the sexes here and equal protection of the laws'.[72] The court was only concerned with formal equality, that is, with whether women and men were treated formally equally under the law. There is no consideration of the impact of the law, nor in turn, whether there is a disparate impact of the law on women.

In rejecting the challenge, the court further held that the Constitution ought not to be applied to the family.

> Introduction of Constitutional Law in the home is most inappropriate. It is like introducing a bull in a china shop. It will prove to be a ruthless destroyer of the marriage institution and all that it stands for. In the privacy of the home and the married life, neither Article 21 nor Article 14 have any place. In a sensitive sphere which is at once most intimate and delicate, the introduction of the cold principles of Constitutional Law will have the effect of weakening the marriage bond.[73]

In the court's view, the application of constitutional law would encourage litigation within the marital relationship—litigation which should be discouraged as far as possible.

The reasoning in *Harvinder Kaur* is a classic statement of the understanding of the family as private and of the public/private distinction. The family is understood as private, and thus beyond the appropriate intervention of the law. This public/private distinction has been an important dimension of the legal regulation of women's subordination.[74] Women have traditionally been confined to the private sphere of the family, as wives and mothers, sisters and daughters; and their access to the public sphere has been denied. The public/private distinction has been used to insulate the discrimination that women face within the private sphere of the family from legal review. Discriminatory practices ranging from unequal inheritance rights to sexual assault to dowry death have been, and continue to be, justified on the ground that they occur within the private sanctuary of the family, and thus beyond the scope of the law.

The constitutionality of section 9 was considered by the Supreme Court in *Saroj Rani* v. *Sudarshan Kumar*.[75] The court held that restitution of conjugal rights did not violate Article 14, thus affirming the decision in *Harvinder Kaur* and overruling the decision in *Sareetha*. According to the court:

> In India it must be borne in mind that conjugal rights i.e. the right of the husband or the wife to the society of the other spouse is not merely a creature of the statute. Such a right is inherent in the very institution of marriage itself.[76]

In the court's view, there were sufficient procedural safeguards to prevent section 9 'from being a tyranny,' and that the decree was only intended where the disobedience was willful. The court further held that the decree for the restitution of conjugal rights 'serves a social purpose as an aid to the prevention of the break-up of marriage,' and thus concluded without any further equality analysis that it did not violate Article 14. While the court implicitly adopts the approach to equality and gender of the Delhi High Court in *Harvinder Kaur*, it does not expressly state or develop on its own views in this regard.[77] In this case, the roles and responsibilities of spouses within marriage are again naturalized, and thereby placed beyond reasonable interrogation. The concept of conjugal rights is not recognized as a social and legal construction, but posited as a natural and inherent part of marriage, that precedes the social or legal regulation of the institution of marriage.

■ Succession Laws

Several challenges have been made to the laws of succession. These challenges have been unsuccessful in striking down provisions on the basis of sex discrimination. Some of these challenges have been brought by women who are restricted from making claims on their fathers estates. In *Mukta Bai* v. *Kamalaksha*,[78] Hindu personal law which excluded illegitimate daughters from maintenance from the estate of their putative fathers was challenged as violating Article 14. In rejecting the challenge, the court held:

> The fact that the law makes no provision for the maintenance of an illegitimate daughter cannot be said to amount to discrimination against illegitimate daughters, such as would amount to violation of Article 14 of the Constitution.[79]

The reasoning in the decision is entirely conclusory. There is no consideration of Article 14 case law, nor any analysis of why the distinction did not amount to discrimination. Presumably the distinction between legitimate and illegitimate daughters was so obvious to the court that it was not in need of any explanation. The absence of any legal analysis is indicative of the extent to which the court assumed it was simply appealing to common sense. The assumptions underlying this distinction rest on the assumptions that have traditionally informed succession—that property is to be inherited by children, primarily, male children, born within marriage. Illegitimate children—that is children born outside of marriage—have not traditionally had any claims to their father's property. While only legitimate sons were entitled to inherit property, legitimate daughters were entitled to maintenance from the estate of their fathers. In the same way as illegitimate sons were disentitled, so too were illegitimate daughters disentitled from maintenance. The social practice whereby only children born within marriage are entitled to make any claim on their father's estate is so deeply embedded that there is simply no question as to the appropriateness or justification of the practice nor of the impact of this practice on the illegitimate children. It is beyond interrogation.

Sex discrimination challenges to the *Hindu Succession Act, 1956*, have been brought largely by men, and have been rejected by the courts. In *Kaur Singh* v. *Jaggar Singh*,[80] section 14, which provides a female Hindu with the right of absolute ownership over her property, was challenged as discriminatory.[81] While the court acknowledged that the *Hindu Succession Act* did create an apparent anomaly in the powers of alienation of property, it held that the removal of such remained the prerogative of the legislature, not the courts. The court stated that 'it may well be that in view of the inferior status enjoyed by the females, the legislature thought fit to put the females on a higher pedestal,' which was within the purview of Article 15(3). It further held that women as a class were different from men as a class and the legislature had merely removed the disability attaching to women.

In *Partap Singh* v.*Union of India*,[82] section 14(1) was again challenged as violating Articles 14 and 15(1). The court found that section 14(1) was enacted to address the problem faced by Hindu women, who were unable to claim absolute interest in properties inherited from their husbands, and who could only enjoy these properties with the restrictions attached to widow's estates under Hindu law. In the court's view, as a special provision intended to benefit and protect women who have traditionally been discriminated against in terms of access to property, it was not open to Hindu males to challenge the provision as hostile discrimination. The court concluded that the provision was protected by Article 15(3), which in its view, 'overrides clause 15(1)'.[83]

In both *Kaur Singh* and *Partap Singh*, section 14 was upheld. In both cases, the provision was seen to fall within the ambit of Article 15(3) as a special provision for women. In *Kaur Singh*, the court adopted a formal model of equality, and further supported its finding by the fact that women and men were different, and thus, any different legal treatment could be justified. At the same time, however, the court observed that the legislation might be directed at compensating women for their inferior status. Although the court does not adopt the language of compensation or disadvantage, it does seem to understand section 14 within the content of the past discrimination suffered by women. Any underlying shift is limited, however, by the court's explicit adoption of the reasonable classification approach. In *Partap Singh*, the approach to equality and to gender is less obvious. The decision could be informed by either a protective approach (women need special provisions to protect them) or a corrective approach (women have historically been discriminated against and special provisions are required to correct this discrimination). The court's reference to the traditional problems that women faced in property ownership is suggestive of the latter and of a more substantive approach to equality focusing on disadvantage. Notwithstanding the difference in reasoning and approaches, in both *Kaur Singh*, and *Partap Singh*, the courts upheld a provision that was specifically intended to remedy the traditional discrimination that women had faced in Hindu personal law.

It is also worth noting that familial ideology did not operate in these cases to defeat the legislation. At one time, prior to the legislative amendment, it would have been the very construction of women as wives, mothers and daughters-in-law that supported their limited property rights. Women's inability to own and control inherited property was understood as a natural and inevitable result of their difference. The legislative amendments to those legal disabilities successfully challenged and displaced this understanding. As both *Kaur Singh* and *Partap Singh* illustrate, this understanding of women as different could no longer operate as a 'common sense' justification for limiting women's property rights. At the same time, however, the findings in the two cases remains at least partially based on the understanding of women as different.

In *Sonubai Yeshwant Jadhav* v. *Bala Govinda Yadav*,[84] section 15(2) of the *Hindu Succession Act, 1956*, was challenged as discriminating on the basis of sex, and thus in violation of Articles 14 and 15. Section 15(2)(b) provides that where a female Hindu dies intestate, any property that she inherited from her husband will devolve upon the heirs of the husband, whereas section 8, dealing with the property of a male Hindu dying intestate does not make any such provision regarding property inherited from his wife. In rejecting the challenge, the court held that the rules were enacted with the clear intention of ensuring the continuity of the property within the husband's line. Again, we see an example of familial ideology operating to preclude a substantive analysis of inequality and disadvantage. The assumption that property should be passed down through the male line is so deeply held that the court does not question the gender bias of the assumption. The historic discrimination against women in inheritance has created a norm—that property is passed through the male line—and it is against this norm that any challenges to the practice are measured, and ultimately rejected.

■ Maintenance

Constitutional challenges have been directed to the maintenance provisions of several family law statutes and the Criminal Procedure Code. In *Purnananda Banerjee* v. *Sm. Swapna Banerjee*,[85] section 36 of the *Special Marriage Act, 1954*, which provides for a grant of alimony *pendente lite* to a wife was challenged as violating Article 15. In upholding the section, the court held that it did not discriminate only on the basis of sex, but rather provided maintenance where the wife had no independent income sufficient for her support. The court further held that even if section 36 did discriminate on the basis of sex alone, it would be protected by Article 15(3).

The court approached the question of the constitutionality of section 36 from the perspective of formal equality. Article 15 is seen as prohibiting any classification based on sex—or more specifically, any classification based 'only on the ground of sex'. In order to uphold section 36, the court thus had to find that the section did not discriminate only on the ground of sex, but on other grounds as well. In the court's view, the classification was based not only on sex, but on a wife's need for economic support where she had no independent mean's of support. Women's economic dependency within the family is thereby separated from sex, for the specific purpose of upholding legislation intended to address this economic dependency. The formal model of equality is further echoed in the court's approach to Article 15(3), which is understood as an exception to the principle of non-discrimination set out in Article 15(1).

The case is an interesting example of the judicial gymnastics made necessary by the formal model of equality. The technical approach of 'only on the ground of sex' is used to uphold legislation that would otherwise be seen to violate Article 15, by drawing artificial distinctions between sex and socially constructed gender differences, or in the words of other courts who have been critical of this approach, between 'sex and what sex implies'. The formal understanding of equality, within which any classification on the basis of sex is seen to constitute discrimination, requires that economic dependency be seen as something other than a difference based on sex, if the provision is to be upheld.

By way of contrast, a substantive model of equality would similarly allow the court to uphold such legislation, without 'serving sex from what it implies'. A substantive approach to equality and a corrective approach to gender would direct attention to whether the rule in question contributes to the disadvantage of women and would allow a recognition that women may need to be treated differently to compensate for past disadvantage. Within such an approach, the maintenance provision could be upheld on the ground that it takes gender difference into account to compensate for past disadvantage. The reality of women's economic dependence, resulting from the sexual division of labour within the family, could be seen to require provisions that to recognize and compensate women for this dependence.[86]

The case is also illustrative of the often contradictory nature of familial ideology. The way in which the court casually draws a distinction between sex and women's financial needs rests, at least partially, on the naturalization of women's economic dependency within the family. Economic dependency is not seen as a socially constructed gender difference, but simply as a natural and inevitable consequence of family life for many women. It is, at least in part, the way in which this assumption operates at the level of common sense that allows the court to hold that section 36 of the *Special Marriage Act, 1954*, is not a classification on the basis of sex only, and in turn, to uphold the section from constitutional challenge. This result, which both draws upon and reinforces familial ideology, is at the same time an important victory both for the individual woman in *Banerjee*, who was awarded maintenance, and for all women who may otherwise qualify for maintenance under section 36 of the *Special Marriage Act, 1954.* The case thus illustrates the extent to which familial ideology does not necessarily always work against women's immediate interests. Rather, in effectively blocking the equality challenge to a provision intended to address women's socio-economic inequality, familial ideology can be seen to have protected these interests.

Several challenges were made to the maintenance provisions of the *Code of Criminal Procedure* which requires men to pay maintenance to their wives, but imposes no corresponding duty on women to maintain their husbands (section 488, now section 125). In *Thamsi Goundan* v. *Kanni Ammal*,[87] this provision was challenged as violating Article 14. The court, in adopting the reasonable classification approach, held that the classification was based on the difference between men and women.

> Women as a whole suffer from several disabilities from which men do not suffer. They have no right at least under Hindu law to participate along with their brothers in the inheritance to the property of their parents.... Instances can be multiplied without number to show how women have not equal rights with men. That as a class they are weaker than men cannot also be disputed. In fact they are even called by the appellation 'Weaker Sex'. The very provision in clause 3 of Article 15, that special provision may be made for women, suggests the existence of disparity.[88]

The court held that section 488 'applies to all women in similar circumstances,' that is, to all women deserted by their husbands, and that '(l)egislation in favour of this class of people' is not arbitrary.[89] The challenge was rejected, and section 488 upheld.

In this case, the court upheld the maintenance provisions in the face of a sex discrimination challenge brought by a man who attempted to escape his spousal support obligation by having section 488 struck down. The result in the case was important, from the perspective of the individual woman who was seeking, and received, an award of maintenance from her husband. At the same time, it is important to recognize that the reasoning on which this result was based was not unproblematic. The court adopted a formal approach to equality to Article 14 according to which only those who are similarly situated are to be treated the same. In the court's view, women, and more specifically, wives deserted by their husbands, are not the same as men, and therefore need not be treated the same. Further, Article 15(3) allows for special treatment of this class. The court's approach to gender is thus one of emphasizing the difference. The particular approach that the court adopts on gender is somewhat ambiguous. On the one hand, the court recognized that there has been historical discrimination against women in so far as they have been denied property rights. This recognition of the historic and specifically legal discrimination against women is suggestive of a corrective approach to gender. However, the court then seems to treat the difference between men and women as natural. The court explicitly states that women are weaker than men and thus, in need of special treatment. This language, in contrast, is suggestive of a protectionist approach to gender. There is no further interrogation of the deeper relationships of oppression that create these inequalities such as the sexual division of labour that renders women economically dependent on men.[90]

Familial ideology again picks up from where equality discourse leaves off: women and men are different not simply because the law has treated them differently but because they are different. The nature of this difference is accepted as self-evident—women simply are weaker than men. The language of 'the weaker sex' has strong biological overtones—that women have less physical strength than men. These biological differences are conflated with the legal discrimination that women have faced. By failing to interrogate the socially constructed reasons that women have needed and continue to need economic support from men, legal discourse operates to reinscribe the construction of women as naturally different from and weaker than men. The sexual division of labour, and the economic dependency engendered by it remains invisible, and women's difference remains natural. Once again, familial ideology remains immune from the challenge of equality discourse. Yet, we can also see that once again the impact of this familial ideology is contradictory. While reinscribing problematic assumptions about women's roles within the family, familial ideology operated to allow the court in this case to uphold the maintenance provisions designed to address women's economic dependency.

A rather different constitutional challenge was brought to the maintenance provision in *K. Shanmukhan* v. *G. Sarojini*.[91] In this case, section 124(1)(b) of the *Code of Criminal Procedure* was challenged as discriminating between divorcees and wives whose marriages were subsisting and thus in violation of Article 14. The provision entitles a divorced woman to maintenance while a married woman is not entitled to maintenance if she refuses to live with her husband without sufficient reason, lives in adultery or lives separately by mutual consent. The court adopted the reasonable classification test, and held that the classification was based on intelligible differentia. In the court's view, divorced women and married women were differently situated. The conditions stipulated in the impugned legislation could only apply to married women; they were, by their very nature inapplicable to divorced women. Similarly, the court observed that divorced women were disentitled to maintenance in situations that do not apply to married women, such as, when divorced women remarry. The court adopts a formal approach to equality, according to which the difference between married and divorced women is seen to defeat the challenge. There is no interrogation of whether the legal treatment disadvantages married women.

The approach to difference is essentialist: in the court's view, the differences between married women and divorced women are seen as natural, as part of the nature of the institution of marriage. The deeper question of why married and divorced women are different remains unexamined. There is no consideration of the extent to which these differences are a product of the legal regulation of marriage, that is, married women and divorced women are different because the law treats them differently. Rather than considering the question of economic dependence and economic need, a criteria according to which married and divorced women may be similarly situated, the court justifies the differential entitlement of maintenance on the basis of what it considers to be accepted differences. The case illustrates how virtually any difference, including those differences created solely through law, can be found to be intelligible criteria, and thereby satisfy the reasonable classification test of the formal equality approach.

Nor is there any consideration as to why the law has seen fit to treat these women differently. In examining the assumptions that underlie the law, it is important to recognize that the law does not distinguish between divorced women and all married women, but rather, only those married women who refuse to live with their husbands without sufficient reason, who live in adultery, or who live separately through mutual consent. The category of married women who are disentitled from maintenance are those who have chosen not to live with their husbands. The question which is nowhere addressed in the decision is why women who choose not to live with their husbands should be any less entitled to maintenance than divorced women (many of whom no doubt also choose not to live with their husbands). The answer lies in the assumptions about women's roles and responsibilities in marriage. As the restitution of conjugal rights cases made clear, the institution of marriage is seen to involve, first and foremost, the obligation of the wife to live with her husband. The status of being married precludes the idea that a woman can choose to not live with her husband.

These assumptions about the nature of marriage and about women's roles within marriage remain uninterrogated. According to the formal model of equality, the court is able to simply point to what it understands to be significant differences. The mere existence of these differences precludes any further analysis of the source of these differences. As with so many of the cases involving challenges to family laws, women's discursively constituted roles as wives and mothers are accepted as natural, without any further consideration of the inequalities that these roles have produced, nor of the unequal social relations that have produced these roles. Again and again, the formal model of equality, and familial ideology which constructs women as naturally wives and mothers preempt any substantive interrogation of inequality and disadvantage. At the same time, within the context of maintenance laws, familial ideology has largely operated to uphold these laws from equality rights challenges by men who have sought to escape from their legal obligations to support their wives.

Sex Discrimination and the Legal Regulation of Employment

Many rules, regulations and practices that impose restrictions on women's employment have been challenged as violating the equality guarantees. These challenges have been overwhelmingly brought by women who were denied employment on the basis of these restrictions. In this section, we will focus on sex discrimination challenges that have been brought to rules that restrict the employment of married women. Many of the challenges have been successful in striking these restrictions down. However, the decisions in this area are not entirely unproblematic. First, some of the rules and practices which restrict women's employment have been upheld. Second, the approach to equality and gender difference in forming these decisions is often problematic.

In *Bombay Labour Union* v. *International Franchise*,[92] a rule requiring an unmarried woman to give up her position when she married was challenged. The rule only applied to a particular department of the company. The justification offered by the company for this rule was the need to work in teams, the need for regular attendance and greater absenteeism among married women. The Supreme Court held that there was no evidence that married women were more likely to be absent than unmarried women.

If it is the presence of children which may be said to account for greater absenteeism among married women, that would be so more or less in the case of widows with children also...The only difference in the matter of absenteeism that we can see between married women...and unmarried women...is in the matter of maternity leave which is an extra facility available to married women. To this extent only, married women are more likely to be absent than unmarried women and widows. But such absence can in our opinion be easily provided for by having a few extra women as leave reserve and can thus hardly be a ground for such a drastic rule...[93]

The court struck down the restriction on women's employment.

In this case, the court was of the view that marital status was not a reasonable classification in light of the employment needs of the company. Rather, the more relevant indicia of women's ability to meet the company's requirements was whether or not women had child care responsibilities, which could apply equally to married and widowed women. Interestingly, the question of bearing children, is not, in the court's view, equally applicable to married and unmarried women. The assumption is that women only bear children in marriage (or at a minimum, that maternity leave only needs to be extended to women who bear children in marriage). Notwithstanding this assumption, the court was of the view that there was a duty of reasonable accommodation on the part of the employer. Women on maternity leave could, without undue hardship on the employer, be accommodated by hiring women who could fill in for those who were on leave.

In *C. B. Muthamma* v. *Union of India*,[94] the petitioner, an employee of the Indian Foreign Service, was denied promotion, which she alleged to be on the basis of pervasive discrimination against women in the foreign service. She challenged the rules of the Indian Foreign Service (IFS), including those rules prohibiting the appointment of married women, and requiring that unmarried women in the employment of the IFS obtain permission before marrying. The Supreme Court held:

If a woman member shall obtain the permission of government before she marries, the same risk is run by government if a male member contracts a marriage. If the family and domestic commitments of a woman member of the Service is unlikely to come in the way of efficient discharge of duties, a similar situation may well arise in the case of a male member. In these days of nuclear families, intercontinental marriages and unconventional behaviour, one fails to understand the naked bias against the gentler of the species.[95]

The court held that although the rule is discriminatory, the application should be dismissed in light of the subsequent promotion of the petitioner.

The court concluded, however, by strongly urging the government to 'overhaul all Service Rules to remove the stain of sex discrimination'.[96]

The court adopted a formal approach to equality, and a sameness approach to gender. For the purposes of employment in the IFS, women and men are to be considered the same. According to the court, women and men must both balance the demands of work and family. Women and men must therefore be treated the same in law. The court was able to see beyond the dominant familial ideology that at one time had justified the restriction on the employment of married women. In the court's view, women's roles as wives and mothers could no longer justify the blanket prohibition on employment. For the purposes of employment, women and men were the same. In this respect, the Supreme Court in *C. B. Muthamma* was able to go considerably further than it had in *Bombay Labour Union* a decade earlier, where it had not compared women and men, but rather, married and unmarried women.

The willingness of the court to hold that women and men are the same in relation to family obligations stands in stark contrast to the many cases in which the construction of women through familial ideology as wives and mothers precludes any such comparison. In light of the power once exercised by this familial ideology in the area of employment, and the continuing discursive significance of women as wives and mothers in constructing of gender difference that precludes equality analysis in other areas, the decision of the court is an important one.

The court is cautious, however, in its adoption of this sameness approach, and in fact, goes on to limit its applicability:

> We do not mean to universalise or dogmatise that men and women are equal in all occupations and all situations and do not exclude the need to pragmatise where the requirements of particular employment, the sensitivities of sex or the peculiarity of societal sectors or the handicaps of either sex may compel selectivity.[97]

In the court's view, although gender should not be relevant for the specific purposes of employment in foreign services, it might be a relevant factor in relation to some other legislative objective. The sameness approach to gender is thereby expressly limited to the particular circumstances of the particular case. The court leaves open the possibility of the need to adopt an approach which recognizes differences in other cases. At the same time, however, the discourse of the decision suggests an underlying protectionism. The references to women as 'the gentler of the species,' suggests that the court does see women as different, as weaker, and as in need of protection. Indeed, the recurring references to women as 'the weaker' and 'the gentler' sex reinforces images of women as weak, and in need of protection.[98]

In *Air India* v. *Nergesh Meerza*,[99] air hostesses challenged the discriminatory employment conditions for air hostesses and stewards. Air India contractual conditions required that an air hostess retire (*a*) if she marries within four years of her recruitment, and (*b*) at the time of her first pregnancy. The Supreme Court upheld a contractual condition permitting the termination of an air hostess's services on her marriage within the first four years, but invalidated a condition that terminated her services on her first pregnancy. On the basis of the reasonable classification test, the Supreme Court found that air hostesses constituted a separate class of Air India employees. The court considered the list of circumstances, noting the differences in recruitment, terms and conditions of service, the promotional avenues, and other 'special attributes' between an air hostess (female flight attendants) and assistant flight pursers (male flight attendants), and concluded that air hostesses were distinct from the class of assistant flight pursers. The category of male employees was thus seen as distinct from the category of female employees, and any difference in treatment could therefore be justified on this basis.

The formal approach to equality, and its similarly situated test was used to preclude any analysis of inequality between male and female employees. The court used the very discrimination between these two groups of employees to distinguish between them, that is, the practice of institutional discrimination against female flight attendants is used in the very definition of classes. As a result of the history of discriminatory treatment between a group of female and male employees, the court was able to conclude that the classes are distinct, and that no comparison need to be made between them for the purposes of Article 14. For example, rather than considering the problematic nature of the distinctions between the recruitment requirements for the male and female flight attendants, the court uses the different requirements regarding marital status between these groups as a factor in concluding that these employees are different. The circularity of the approach is evident—past institutional discrimination (female flight attendants must be unmarried; male flight attendants need not be) is thereby used to preclude any analysis of institutional discrimination (male and female flight attendants are distinct classes).

The court then turned to consider the distinction and restrictions that existed within the category of women employees, namely, the distinctions on the basis of marriage and pregnancy. Because of the court's finding that female flight attendants were a distinct class from male flight attendants, the question of whether these marriage and pregnancy restrictions constitute sex discrimination is never addressed. Rather, the court simply considers whether these restrictions are arbitrary or unreasonable without any comparison to the treatment of male employees. The way in which the issue of sex discrimination is written out of the equation in this case is an extraordinary example of the problems that a formal equality model and its similarly situated test presents to women who attempt to challenge discriminatory rules and practices. The employment restrictions on marriage and pregnancy apply only to women—the restrictions are explicitly and exclusively based on sex. Yet, within a formal approach to equality, wherein virtually any difference can be used to support the conclusion that women and men are not similarly situated, distinctions based on sex are not considered as sex discrimination. Assumptions about gender difference are so naturalized that rules and practices that institutionalize these differences are rendered virtually immune to any challenge of sex discrimination.

The court first considered whether the employment condition prohibiting air hostesses from marrying during their first four years of employment was arbitrary or unreasonable. The restrictions were upheld on the grounds that they fostered the state family planning programme, that women would be more mature to handle and make a marriage work successfully if forced to wait four years, as well as on the grounds of the financial hardship the corporation would incur should the bar to marriage be removed.[100] The court concluded that the treatment of the 'fair sex' in this regulation is neither arbitrary nor unreasonable, and thus does not violate Article 14.

In contrast, the court held that the employment restriction on pregnancy was unconstitutional. The court held that the dismissal of a pregnant air hostess 'amounts to compelling the poor air hostess not to have any children and thus interfere with and divert the ordinary course of human nature'. In the court's view:

It seems to us that the termination of the services of an air hostess under such circumstances is not only a callous and cruel act but an open insult to Indian womanhood—the most sacrosanct and cherished institution. We are constrained to observe that such a course of action is extremely detestable and abhorrent to the notions of a civilized society. Apart from being grossly unethical, it smacks of a deep rooted sense of utter selfishness at the cost of all human values.[101]

The court concluded that the pregnancy restriction was unreasonable and arbitrary, and thus in violation of Article 14.[102]

The Supreme Court decision in *Nergesh Meerza* is often applauded as a vindication of the constitutional rights of women. On one hand, the court's willingness to strike down the pregnancy restrictions was an important improvement in these women's employment conditions. On the other hand, it is also significant that the court was not willing to strike down the marriage restriction. At best, the decision in *Nergesh Meerza* was a partial victory for the women involved, but, at another level, there is reason to be concerned with the assumptions about women that informed the court's reasoning, in terms of its finding on both the marriage and pregnancy restriction.

For example, the factors listed by the court in upholding the marriage restrictions are quite problematic, particularly when considered in relation to the treatment of male employees. There is some question about the appropriateness of using the employment practices of corporations to promote family planning. Why is this a legitimate objective of employment practices? What is the rationale connection between family planning and employment? Even if some reasonable nexus could be established, there is a further question of why this connection only applies to women. If the reason for making women wait for four years before marrying is to be seen as a legitimate family planning issue, then it is an issue that is equally applicable to men, who should also be forced to wait for at least four years before marrying. Yet, the way in which sex discrimination was written out of the case precludes any such interrogation. A very similar question is raised by the second reason offered by the court, that is, the restriction will operate to make women more mature, and thus, lead to more successful marriages. What is the nexus between promoting successful marriages and employment practices? Why is it a legitimate objective for employers to effectively raise the age of marriage well beyond that provided by law in India? And why would this objective only apply to women? Again, the way in which the question of sex discrimination was effectively obscured in the case allows the court to escape from any consideration of why these factors should not also be applied to men.

The last factor which is seen to justify the restriction on marriage is illustrative of the court's approach to gender difference. The restriction on marriage is based in part on the company's desire to avoid the expense associated with maternity leave. By forcing its female employees to wait for four years before they are allowed to marry, Air India argued that it was able to avoid the 'huge expenditure' of training additional employees to replace those employees on maternity leave. The restriction is an explicit attempt to avoid the costs associated with maternity leave, as legally mandated by the *Maternity Benefits Act*. Yet, the court fails to consider the obvious connection between the restrictions on marriage and the restrictions on pregnancy. The employment restrictions on marriage are an effort to delay women's pregnancies, by delaying their marriages. These restrictions are justified, in part, by women's reproductive roles—that women become pregnant, and give birth to children. Indeed, the other factors which the court lists as justifying the restriction—health, family planning, and maturity—can similarly be seen in this reproductive light. It is this biological difference between women and men that underlies the court's willingness to find the marriage restriction to be reasonable, and which at least implicitly operates to justify the non-applicability of those restrictions to male employees.

But it is not only the court's reasoning in relation to the marriage restriction that is problematic. The basis on which the court struck down the pregnancy restriction is also cause for concern. Indeed, women's roles as mothers become synonymous with 'Indian womanhood'. To be an Indian woman is, in other words, to be a mother. Denying a woman the right to have children is not simply 'cruel and callous,' but amounts to a denial of her very essence. Women's roles as mothers are not only naturalized, but are unequivocally celebrated and essentialized.

In *Maya Devi* v. *State of Maharashtra*,[103] a requirement that married women obtain their husbands' consent before applying for public employment was challenged as violating Articles 14, 15 and 16. The Supreme Court held:

> This is a matter purely personal between husband and wife. It is unthinkable that in social conditions presently prevalent a husband can prevent a wife from being independent economically just for his whim or caprice.[104]

The court emphasized the importance of economic independence for women, and thus, the importance of not creating conditions that discourage such independence. The consent requirement was thus held to be unconstitutional. In this case, the court was of the view that consent requirements were an anachronistic obstacle to women's equality. In order to achieve economic independence women must not, at least in this regard, be treated differently than men. The decision might be seen to be informed by a formal model to equality, and a sameness approach to gender difference which requires that women and men be treated the same. However, the decision can also be supported by a more substantive approach to equality, that is, the consent requirement contributed to the subordination of women. The case exemplifies how a substantive approach to equality may still require a choice to be made about the relevance of gender. In this case, an inquiry into whether the rule contributed to or reinforced women's subordination revealed that in this particular context gender ought to be irrelevant, and thus, a sameness approach was appropriate.

Sex Discrimination and the Legal Regulation of Civil and Political Rights

■ Restrictions on Land-ownership

Statutory provisions that have restricted women's right to own land exclusively on the basis of sex have been struck down by the courts as discrimination on the basis of sex. For example, in *Pritam Kaur* v. *State of Pepsu*,[105] section 5(2) of the *Pepsu Court of Wards Act* was challenged as violating Article 15(1). The provision authorized the government to make an order directing that property of a landholder be placed under the supervision of the Court of Wards if the landholder was incapable of managing his affairs. Sub-section (a) authorized such an order if a landholder 'by reason of being a female' was incapable of managing the property. The provision was challenged by Pritam Kaur, a widow whose deceased husband's estate had been placed under the supervision of the Court of Wards in 1928. After independence, possession of the property came to be held under the Pepsu law.[106] The court noted:

> To be a woman is an additional reason on the basis of which the Government can deprive her of the management of her estate. In other words, if a man mismanages his estate, that mismanagement will not render his estate liable to be taken over by the Court of Wards unless his case falls under any one of clauses (b), (c) and (d) of section 5(2) of the Act. Whereas in the case of a woman it can be so taken merely for the reason that she is a woman.[107]

The court concluded that section 5(2) of the Act discriminated on the basis of sex, and thus violated Article 15. As a result, the Court of Wards was ordered to return possession of the property to the petitioner.

Statutory provisions that have restricted ownership of land on the basis of their family status as daughters or wives, however, have been upheld. Restrictions based on distinctions between sons and daughters, for example, have been upheld. In these cases, we can again see the interaction between equality discourse and familial ideology; on interaction in which familial ideology precludes any substantive analysis of discrimination. In *Sucha Singh Bajwa* v. *The State of Punjab*,[108] section 5 of the *Punjab Land Reforms Act, 1973*, was challenged as violating Article 15 on the grounds that it allowed the holder or owner of the land to select the separate permissible area in respect of adult sons, but not adult daughters. The High Court held:

> The subject of the legislation is the person owning or holding land, and not his or her children...[Since] every person described in section 5 whether male or female is allowed the same permissible area and there is no discrimination qua one land owner and the other on the ground of sex...[109]

The court further held that the distinction was not made on the ground of sex alone, but rather 'also for reason that a daughter has to go to another family after her marriage in due course'. The court upheld the restriction.

The decision highlights the ways in which classification and comparison can be manipulated within a formal equality approach. The court defines the relevant comparison as one between the landholders. Accordingly, since there is no discrimination between male and female *landholders*, the provision is not seen to discriminate on the basis of sex. While the discrimination as between sons and daughters on the face of the legislation might be seen to offend even a formal approach to equality, the court evades this question by simply defining this comparison between potential recipients as irrelevant.

The court's approach to gender is also problematic. In support of its decision, the court resorts to the doctrine of 'only on the grounds of sex' and argues that there are factors not based on sex that justify the differential treatment of a daughter, such as the fact that daughters go to another family after marriage. The status of being a daughter is seen as distinct from the status of being a woman. The social norms and practices associated with daughters are thereby disassociated from sex. The reasoning in *Bajwa* provides yet another illustration of the problematic distinction between sex and what it implies in Article 15 jurisprudence. The distinction allows the court to obscure the connections between such customary practices and the social construction of gender. The practice of daughters leaving their birth families on marriage is a product of the social organization of gender, and the roles that women are expected to assume. It is part of a familial ideology which constitutes women as being only temporarily members of their birth family. When women are married, they are reconstituted as wives, and as wives, they belong to their husband's family. In marriage, women are conveyed, in property-like terms, from one family to another. This social practice is part of a host of familial practices (including daughter's ineligibility to own or inherit family property) which have historically reinforced women's inequality within the family. It is a practice that is firmly rooted in the social construction of gender, as constructed in and through familial ideology.

The court does not, however, consider the historic and discursive basis of this deeply gendered social practice. By focusing narrowly on sex, which presumably involves biological difference alone, the court obscures the connection between sex and the social practice of daughters leaving their birth families on marriage. Indeed, the court's ability to unproblematically assert that the practice is based on something other than sex is a testament to the discursive power of the familial ideology which operates to naturalize the practice. The assumption that daughters will go to another family is so deeply embedded that it becomes a matter of common sense. And as common sense, it need not be interrogated. As a result, the socially constituted understanding of women as daughters, and subsequently, as wives and daughters-in-law is used to justify the differential treatment, without the need for any analysis of the extent to which these identities have been a site of women's oppression.

In *Nalini Ranjan Singh* v. *The State of Bihar*,[110] section 2 (ee) of the *Bihar Land Reforms Act, 1962*, was challenged as violating Article 15. The definition of family in the section did not include an adult daughter, for the purposes of claiming a separate unit of land and was thus alleged to discriminate as between adult daughters and adult sons. On the basis of principles of Hindu personal law, the court held that daughters are not members of the coparcenary.

> Although a daughter can be a member of a joint Hindu Undivided Family, she cannot be given a status as a coparcener in a coparcenary, even after the commencement of the Constitution.... There are various factors which sanction that while a son may be a member of a coparcenary, a daughter may not. As a necessary corollary it follows that the very same reasons which justify the discrimination between a son and a daughter in a coparcenary apply with force to any attack on the validity of the impugned legislation as being violative of Article 15(1).[111]

The court thus upheld the restriction.

In this case, the discriminatory component of one law (Hindu personal laws in relation to coparceny) was used to justify the discriminatory component of the impugned law (*Bihar Land Reforms Act*). Further, the case again illustrates the extent to which the socially constructed differences between sons and daughters have become so naturalized—so much a part of common sense as to be beyond reproach. Adult daughters are not seen to be members of their birth family, but rather, as members of husband's family. Adult daughters are constructed, through familial ideology, as wives and daughters-in-law; their identity constructed entirely in relation to their husbands family. This identity comes to be a natural difference, which in turn operates to forestall any analysis of the extent to which these practices have contributed to women's social and economic inequality.

■ Restrictions on Public Worship

In *S. Mahendran* v. *The Secretary, Travancore Devaswom Board, Thiruvananthapuram*,[112] the petitioner complained of young women trekking the Sabari Hills, and offering prayers at the Sabrimala Shrine, contrary to the customs of the temple. The question raised for the court was whether the denial of entry of women between the ages of 10 to 50 is discrimination, and in violation of Article 15.[113] According to the court, 'the entry in Sabrimala temple is prohibited only in respect of women of a particular age group and not women as a class'. In the court's view, the restriction on this class of women was reasonable.

> Pilgrims are expected to observe penance. Purity in thought, word and deed is insisted during the period of penance. A pilgrim starts trekking the Sabarimala only after completing the penance period of 41 days (Vratham). Women of the age group 10 to 50 will not be in a position to observe Vratham continuously for 41 days due to physiological reasons.[114]

In the court's view, this was the main reason restricting women from the pilgrimage. But, the court further held that there is another 'vital reason for imposing this restriction on young women,' which in its view 'appears to be more fundamental'.[115] According to the court, the deity at the temple at Sabarimala is in the form of a Naisthik Brahmachari—a strict and self-disciplined celibate. Quoting from the Manu Smriti, Chapter II, Sloka 179, the court observed that a brahmachari must refrain from a host of activities, including 'casting his lustful eyes on females'. The court then concluded that because the deity at the temple was in the form of a Naisthik Brahmachari:

...it is therefore believed that young women should not offer worship in the temple so that even the slightest deviation of celibacy and austerity observed by the deity is not caused by the presence of such women.[116]

The restriction on women was thus held to be reasonable, and not in violation of Article 15. The reasoning in *Mahendran* is an extraordinary example of the way in which classification can obscure issues of discrimination and disadvantage. The court tells us that the denial of entry is not to women as a class, but only to women between the ages of 10 and 50.

In the court's view, discrimination against a sub-class of women does not constitute discrimination on the basis of sex. There is virtually no explicit interrogation of the classification itself—of why women between 10 and 50 are the excluded category. Although it is implicit in the court's subsequent reasoning, the court does not acknowledge that it is women of child-bearing years that are excluded, specifically because of the assumptions in relation to menstruation. It would be difficult to find a classification more clearly and explicitly based on sex—on physiological sex differences between women and men—than the classification in question in *Mahendran*. It is equivalent to classifications on the basis of pregnancy, and the dubious argument that discrimination on the basis of pregnancy is not discrimination on the basis of sex. Yet, by obscuring the basis of the classification, the court in *Mahendran* evades the extent to which the denial of entry to women between 10 and 50 is very clearly based on sex.

At the same time, the court goes on to use these physiological differences to justify the exclusion of this sub-class of women. In so doing, physiological differences are conflated with a host of socially constructed assumptions about menstruation. Assumptions about women's 'impurity' during menstruation are naturalized, and seen as an inherent and inalienable dimension of the biological differences. Once again, biological differences are conflated with socially constructed differences, and used to justify the blanket exclusion of women of child-bearing years. Interestingly, in this case, the woman's identity as a mother is not idealized, but rather, her reproductive functions are denigrated, in so far as it is these functions that render them 'impure'. Removed from the immediate sphere of the family, women's reproductive abilities are no longer revered, but constructed as a threat to spiritual pursuits.

■ Civil Procedure

In *Mahadeb Jiew* v. *Dr. B. B. Sen*,[117] a provision of the *Civil Procedure Code, 1908*, which gave the courts discretion to order security for costs where the plaintiff is a woman and does not possess sufficient immovable property in India, was challenged as discrimination on the basis of sex.[118] The court held that the discrimination was not on the basis of sex alone, but rather, also involved property considerations.

> Possession of sufficient immovable property in India is not a consideration bearing on sex at all.... The basic criterion is...that the person who is ordered to secure for costs is one who has not sufficient property out of which to pay the successful litigant's costs.[119]

The court upheld the provision. The fact that men without sufficient immovable property in India were not required to provide security for costs was not considered relevant. In the court's view, the discrimination could not be said to be on the basis of sex alone, but on the combined grounds of sex and property.

The case illustrates once again the rather odd reasoning to which the doctrine of 'only on the ground of sex' can give rise. A legislative distinction that was explicitly based on sex was held not to constitute sex discrimination because the distinction was not based on sex alone. Yet, the additional ground on which the distinction was based, namely, property, was directly related to assumptions of gender and gender difference. The legislative provision assumed that women did not have any independent source of income. It assumed that women do not work outside of the home in paid labour and as such, they will not be able to pay for costs, unless they have 'sufficient immovable property'. Men, on the other hand, are assumed to inherit property and/or to have an independent source of income through paid work, and are therefore presumed to be able to pay for costs. The doctrine of 'only on the ground of sex,' however, allows the court to avoid examining these underlying assumptions. The court simply asserts that the distinction is not on the basis of sex alone, and notwithstanding the connection between sex and property, the legislative provision is thereby found not to discriminate on the basis of sex.

This critique of the reasoning, and of the doctrine of 'only on the ground of sex' is not to suggest that the court should necessarily have found the legislation to be discriminatory on the basis of sex. On the one hand, the objective of the provision is legitimate, that is, ensuring that plaintiffs have sufficient means to pay costs. Familial ideology, and the sexual division of labour has historically operated to deprive women from achieving any significant degree of financial independence. As such, there is arguably a nexus between the objective of the legislation and the legislative distinction. At the same time, it is arguable that the distinction is too broad. While the sexual division of labour has operated to make many, or even perhaps most, women economically dependent on men, it is not the case that all women are economically dependent. As discussed in chapter 2, some women inherit property, and some women work outside of the home. But, the provision effectively deems all women to be economically dependent. The difficult question for an equality analysis is whether this deemed dependency is an appropriate basis for a legislative distinction. Recognizing this difference may further reinforce and naturalize the assumption of women as economically dependent. The same legislative objective of securing costs could be meet with a different distinction. For example, the *Civil Procedure Code* could allow the court discretion to order security for costs where a plaintiff (regardless of sex) does not have access to either sufficient immovable property or sufficient income. Such an approach would not expressly discriminate against women. Nor would such an approach be based on and operate to reinforce assumptions about women's access to financial support. These questions about women's economic dependence, however, are simply never addressed within the framework on the 'only on the grounds of sex' doctrine. Difficult questions of the substantive inequalities confronting women, and of the legal relevance of these inequalities are obscured by a doctrinal approach that asserts without substantiation that sex and property are conceptually distinct classifications. The assumptions at work in the legislative distinction thereby remain invisible, and beyond interrogation.

In *Shahdad* v. *Mobd Abdullah*,[120] the provisions of the *Civil Procedure Code, 1908*, which state that service of a summons must be made on a male member of the family were challenged as violating Article 15. In this case, a dispute arose in a business partnership that resulted in an arbitration. The respondents to the dispute raised a question of the validity of the service of notice of the summons to appear before the arbitrator. The notice of summons had been served only on one of the respondents—who was the mother of one of the other named respondents, contrary to Order 5 rule 15 of the *Civil Procedure Code, 1908*, which stated that the service be made on the male member of the family. Accordingly, the respondents argued that the notice was not valid.

It was within this context that counsel for the petitioner brought a constitutional challenge to the service provisions of the *Civil Procedure Code, 1908*, arguing that these rules amounted to sex discrimination. In rejecting the challenge, the Court held:

...we have to analyze the background in which this rule was enacted. The functions of females in Indian society is that of housewives. Until very recently it was in exceptional cases that ladies took part in any other activity than those of housewives. Females were mostly illiterate and some of them Parda Nashin. Therefore in enacting this rule, the legislature had in view the special conditions of the Indian society and therefore enjoined service only upon male members and did not regard service on females as sufficient.[121]

The court noted that Article 15(3) is intended 'to cover any provision specially made for women' and that the impugned provision '...does not give them any disadvantageous position but rather exonerates them from the responsibility of fastening notice of service as service of the other members of the family'.[122] After noting other provisions which 'confer special privileges upon a protection to women' which have been upheld by the courts, the court concluded that the service provisions of the *Civil Procedure Code, 1908*, did not constitute discrimination on the basis of sex.

The decision is based on a formal approach to equality, in which any difference can be used to justify differential treatment, and a protectionist approach to gender, in which women are seen as different and as in need of protection. Informed by familial ideology, the court seized upon women's roles as wives as a difference which justified their differential treatment in law. The approach did not challenge the social construction of women as housewives; it did not examine the extent to which this socially constituted identity has served to reinforce women's inequality—nor the extent to which the underlying sexual division of labour has produced such inequality. Rather, the 'difference' as constructed in and through familial ideology, is taken as natural.

Further, the court simply accepts that this differential treatment is preferential treatment. There is no consideration as to whether the rule which prohibits service on a female member of the family contributes to women's socio-economic inequality, or to overcoming this inequality. There is at least an argument to be made that this differential treatment accords women less than equal rights and responsibilities, and thus renders them less than equal members of the family. An equality analysis based on a substantive model, would require a consideration of whether the legislation could be seen to disadvantage women.

The answer to this question is not a foregone conclusion. A substantive equality analysis might conclude that gender difference is relevant, and needs to be recognized in relation to service. It could be argued that the continuing sexual division of labour and the resulting inequalities of women within the family is such that they should not be burdened with equal responsibilities until such time as they have equal rights. A substantive equality analysis thus does not necessarily produce a different result than a formal equality analysis even though the reasoning will substantially differ. Moreover, the court's approach in *Shahdad* illustrates yet again the often contradictory nature of a formal approach to equality informed by familial ideology. This approach can result in a court upholding legislation that promotes women's substantive equality, on the grounds that women are different. Paradoxically, a protectionist approach which effectively precludes an equality analysis within the formal model can have the effect of upholding legislation that promotes women's substantive equality.

It is also important to recognize that this constitutional challenge was not raised in furtherance of the political objectives of the women's movement, nor even in the furtherance of the interest of an individual woman litigant. Rather, the challenge was raised as one of a number of technical arguments of individuals involved in a private dispute of a commercial nature. Indeed, as this chapter has demonstrated, many of the cases involving allegations of sex discrimination have been brought within the context of private disputes, and as part of the efforts of one party of the dispute to avoid the consequences of the impugned law. Often, the challenges have been brought by men to strike down provisions that treat women differently. Male petitioners have argued that laws that treat women differently constitute sex discrimination against women. The constitutional challenge is not only motivated by the broader political concerns of the women's movement, but it is not even propelled by the particular interest of the particular woman in the dispute at hand.

Conclusion

In this chapter, we have attempted to illustrate the extent to which Indian sex discrimination case law has been informed by a formal approach to equality, within which almost any differences can justify the differential treatment of women in law. Sometimes this approach has the effect of upholding legislative provisions designed to benefit women. But, often times, this approach has the effect of upholding legislative provisions that have disadvantaged women. The formal approach to equality, coupled with a protectionist approach to gender difference, preempt any consideration of disadvantage: women are just different. We have further examined the way in which familial ideology interacts with this dominant discourse of equality and undermines any consideration of substantive inequality. Familial ideology which constitutes women as wives and mothers reinforces the construction of gender difference. The woman is different, and thus, is precluded from any entitlement to be treated the same. Familial ideology thereby operates to immunize laws that treat women differently than men from constitutional challenge.

As we have also argued, however, the impact of this familial ideology on women in the context of equality rights challenges is contradictory. In many cases where men have sought to have legislation that is intended to promote women's interests struck down as discriminatory, familial ideology has operated to defeat the challenge. The understanding of women as wives and mothers, as naturally different from men, lead the courts to conclude that women need not be treated the same as men, and that legislation that treats women differently is not unconstitutional. Maintenance laws, for example, are thus upheld on the ground that women are different, and in need of protection. Paradoxically, within a formal approach to equality, this understanding of women as different has had the effect of upholding laws that promote women's substantive equality.

In contrast to formal equality, we have described a second substantive model of equality, in which the central question is whether the impugned legislation contributes to the subordination of the disadvantaged group, or to overcoming that subordination. Throughout this chapter, we have suggested ways in which a substantive equality analysis might alter both the reasoning and results of the cases, by directing attention to the question of disadvantage. We have also attempted to illustrate that such an approach to equality does not, in and of itself, answer the question of the relevance of gender difference. Rather, this substantive approach simply directs the interrogation to whether gender difference needs to be taken into account in furtherance of the substantive equality of women. This approach opens space within which the difficult question of gender difference can be examined. By directing attention to this question of disadvantage, this approach creates space for an analysis of the relationship between difference and disadvantage. In this way, difference is not assumed to be natural, nor assumed to be relevant. Rather, difference must itself become part of the analysis, rather than a justification for not pursuing an equality analysis. Substantive equality redirects our attention to disadvantage, and to a critical interrogation of the dilemmas of difference; to the ways in which difference has been socially constructed, to the ways in which difference has very real material implications in individual's lives, and to the ways in which judicial approaches cannot simply proclaim on the relevance or irrelevance of difference, but rather, must begin to deconstruct the assumptions that are deeply embedded in the way we see the world.

The relationship between the discourses of equality and familialism will not be automatically resolved by a shift to a substantive model of equality. Familial ideology can still operate to blind courts to the socially constructed nature of women's roles as wives and mothers in the family. The substantive approach to equality simply opens the space within which this familial ideology, and the way in which these discourses constitute women as naturally different, can be further scrutinized and deconstructed. By redirecting our attention to disadvantage instead of difference, this approach may facilitate an analysis of the ways in which women's position in the family has contributed to their social, economic and political inequality. It does not in any way guarantee that the ideological grip of the family will be loosened. But, it might take us a few steps further in the project of destabilizing assumptions about gender difference. And as we will further discuss in chapter 5, a substantive approach to equality may provide feminists engaged with law with a way to make more complex legal arguments.

NOTES

1. For a more comprehensive review of sex discrimination cases, see Ratna Kapur and Brenda Cossman, 'On Women, Equality and the Constitution: Through the Looking Glass of Feminism', (1993) 1 *National Law School Journal* 1.
2. Joseph Tussman and Jacobus Tenbroek, 'The Equal Protection of the Laws', (1948) 37 *California Law Review.* 341. Y. R. Haragopai Reddy in 'Equality Doctrine and the Indian Constitution' [1982] *Andhra Law Times.* 57, similarly has written, at 58, '[a]ll persons are to be treated alike, except where circumstances require different treatment'.
3. As Parmanand Singh notes, in 'Equal Opportunity and Compensatory Discrimination: Constitutional Policy and Judicial Control' (1976) 18:2 *Journal of the Indian Law Institute* 300 at 301, '...legal equality requires the absence of any discrimination in the words of the law'. K. C. Dwiredi, in *Right to Equality and the Supreme Court* (Delhi: Deep, 1990) at 11, defines equality as signifying 'that among equals law should be equal and equally administered'.
4. Gwen Brodsky and Shelagh Day, *Canadian Charter Equality Rights for Women: One Step Forward or Two Steps Back?* (Ottawa: Canadian Advisory Council on the Status of Women, 1990) at 153:

   The way the court defines a class, or its willingness to recognise a class, can make the difference between winning and losing. The Court can justify making a comparison between classes or refusing to make a comparison by the way they define the class, or whether they recognise it at all.

And at 155:

Just as the way the Court defines a class can determine the outcome, so can the way the Court compares or fails to compare the classes it has identified. Sometimes the courts simply fail to make a comparison; and sometimes comparisons are tautological because the courts compare classes only within the terms already set out in the law.

5. Martha Minow. 'Learning to Live with the Dilemma of Difference: Bilingual and Special Education' (1985) 48 *Law & Contemporary Problems* 157. In exploring the problematic connection between equality and sameness, Minow has observed: 'The problem with this concept of equality is that it makes the recognition of difference a threat to the premise behind equality. If to be equal you must be the same, then to be different is to be unequal'. (*Ibid.* at 207).

6. As Maureen Maloney has written in her article, 'An Analysis of Direct Taxes in India: A Feminist Perspective' (1988) 30:4 *Journal of the Indian Law Institute* 397: 'Such inequality results from provisions which though seemingly neutral in their application (and therefore conforming to notions of formal equality) in reality result in discrimination. Certain provisions have the effect of discriminating between men and women because in practice they only affect women'.

7. Singh, *supra* note 3 at 301. He describes this approach as one of equality in fact, or compensatory discrimination. See also Andre Beteille, *The Idea of Natural Inequality and Other Essays* (Delhi: Oxford University Press, 1983), who discusses the compensatory principle, that is, the idea that those who have been denied access to social resources—education, employment, power—'…need some compensation if there is to be any prospect of achieving substantive as opposed to merely formal equality' (at 95). Beteille notes that, this compensatory principle has achieved some recognition in India, where it is known as 'protective discrimination'.

8. Helena Orton, 'Litigating for Equality: LEAF's Approach to Section 15 of the Charter', in Karen Busby, Lisa Fainstein, and Holly Penner, eds., *Equality Issues in Family Law: Considerations for Test Case Litigation* (Winnipeg: Legal Research Institute of the University of Manitoba, 1989), discusses the approach advocated by LEAF—the Women's Legal Education and Action Fund in Canada. See also K. Lahey, 'Feminist Theories of (In) Equality,' in S. Martin and K. Mahoney, eds., *Equality and Judicial Neutrality* (Toronto: Carswell, 1987). Lahey argues that courts must adopt an approach which considers the effect of the rule or practice being challenged, to determine whether it contributes to the actual inequality of women, and whether changing the rule will actually produce an improvement in the specific material conditions of the women affected (*ibid.* at 71).

9. Orton, *supra* note 8 at 9.

10. R. K. Gupta, 'Justice: Unequal but Inseparate' (1969) 11 *Journal of the Indian Law Institute*, 57 at 76. Within this approach, the important question is not whether there are 'natural' differences between people, but rather, about when particular differences between people (such as race or sex) are systematically transformed into inequalities. As Andre Beteille writes, *supra* note 7 at 29, 'My argument is not about the fact of individual variations among human beings which are universal and undeniable, but about the significance of these variations. It is difficult to see how one can deny some role to genetic factors in the perpetuation of individual variations. As soon as some of these variations are marked out and transformed into inequalities by being ordered on a scale, such inequalities come rightly to be regarded as hereditary. It is the crucial step by which differences are transformed into inequalities that I consider to be a social construction rather than a gift of nature'. An approach which only examines

differences between individuals can be blinded to the possibility that such differences have been produced as a result of social relations of inequality.

11. *Budhan Choudhry* v. *State of Bihar*, A 1955 SC 191.

12. *R. K. Dalmia* v. *Justice S. R. Tendolkar*, A 1958 SC 538. More recently, the Supreme Court has emphasized a new dimension of Article 14 as a guarantee against arbitrariness. See *Ajay Hasia* v. *Khalid Mujib*, A 1981 SC 487 at 499, and *E. P. Royapappa* v. *State of Tamil Nadu*, A 1974 SC 555 at 583. See also *Maneka Gandhi* v. *Union of India*, A 1978 SC 597 at 624. While many commentators have argued that this new doctrine constitutes a significant shift in judicial approach to Article 14, the underlying understanding of equality has not been significantly altered, in so far as the new approach has incorporated the doctrine of classification.

13. For a detailed discussion of the way in which these approaches to equality have informed Indian constitutional law, and the extent to which the formal discourse of equality has been dominant in the case law, see Ratna Kapur and Brenda Cossman, *supra* note 1. See also Beteille, *supra* note 7, who discusses the extent to which both meritarian principles (a liberal notion based on equality of opportunity and on removing obstacles) and compensatory principles (which he describes as a more 'socialist inspired conception of equality, which seeks to take into account the unequal needs of individuals who are unequally placed': at 95) can be seen to have informed and shaped the Indian Constitution.

14. A classic statement of this approach is found in *Anjali Roy* v. *State of W. B.*, A 1952 Cal 825 at 830–31, in which the Calcutta High Court held that Article 15(3):

> …is obviously an exception to clause (1) and (2) and since its effect is to authorise what the Article otherwise forbids, its meaning seems to be that notwithstanding that clause (1) and (2) forbids discrimination against any citizen on the grounds of sex, the State may discriminate against males by making a special provision in favour of females. This exception approach has been overwhelmingly supported by the commentators.

> H. M. Seervai in *Constitutional Law of India*, 3d ed. (Bombay: Tripathi, 1983) at 396, argues for example, that Articles 15(3) and 15(4) must be seen as exceptions to the general guarantees of equality.

> Article 15(1) prohibits discrimination only on the ground of sex; therefore a discrimination in favour of women would necessarily discriminate against men only on the ground of sex and would be void. The discretionary power in Art. 15(3) relaxes this prohibition in favour of women by expressly authorising such discrimination by way of an exception.

> M. P. Jain in *Indian Constitutional Law*, 3rd ed. (Bombay: N. M. Tripathi, 1978), and D. D. Basu in *Constitutional Law of India*, 10th ed. (New Delhi: Prentice Hall of India, 1988), similarly argue that Articles 15(3) and 15(4) are exceptions: clause (4) cannot be so extended as in effect to destroy the guarantee in clause (1).

15. This approach was endorsed in *Motiram More Dattatrava* v. *State of Bombay*, A 1953 Bom 311 at 314, wherein the Bombay High Court held:

> …Article 15(3) is obviously a proviso to Article 15(1) and proper effect must be given to that proviso…The proper way to construe Article 15(3) in our opinion is that whereas under Article 15(1) discrimination in favour of men only on the ground

of sex is not permissible, by reason of Article 15(3) discrimination in favour of women is permissible, and when the State does discriminate in favour of women, it does not offend against Article 15(1).

See also *Ram Chandra Mahton* v. *State of Bihar*, A 1966 Pat 214. Basu, *supra* note 14 at 430, is extremely critical of this approach. With regard to the decision in *Dattatraya*, he writes:

…such discrimination in favour of women would be justifiable only if clause (3) could be regarded as a complete exception to clause (1) of Article 15. The use of the word 'women' in juxtaposition to children in (3)(d) suggests that the special provision referred to in it must be related to such disabilities which are peculiar to women and children.

16. In *Dattatraya, supra* note 15, for example, the court states: 'The proper way to construe Article 15(3)…is that…discrimination in favour of women is permissible, and when the State does discriminate in favour of women, it does not offend against Article 15(1)'.

17. For example, in *All India S. M. and A. S. M.'s Assn.* v. *Gen. Manager Central Railway*, A 1960 SC 384, the Supreme Court held that equality of opportunity in matters of promotion guaranteed by Article 16(1) must be interpreted to mean equality among members of the same class of employees, and not equality among members of different classes. The similarly situated test with its emphasis on sameness as the basic entitlement to equality thus infused the courts understanding of equality of opportunity and reinforced the formal model of equality.

18. A 1976 SC 490.

19. The relationship between Articles 16(1) and 16(4) had been the subject of a controversy similar to that around the relationship between Articles 15(1) and 15(3). Some cases had interpreted Article 16(4) as an exception to equality, whereas others had suggested that it was part of equality.

20. For a detailed discussion of the doctrinal shift in *Thomas, supra* note 18, see Marc Galanter, 'Symbolic Activism: A Judicial Encounter with the Contours of India's Compensatory Discrimination Policy', in Marc Galanter, ed., *Law and Society in Modern India* (Delhi: Oxford University Press, 1989) 112.

21. Formal equality is achieved by treating all persons equally: 'Each man to count for one and no one to count for more than one. But men are not equal in all respects…. We, therefore have to resort to some sort of proportionate equality in many spheres to achieve justice' (*Thomas, supra* note 18, at para. 78, 79). Mathew J. continues: 'The principle of proportional equality is attained only when equals are treated equally and unequals unequally. This would raise the baffling question: Equals and unequals in what?' Mathew J. notes that the formal approach to equality requires criteria by which differences, and thus differential treatment, can be justified, and observes that '[t]he real difficulty arises in finding out what constitutes a relevant difference'. (*ibid.*).

22. *Ibid.* at para. 82. At para. 89, he writes '…if we want to give equality of opportunity for employment to the members of the Scheduled Castes and Scheduled Tribes, we will have to take note of their social, educational and economic environment'.

23. See *Jagdish Rai* v. *State of Haryana*, A 1977 P&H 56 at 61, in which *Thomas, supra* note 18, is interpreted as having 'introduced a new dynamic and a new dimension into the concept of…equality of opportunity'. See Singh, *supra* note 3, at 304–19; and Galanter, *supra* note 20.

24. Basu, *supra* note 14 and Seervai, *supra* note 14 at 428–41.
25. Both the doctrinal techniques and the discourses used by the Supreme Court has restricted the transformative potential of the case. For example, the court adopted 'the theory of legislative device'. The court cites with approval this passage from *Devadasan* v. *Union of India*, A 1964 SC 179:

    The expression 'nothing in this article' is a legislative device to express its intention in a most emphatic way that the power conferred thereunder is not limited in any way by the main provision but falls outside it. It has not really carved out an exception, but has preserved a power untrammeled by the other provisions of the article. (*supra* note 18 at 554.)

    While this theory of legislative device can be seen to support the view that Articles 15 and 16 must be broadly construed, the reasoning of the Supreme Court has remained predominantly at the level of technical doctrine. It has not gone far enough in articulating its substantive theory of equality that ought to inform this doctrine. Opponents of this approach remain free to engage exclusively at the level of technical interpretation from the unstated vantage point of formal equality. Seervai, *supra* note 14, and Basu, *supra* note 14, continue to chip away at the reasoning without having to confront the fundamental differences in their normative vision of equality informing the Constitution. Similarly, the court continues to invoke the term 'compensatory discrimination'. Discrimination thus continues to mean any distinction, rather than distinctions that disadvantage within the broader understanding of substantive equality.
26. A 1989 SC 307.
27. The Supreme Court held that '[t]he over-emphasis on the doctrine of classification or any anxious and sustained attempts to discover some basis for classification may gradually and imperceptibly deprive the article of its previous content and end in replacing the doctrine of equality by the doctrine of classification.... The idea of similarity or dissimilarity of situations of persons, to justify classification cannot rest on merely differentials which may, by themselves be rational or logical, but depends on whether the differences are relevant to the goals to be reached by the law which seeks to classify'. (*ibid.* at 312).
28. (1990) 3 SCC 130 (India).
29. *Ibid.* at 138.
30. A 1993 SC 477.
31. *Ibid.* at paras. 396, 397.
32. This approach is exemplified by S. Jahwari, 'Women and Constitutional Safeguards in India' (1979) 40:11 *Andhra Law Times Journal* 1, who writes, at 1: 'The true meaning of the principle of equality between men and women is that certain natural differences between men and women [are] to be treated as normally irrelevant in law; ...consequently [these differences are] not to be treated as constituting in [themselves] sufficient [justifications] for unequal treatment'.
33. This approach is associated with the work of Wendy Williams: 'The Crisis in Equality Theory and Maternity, Sexuality and Women' (1982) 7 *Women's Rights Law Reporter* 179; and 'Equality's Riddle and Pregnancy and the Special Treatment/Equal Treatment Debate: Towards a Redefinition of Sexual Equality' (1981) 95 *Harvard Law Review* 487.
34. See Williams, 'The Crisis in Equality Theory and Maternity, Sexuality and Women', *supra* note 33.

35. Williams, 'Equality's Riddle and Pregnancy and the Special Treatment/Equal Treatment Debate,' *supra* note 33; Linda Krieger and Patricia Cooney 'The Miller-Wohl Controversy: Equal Treatment, Positive Action and the Meaning of Women's Equality' (1983) 13 *Golden Gate University Law Review* 513.
36. Nadine Taub, Book Review (1980) 80 *Columbia Law Review* 1686 at 1694. As Brodsky and Day, *supra* note 4 at 149, further note:

    The extreme and persistent economic and social inequality of women, which is the result of society's bias and oppression, is obscured by a definition of equality that focuses only on differences in the form of law. Women are poorer than men, they work in ill-paid female ghettos, they are the primary caregivers for their children and parents, and they are overwhelmingly the victims of rape and battery. Simple gender neutrality in law based on male standards does not address those major inequalities.

37. Some feminist scholarship has reflected on the relationship between equality rights and familial ideology. Carol Smart and Susan Boyd, for example, have argued that the realization of equality rights within family law has not operated to eliminate women's oppression within the family. Rather, the arrival of formal equality rights within the family, and specifically within the context of child custody determinations, has changed the form that the oppression and discrimination may take. See Susan Boyd, 'Child Custody, Ideologies and Employment' (1989) 3 *Canadian Journal of Women and Law* 111–33; Susan Boyd, 'Child Custody and Working Mothers', in S. Martin and K. Mahoney, eds., *supra* note 8 at 168–83; Carol Smart, *Feminism and the Power of Law* (London: Routledge, 1989).
38. For a discussion of the sameness/difference debates within feminist scholarship, see Lucinda Finlay, 'Transcending Equality Theory' (1986) 86 *Columbia Law Review* 1118; Catharine MacKinnon, 'Difference and Dominance', in her *Feminism Unmodified: Discourses on Life and Law* (Cambridge: Harvard University Press, 1987); Joan Scott, 'Deconstructing Equality—Versus—Difference or the Uses of Poststructuralist Theory for Feminism' (1988) 14 *Feminist Studies* 33.
39. Joan W. Scott, *Gender and the Politics of History* (New York: Columbia University Press, 1988) at 172.
40. Scott, 'Equality—Versus—Difference', *supra* note 38 at 39.
41. Scott, *Gender and the Politics of History*, *supra* note 39 at 172.
42. Martha Minow, *Making All the Difference* (Ithaca, NY: Cornell University Press, 1990).
43. Martha Minow, 'Foreword: Justice Engendered' (1987) 101 *Harvard Law Review* 10 at 13.
44. *Ibid.* at 34–54.
45. Minow, *supra* at note 42. See also Minow, *supra* note 5.
46. For a more detailed discussion of the dilemma of difference in the context of economic dependency, see Brenda Cossman, 'A Matter of Difference: Domestic Contracts and Gender Equality' (1990) 28 *Osgoode Hall Law Journal* 803.
47. A 1953 Mad 792.
48. *Ibid.* at 800.
49. A 1989 Cal 1.
50. *Ibid.* at 3.
51. The court noted that the only defense for the provision was that stated in *Dwaraka Bai*, *supra* note 47 at 800, namely, where the court held that since the husband even

by committing adultery 'does not bear a child as a result and make it a child of his wife to be maintained by the wife,' the wife by committing adultery 'may bear a child as a result of such adultery and the husband will have to treat it as his legitimate child and will be liable to maintain that child under Section 488, Criminal Procedure Code'.

52. *Swapna Ghosh*, *supra* note 49 at para. 3.

53. *Ibid.* at para. 4.

54. *Ibid.* at para. 9. More specifically, the divorce decree was confirmed 'on the ground that the husband-respondent is guilty of adultery coupled with such cruelty as without adultery would have justified a decree of judicial separation and also of adultery coupled with desertion without reasonable excuse for two years and more'.

55. This interpretation of Article 15 as prohibiting discrimination 'on the grounds only of sex' was developed by the courts primarily as a way of upholding legislation that accorded women preferential treatment. For example, legislative distinctions based on the 'backward' social position of women, or on the financial need of wives, have not been found to be distinctions on the basis of sex alone, and the laws have thus been upheld. This approach, although primarily motivated by the courts desire to uphold legislation that benefits women, must be seen within the context of a formal model of equality, wherein any and all distinctions are seen as a violation of equality. Rather than understanding the backward social position of women or the financial needs of wives as a product of the historic disadvantage that women have suffered, and that equality should remedy, these distinctions are seen to be based on something other then sex.

56. The Delhi High Court, in *Walter Alfred Baid* v. *Union of India*, A 1976 Del 302, although dealing primarily with a challenge under Article 16(2), recognized some of the problems implicit in this approach to 'only on the grounds of sex'. The court observed:

> ...it is difficult to accept the position that a discrimination based on sex is nevertheless not a discrimination based on sex 'alone' because it is based on 'other considerations' even though these other considerations have their genesis in the sex itself. It virtually amounts to saying that woman was being discriminated against...not because she belonged to a particular sex but because of what the sex implied...(*ibid.* at 306).

The court concluded:

> Sex and what it implies can not be severed. Considerations which have their genesis in sex and arise out of it would not save such a discrimination. What could save such a discrimination is any ground or reason independently of sex such as socio-economic conditions, marital status, and other disqualifying conditions such as age, background, health, academic accomplishments, etc. *Ibid.* at 308.

The approach in *W. A. Baid* recognized the connection between sex and the social implications of sex and criticized the narrow doctrinal approach to only on the ground of sex. However, the decision is rooted firmly within a formal model of equality, and the result of the case was to strike down a recruitment rule that had been advantageous for women.

57. A 1954 SC 321.

58. *Ibid.* at 322.

59. A 1985 SC 1618.
60. *Ibid.* at para. 6.
61. *Ibid.* at para. 7.
62. A 1988 SC 835.
63. *Ibid.* at 838.
64. See Ursula Vogel, 'Whose Property? The Double Standard of Adultery in Nineteenth-Century Law', in Carol Smart, ed., *Regulating Womanhood: Historical Essays on Marriage, Motherhood and Sexuality* (London: Routledge, 1992).
65. See Vogel, *ibid.*, at 61, discussing the passage of the *Matrimonial Causes Act of 1857* in England: 'When the Act passed through Parliament there was a general consensus that the sin committed by adultery was the same for both spouses but that different treatment stood justified by the significance of different consequences:

A wife might without any loss of caste...condone an act of adultery on the part of the husband; but a husband could not condone a similar act on the part of a wife. No one would venture that a husband could possibly do so, and for this, among other reasons...that the adultery of the wife might be the means of palming suspicious offspring on the husband while the adultery of the husband could have no such effect with regard to the wife (McGregor, 1957: 20)'.

66. See also *Swaraj Garg* v. *K. M. Garg*, A 1978 Del 296, in considering the interpretation of section 9, wherein the court held that any law that gave husbands the exclusive right to decide the place of the matrimonial home without considering the merits of the wife's claim would violate Article 14.
67. A 1983 AP 356.
68. *Ibid.* at para. 38.
69. *Ibid.*
70. A 1984 Del 66.
71. *Ibid.* at para. 15.
72. *Ibid.* at para. 44.
73. *Ibid.* at 75.
74. Madhu Kishwar, 'Some Aspects of Bondage: The Denial of Fundamental Rights to Women' (1983) 12 *Manushi* 31–37 (arguing that the family structure in India reinforces the subordination of women in a way that precludes women's access to fundamental rights); Nandita Haksar and Anju Singh, *Demystification of Law for Women* (New Delhi: Lancer Press, 1986) at 58; Nadine Taub and Elizabeth Schneider, 'Perspectives on Women's Subordination and the Role of Law', in David Kairyns, ed., *The Politics of Law: A Progressive Critique*, rev. ed. (New York: Pantheon Books, 1990); Nicholas Rose, 'Beyond the Public/Private Division: Law, Power and the Family' (1987) 14 *Journal of Law and Society* 61; Frances Olsen, 'The Myth of State Intervention' (1985) 18 *Michigan Law Review* 835; Judy Fudge, 'The Public/Private Distinction: The Possibilities of and the Limits to Further Feminist Struggles' (1987) 25 *Osgoode Hall Law Journal* 485.
75. A 1984 SC 1562.
76. *Ibid.* at para. 15.
77. It should be noted that the Supreme Court did not comment on the holding in *Harvinder Kaur*, regarding the non-applicability of the Constitution to the legal regulation of the family. Further, more recent cases involving challenges to personal laws have not strictly followed *Harvinder Kaur* in so far as the non-applicability of the Constitution to the legal regulation of the family is concerned. For example, in *P. S. Krishna*

Murthy v. *P. S. Umadevi*, A 1987 AP 237, *Swapna Ghosh* (*supra* note 49), and *Lalitha Ubhayakar* v. *Union of India*, A 1991 Kant. 186, the courts were willing to consider constitutional challenges to the *Hindu Marriage Act, 1955*, the *Divorce Act, 1869*, and the *Hindu Adoptions and Maintenance Act, 1956*, respectively. The ideology of privacy was not invoked, as in *Harvinder Kaur*, to preclude an analysis of the operation of the provisions relating to the legal regulation of the family.

78. A 1960 Mys 182.
79. *Ibid.* at 183.
80. A 1961 Punj 489.
81. The plaintiffs argued that the effect of section 14 was discrimination in the powers of alienation of property between women and men. While women had by virtue of section 14 absolute ownership and thus absolute rights of alienation, men who were still governed by the Punjab Customary Law were not free to dispose of ancestral immovable property at will.
82. A 1985 SC 1695.
83. *Ibid.* at 1698.
84. A 1983 Bom 156.
85. A 1981 Cal 123.
86. In *Krishna Murthy supra* note 77, section 24 of the *Hindu Marriage Act, 1955*, was challenged as violating Article 14, on the basis that a spouse's liability for alimony was vague, particularly as compared to the *Indian Divorce Act*, where a husband's liability for alimony was expressly limited to a maximum of one-fifth of his income. In a brief decision, the High Court rejected the challenge, and held that there was no invidious discrimination or undue disability to the wife or the husband.
87. A 1952 Mad 529.
88. *Ibid.* at 530.
89. *Ibid.*
90. In *Gupteshwar Pandey* v. *Smt. Ram Peari Devi*, A 1971 Pat 181, the court again held that section 488 was a special provision designed for the benefit or protection of women or children whose husbands or fathers failed to maintain them in spite of sufficient means, and thus within the scope of Article 15(3). The court again adopts a formal approach to equality, within which Article 15(3) is understood as an exception to equality, and a protectionist approach to gender difference, according to which section 488 is justified on the basis that women are the weaker sex, and in need of special protection.
91. (1981) *Criminal Law Journal* 830 (Kerala High Court).
92. A 1966 SC 942.
93. *Ibid.* at para. 3.
94. A 1979 SC 1868.
95. *Ibid.* at para. 5.
96. *Ibid.* at para. 9.
97. *Ibid.* at para. 7.
98. While the court's references to misogynous and masculinist culture suggest that women's differences are the product of these oppressive relations (the court writes, for example, 'This misogynous posture is a hangover of the masculine culture of manacling the weaker sex forgetting how our struggle for national freedom was also a battle against men's thralldom'. *Ibid.* at para. 3.), these references are at least in part undermined by references which suggest that women are naturally and essentially weak.
99. A 1981 SC 1829.

100. The court held:

> Apart from improving the health of the employee, it helps a good deal in the promotion and boosting up of our family planning programme. Secondly, if a woman marries near about the age of 20 to 23 years, she becomes fully mature and there is every chance of such a marriage proving a success all things being equal. Thirdly, it has been rightly pointed out to us by the Corporation that if the bar of marriage within four years of service is removed then the Corporation will have to incur huge expenditure in recruiting additional AHs either on a temporary or on ad hoc basis to replace the working AHs if they conceive and any period short of four years would be too little a time for the Corporation to phase out such an ambitious plan. (*Ibid.* at para. 78).

101. *Ibid.* at para. 80.
102. In a more recent case against Air India, *Lena Khan* v. *Union of India*, A 1987 SC 1515, the regulations which required air hostesses employed in India to retire at age 35, with extension to age 45, but which allowed air hostesses employed outside India to continue employment beyond age 45, was challenged as violative of Articles 14 and 15. The Supreme Court held that such discrimination should not be allowed merely because it complies with local law abroad. However, in light of Air India's submissions that it would phase out air hostesses recruited outside of India at age 45, the court concluded that no intervention was required at that time. Finally, the court examined whether the mandatory retirement of air hostesses at the age of 35, extendible to 45 years at the discretion of the Managing Director, was an arbitrary or unreasonable restriction. In considering the arguments offered by Air India in support of this provision, the court expressly rejected the argument that air hostesses must be 'young and attractive'. In considering the other arguments in favour of the provision, the court was particularly concerned with the discretion exercised by the Managing Director. Since the regulation did not provide any guidelines, rules or principles to govern the exercises of the discretion, it was held to be arbitrary.
103. (1986) 1 SCR 743 (India).
104. *Ibid.* at 745.
105. A 1963 Punj 9.
106. The case arose within the context of a separate petition brought by Pritam Kaur, against her co-widow, for inappropriately withdrawing funds from the estate.
107. *Supra* note 105 at 16.
108. A 1974 P&H 162.
109. *Ibid.* at 171.
110. A 1977 Pat 171.
111. *Ibid.* at 179.
112. A 1993 Ker 42.
113. The court further considered whether the denial of entry violated Articles 25 and 26.
114. *Supra* note 112 at para. 26.
115. *Ibid.* at para. 39.
116. *Ibid.* at para. 41.
117. A 1951 Cal 563.
118. *Civil Procedure Code* O.25 r.1(3).
119. *Supra* note 117 at para. 29.
120. A 1972 J&K 120, at para. 32.
121. *Ibid.* at para. 32.
122. *Ibid.* at para. 33.

4

Women, the Hindu Right and Legal Discourse

The women's movement, the struggles against communalism, and for survival and land, deny an easy polarization of 'theory' and 'practice'...They are some of the spaces where many men and women have to intervene in structures worked through by colonialism, as well as earlier and later histories of domination. Such intervention is difficult, and, at the moment, often ineffective. It is also limited to relatively small sections of people, but is significant because it has to reclaim some earlier histories—such as those of secularism, or women's struggles, while contesting revisionism, or nostalgia.... To say that if the subaltern could speak she/he would not be subaltern is a neat enough formulation, but somewhat inadequate if the 'Third Word' is not to be, yet again, theorized into silence.

Ania Loomba
'Overworlding the "Third World"'*

...one should totally and absolutely suspect anything that claims to be a return. One reason is a logical one; there is in fact no such thing as a return.

Michel Foucault
'Space, Knowledge and Power'†

---

* In Patricia Williams and Lauran Chrisman, eds., *Colonial Discourse and Post-colonial Theory: A Reader* (New York: Columbia University Press, 1994).
† In Paul Rabinow, ed., *The Foucault Reader* (New York: Pantheon Books, 1984).

The preceding chapters have examined some of the ways in which familial ideology is deeply embedded in the legal regulation of women, as well as the ways in which this ideology has operated to preclude equality challenges to this regulation. In this chapter, we turn to examine yet another formidable challenge to the women's movement's engagement with law: the resurgence of Hindu nationalism and its reliance on legal discourse. We will examine some of the ways in which legal discourse is being used to advance the political agenda of the Hindu Right. The language of equality and secularism, so central to the struggles of the women's movement, has been appropriated by communalist and reactionary political groups. Similarly, many legal issues, long associated with the women's movement, from violence against women to the Uniform Civil Code, have been taken up by communalist organizations whose political agenda is in many respects antithetical to that of the women's movement.

Equality and secularism—concepts central to India's democratic tradition—have become powerful weapons in the Hindu Right's attack on minority rights. The concepts have become the site of a contest for meaning, as the Hindu Right seeks to redefine both equality and secularism in accordance with Hindutva's vision of political life. This redefinition is part of a much broader campaign. The Hindu Right is engaged in a discursive struggle, that is, a contest over the way in which individuals understand the world around them. Hindutva represents a particular set of beliefs and categories; it is a way of giving meaning to the world and of organizing social institutions. The Hindutva campaign is also ideological, that is, it is related to the social, economic and political conditions of contemporary India and to the legitimation of social and political power. It is part of a contest over the dominant or hegemonic way of understanding the world, and of establishing an understanding that contributes to the legitimation of social power and inequality.

In this chapter, we explore the discursive strategies of the Hindu Right in relation to law, and the way in which they are seeking to displace dominant understandings of the concepts of secularism and equality, and redefine these concepts in accordance with their vision of Hindutva. We focus on the impact of these strategies on women, and the extent to which women have become a site of contest in the struggle to redefine Indian identity. We consider the important role of familial ideology in this discursive strategy. Hindutva's discourse on women is seeking to rearticulate women's identities as wives and mothers, in and through familial ideology. 'Women's issues' as taken up by the Hindu Right are being cast within a revivalist and familial discourse that seeks to restore women to the position of respect in their roles as wives and mothers that they are alleged to have enjoyed in the mythical, golden age of Hindu society. We begin this chapter with a brief review of Hindu communalism and the ideological agenda of the Hindu Right. We then turn to examine the way in which the Hindu Right has sought to deploy law in furtherance of its Hindutva agenda. We examine the role of law at two interrelated levels: (*a*) the struggle to redefine basic legal and political concepts of secularism and equality, and (*b*) the appropriation of specific legal issues relating to women. We attempt to reveal the extent to which the women's issues being adopted by the Hindu Right are being articulated through the discourses of equality and secularism, and the central role of familial ideology in this discursive strategy. We then consider the implications of this discursive strategy in terms of the broader identity that the Hindu Right is attempting to constitute for women. The chapter attempts to relate this discourse of equality, women, and familial ideology to the broader discursive struggle to constitute a new identity for Indian women—an identity imbued with the rhetoric of tradition and culture, but which is thoroughly modern, responding to contemporary social and economic demands placed on women.

The Hindu Right

The Hindu Right refers to the contemporary political movement in India, informed by the ideology of Hindutva, which seeks to establish a Hindu Rashtra (Hindu state). We use it to refer to the central organizations and movements of the current phase of Hindu communalism in India—the triumvirate of the Bharatiya Janata Party (BJP), the Rashtra Swayamsevak Sangh (RSS), and Vishva Hindu Parishad (VHP), collectively known as the Sangh Parivar, as well as the militantly anti-Muslim, Shiv Sena. Communalism has been defined as a discourse based on the 'belief that because a group of people follow a particular religion, they have as a result, common social, political and economic interests'.[1] It is a discourse that attempts to constitute subjects in and through community attachment, particularly through religious community. It constitutes the way in which these subjects see and give meaning to the world around them. Through communal discourses, subjects come to understand the world around them as one based on the conflict between religious groups; Indian society is understood as fractured by the conflict between these groups. This community identity becomes the basis for social, economic and political demands, and for political mobilization around these demands.

The Hindu Right has its basis in revivalist and nationalist movements of the nineteenth century, and began to take on its distinctive form in the 1920s, with the publication of Sarvarkar's *Who is a Hindu?* and with the founding of the RSS.[2] Sarvarkar developed his idea of Hindutva, a communal discourse which seeks to constitute Hindu subjects to understand the fractured society in a particular way. As Basu et al. describe:

> At the heart of Hindutva lies the myth of a continuous thousand year old struggle of Hindus against Muslims as the structuring principle of Indian history. Both communities are assumed to have been homogenous blocks—of Hindu patriots, heroically resisting invariably tyrannical, 'foreign' Muslim rulers.[3]

More recently, it is said, the policy of appeasing minorities, that is, of special treatment for Muslims and other religious minorities, has perpetuated the oppression of Hindus. The contemporary social, economic and political malaise that is allegedly gripping Hindu society is seen as the result of this policy of appeasement. The answer to this crisis, according to Hindu communalism, is Hindu Rashtra—India must be a Hindu state. Only then can Hindu culture and pride be restored. The subjects of Hindu communalist discourse are being constituted to understand the world around them through this lens.

The Hindu Right has sought to promote and spread this communalized discourse to an increasingly large segment of Hindu society, with the creation of the VHP in 1964. Founded at the behest of the RSS, the VHP was intended to infuse the politics of Hindutva with a specifically religious vision. Unlike the RSS, which has functioned as an elite organization, the VHP was intended to popularize Hindutva identity among the masses.[4] The RSS–BJP–VHP combine are seeking to forge an ideologically dominant discourse, through the organization of consent and the production of common sense. The discursive strategies are aimed at naturalizing the ideas of Hindutva, by making these ideas a part of the common sense of an increasingly large segment of Hindu society. The strategy has been particularly successful since the advent of the VHP and its mass campaigns, through which an increasingly large group of Hindus are beginning to accept the Hindu Right's version of history and politics as universal and natural. The discourse of 'Muslim domination,' 'appeasement of minorities,' and 'Hindu pride' has become commonplace. As the discourse becomes more commonplace, so too does the support for the Hindu Right.

The Hindu Right's discursive struggle for ideological hegemony stretches across a broad range of discursive fields—history, politics, religion, economics. Our focus is on the struggle for meaning within the field of law, as legal discourse becomes yet another contested site. We will consider the way in which law and legal discourse is being deployed by the Hindu Right to advance its political agenda. The legal and political concepts of secularism and equality have come to play an increasingly central role in this discursive struggle for the hearts and minds of Hindu subjects. The Hindu Right has made considerable inroads in its efforts to infuse these concepts with new meaning, consistent with the discourse of Hindutva, even in the courts.[5] Secularism and equality, in the hands of the Hindu Right, are being used to advance the attack on minority rights—the central ideological plank of Hindutva.

We will also examine the ways in which the discourse of equality is being deployed in relation to women. While the attack on minority rights provides the central rallying cry for the forces of Hindutva, its agenda embraces a broad range of conservative social and political issues. Like other conservative and religiously motivated political movements in many parts of the world, the Hindu Right's ideological agenda includes a focus on the importance of the family. It is part of an effort to reinscribe a modernized, but thoroughly patriarchal family, with its role for women as wives and mothers. At the same time, this ideological agenda has been shaped by the participation of women within the Hindu Right; the discourse of equality, and the particular women's issues that have been taken up, have been given shape by the significant participation of women within the women's wings of the Hindu Right. While we will attempt to illustrate the extent to which the issues are framed within familial ideology, we will at the same time try to reveal the complexities of this discourse, as women within the Hindu Right have come to voice their own concerns and needs in the changing world in which they live.

Hindutva and the Discourse of Equality

The concept of equality may not, at first glance, appear to be a cornerstone in the Hindu Right's deployment of legal and political discourse. As we will attempt to reveal, however, 'equality' has become a foundational discourse in Hindutva's attack on minority rights and in its agenda for women. The Hindu Right's approach to equality provides the basis of their understanding of secularism through which they are seeking to redefine the relationship between religion and politics in Indian society. The concept of equality is, at the same time, a central discursive element in the communalist efforts to rearticulate the role and identity for women in India. As discussed in chapter 3, equality is a highly contested concept, which defies any simple or uniform definition. Even within the context of the Hindu Right, the concept of equality similarly eludes a consistent definition. As we will argue in the sections that follow, the precise meaning of the concept within the Hindu Right depends on the context in which it is being deployed. In much of its contemporary political rhetoric, the Hindu Right deploys a formal understanding of equality. In the context of the attack on minority communities and the discourse of secularism, 'equality' refers to the requirement of formally equal treatment. In the context of women, however, the understanding of equality that emerges from the Hindu Right is very different. It no longer requires formally equal treatment, but rather, embraces an affirmation of difference and diversity.

■ Formal Equality, Secularism and the Assault on Minority Rights

In much of its political rhetoric, the Hindu Right deploys a formal approach to equality, that is, an approach based on equal treatment.[6] References can be found throughout BJP literature and speeches to the importance of non-discrimination, and to the equal treatment of all citizens.[7] This approach to equality is most evident in their approach to a second and more central concept in the discourse of Hindutva: secularism. The dominant approach to secularism in India, and the approach adopted by the Hindu Right is based on the Gandhian notion of *sarva dharma sambhava*—the equal respect of all religions. Unlike Western notions of secularism, this approach does not require a wall of separation between religion and politics, but rather, an equal respect of all religions within both the public and private spheres. Despite this general agreement on *sarva dharma sambhava* as the prevailing understanding of secularism, there is considerable disagreement on the precise meaning of the equal respect of all religions. Equal respect of all religions could mean either that all religions must be treated the same (formal equality), or that religions should be treated substantially equally, which may require the accommodation of differences and past disadvantages (substantive equality). The contest over the meaning of secularism turns on the underlying contest over the meaning of equality.

The Hindu Right argues in favour of *sarva dharma sambhava*, and positive secularism. The BJP manifesto states: 'The BJP believes in positive secularism which, according to our constitution-makers, meant Sarva-Dharma-Sambhava and which does not connote an irreligious state'. Similar statements are seen in RSS literature, from Golwalkar to the contemporary ideologues such as Deoras and Malkani. This discourse of the BJP and the RSS is based on a particular vision of equal respect of all religions, that is, on formally equal treatment. Within this view, the equality of all religions requires that all religious communities be treated the same in law. Any special or different treatment, on the basis of religion, is seen to violate secularism. For example, the BJP manifesto states:

> The idea of a theocratic state is an anathema to the Indian mind. The BJP believes that the State in India has always been a civil institution which respects all religions equally and makes no discrimination between one citizen and the other on the grounds of language, caste or religion.... It is the duty of the State to guarantee justice and security to all minorities—linguistic, religious or ethnic. The BJP considers that it is also imperative for national integration that minorities do not develop a minority complex.[8]

The same emphasis on formally equal treatment can be seen in much of RSS political rhetoric. In a typical statement, an RSS publication states:

> The RSS...never demands any special rights to the Hindus. At the same time, it is against giving any concession to other religious minority groups and it opposes religious discrimination.[9]

The particular meaning that the Hindu Right gives to *sarva dharma sambhava* is one based on formal equality. Accordingly, any laws or policies that provide special treatment for minorities are opposed as pseudo-secularism and appeasement of minorities. First among its targets are the provisions of the Constitution which condone such 'appeasement': Article 30 of the Constitution, which allows minorities to run their own educational institutions, and Article 370 which provides special status for Jammu and Kashmir. A BJP policy document states, for example: 'Article 30 permits minorities to run their own schools. It will be rationalised and suitably amended to ensure justice and equality to all irrespective of religions'.[10] The document similarly recommends that the Minorities Commission 'which entertains complaints of discrimination only from minority sections' should be replaced by a Human Rights Commission 'to look into complaints of injustice against any section of society'. Among the first steps taken by the Shiv Sena-BJP government in Maharashtra has been to dismantle the Minorities Commission.[11] In making the announcement, chief minister Manohar Joshi stated '[t]his government will not appease anyone, there will be no special treatment for anyone'.[12] Similar references to pseudo-secularism and appeasement of minorities are repeated in BJP speeches. L. K. Advani repeatedly attacks pseudo-secularism and appeasement of minorities in his speeches. A typical example: '...secularism has come to mean a premium on belonging to a minority'.[13] It is this emphasis on secularism as equal treatment that informs their support for a Uniform Civil Code, that is, all religious communities must be treated exactly the same. In contrast, the prevailing notion of secularism in Indian constitutional law and politics, which has allowed for the special treatment of minorities, is cast as 'pseudo-secularism'.

Within the political rhetoric of the Hindu Right, secularism has become virtually synonymous with equality, and the approach to equality appears unequivocally formal, insisting that equality dictates equal treatment. It is this emphasis on formally equal treatment of all religions that allows the Hindu Right to attack minority rights, and particularly, any provisions designed to protect the rights of religious minorities, as 'special rights' in violation of secularism and equality.

Ironically, it is through this emphasis on secularism, and on the secular value of equality that the Sangh Parivar is attempting to advance its rather non-secular agenda: the establishment of a Hindu state. The Hindu Right repeatedly denies that this Hindu Rashtra represents a theocratic state, insisting instead on its commitment to the democratic institutions of a secular state. L. K. Advani, addressing the National Executive of the BJP, in March 1994, stated:

> The Bharatiya Janata Party believes that Indian secularism has its roots in Hindutva. India is secular because it is essentially Hindu. Theocracy is alien to Hindu tradition.

At the same time, a close examination of some of the statements of the ideological leaders of the Sangh Parivar reveals the underlying spirit of the Hindu Right's version of secularism. Deoras, for example, in defending the secularism of the RSS and of Hindu Rashtra, has argued that only Hindus are capable of real secularism.

> If secularism means treating all religions on an equal footing, prose-lytisation and secularism can't go together. Those who believe in conversion do so because they feel that their religion is superior to all others. Their organisations therefore can not claim to be secular. Hinduism, on the other hand, does not believe in conversions and

Hindus have never been proselytisers. As such, organisations of Hindus alone can truly be secular.[14]

There is an underlying, though somewhat perverse logic to this RSS argument, based on their ability to define the terms of debate. Secularism is defined as the toleration of all religions; Hinduism is defined as the only religion with a true tolerance for all other religions; it follows, according to these terms, that only a country based on Hinduism can be truly secular.

Within this vision, the sharp distinction between secularism and theocracy begins to blur. Although the Hindu Right does not advocate replacing the secular and democratic institutions of governance with religious leaders or structures, it does encourage the politicization of religious leaders. The ranks of the BJP are filled with sants and sadhus, who have come to play an increasingly visible and vocal role in the Hindutva movement, some going so far as to call for a return to the laws of Manu. And the very mandate of the VHP is the promotion of a unified and politicized religious identity. Yet, this infusion of politics with religious leaders and religious identity is done under the guise of secularism.

The Hindu Right's discourse of 'secularism' does not conform to any of the prevailing definitions of secularism. There is, of course, no wall of separation between religion and politics. But even as measured against the standards of *sarva dharma sambhava*, the Hindu Right's vision undermines the spirit of secularism. There is no real respect or accommodation for any other religion. The state becomes a Hindu Rashtra, and state policy comes to be modeled on Hindu norms and practices. There is no real respect for other religions, since these religions are not seen to be as tolerant as Hinduism, and therefore, not as worthy of respect. Within this vision the objective becomes the assimilation of minorities into the broader and ostensibly more tolerant fabric of Hinduism. This discourse of secularism thus comes to represent little more than the politics of Hinduism, and freedom of religion represents the assimilation of religious minorities.

It is important to recognize the extent to which it is the very model of equality that allows for such manipulation, and ultimately, for this unmodified majoritarianism. Formal equality's insistence on equal treatment begs the question of who should be treated equally with whom. As we discussed in chapter 3, a formal approach to equality will only treat equally those who are the same, or can act the same, as the dominant group. Women are only treated equally if they can be the same as men. The vantage point of the dominant group is not questioned, but rather, unproblematically deployed as the reference point against which 'others' are judged.[15] This formal model of equality is similarly deployed by the Hindu Right in the context of religious minorities. Equal treatment is understood to mean treating minority groups the same as the majority. The reference point of the Hindu majority is uninterrogated, and thereby remains the norm against which all 'other' groups are judged. This majoritarianism implicit in the very approach to equality is simply brought to the surface in the discursive shifts of the RSS ideologues, who articulate the otherwise unstated assumptions. Deoras, and others before him, are unabashed and unapologetic in their admission that Hinduism is to be the norm against which other religions are to be judged, and in their view, ultimately rejected. It is their candor, rather than their understanding of equality, that makes their arguments exceptional.

■ Equality as Harmony

A second understanding of equality is also apparent in the writings and speeches of proponents of Hindutva, particularly among the ideologues of the RSS. On the one hand, their rhetoric often echoes the equal treatment approach of the BJP, particularly in relation to religious minorities. 'Equal treatment', and 'equality before the law' are invoked to attack any special treatment of minorities.[16] However, these same RSS intellectual leaders have elsewhere displayed a rather different understanding of equality. Golwalkar explicitly rejected the 'Western' concept of equality.[17] In contrast to this understanding, which in his view emphasizes 'equality of men...on the material plane because all men were equally in need of all...basic material needs,'[18] Golwalkar argued that it is only on the spiritual plane that it can be said that all men are equal.

> It is in this sense, i.e., the same spirit being immanent in all, that men are equal. Equality is applicable only on the plane of the Supreme Spirit. But on the physical plane the same spirit manifests itself in a wondrous variety of diversities and disparities.[19]

Golwalkar argued that 'disparity is an indivisible part of nature and we have to live with it,' and concluded that harmony, not equality, should be the organizing principle.[20] A similar emphasis on harmony is echoed by contemporary RSS leaders. H. V. Seshadri writes:

> [T]he principles of equality propounded by Hinduism envisages an all round harmonious synthesis...All members of a family mete out equal

treatment to each other and they also perform different roles. It is possible because they love each other and they live in harmony. The body of man itself has different organs which perform diverse functions but a harmonious order prevails among them. Hence the Hindutva and RSS primarily lay an emphasis on harmonious order. This harmony spontaneously leads to equality, which is the prominent characteristic of Hindutva and RSS.[21]

He further explains the spiritual nature of this concept of equality:

It is our basic approach to find every person and creature, birds and animals, as the embodiment of God. We believe that God pervades in all.... This is the type of equality which alone can bring harmonious synthesis.[22]

Like Golwalkar, the emphasis is on equality within the spiritual domain—on the equal embodiment of 'atma'.

Despite the similar emphasis on harmony in difference, and on the spiritual dimension of equality, there is a subtle shift from Golwalkar to the contemporary discourse of Seshadri. In this more current RSS rhetoric, the outright rejection of equality within the material sphere is tempered. Rather than rejecting equality in favour of harmony, equality is conflated with harmony. Golwalkar's vision of harmony in diversity and difference is retained, but recast within the discourse of equality: equality becomes harmony. While the shift is a very subtle one, it may be indicative of the broader discursive transformations in Indian law and politics in which equality has emerged as a dominant discourse. Rather than arguing against equality, it has become far more politically expedient to attempt to redefine its meaning.

This redefinition is, in turn, achieved in a manner consistent with Golwalkar's earlier version. Seshadri, for example, further elaborates on the meaning of equality by analogy to the family:

The young child in the family holds the parents and his elders in high regard, but the elders do not treat the child as low. Similarly, there can be inequality on the basis of intelligence and wisdom. But the Hindu view point does not allow to treat them as higher or lower classes'.[23]

Based on this vision, Seshadri concludes

We cannot contemplate a society, a life or a world without the elements of diversification. When we visualize the unity in diversity, we would be able to bring equality and harmony.[24]

Equality, in the RSS view, does not mean that all persons must be treated the same. Rather, equality means harmony within difference. The RSS approach to equality as harmony in diversity is distinct from both formal and substantive equality. It does not seek to promote formally equal treatment, but rather, expressly rejects this emphasis on sameness. Nor is the RSS approach consistent with a substantive approach to equality. While it does embrace difference, the objectives and orientations of the RSS approach are markedly different from that of substantive equality. The RSS approach does not address questions of systemic or historic discrimination. There is little or no effort within this approach to eliminate material inequalities. Rather, diversity is emphasized as a good in and of itself. It contemplates equality as harmony within explicitly unequal material conditions.

This equality as harmony approach sits in stark contrast to the formal equality approach adopted in much of the Hindu Right's political rhetoric. Indeed, the equality as harmony approach could operate to undermine the very discursive basis of the Hindu Right's attack on minority rights. In the context of religious minorities, equality as harmony could be taken to mean that Muslims do not have to be treated the same as Hindus; it could be deployed to affirm the value of religious diversity and the legitimacy of differential legal treatment. But the equality as harmony approach is not so deployed. In the context of secularism and religious minorities, the Hindu Right is unequivocal in its insistence on formal equality. Yet, as we will examine, in other contexts dealing with issues of social inequality such as gender relations, the rhetoric of the Hindu Right shifts back to an emphasis on harmony in diversity. The tension between these two approaches to equality are never resolved in Hindutva thought and rhetoric, but instead co-exist in awkward and unstated juxtaposition.

■ Women and Equality in Hindutva

It is important to recognize at the outset that the Hindu Right does not speak with a single voice on the issue of women and equality rights. Some of the more orthodox elements within the RSS–VHP–BJP combine have adopted a reactionary position on women and the family, calling for example for a return to the laws of Manu, a restoration of polygamy, and the glorification of sati.[25] These views, however, are not representative of the position of the Hindu Right as a whole on the question of women's issues. The women's wings of the Hindu Right organizations—such as the Rashtra Sevika Samiti, and the Mahila Morcha of the

BJP—have all begun to articulate more moderate positions, denouncing discrimination against women, and promoting equality.[26] The BJP has similarly begun to adopt positions formally denouncing atrocities against women, and promoting women's equality. The Hindu Right does not speak with a single and homogenous voice on the question of women, but rather, is characterized by diverse and conflicting positions. The recent controversy arising from Swami Nischąlananda, the Sankaracharya of Puri, who pronounced that the scriptures did not permit women to recite the Vedas exemplifies these divisions. While the General Secretary of the VHP defended these views, and denounced those who dared to criticize the Sankaracharya as an attack on Hindutva itself,[27] many within the BJP were quick to denounce the views of the Sankaracharya. Sushma Swaraj, a BJP spokesperson, responded sharply, saying that the Sankaracharya and other religious leaders 'must change their thinking with the times'.

In the sections that follow, we focus on this more moderate position promoting women's equality that is increasingly visible within the Hindu Right, and the discourse within which women's issues are being appropriated and articulated. The particular discourse of equality adopted by the Hindu Right in relation to women is one that does not fundamentally challenge women's traditional role as wives and mothers within the family. Rather, as we will attempt to demonstrate, the discourse of equality is one that is deeply imbued with familial ideology, such that the Hindu Right is able to advocate seemingly more moderate positions, while at the same time reinscribing the patriarchal family and women's roles therein. The legal discourse of equality, as we will illustrate, thus plays an increasingly important role in the discursive struggles of the Hindu Right, not only in its assault on minority rights, but also in its efforts to forge a new identity for women.

The Discourse of Women's Equality: Beyond Equal Treatment

The Hindu Right's official position on women is filled with commitments to equality.

> The BJP pledges itself to restore to women the position of equality with men that the Indian tradition proposed and accepted.[28]

The discourse of equality is fused with a more specifically revivalist discourse that seeks to reclaim a glorious and ancient past. The objective of equality becomes the restoration of women to the position that they ostensibly enjoyed in this 'golden age'. But what is the meaning of their commitment to women's 'equality with men'? In the context of secularism, the BJP has endorsed a formal approach to equality, which demands formally equal treatment. In the context of women's equality, however, the equal treatment of women and men is not what they seem to have in mind. In a telling statement, the BJP asserts: 'Men and women are equal but they are not the same'.[29] Since women and men are not the same, then according to the logic of formal equality, they do not have to be treated equally. With a single stroke, the BJP both invokes the discourse of women's equality, and at the same time undermines any real entitlement to it by stating that women are different. One way of reading this statement is as a formal model of equality coupled with a protectionist approach to gender difference. Since sameness is the prerequisite for equality, women, who are different, do not have to be treated the same. Yet, the BJP does specifically say that women are equal. If women and men are equal, at the same time as women and men are not the same, then equality cannot mean sameness and equal treatment. The question of what equality does mean in this context, however, remains unanswered.

The answer to this riddle of equality lies in a deeper exploration of the BJP's policies and statements on women. It is within these policies and statements that we can begin to see more clearly the way in which women are to be treated, the position of 'equality' to which they are to be restored, and the understanding of equality that underlies this policy. BJP policy on women often focuses on the roles in the family that have traditionally been allocated to women according to the sexual division of labour. For example, health care, particularly maternal and natal care, is taken up, as are smokeless chulas and sanitation facilities for poor, rural, and slum women. Policies that reinforce women's role in the family as mothers and wives are supported as part of women's equality rights. In so doing, the Hindu Right reinforces the assumption of natural and essential differences between women and men. Women are mothers and wives—they are *matri shakti*—they are different, and these differences must be honoured and protected.

The extent to which BJP policy supports women in their familial roles can be seen by the political issues that are expressly excluded from their agenda. For example, writing in regard to the UN Conference on Women in Nairobi:

The BJP women's wing expressed its profound appreciation of the conference. However, it also expressed its sharp disagreement with certain subjects that were discussed at the conference, subjects that are antithetical to Indian social order and our cultural moorings. Evaluation of women's domestic work in terms of money is an insult to Indian motherhood.... Likewise the demand for legal sanction of lesbianism is too vulgar and irrelevant in the Indian context.[30]

Wages for housework and lesbianism are both considered to be antithetical to Indian womanhood—defined in and through women's natural roles as mothers and wives. Wages for housework and lesbianism undermine these roles; thus, they cannot be supported.

Political claims that, in their view, go too far beyond these traditional roles are dismissed. Atal Bihari Vajpayee's statement is particularly revealing: 'Women who want to become men and want to make other women [like] men are worthy of ridicule'.[31] Implicit in this statement is the assumption of natural differences between women and men. These differences can be strategically deployed to justify any differential, protective and discriminatory treatment. To argue counter to their policies—to argue that any particular legislation discriminates against women, runs into the trap of the Hindu Right's discourse: it is simply met with the refrain that women are trying to become men. Political claims that go too far beyond the traditional roles of women in family are rejected as attempts to make women into men, and thus ridiculous.

The BJP policy on women also includes issues of women's education and employment—issues which seem to bring women out from within the narrow confines of the family. The BJP has identified women's socio-economic dependence as a main cause of women's oppression, and accordingly, the party supports programmes designed to improve their socio-economic status, including increased employment opportunities, particularly in areas that 'suit [women] most'.[32] Women's illiteracy is also seen to contribute to this poor status and must therefore be eliminated through improved access to education. However, even the support given to improving such educational and employment opportunities for women is justified in the name of the family:

> An Indian woman will command the affection of the father, the love of the husband, and the respect of her son only when she has been provided with equal rights and opportunities.[33]

Women's role in the family—as mothers and wives—remains the cornerstone of the BJP approach to restoring women to the position of equality reserved for them in Indian tradition. We can begin to see the extent to which the traditional discourse of women as *matri shakti* infuses the BJP policies. Indeed, it is this image of *matri shakti* that can be seen to underlie the very understanding of women's equality.

Man and woman will remain the two wheels of the chariot of the family, and the nation. There can be no better concept of unity and equality of man and woman than the concept of 'Ardhanarishwar'.[34]

We can begin to see here echoes of the RSS vision of equality, that is, of equality as harmony in diversity. Equality does not mean treating women the same as men. Rather, equality becomes an affirmation of the difference between women and men. These different roles of women and men, in the family and in society, are affirmed and celebrated as harmonious synthesis. The BJP approach to equality within the context of women, initially somewhat elusive, begins to emerge. The very meaning of the concept of equality begins to shift away from sameness and equal treatment towards diversity and differential treatment.

This harmony in diversity approach is also very different from a substantive approach to equality. It has little to do with the systemic or historic disadvantage of women. While there are overtones of historic disadvantage in the discourse of restoring women to the position they once occupied in the golden age of Hindu culture, the vision of the Hindu Right is very different from the one contemplated by substantive equality. Within this vision, 'historic oppression' refers only to the oppression and degeneration of Hindu society at the hands of foreign (Muslim) invaders. There is virtually no attention to systemic or historic disadvantage or discrimination against women within Hindu culture. There is no recognition of gender as a socially constructed category, but simply an affirmation and celebration of natural and essential differences.

The 'Women's Rights' Agenda Within the Hindu Right

This general discourse on equality and women sets the discursive framework for the 'women's rights' agenda of the Hindu Right. In recent years, the women's wings of the Hindu Right organization have taken on a number of specific women's rights issues that have been associated with the secular women's movement. The Uniform Civil Code, violence against women, obscenity, women's education and employment have all been taken up by women within the Hindu Right, and articulated as a part of the Hindutva agenda for women. In this section, we will examine the way in which some of these women's issues are being articulated within the Hindu Right. We will attempt to reveal the revivalist and familial discourses through which these issues are being constituted and given meaning. More specifically, we will illustrate the extent to which women's issues are being framed within (*a*) a revivalist discourse that seeks to restore women to the position of honour and respect they enjoyed in a reconstructed and mythical 'golden age,' and (*b*) a dominant familial discourse, through which women's identities and roles as wives and mothers within the family are being reinscribed. We will attempt to further reveal the approach to equality that underlies the Hindu Right's appropriation of these women's issues—an approach that emphasizes women's differences in relation to men, but women's sameness in relation to all other women.

■ Atrocities against Women

'Atrocities against women' has become a prominent issue within the Hindu Right. The resolutions of the Mahila Morcha of the BJP, and more recently, the All India Women's Association, have come to routinely condemn 'atrocities against women'. Rape, dowry, female infanticide, and sex selection have each been taken up, and condemned. To the extent that the manifestos of the BJP have addressed issues of concern to women, violence against women is always condemned. Uma Bharati repeatedly denounces atrocities against women. Buried within the long shopping list of the BJP's manifesto for the Delhi assembly elections in November 1993 was a promise to establish a special court to deal with crimes against women.[35] Chief Minister of the Shiv Sena–BJP government in Maharashtra has stressed the need for more district courts for women to deal with cases of atrocities.[36] RSS training for women is often justified specifically in relation to this violence, since physical training and strength will empower women to resist this violence.

The Sangh Parivar's appropriation of the issue of violence against women should not be seen as a wholesale adoption of the framework within which the women's movement has understood this violence. In stark contrast to the women's movement's emphasis on women's rights and men's violence, the Hindu Right has framed the issue of violence against women within the broader political and cultural discourses of Hindutva. As we will illustrate, the discursive strategy is twofold: it involves both (*a*) the communalization of sexual violence, through which responsibility for violence against women is seen to lie within the Muslim community, and specifically, with Muslim men, and (*b*) the feminization of violence against women, through which the violence that occurs within the family is seen to be the responsibility of women. This twofold discursive strategy corresponds to a public/private distinction in the types of violence identified, and in the ways in which this violence is addressed. Violence within the public sphere is associated with rape, sexual assault, and sexual harassment, whereas violence within the private sphere is associated with issues such as dowry, sex selection, and female infanticide. Public violence is constituted within the communalizing discourse, whereas private violence is constituted through the feminization discourse. This discursive strategy operates to reinforce the construction of the Muslim community as a dangerous 'other,' as well as to absolve Hindu men of any blame for violence, either inside or outside of the family. As we will further argue, the solution to this violence comes to lie in further reinforcing women's roles in the family, by making them strong mothers and wives.

Communalizing Sexual Violence

The recognition of sexual violence within the public sphere is framed within a communal discourse. The perpetrators of sexual violence are constructed as the Muslim 'other'. Sexual violence is thereby seen as that which (Hindu) women experience at the hands of Muslim men. The rape of Hindu women by Muslim men during communal riots is highlighted.[37] The rape of Hindu women in Kashmir by 'Muslim fundamentalists' is a recurrent theme in RSS literature, and often provides the rationale for providing Hindu women with RSS style physical training.[38] Atrocities against women in the Muslim countries of the subcontinent are also frequently highlighted.[39] This construction of the Muslim 'other' as the perpetrator of sexual violence fits all too neatly with the stereotype of Muslim men as lustful that has long been part of the discourse of Hindutva. As Sarkar has observed:

> From Sarvarkar's formative writing on Muslim rule in India, the stereotype of an eternally lustful male with evil designs on Hindu women has been reiterated and made a part of a historical common sense.[40]

This communalization of sexual violence operates simultaneously to reinforce the demonization of the Muslim community, while deflecting attention away from sexual violence within Hindu communities.[41] The violence that women may experience within the public sphere can thereby be addressed with demands for harsher penalties for the perpetrators, without threatening the patriarchal authority of Hindu males. The call for harsh penalties becomes in effect a call for the punishment of Muslim men who have dishonoured Hindu women, and by implication, the Hindu community.

Within this communalized discourse of sexual violence, the harm associated with rape becomes the harm to the community. Rape is understood not as a violation of an individual woman's right to bodily autonomy, but rather, in a more traditional and patriarchal discourse as a violation of a woman's honour. This honour is in turn closely associated with a family's honour, and the honour of the broader community. As Amrita Basu has observed: 'The BJP has made the raped Hindu woman symbolic of the victimization of the entire Hindu community'.[42] This communal discourse further provides women within the Hindu Right with a legitimate focus for their personal and political anger about sexual violence. As Sarkar suggests: 'The hindu woman is given an externalized enemy to focus on that helps obliterate and displace personal and immediate experiences of oppression within the family'.[43]

Feminization of Violence

Within the political rhetoric of the Sangh Parivar, atrocities against women that are located within the family, that is, issues such as dowry, sex selection and female infanticide, are rarely treated differently. These issues are constituted through a discourse of feminization in which responsibility for violence is placed on women themselves. Within this private sphere, women are seen as responsible for both the atrocities and for ending the atrocities. Emphasis is placed on educating women against the practices in which they are complicitous. For example, the practice of sex selection is constructed as a practice engaged in by women. Eliminating sex selection must therefore begin with women, who must be educated against it. In an article against sex selection in the *Organiser*, Kelkar argues that women must be educated against this practice.[44] Men's role in the practice of sex selection is nowhere addressed. Indeed, the desire of Hindu men for sons, who must light their father's funeral pyre, is noticeably absent. Only women's role in the practice, and in ending the practice, is addressed. Even dowry and dowry deaths are seen to be at least partially the responsibility of women—who must not agree to this practice in the first instance, and who, as mothers-in-law, are often seen to be involved in the dowry murder.

Underlying this feminization of violence in the Hindu Right's approach to violence against women is a heavy reliance on dominant familial ideology. The arguments used by Kelkar in support of the basic proposition that women are to be educated against the practice of sex selection are illustrative:

Women's status and importance as an emotional link of the family is beyond any doubt. It is universally accepted by human beings. It is the mother who speaks to the child first and links him to society. She is first teacher and the model of social relationship. It is attachment to the mother that keeps all members of the family emotionally linked. The mother, therefore, is identified with the family. In India, the family is the fundamental unit of society.[45]

It is women's quintessential role as mother that is seen to lie at the root of the problem. And it is in and through women's roles as mothers that the problem is to be addressed.

The selective recognition of atrocities against women that occur within the family leads to a call for education. While educating and empowering women is an important strategy of the secular women's movement as well, what is particularly notable about the rhetoric and strategies of the Hindu Right is the extent to which men's roles and responsibility in violence against women within the family is virtually untouched. Issues such as wife assault, marital rape and/or child sexual abuse which directly implicate men within their families are not raised. It is not men who must stop abusing women, but women who must become the objects of men's respect. Responsibility for these practices is implicitly seen to lie with the women themselves. And men's responsibility in the practices of dowry, dowry death, sex selection and infanticide is obscured by the focus on women. It is women who are seen to have become weak, to have become objects of degradation and maltreatment. And so it is women who must make themselves strong, and who in turn can then make their families strong.

Within this discourse of the Hindu Right, violence against women has become, quite literally, a women's issue. The responsibility for the violence, and in turn, the responsibility for eliminating the violence, lies with women alone. Yet, women are not accountable to women alone: they are accountable to their families, and to their Hindu culture. It is their duty and obligation, as mothers and wives, to make their families strong. It is in turn this duty to their families which creates their obligation to eliminate violent practices. Women must resist the violence in their lives—not as an issue of individual rights, but as an issue of family honour.

While the condemnation of violence against women is shared by the secular women's movement and the women's wing of the Hindu Right, the underlying understandings are very different. Within the secular women's movement, violence against women is an issue of individual women's rights—the right to be free from violence, the right to bodily integrity, the right to life. Within the Hindu Right, resisting violence against women is framed as an issue of restoring the role and respect of women within Indian tradition, particularly within the family. Atrocities against women are a sign of the degeneration of Hindu society, so that the revival of the ancient tradition—of the golden age—must restore women to their rightful position. Women who are victims of violence are not objects of respect, either from those who subject them to violence, or from themselves. It thus becomes women's duty to their families, their community and their nation to restore themselves to a position of respect. As a BJP leader stated at a Rashtra Sevika rally, 'one of the important tasks before women leaders is to instill self respect and self confidence among women who were maltreated in the society in spite of the fact that the constitution gave them equal rights with men'.[46]

Within the discourse of the Hindu Right, a strong Hindu woman becomes essential to a strong Hindu society, particularly since women are responsible for raising the next generation, with appropriate values, discipline, and culture. Although women are constituted as different from men, they must not be weak. Rather, Hindutva's gender discourse seeks to reconstitute women as strong. The RSS provides physical training of women for this purpose. And BJP policy takes a strong stand against violence against women, including organizing women to defend themselves. Strong Hindu women are to be important conduits of a strong Hindu culture. And yet, the very discursive framework ensures that women's strength does not challenge or undermine their position within the family. Women's strength is constituted not in individualistic terms, but in strictly familial terms. Women's strength is located and contained within the confines of the family—their strength is intended to serve the higher cause of the family, and through it, the higher cause of the community and the nation.

Atrocities against women have been taken up by the Hindu Right in a way that does not challenge the authority or legitimacy of the patriarchal family. Hindu men are not called to account for the violence against women. Rather, public violence is blamed on Muslim men, and private violence is made the responsibility of women. And in both public and private violence, women are made responsible for eradicating these violent practices, and restoring their own place of respect, as wife and mother, within their families. The denunciation of violence against women by the Hindu Right is far removed from the discourse of formal or substantive equality for women. Ending violence against women has nothing to do with treating women the same as men. Nor does it have much to do with the historic and systemic oppression of women. The issue is articulated within the language of restoring women to the position of respect that they once enjoyed. While there are overtones of historic disadvantage within this discourse, it is clearly a very different vision than that contemplated within a substantive model of equality. In the revivalist discourse of the Hindu Right, 'historic oppression' refers to the oppression and degeneration of Hindu society (and thus Hindu women) at the hands of foreign (Muslim) invaders. Overcoming this historic disadvantage means restoring women to the pedestal of respect and honour that was rightfully theirs in the golden age. This position of respect and honour is not, however, one in which women and men were the same. It is, rather, a vision of equality that celebrates their harmonious difference. Ending violence against women can thus be seen within the context of the RSS model of equality as harmony in difference. Ending violence is intended to restore the harmony that has been lost, and celebrate the natural differences between women and men. It is intended to restore a women's 'natural' place of respect and honour in her family as mother and wife.

■ Obscenity and the Indecent Representation of Women

Obscenity and the indecent representation of women has also been taken up as an issue by the Hindu Right. The resolutions from the meeting of the All India Women's Sammelan included a condemnation of vulgar and obscene representations of women in film and television. Uma Bharati repeatedly denounces the indecent representation of women in the mass media.[47] A BJP election manifesto states:

> BJP recognises the great role of cinema in entertainment, education and national integration. BJP will have 50 per cent women on Film Censor Board—to keep violence and vulgarity out of films.[48]

This condemnation of obscenity and vulgarity is followed by a call for stricter censorship. The criminal law of obscenity, the civil law of the indecent representation of women, and the regulations/guidelines of the Film Censor Board should all be more strictly enforced.

Recently, there has been considerable focus on the Hindi film industry, and on the allegedly vulgar and indecent representations of women within these films. The controversy surrounding the song 'Choli Ke Peechey Kya Hai'(What's behind the blouse?),from the film *Khalnayak* became the focus of a legal challenge, as a BJP supporter brought a petition alleging that the song was 'vulgar, against public morality and decency'. The case was dismissed by the trial court, and subsequently on appeal, dismissed by the High Court. While the case was not successful in legal terms, the petition did assist in the mobilization of public opinion around the controversy—a controversy which has been taken up by politicians, and lead to a call for stricter censorship by the Central Board of Film Certification (Censor Board). The controversy was heightened again following the release of the song 'Sexy, Sexy, Sexy' from the film *Khuddar*. Following an uproar in parliament on the increasing 'vulgarity and obscenity' in Hindi films, a meeting was convened in May 1994 by the Minister for Information and Broadcasting, with the Censor Board, members of the National Commission for Women, cable television operators, and members of the film industry. Uma Bharati, one of the BJP members of parliament present at the meeting, argued strongly in favour of increased censorship. The Censor Board undertook to ensure that vulgar songs and dances will be prohibited.

'Vulgarity' in advertising has also attracted the attention of the Hindu Right. Among the first actions of Pramod Navalkar, Minister for Cultural Affairs of the Shiv Sena–BJP government in Maharashtra was a call to 'clean up' culture. Navalkar condemned the use of sexually explicit imagery in advertising, and the widespread availability of pornographic books and magazines. Navalkar has declared: 'I only want to repel the attack on our culture by sexual permissiveness'.[49] The Minister has promised to pursue an 'anti-vulgarity' campaign, and to provide the police with the government assistance required to seize and destroy such vulgar materials.[50] In an interview with the women's magazine, *Savvy*, Navalkar elaborated on his understanding of vulgarity, which he defined as 'whatever cannot be enjoyed in the company of children'. In his view, then, the problem with vulgarity in the media like magazines and billboards is that 'it is a family media which I cannot avoid from reaching my family'.[51]

The sexist representation of women in mass culture has been an issue of concern within the secular women's movement.[52] Despite the similarities between the secular women's movement and the Hindu Right in condemning obscenity, there are significant differences in the understanding of the underlying problem of obscene representations. The secular women's movement has framed the issue as one of women's rights—the right to equality, the right to be free from sexual harassment. Indecent representations are, within this view, connected directly or indirectly to violence against women. The Hindu Right, however, frames the issue quite differently. As with the issue of violence against women, obscenity is framed as a violation of women's traditional identity. These representations of women are seen to be a violation of women as *matri shakti*, of women's roles as wives and mothers, and of the respect for women in these roles. The attack on vulgarity in the media is justified on the basis of family values, of women's roles in the family to protect and foster tradition and culture.

The denunciation of obscenity and vulgarity is framed within the same revivalist and familial discourses as the denunciation of violence against women. The Hindu Right is concerned with restoring women to their position of respect and honour of the mythic past, a position in which women were respected and honoured as mothers and wives. But the concern with obscenity is further constituted within a discourse of gender that focuses on women's sexuality. The threat of obscenity is seen as a threat to the purity of women's sexuality. If women's sexuality is not protected within the confines of the family, then men cannot be held responsible for their actions of violating this sexuality. As BJP Shatrughan Sinha has stated, rather explicitly in relation to Hindi films' values becoming degenerate:

> Girls are appearing on magazine covers their bodies painted naked. They argue that it is their freedom, their bodies…. They can do what they want but they shouldn't raise a hue and cry if men react on seeing such explicit pictures…all that we are saying is that 'mandir ka apman na karo, aurat ka apman na karo.[53]

The way in which the problem of obscenity is framed operates to deflect responsibility for sexual violence away from men. Obscenity is seen to cause sexual violence, so that men cannot be held to be at fault. Rather, the blame lies with the obscene representation, and those who produce these representations, including the women who appear in them.[54]

The Hindu Right's denunciation of obscenity has little to do with either a formal or substantive model of equality. The harm associated with obscenity is the harm to women's dignity and sexual modesty. There is no corresponding concern with men's dignity or sexual modesty. This is not a question of treating women the same as men, but rather, quite explicitly about treating women differently than men, because of their sexual differences—differences that are assumed to be natural. Nor does this differential treatment have much to do with substantive equality. Unlike those within the secular women's movement who argue that obscenity is a violation of women's equality, the Hindu Right's concern is about traditional sexual morality, and women's rightful place within this morality. The only vision of equality that is consistent with the way in which the issue of obscenity has been framed, is the RSS harmony in diversity model. Obscenity is seen to threaten the harmonious balance between the sexes, and thus, ending this obscenity will help to restore the balance, and women's place of respect and honour therein.

■ The Uniform Civil Code

One of the issues long advocated by the Hindu Right has been the demand for a Uniform Civil Code. In the 1980s, the Shah Bano case became the focus of a campaign for the reform of personal laws, and the enactment of a Uniform Civil Code in accordance with the Directive Principles of the Constitution. But, this issue is rather different in its focus than the other women's rights issues that have subsequently been appropriated by the Hindu Right. The demand for a Uniform Civil Code is articulated within the discourse of formal equality. The Hindu Right deploys this discourse to claim the sameness of all women, and that all women must be equal. When the Hindu Right argues that all women must be treated equally, they mean that Muslim women should be treated the same as Hindu women. In this respect, their approach to equality corresponds to their approach to secularism, where any recognition of difference is seen to constitute a violation of secularism. Thus, any recognition of difference as between the women in different religious communities is seen to violate the constitutional guarantees of equality, which in their view, requires the formally equal treatment of all those who are the same. Muslim women, as women, should be the same as Hindu women—and therefore they should be treated the same in law.[55] The demand for the UCC can thus be seen to have more to do with the discourse of secularism than it does with the discourse of women's rights. The issue is deployed as a means of attacking minority communities, particularly the Muslim community, on the basis of their personal laws which discriminate against women. Muslim personal law, and the *Muslim Women's (Protection of Rights on Divorce) Act* within the Hindutva discourse of secularism is cast as yet another example of pandering to minorities. It is used as a focus for the rallying cry of 'pseudo-secularism'—which according to the Hindu Right means the failure of law to treat all religious communities formally equally.

The paradoxical ways in which the discourse of equality is invoked by the BJP is vividly illustrated in their response to the Shah Bano case, and particularly to the enactment of the *Muslim Women's (Protection of Rights on Divorce) Act*.[56] The BJP campaigned against the Act on the ground that it violated the rights of Muslim women.[57] The Muslim community, supporting this Act, was thereby constituted in terms of its opposition to women's equality. Yet, both the Act, and its alternative—section 125 of the *Criminal Procedure Code*—are based on treating women differently than men. Women are different than men and need to be protected from men. The discourse of equality is at one and the same time being used to reinforce the idea that all women are or should be the same, as well as the idea that women are not and should not be the same as men. Two models of equality converge to allow the Hindu Right to delegitimize the recognition of religious and cultural difference without challenging the assertion of natural gender difference.

This response to the Shah Bano controversy begins to reveal the extent to which the discourses of secularism and equality are mutually constituting. In the BJP's view, the Act violates both secularism and equality. It violates secularism because the Muslim community is treated differently. It violates equality because Muslim women are treated differently than Hindu women. Both discourses are used to reinforce the image of the Muslim community as 'other'. And in so doing, the discourse of equality is being used to undermine substantive equality, that is, real equality between women and men, and substantive secularism, that is, equal respect and accommodation for minority communities.

A number of more recent judicial decisions have again provided the BJP with an opportunity to push forward its demand for a Uniform Civil Code. For example, the Allahabad High Court held that the practice of triple *talaq* was unconstitutional. Hari Nath Tilhari J. held that the pronouncement of triple *talaq* at a single sitting was in violation of both Muslim law and the Constitution. 'Giving an irrevocable talaq at once or during one tuhar or at one sitting has been regarded by all under Islam-Sunnat to be against the mandate of the Holy Quran'. On the constitutional issue, Tilhari J. held:

> Any customary or codified law, if it perpetuates against the dignity of women and runs counter to the fundamental duty imposed on every citizen to denounce or renounce practices which denigrate women, cannot be deemed to be operative in case a conflict arises between the constitutional provisions and the customary or codified law.

The practice of triple *talaq* was, in the court's view, a practice which denigrates women, and which was in violation of the Constitution. Leave to appeal to the Supreme Court has been granted, and the High Court decision has been stayed.

The response to the decision has come primarily from the Muslim community. And the response has been divided. The conservative and orthodox voices have denounced the decision, largely on the basis that the courts should not have jurisdiction to interfere with Muslim personal law. Some moderate and liberal voices have cautiously welcomed the decision. Husna Subhani, president of the All-India Muslim Women's Association has endorsed the decision, noting that 'since the high court verdict is based on the Shariat Application Act, it is in conformity with

Islamic law. We are now going to demand a similar law to be passed by the Muslim Personal Law Board'.[58]

Unsurprisingly, the Hindu Right has come out in favour of the decision of the High Court. An editorial in the *Organiser* on the *talaq* decision speaks of the 'gross violation' of Muslim women's equality rights under the practice of triple *talaq*.

> The Constitutional rights of Muslim women cannot be different from those of Muslim men. For that matter, there cannot be a different set of rights for women and men, no matter what religion they belong to. If the provisions of the Muslim Marriage Act, 1939, govern the rules and procedures regarding the rights of Muslim women in case of divorce, how can a Muslim male enjoy such exclusive and atrocious 'right' to arbitrarily pronounce the dreaded word thrice and plunge the woman in misery for life.[59]

Interestingly, the argument is cast in the rhetoric of pure formal equality—that Muslim women should have same rights as Muslim men—an argument that is conspicuously absent in other contexts of women's rights, Muslim and Hindu alike. Even in the context of a Uniform Civil Code, where the Hindu Right deploys a formal model of equality to argue that the Muslim community should be treated the same as the Hindu community, no mention is made of treating women just the same as men. But the issue of divorce, and triple *talaq*, is apparently a rare issue on which the Hindu Right is comfortable in insisting that women and men should be treated the same, at least for the purposes of attacking the Muslim community.[60]

The focus of the *Organiser* editorial then shifts to an attack on the orthodox within the Muslim community, who would continue to threaten 'national integration and communal fraternity'. The rhetoric, informed by the underlying discourse of secularism, calls for the moderates within the Muslim community to join the ranks of those demanding a UCC. It commends the All-India Muslim Women's Association for supporting the decision, and promoting the rights of Muslim women. Once again, the Hindu Right tries to position itself as the guardians of the rights of Muslim women, and attempts to align itself with the moderate voices within the Muslim community. The arguments are cast within the language of formal equality, in which Muslim women must be treated the same as Muslim men, and ultimately, in which all women should have the same rights under a UCC. While the All-India Muslim Women's Association has very clearly articulated its opposition to a UCC, preferring instead to see reforms brought through the Muslim Personal Law

Boards within the community, the Hindu Right attempts to frame the All-India Muslim Women's Association's support for the judgement as the first step in a movement towards supporting a UCC. 'Muslim women will themselves have to come forward and fight for their own rights. They will realize that their salvation lies in a Uniform Civil Code'.

Following closely on the heels of the *talaq* decision was the Supreme Court's decision in *Sarla Mugdal, President, Kalyani and Ors.* v. *Union of India and Ors.*[61] The case involved the legal implications of Hindu men, originally married under Hindu law, who subsequently convert to Islam, and enter into second marriages. The court had to consider whether the second marriage could be solemnized, whether the first marriage would subsist, and whether the husband would be guilty of an offense of bigamy under section 494 of the *Indian Penal Code*. Kuldip Singh J. delivering one of the two concurring opinions, held that the second marriage would not be valid without having dissolved the first marriage. Singh J. further commented on the need for the central government to enact a Uniform Civil Code:

> Article 44 is based on the concept that there is no necessary connection between religion and personal law in a civilised society. Article 25 guarantees religious freedom whereas Article 44 seeks to divest religion from social relations and personal law. Marriage, succession and like matters of a secular character cannot be brought within the guarantee enshrined under Articles 25, 26 and 27. The personal law of the Hindus, such as relating to marriage, succession and the like all a sacramental origin [sic.], in the same manner as in the case of the Muslims or the Christians. The Hindus along with Sikhs, Buddhists and Jains have forsaken their sentiments in the cause of the national unity and integration, some other communities would not, though the Constitution enjoins the establishment of a 'common civil code' for the whole of India.[62]

These comments suggest that all other religious communities have been secularized, and that it is only the Muslims and Christians who are standing in the way of 'national unity and integration'. But, in his subsequent comments, Kuldip Singh J.'s view of the Muslim community come into sharper focus. First, he expressly criticizes the practice of polygamy, by approvingly noting that the practice has been prohibited in the United States, in the name of public morality.[63] Kuldip Singh J. then states:

> Those who preferred to remain in India after the partition, fully knew that the Indian leaders did not believe in two-nation or three-nation

> theory and that in the India Republic there was to be only one
> Nation—the Indian Nation—and no community could claim to remain
> a separate entity on the basis of religion.... In this view of the matter
> no community can oppose the introduction of human civil code for all
> citizens in the territory of India.[64]

This reference to Partition and to the choice to remain in India is, like
the reference to polygamy, a reference to the Muslim community alone.
Christians did not have another 'choice' to make in relation to Partition.
Rather, the discourse of 'choosing' to remain in India after Partition has
long been a message—indeed a warning—to Indian Muslims from the
Hindu Right.[65] Moreover, the references in these passages to 'civilized'
and 'human' in relation to the Uniform Civil Code suggests that those
who oppose the code [read 'Muslims'] are barbaric and uncivilized. The
decision is deeply problematic, both in its suggestion that Hindu family
laws are entirely secularized and absolved of all discrimination against
women; and in its construction of the Muslim community as the uncivilized, enemy to national integrity. The language of the decision, in
deflecting attention away from the continuing religious and discriminatory aspects of Hindu personal law, and in attacking the Muslim community, is disturbingly similar to the political rhetoric of the Hindu Right.
In this view, all religious communities must be treated the same; and in
this view, it is the dominant Hindu community which is to be the norm
against which equality is judged.[66]

Not surprisingly, the Hindu Right has welcomed the decision with open
arms, and begun to deploy it in support of their continued call for a
Uniform Civil Code. The chief minister of the Shiv Sena–BJP government in Maharastra has stated that his government is considering imple-
menting a Uniform Civil Code.[67] Joshi has indicated that he is seeking
legal advice on how to implement the Code, and referred to the comments
of Supreme Court Justice Kuldip Singh to further justify the legal
necessity for this implementation.[68] In an effective discursive move, Joshi
attempts to construct his government's position as simply complying with
the rule of law: 'The Supreme Court has asked the Centre to implement
the Code and the Maharashtran government feels that the Supreme
Court's instruction should be complied with'.[69] The Hindu Right continues to support a Uniform Civil Code, as a means realizing its vision of
secularism (formally equal treatment of all religious communities) and
its vision of equality for women (treating all women the same, but treating
them differently from men). It is advanced as a women's rights issue, in
which the Hindu Right attempts to position itself as the defender of the
rights of women within minority communities. Yet, it does so in a way

that does not fundamentally challenge its position on gender difference within its own community. Moreover, the campaign to have all religious communities treated according to the same basic legal provisions is not seen as a threat to Hindu norms and practices, since the Hindu Right's version of the Uniform Civil Code would be one that would be based most closely on existing Hindu norms and practices. The Hindu Right's position on the Uniform Civil Code again highlights the majoritarianism implicit in a formal model of equality. The unstated norm of the Hindu majority remains the reference point against which others are judged, and into which these others are expected to assimilate.

■ The Rights of Muslim Women

While Muslim personal laws, and the campaign for a Uniform Civil Code has provided the most frequent focus of the Hindu Right's effort to position itself as the great defender of Muslim women's rights, it has not been the only focus. The Hindu Right avails itself of virtually every opportunity that comes along to denounce the Muslim community because of the way women are treated. The *Organiser* never fails to report on some atrocity or indignity committed against Muslim women, either within the Muslim community in India, or within the surrounding Muslim countries. For example, the Hindu Right took up the cause of Taslima Nasreen, in the fatwa controversy that has emerged around this Bangladeshi writer. The fatwa was first issued in September 1993, after the publication of her novel *Lajja*—a story of the plight of a Hindu family in Bangladesh persecuted in the aftermath of the destruction of the Babri Masjid in December 1992. The stakes were increased following an interview in the *Statesmen*, in May 1994, in which Nasreen called for a reform of religious texts that oppress women. The fatwa was reasserted. Facing increasing protests and calls for Nasreen's death, the Bangladeshi government brought blasphemy charges against her. Nasreen has since fled the country, and is living in exile.

In this controversy, the Hindu Right has again attempted to position itself as the great defender of free speech from the threat of fundamentalist censors. The obvious parallel is drawn between the fatwa issued against Salman Rushdie, and the banning of *Satanic Verses* in India in 1989. In the hands of the Hindu Right, the parallel serves the equally obvious purpose of an attack on the Muslim community. The rhetoric of freedom of expression, much like that of equality, is deployed to construct the Muslim 'other' as the great violator of democratic rights, and to deflect attention away from the similar absence of a respect for free expression within its own ranks.[70] And once again, within the context of the Nasreen controversy, the Hindu Right becomes the self-appointed champion of the rights of Muslim women, and deploys the violation of these rights as a way of attacking the Muslim community as a whole. Taslima Nasreen comes to play the same discursive role as Shah Bano; only more so, because her very life is at risk. In taking on this issue, the Hindu Right aligns itself with the secular movements, opposed to this fundamentalist attack on Nasreen, and in so doing, endeavours to further constitute itself in and through the discourse of secularism. Within the context of the Muslim 'other,' freedom of expression is deployed by the Hindu Right to construct itself as the real secularists.

Freedom of expression proves to be as elastic a concept in the hands of the Hindu Right as equality. The violation of freedom of expression, like the violation of the right to equality, is located exclusively within the community of the 'other'. It is the Muslim community that violates women's rights to equality, just as it is the Muslim community that violates women's rights to freedom of expression. By focusing attention on the violation of rights within the 'other' community, the Hindu Right is able to deploy the concept of freedom of expression in a manner that deflects attention away from the extent to which its own position on other expression issues could be seen to be a violation of this right.

There is an interesting correspondence between the Hindu Right's understanding of freedom of expression and equality. In the context of the Muslim community, the violation of freedom of expression is seen through the lens of formal equality—to allow Muslims to violate freedom of expression by censoring speech is yet another marker of a 'pseudo-secularism,' which gives special treatment to the minority community. But, within the context of 'obscene' representations of women, the violation is seen through and obscured by the lens of a very different understanding of equality. State censorship of obscene representations is seen to be required in the interests of women's equality. Women must be treated differently; they must be respected; returned to the position of respect that is rightfully theirs as wives and mothers. These two very different positions on freedom of expression can thus be seen to reflect the two very different positions of equality. For Muslims, it is measured as sameness, but for (Hindu) women, it is measured as difference.

The Gendered Discourses of Hindutva

Equality, in the hands of the Hindu Right, remains an elusive, but enormously useful concept. It is, on the one hand, consistently deployed as equal treatment to attack the rights of religious minorities. But, in the context of gender, such consistency seems to evaporate. Two very different models of equality are simultaneously deployed in the Hindu Right's political rhetoric on women. In the context of Hindu women, equality for women is understood as harmony in diversity. Hindu women need not be treated the same as men in order to be treated equally. Rather, they need only be treated with respect, and with due recognition of the 'natural' differences between the sexes. Within this model, there is a celebration of difference and a quest for harmony. But, in the context of minority women, the two models of equality converge. There is an insistence that all women be treated the same—that Muslim women be treated the same as Hindu women. The equality rights of minority women are framed within the Hindutva discourse of secularism and formal equality—wherein all religious communities must be treated the same, and in turn, wherein all women within different religious communities must also all be treated the same. Here, there is no talk of harmony, nor celebration of difference, only a quest for assimilation and sameness.

But, this formal model of equality and its insistence on sameness is not extended to the relationship between women and men. Women's 'natural' differences from men are maintained, while women's 'artificial' differences from one another are erased. The underlying discourses of gender difference for Hindu and Muslim women are, then, strikingly similar. The reference point for equal treatment is religion, rather than sex. It is different religious communities that must be treated the same, not different sexes that must be treated the same. Equality for Muslim women thus means equal treatment with Hindu women—it does not as a rule mean equal treatment with either Muslim men or Hindu men. For both Hindu and Muslim women there is an affirmation of gender difference, in which women are understood as different from men, and a common understanding of the relevance of this gender difference. Women and men are different, and these differences must be respected and accommodated in law. While the nature of these differences is simply asserted as natural and inevitable, we have tried to reveal the extent to which these differences are constituted in and through discourses of revivalism and familialism. For Hindu and Muslim women alike, gender difference is constituted through a familial ideology, which constructs women as wives and mothers. Alongside a revivalist discourse, emphasizing the return to a glorious past, the gendered discourse of Hindutva insists that women be respected and honoured in these roles as wives and mothers. The problems that women face in contemporary society are seen through this lens of a fall from grace—that the harmony that came of respect and honour of women's distinctive roles as wives and mothers in the past has been lost and must be restored.

While both Hindu and Muslim women are constituted through this discourse, they are differently located in relation to it. Hindu women are to be restored to the position of respect they enjoyed within their own culture. Muslim women, however, must be restored to the position of respect enjoyed by Hindu women before they were degraded by the influence of and conversion to Islam. The phenomenon that lead to the downfall of women is ultimately identified as the same: the invasion of India by foreign (Muslim) influences. As one VHP poster rather blatantly states: 'Women lost all their glory and liberty in the dark period of history when India was invaded by barbarians'.[71] The revivalist discourse attempts to restore all women to the position they enjoyed prior to the invasion of, and resulting downfall of, Hindu culture. The unstated reference point is the Muslim invasion of Hindu culture. At the core of this revivalism is a highly communalized discourse, deployed to promote anti-Muslim sentiment. In this respect the gendered discourses of Hindutva can be seen as part and parcel of the Hindu Right's assault on minority communities. The problems that women face in contemporary society can be blamed on a fall from grace—but blame for this fall from grace can be placed on Muslims.

At the same time, the communalized dimension of the gendered discourse of Hindutva is not sufficient in itself to understand the complexity of this discourse. The women's rights agenda is not entirely derivative of the communalism of the Hindu Right. The discourse of women's equality and the appropriation of particular women's issues must also be seen within the context of the lived realities of women within the Hindu Right, and the changing demands on these women at the end of the twentieth century. Women's issues are being taken up, in part, because women within the Hindu Right themselves have named them as issues. And the way in which these issues are being articulated, the discursive framework within which these issues are being named and taken up, must be seen within the broader context of a fundamental redefinition of women's identities.

In many ways, the emphasis on respecting women as wives and mothers in the gendered discourse of Hindutva sounds unchanged from the early days of cultural revivalism and nationalism in the nineteenth century. Indeed, there are important similarities and discursive continuities between the contemporary discourse and its historical antecedents. But, there are also many important ways in which this discourse is not just like its earlier version. The contemporary discourse is very much a product of the historically and materially specific conditions of women's lives in the last decades of the twentieth century. In this section, we will examine this specificity of the discourse on women. We attempt to draw some connections between these gendered discourses of equality and women's rights, and the broader discursive project of reconstituting and renegotiating Indian women's identity in a period of rapid socio-economic transformation. We will consider the specifically ideological nature of the gendered discourse of Hindutva, in attempting to reveal the connections between ways of seeing the world, and the underlying socio-economic conditions of contemporary India. We are not suggesting that the discourse of Hindutva can be seen as a simple reflection of economic change; rather, simply that it is important to understand the particular nature of Hindutva's discursive strategies and their discursive power within the broader context of these underlying material realities.

■ Women and the New Tradition

As we have argued in our discussion of equality and the women's rights agenda, the contemporary discourse of the Hindu Right relies heavily on the language of tradition. The language of respecting and honouring women, of returning women to their rightful place of honour bears more than a slight resemblance to the debates throughout the nineteenth century of the women's question, where women became the site of the rearticulation of tradition, and the reconstruction of Indian history and identity.[72] It is reminiscent of the discourse of women's uplift, used by the social reformers in the nineteenth century, and one faction of the women's movement in the early twentieth century. The discourse of women's uplift was deeply imbued with familial ideology, emphasizing women's roles within the family. Campaigns to improve women's conditions were justified in the name of improving women's ability to perform their roles as wives and mothers, thereby strengthening the family.

But, the emphasis on culture and tradition, and on the important role of women in upholding this tradition, bears a greater resemblance to the gendered discourse of the cultural revivalism and nationalism of the nineteenth century. The language within which the Hindu Right is appropriating and articulating women's issues draws on many of the same discursive elements: the need to restore respect for women in their roles as wives and mothers within the family, and the focus on women as the site of Hindu culture and tradition more generally.[73]

This discursive continuity lies not only in the rhetoric of tradition but, perhaps more significantly, in the extent to which the rhetoric of tradition represents a selective and modern reinterpretation of history. Feminist historians in India have examined the extent to which the discourses on women in the nineteenth century, imbued with the rhetoric of tradition and culture, were in fact thoroughly modern discourses.[74] As Lata Mani has argued in relation to the nineteenth century discourse on sati:

> ...it was a modern discourse on tradition. It exemplifies late eighteenth century colonial discourses that elaborated notions of modernity against their own conceptions of tradition. I suggest, in other words, that what we have here is not a discourse in which pre-existing traditions are challenged by an emergent modern consciousness, but one in which both 'traditional' and 'modernity' as we know them are contemporaneously produced.[75]

Feminist historians, along with others, have persuasively demonstrated the need to subject the discourses of tradition to historical interrogation, to reveal the extent to which these discourses are reflections of the period within which they are articulated. Historians have similarly attempted to reveal the extent to which the contemporary discourse of the Hindu Right, and its emphasis on tradition, are selective and thoroughly modern reinterpretations of the past.[76] As we will attempt to illustrate, the contemporary gendered discourse of the Hindu Right is similarly one in which both 'tradition' and 'modern' are, as Mani suggests, 'contemporaneously produced'.[77]

Notwithstanding the discursive continuity of the language within which the Hindu Right is articulating women's issues, there are important ways in which the discourse represents a break from its historical antecedents. First, the appropriation of the language of equality marks a significant departure from the language of Hindu revivalists in the nineteenth century. The claim that women are equal was not one that was characteristic of the cultural revivalists. Indeed, the language of equality was not part of this early nationalist discourse. Even well into the twentieth century, Hindu nationalists rejected the language of equality as western.[78] In the discourse of the cultural revivalists, women were seen to represent the spiritual domain far removed from the material influences of the public sphere.[79]

Second, the contemporary discourse on women can also be seen to mark a significant departure from past discursive practice in its attention to women's employment. In the past, women's identity was constituted as exclusively within the private sphere. Debates over women's education in the nineteenth century extended this sphere somewhat, as social reformers advocated schooling for girls. Yet, these debates over education remained firmly located within women's roles as wives and mothers within the family. Those who supported women's education argued that such education would only strengthen women in their familial roles.[80]

Education was not supported as a means of changing or challenging the private, familial sphere as women's appropriate domain. In contemporary discourse, however, women's identity includes their roles in the labour market. While these new roles continue to be framed within the discourses of tradition and familialism, women's identity is moving beyond the private sphere of the family, and into the public sphere of work.

This emphasis on the need for women to attain equality, and to work outside of the home, has lead to a new emphasis within the rhetoric of the Hindu Right on meeting the challenge of modernization. For women, modernization is posited in opposition to westernization. A central discursive component of Hindu communalism for women has become one of constituting the identity of 'modern, but not western'. This identity for women was clearly articulated by Uma Bharati at the All India Women's Sammelan in New Delhi in May 1994.

> Modernization does not mean Westernization. Our women should become doctors, scientists and engineers, but this modernization need not take away Indian Culture and values from our women.[81]

The theme of 'modern but not western' is directed specifically at women.[82] It is women who must guard against losing their cultural traditions and identity. This message is directed specifically to women's roles in the family. As is common to many nationalist movements, women are identified not only as biological reproducers, but as cultural reproducers, with the special responsibility of transmitting 'the rich heritage of ethnic symbols and ways of life to the other members of the ethnic group, especially the young'.[83] It is in their roles as wives and mothers, as guardians of the tradition to be passed on to younger generations, that women of the Hindu Right must guard against encroaching westernization. As an article in the *Organiser* supporting the need to educate women against the practice of sex selection argues:

> Indian woman today is at the crossroads. Firstly, she has to attain her status in society which will be consistent with modernity. Secondly, she has to perform her duty as the vehicle of culture and nationalism. She has to preserve the ancient culture of India, rear the children and make them ideal citizens.[84]

This identity of 'modern but not western' which recurs throughout the rhetoric of the women's wings of the Hindu Right, corresponds to what Rajeswari Sunder Rajan has described as 'the new Indian woman,' 'perennially and transcendently wife, mother and homemaker, who saves the project of modernization—without westernisation'.[85]

This distinction between modernization and westernization is important in the way the women's wings of the Hindu Right distinguish themselves from the secular women's movement. The Mahila Morcha writes, for example:

We conceptually differ from what is termed as the women's liberation movement in the west. We require a sort of readjustment in the social and economic set up. No fundamental change in values is desirable. Women in India ever had a pride of place within the household, and the society. That has only to be re-established and re-affirmed.[86]

Mridula Sinha similarly writes: 'In spite of all this glorious background the Indian woman today has to fight a sustained and long drawn battle to achieve the goal of complete equality. This can be fulfilled not by blind imitations of the modes and techniques of struggles adopted by the so-called liberated women of the west'.[87] Manohar Joshi, criticizing the dominance of western feminism and its emphasis on 'free sex, physical relationships with men, unmindful of marital status, the growth of lesbianism and in this situation artificial pregnancy' at the Fourth World Women's Conference in Beijing, similarly admonished Indian feminists for 'imitating the western women libbers' and 'aping the failure of their western sisters'.[88] A more extreme, though not entirely dissimilar, position is found in the writings of RSS ideologues. K. R. Malkani argues that 'the position of women is better in India than anywhere else in the world,' and that the RSS '...would consider women's "libbers" as the worst enemies of woman kind'.[89] The secular women's movement is thereby dismissed by its association with the West, and the women's wings of the Hindu Right become the 'authentic' voice and guardians of the interests of Indian women.

This emphasis on 'modern but not western' has parallels with nineteenth century revivalist discourse on women. Much like this earlier discourse, women continue to be posited as the site for retaining and reconstituting Hindu tradition and culture. In the contemporary discourse of the Hindu Right, culture is again designated as a sphere distinct from material life.[90] Women's identity continues to be constituted through the discourse of tradition and culture, in which women are the site of the opposition to the crass materialism of westernization. The discourse of tradition is very similar, in so far as it posits culture as a separate sphere. At the same time, much like the discourse of tradition in the nineteenth century was a response to nineteenth century conditions, this discourse of tradition is a thoroughly modern discourse, responding to the materially and historically specific context of late twentieth century India. And in much the same way as revivalist discourse in the nineteenth century disguised the fundamental social, economic and political changes that were taking place, Hindutva discourse in the late twentieth century is also operating to 'disguise, mitigate, compensate, contest' fundamental transformations in the social, economic and political landscape, and the role of women therein.

At one level, this new identity can be seen as a response to the contradictory effects of the politicization of women within the Hindu Right. As Tanika Sarkar has argued, the politicization and mobilization of women has become an important dimension of the mass character of the Hindu Right. At the same time, this politicization 'makes it imperative...to reinforce the boundaries of control over women'.[91]

> At this peak moment within the right-wing mass movement, when women of its own circles need to be mobilized for the spread of the movement, when the movement itself grants women as unprecedented visibility and voice, it becomes ever more imperative to recover, gather, and articulate the submerged patriarchal assumptions, to tighten them up and indicate firmly that the new public role needs to be contained within a war against the Muslims.[92]

The need to reinforce the boundaries of control over women becomes all the more imperative in the context of the fundamental economic transformations in contemporary India. Amrita Chhachhi has argued that the development of state sponsored religious fundamentalism, alongside the increased demand for women's labour market participation may not be coincidental.[93] She suggests that religious fundamentalism may be providing an important new legitimating ideology, to keep women under patriarchal control, at the same time as they are moving beyond the narrow confines of the private sphere. We can see this discursive strategy in the context of the new Hindu woman of Hindutva. The new identity of 'modern but not western' is providing legitimacy not only for the increasing political role of women, but also for their increasing economic role, that is, the increasing demand for women's work within the labour market. This identity, which recognizes women's role in the public sphere, while protecting their cultural integrity as the guardians of culture and tradition, is in many respects, the perfect ideological companion to the economic restructuring of the new economic policies. Women may work outside of the home—but their identity remains first and foremost as wives and mothers. And as wives and mothers, women are the guardians and purveyors of Indian tradition and culture. The Hindu Right is attempting to reconstitute an identity for women that firmly reinscribes women's roles within the family, while embracing the demands of contemporary consumer capitalism and global economic restructuring.[94]

This new identity of 'modern but not western,' of the new Hindu woman as strong wife and mother, is all the more useful in the context of the renegotiation of the public and private spheres engendered by the new economic policies. As we discussed in chapter 2, the new economic policies are resulting in a reduction of the public sphere, and an expansion of the private. It is a process within which services provided by the state are being reprivatized, and in which the role of both the market and the family are being expanded. This renegotiation of the public and private sphere includes a formidable increase in women's roles, not only within the economy, but also within the family, as the family is called upon to provide more and more of the services once provided by the state. Women are being called upon not only to work outside of the home, but also to perform and/or manage more work inside the home. The identity of the new Hindu woman, as strong wife and mother, is an identity that corresponds to the call for women to perform more work—both inside and outside of the family. The new Hindu woman is a woman who can respond to all of the demands of contemporary consumer capitalism—she can rise to the call of modernization, yet she can continue her role as the guardian of culture within her family. This renegotiation of the public and private, and the process of reprivatization is producing what Janine Brodie has referred to as the 'reconstitution of the domestic,' which she argues '...rests on imposition claims about the role and value of the hetero-patriarchal family as foundation for society'.[95] This reconstitution of the domestic is evident in the increasing emphasis on the family and family values within the political rhetoric of the Hindu Right. The importance of family was very clearly articulated at the 1994 All India Women's Sammelan in New Delhi. According to Usha Tai Chati, head of the Rashtriya Sevika Samiti, the 'family [is] the bedrock of a society and any evil in society first takes root in the family and then spreads. Therefore, women have to safeguard the values and culture in the family'.[96] Women are being explicitly called upon to protect the family, and in so doing, to protect Hindu society from moral degeneration.

Efforts to shore up the family, and women's role therein often accompany periods of political, social and economic transformation. As Valentine Moghadam has argued, 'Crisis and transition seem to bring about an exaggerated reliance on the home and family as refuge for the assaulted identity'.[97] The increasing role of the family in the political discourse of the Hindu Right can be seen within the context of the

fundamental transformations occurring in social and economic relations
in India. The Hindu Right's discourse on women is an effort to ensure
that neither the mass politicization of women, nor their increasing integration into the labour market, undermine the patriarchal family, nor
women's roles as wives and mothers therein. Unlike the revivalist discourse of the nineteenth century, women's identities are being reconstituted to explicitly include their roles within the public sphere. The Hindu
Right's discourse on women and equality can be seen as an effort to
contain the challenge that this renegotiation presents to the traditional
patriarchal family. Within this discourse, women remain the repositories
of tradition and culture, and the primary site for performing the role of
cultural progenitor remains the family. Familial and revivalist discourse
become the terms on which women are permitted to move beyond the
confines of the private sphere. It is the discourse through which women's
new political and economic roles are being negotiated and articulated.

The particular 'women's issues' which have been appropriated by the
Hindu Right can be seen as part of this effort to renegotiate the boundaries
between the public and private, and reconstitute women's identity without
undermining the patriarchal family. The issues of employment and education are taken up, in recognition of the new economic role of women
with the new economic policies. At the same time, these roles are
controlled and justified in the name of the family. For example, while
supporting women's education and employment, parental consent is the
sine qua non for such opportunities for young women of the Hindu
Right.[98] Similarly, issues of violence against women must be addressed
as women come more and more into the public sphere.[99]

> Thrust into public and mixed spaces for the first time, women encoun-
> ter yet new forms of overt or covert sexual discrimination and violence.
> It is no wonder that the physical training programmes of the shakhas
> prove extremely attractive to such women, with the promise of a
> powerful body and the attendant self-confidence. That body and that
> mental attitude that it generates would be vital [sic] shield against
> gender oppression within domestic as well as public spaces.[100]

It is the violence that women experience within the public sphere that is
the easiest for the Hindu Right to address. Violence in the public sphere
operates as an obstacle to women's employment and education, and
constitutes a threat to women's identities as wives and mothers.

Indecent representations of women are similarly cast as a threat to
women's identity as the site of culture and tradition, and to the precarious
balance that is being negotiated between their roles within the public and

private spheres. While the issue of the indecent representation of women can be seen as a product of the mass media revolution in India, alongside the increasing visibility of women within the public sphere, this concern with the representation of women is deeply rooted in the discourses of Hindu revivalism and nationalism. In the nineteenth century, it was women and women's bodies, which as Tanika Sarkar has described, operated as 'a pure space that escaped the transformative effects of colonization'.[101] As in the nineteenth century, it is women—and women's bodies—who are the cultural signifiers of the opposition to westernization. From the importance attached to dress, to the repression of obscene representations, women's bodies continue to symbolize this pure space, which must be continuously protected from corruption and degradation. The concern with the indecent representation of women can be seen as a contemporary form of resistance to the incursion of western culture—where women and women's bodies remain the repositories of tradition; where these bodies must be protected from western corruption.[102] The opposition to sexualized representations of women is part of this resistance to the westernization of women. And the need for the protection of women is only heightened with the increasingly visible role of women within the public sphere. It is part of the 'modern but not western' identity that is being constituted for women.

The reconstitution of women's identity hardly requires a radical disjuncture with dominant representations of women. Rather, the very ideological power of the Hindu Right's discourse on women lies in its reliance on a familial ideology that remains all too dominant. The image of women as wives and mothers is one that remains firmly embedded in legal regulation, as well as in a broad range of social relations. Women within the Hindu Right, whose subjectivities and life experiences are shaped by this dominant familial ideology, are taking up issues that affect them, and articulating these issues in ways that make sense to them. Women experience the world in large part through their roles as wives and mothers—it is in and through this lens that these women are articulating the issues that concern them.[103] In this respect, it is important to emphasize that the 'women's rights' agenda of the Hindu Right is not being imposed by the ideologues of the Hindu Right, but rather, is being taken up and named by women themselves. As Shelley Gavigan has argued, 'ideologies are effective only when not imposed by fiat from above'.[104] The dominant familial ideology which underlies the women's rights agenda of the Hindu Right is effective precisely because it is not being imposed by fiat, but rather, because of the way in which it shapes the subjectivity of women within the movement, who in turn, are shaping the discourse within which these issues are being articulated.

The Hindu Right is playing into an image of women that continues to be part of the collective common sense. And it is doing so in a way that appropriates some of the few incursions that have been made into this familial ideology by the secular women's movement. Women's employment, violence against women, the indecent representation of women—issues that the secular women's movement has fought long and hard to bring into the public arena—are being taken up in ways that do not challenge the dominant ideological construction of women as wives and mothers. While familial ideology once operated to preclude any recognition of employment or violence as political issues, in the hands of the Hindu Right, this familial ideology is now being deployed to ensure that attention to these issues does not challenge the centrality of the patriarchal family. It is the very ideological stronghold of the family that allows and shapes the way in which women within the Hindu Right to take up women's rights issues. Issues like violence and employment are articulated within the legal discourse of rights, without fundamentally challenging or displacing this familial ideology. The way in which the Hindu Right has begun to appropriate women's issues is thus illustrative not only of the elasticity of familial ideology, but also of its resilience.[105] The legal discourse of equality does not challenge or displace this familial ideology. Rather, familial ideology continues to provide the discursive framework within which equality rights are given meaning.[106] In the context of the Hindu Right, and its particular approach to equality as harmony in difference, familial ideology continues to shape the understanding of gender difference. Women continue to be constructed as naturally different—as dutiful wives and self sacrificing mothers—and according to the harmony in diversity model of equality, these differences must be respected and celebrated. Familial ideology and the harmony in diversity model of equality are mutually reinforcing in the gendered discourses of Hindutva. Women's issues can thereby be recognized and addressed in ways that not only do not challenge the family, but which ultimately reinforce its ideological hegemony.

Conclusion

In this chapter, we have examined some of the ways in which legal discourse is being deployed within the discursive strategies of the Hindu Right. We have demonstrated the efforts of Hindu nationalists to redefine the basic concepts of secularism and equality, in accordance with their political vision of Hindutva. We have argued that at the root of their vision of secularism is a particular model of equality—a formal model of equality—which undermines any claim to the recognition of minorities. At the same time, we have tried to reveal that in the context of women, the Hindu Right is pursuing a very different model of equality, based on the principle of harmony in diversity. This model of equality was shown to underlie the Hindu Right's position on a broad range of women's issues, in which the discourse of women's rights is deployed to rearticulate a familial role for women. The exception to this rule is in relation to minority women's rights, when the formal model of equality is again articulated. In the context of women from minority communities, the Hindu Right reverts to the emphasis on sameness, as a means of attacking the legal recognition of religious and ethnic differences. Yet, underlying this formal model of equality is a particular understanding of gender equality: all women are to be treated the same, but they are not necessarily to be treated the same as all men. These two models of equality converge to allow the Hindu Right to delegitimize the recognition of cultural difference, without challenging the assertion of natural gender difference.

Further, we have tried to demonstrate the important role of familial ideology in the discursive strategies of the Hindu Right. The appropriation of a broad range of women's issues is framed within the discourse of familialism, in which women's 'natural' roles as wives and mothers are rearticulated. At least part of the ideological appeal of the Hindu Right lies in the extent to which it deploys this already hegemonic ideology, which we have seen in earlier chapters to deeply imbue the legal regulation of women. Indeed, it is precisely the ways in which women's issues are being appropriated by the Hindu Right within this ideology of familialism that presents the greatest challenge to the secular women's movement. The issues of violence against women, which have become important political issues largely through the efforts of the secular women's movement, are being taken up in a way that is depoliticizing. The critique of the family, and of the systemic subordination of women within the family, is replaced by a discourse which naturalizes and glorifies women's roles within the family. This familial ideology allows the Hindu Right to take up some of the issues that are of increasing concern to the women within its ranks, without threatening the patriarchal structure of the family, and the roles of women therein. The issues are framed in a way that allows them to be addressed and contained at the same time.

The Hindu Right's discursive struggle for ideological hegemony includes an effort to rearticulate an identity for women, thoroughly imbued with the discourses of family and tradition, and yet, thoroughly rooted in the material conditions of the late twentieth century. In this chapter, we have attempted to illustrate the extent to which legal discourse is being deployed by the Hindu Right in this rearticulation of identity. We are not arguing that legal discourse is central to this project. Nor are we suggesting that this project is central to the political and ideological agenda of the Hindu Right. Our arguments are rather more modest in suggesting that legal discourse plays a role in this agenda, and that it plays a particular role in relation to women. It is one among a range of discursive fields that are deployed in the effort to rearticulate women's identity in a way that will forward the general political agenda of Hindutva.

Finally, the chapter has provided an example of the way in which legal discourse and equality rights are not necessarily progressive in nature. While the women's movement, and other progressive marginalized groups have deployed this discourse in pursuit of struggles for social change, we have seen in this chapter an example of groups with less progressive agendas similarly appropriating and deploying this discourse. The Hindu Right has been quite successful in articulating its political agenda within the language of secularism and equality, at the same time as its vision undermines much of the prevailing understandings of these concepts. Within the context of women, the Hindu Right is articulating women's issues within the language of rights, at the same time as it attempts to reinscribe women's traditional roles within the family. The Hindu Right is forwarding a political agenda that is diametrically opposed to the agendas of progressive social and political movements. Yet, much like these movements, the Hindu Right is doing so with the language of rights. This question of the relative political value of rights discourse, and the counter-hegemonic potential of law, will be considered in greater detail in the next chapter, in the broader context of attempting to develop concrete strategies for engaging with law.

NOTES

1. Bipan Chandra, *Communalism in Modern India* (Delhi: Vani Educational Books, Vikas Publishing House, 1984). See also B. Anderson, *Imagined Communities* (London: Verso, 1983).
2. For a discussion of the roots of communalism in nineteenth century colonialism, and of its subsequent shaping by nineteenth century revivalists and nationalist movements, see Gyanendra Pandey, *The Construction of Communalism in Modern India* (Delhi: Oxford University Press, 1990).

3. Tapan Basu et al., *Khaki Shorts, Saffron Flags: A Critique of the Hindu Right* (New Delhi: Orient Longman, 1993) at 2.

4. As Basu et al. have argued, it has done so by claiming to represent the totality of Hindu society: '...[I]t asserts that it already includes the whole of Hindu society as it stands here and now, and that an exact correspondence exists between its own field and the boundaries of an admittedly varied, pluralistic, differentiated Hindu world' (*ibid.* at 56).

5. An example of this inroad can be seen in the decision of the Supreme Court in *Dr. Prabhoo* v. *Kunte* 1995(7) SCALE 1 (and 12 other decisions rendered simultaneously by the court, including *Bal Thackeray* v. *Kunte*, and *Manohar Joshi* v. *Nitin Bhaurao Patil*, all dealing with charges brought against members of the Hindu Right for allegedly violating the *Representation of the People Act, 1951*, which prohibits the use of religion to solicit votes). On the question of whether the use of the term 'Hindutva' constituted a violation of the prohibition of the use of religion to garner votes, Verma J., speaking on behalf of Singh J. and Venkataswami J., stated at 22: '...the term "Hindutva" is related more to a way of life of the people of the subcontinent...Ordinarily, Hindutva is understood as a way of life or state of mind and it is not to be equated with, or understood as religious Hindu fundamentalism'. The court, in equating the term 'Hindutva' with the use of the term 'Hinduism', similarly stated, at 24: 'It is, therefore, a fallacy and an error of law to proceed on the assumption that any reference to Hindutva or Hinduism in a speech makes it automatically a speech based on the Hindu religion as opposed to the other religions or that the use of 'Hindutva' or 'Hinduism' per se depicts an attitude hostile to all persons practicing any religion other than the Hindu religion'. Although the court's statement vis-à-vis the use of the term '*Hinduism*' is not particularly controversial (and is reasonably consistent with past Supreme Court jurisprudence) the equation of 'Hindutva' is a rather extraordinary turn. The term 'Hindutva' has historically been, and remains today the exclusive terrain of the Hindu Right. Yet, the court's willingness to simply equate it with 'Hinduism' erases the political meaning of this term. Moreover, this understanding of Hindutva as 'a way of life of the people of the subcontinent' illustrates the extent to which the Hindu Right has captured the heart and minds of its subjects, and increasingly become a part of the collective common sense. Although the court did find that many of the individuals charged, including Bal Thackeray, the leader of the Shiv Sena were in violation of the *Representation of the People Act*, the judicial comments on Hindutva have set a very dangerous precedent.

6. See chapter 3 for a more detailed discussion of this formal approach to equality.

7. For example: 'The Bhartiya Janata Party urges the...Government to so conduct itself that no citizen gets any feeling that he is discriminated against, or unfavourably treated'. BJP, *Report of the National Executive Committee* (Chandigarh, January 1986) at 7.

8. *Ibid.* as quoted by L. K. Advani, Speech to Parliament (7 November 1990).

9. K. Jayaprasad, *RSS and Hindu Nationalism* (New Delhi: Deep and Deep, 1991) at 93. See also Nana Deshmukh, *RSS: Victim of Slander* (New Delhi: Vision Books, 1979).

10. BJP, *Towards Ram Rajya: Mid Term Poll to Lok Sabha, May 1991: Our Commitments* (New Delhi, May 1991).

11. 'Minorities Commission Scrapped in Maharashtra', *Asian Age* (7 June 1995).

12. *Ibid.*

13. L. K. Advani, quoted in 'Secularism, A Premium on Belonging to a Minority,' Interview with Advani, *Blitz Magazine*; reproduced in *Nation's Hope* (1991) at 25.

14. Balasaheb Deoras, *Balasaheb Deoras Answers Questions* (Bangalore: Sahitya Sindhu, 1984) at 53.
15. See Martha Minow, 'Foreword: Justice Engendered' (1987) 101 *Harvard Law Review* 10; and *Making All the Difference* (Ithaca, NY: Cornell University Press, 1990).
16. See, e.g., H. V. Seshadri, *The Way* (New Delhi: Suruchi Prakashan, 1991) at 51, speaking of the majority Hindu community: 'Give us also the rights which are now enjoyed by others. Apply the principle of equality before the law to all. Stop discrimination against us'. See also Seshadri, 'Strange Political Diction', *Organiser* (4 February 1990). Balasaheb Deoras frequently invokes the same rhetoric of equal treatment and equality before the law. For a typical example, see 'Bharat Bhoomi is Hindu Bhoomi', *Organiser* (14 October 1990) (address of RSS chief Shri Balasaheb Deoras).
17. M. S. Golwalkar, *Bunch of Thoughts* (Bangalore: Vikrama Prakashan, 1966) at 16.
18. *Ibid.* at 18.
19. *Ibid.*
20. *Ibid.* at 19–20.
21. Seshadri, *The Way, supra* note 16 at 113.
22. *Ibid.* at 115.
23. *Ibid.*
24. *Ibid.*
25. See Manini Chatterjee, 'Saffron Extremism', *Frontline* (16–29 January 1993) (on sants and sadhus within the Sangh Parivar calling for a restoration of Hindu polygamy) at 5.
26. See Tanika Sarkar, 'The Woman as Communal Subject: Rashtra Sevika Samiti and Ram Janmabhoomi Movement', *Economic and Political Weekly* (31 August 1991) 2057–62.
27. Mrinal Pande, 'BJP and Puri Sankaracharya', *Mainstream* (19 February 1994) 7.
28. *Ibid.*
29. BJP, 'Our Five Commitments' (Policy Statement, 1984) at 18.
30. BJP Mahila Morcha, 'Women's Decade: Mahila Morcha Response', *Dashak Ke Jharokhe Mein* (1991) at 3.
31. *Ibid.* at 4.
32. 'Our Five Commitments', *supra* note 29: 'Another sure way of producing security for women is to enlarge the employment in areas and sectors that suit them most'. Policy statements include a concern with women's employment. While there is little elaboration as to what areas these might be, another document provides that women should be primary school teachers. The Mahila Morcha, on the other hand, has stated that training for women should not be confined to such traditional areas as sewing and toymaking, but rather should 'be expanded to cover areas like light engineering'. ('BJP Mahila Morcha Decries Rising Crime Against Women', *Organiser* [15 September 1985] at 14.)
33. Mridula Sinha, 'Women's Equality—Miles to March', *Organiser* (1 September 1985) at 5.
34. *Ibid.* See also Murali Manohar Joshi, 'Western Feminism: Second Among Equals', *The Asian Age* (8 December 1995).
35. *Organiser* (31 October 1993).
36. *Asian Age* (4 June 1995).
37. See Pradip Dutta et al., 'Understanding Communal Violence: The Nizamuddin Riots', *Economic and Political Weekly* (10 November 1990).
38. See, e.g., 'Rashtra Sevika Samiti Protests Atrocities Against Kashmiri Women', *Organiser* (Deepawali Special, 1990) at 61.

39. See the following articles: 'Brutal Stoning of a Young Bangladeshi Women', *Organiser* (14 February 1993) 8; 'Inhuman Sex and Family Laws in Pakistan', *Organiser* (13 March 1988) 8 (addressing atrocities against women in Pakistan).
40. Tanika Sarkar, 'The Women of the Hindutva Brigade', *Bulletin of Concerned Asian Scholars* (December 1993) 16–24 at 19.
41. As Paola Bachetta argues in 'All Our Goddesses Are Armed: Religion, Resistance and Revenge in the Life of a Militant Hindu Nationalist Woman', *Bulletin of Concerned Asian Scholars* (1993) 38–52 at 47: '...[T]he violence internal to the regime (the self-hatred, misogyny, aggressiveness and violence that would otherwise cause trouble between Hindu males and between them and Hindu women) is projected onto the entity the "muslims"'.
42. Amrita Basu, 'Feminism Inverted: The Real Women and Gendered Imagery of Hindu Nationalism', *Bulletin of Concerned Asian Scholars* (1993) at 29.
43. Sarkar, *supra* note 40 at 23.
44. 'Ban on Sex Determination by Pre-Natal Tests—Maharashtra Government Bold Step', *Organiser* (31 January 1988) 7.
45. *Ibid.*
46. 'Rashtra Sevika Rally', *Organiser* (11 February 1990) at 7.
47. Amrita Basu, describing an interview with Bharati, writes that she '...spoke vehemently against the exploitation of women's bodies in advertising and the media and favoured strict censorship to control pornography' (*supra* note 42 at 30).
48. *Supra* note 10 at 30.
49. *Times of India* (20 April 1995) 1 at 1.
50. It is perhaps not coincidental that the Minister's promise follows closely on the heels of urging by the Maharashtra police to grant them powers to directly confiscate 'obscene materials'. See 'Police Seek Power to Seize Porn Material', *Times of India* (27 March 1995) 7.
51. *Savvy* (September 1995) 134–38, at 134, 137. Navalkar heavily emphasized the distinction between public and private in the context of vulgarity. Sex shows and cabarets, provided that they were performed in secluded places are not, in his view, a problem. 'When I go for a cabaret show to a small hall on the third floor of a hotel it is okay. But if this same show is performed on the streets, I will not tolerate it'. The Minister even uses this distinction to justify his own attendance at such shows: '...yes, I did attend sex shows in Paris. There is nothing wrong with it, so long as it is not being done on the streets' (at 137).
52. The *Report of the Media Advocacy Group: People's Perceptions: Obscenity and Violence on the Small Screen* (May 1994) [hereafter *MAG Report*], is an important recent example of the issue of obscenity being taken up by some within the secular women's movement. The *MAG Report* concluded that television viewers are increasingly 'angry and disgusted at the rising obscenity levels of films and programmes on television' (*ibid.* at 12). Film songs were identified as 'the worst offenders' which were seen to lead to eveteasing and sexual harassment (*ibid.* at 13). The *MAG Report* was also particularly concerned with the impact of the representation of sex and violence in the mass media on children. The *MAG Report* has set off a national debate on obscenity and vulgarity, and a call, in many quarters, for stricter censorship. At the National Symposium on Violence and Vulgarity in Mass Media, organized by the Centre of Media Studies, many high profile government officials denounced the increasing obscenity, vulgarity and violence in popular culture. Justice Ranganath Misra, Chief Commissioner of the Human Rights Commission, Jayanti Patnaik, Chairperson of the National Commission on Women, Kamala Manekar, member of

the Censor Board, and Kiran Bedi, were among those present who denounced this trend, and called for more stringent censorship. The recent debate illustrates that it is not the Hindu Right alone that is concerned with issues of obscenity. Moreover, the recent debate is illustrative of the way in which feminist arguments on the degrading impact of sexist representations are often appropriated by those with less feminist inclinations. At the National Symposium, many participants were far more concerned with the assault on traditional Indian culture and family values than with sexism and/or sexual harassment. For an opposing feminist view, see *Shifting Boundaries: A Report and Commentary on the Workshop on Women, Law, and the Media* (Center for Feminist Legal Research, New Delhi, October 1994).

53. Shohini Ghosh, 'Masquerade and Carnivalesque as Resistance: A Feminist Reading of the 'Choli' Song from Khalnayak' (unpublished paper, citing *Filmfare*, July 1993) at 28–32.

54. This shifting of responsibility from individual men to sexually explicit representations has appeared in several rape decisions. In *Phul Singh* v. *The State*, A 1980 SC 249, Krishna Iyer J. reduced the sentence of an individual convicted of rape partly on the grounds that 'modern Indian conditions are drifting into societal permissiveness what with proneness to pornos...sex explosion in celluloid and book stalls etc'. More recently, in *Reepik Ravinder* v. *State of Andhra Pradesh*, (1991) *Criminal Law Journal* 595, the court again suggested that sexually explicit representations may need to be taken into account in sentencing. The accused was convicted of raping a five year old girl. The court held that the fact the accused had seen 'blue films' which would have generated the instinct 'to practice the act that culminated in the offence' would be 'an essential factor to be considered before inflicting punishment'. A similar attitude is reflected in the comments of Pramod Navalkar, *supra* note 51, at 137, on the proposed restrictions imposed on barmaids who are to stop work at 8:30 p.m.: 'Barmaids working very late into the night cause a law and order problem. And they can't even take care of themselves. In fact, only recently a case was discovered where barmaids were raped by men of the same gang...Let me be frank. Let them go to hell. Let them work all night long. But somewhere, as guardians of the state, we have to guide them and maybe even prepare certain guidelines regarding this issue'. Instead of placing the blame on men for their violent actions, the blame here is placed on the women, for being in public spaces at 'inappropriate hours'.

55. Mridula Sinha, *supra* note 33 at 7, writes: 'It is a tragedy that in the eyes of the law, the concept of Indian womanhood is non-existent. They are Hindu women, Muslim women, and Christian women.... The emancipation of the Indian women will remain a far of cry as long as a Uniform Civil Code is not passed'. The BJP Mahila Morcha has repeatedly campaigned in favour of a UCC 'so as to equally cover all Indian women' ('BJP Mahila Morcha Decries Crimes Against Women', *Organiser* [15 September 1985] at 14.)

56. The Shah Bano case is discussed in detail in Asghar Ali Engineer, ed., *The Shah Bano Controversy* (Delhi: Orient Longman, 1987); Amrita Chhachhi, 'Forced Identities: The State, Communalism, Fundamentalism and Women in India', in Deniz Kandiyoti, ed., *Women, Islam and the State* (Philadelphia: Temple University Press, 1990) 162; Zakia Pathak and Rajeswari Sunder Rajan, 'Shah Bano' (1989) 12:3 *Signs* 558; Zoya Hasan, 'Minority Identity, the Muslim Women's Bill Campaign, and the Political Process', *Economic and Political Weekly* (7 January 1989).

57. 'The National Executive [of the BJP] regards this move to amend section 125 Cr.P.C. as retrograde, anti-women and a surrender to obscurantism and bigotry' (BJP, *supra* note 7).

58. *[New Delhi] Sunday Times* (24 April 1994). For an insightful discussion of the impact of the triple *talaq* judgement on women, see Flavia Agnes, 'Triple Talaq Judgement: Do Women Really Benefit?' *Economic and Political Weekly* (14 May 1994) 1169. Flavia Agnes argues that the judgement in fact operates to undermine the position of Muslim women by affirming the discriminating provisions of the *Land Ceiling Act.*

59. *Organiser* (1 May 1994) at 2.

60. It is an issue that similarly allows the Hindu Right to attack the divorce practices of another minority—the Christian community. According to Christian divorce law, a man can divorce his wife on the basis of her adultery alone, but a woman can only obtain a divorce from her husband on the basis of adultery plus another ground—cruelty, bigamy, etc. This double standard has periodically been the focus of critique by the Hindu right.

61. *J.T.* 1915 (4) S.C. 331.

62. *Ibid.* at 345.

63. *Ibid.* at 345.

64. *Ibid.* at 346.

65. This message is rampant within the discourse of the Shiv Sena who repeatedly attack 'Muslim traitors' and warn those Muslims who have remained in India to 'shape up' or 'get out'. It was precisely these kinds of messages that were at issue in the case brought against *Saamna*, the Shiv Sena newspaper, discussed at *infra* note 70. And in the court's view, it was the fact that the *Saamna* passages only directed their message at 'Muslim traitors', and not all Muslims that justified the speech, and thereby exempted it from the prohibitions on the promotion of religious hatred.

66. Justice R. M. Sahai, in a concurring opinion, similarly called upon the government to enact a Uniform Civil Code, which in this view 'is imperative both for protection of the oppressed and promotion of national unity and solidarity' (*ibid.* at 348). Although the language of the concurring decision is somewhat more measured that Kuldip Singh J.'s opinion, the implications of the decision are similar: the personal law of minorities violates human rights, and in the interests of national unity should be replaced with a Uniform Civil Code.

67. 'Maharashtra to Try for Uniform Civil Code: Chief Minister Seeks Legal Advice', *Asian Age* (4 June 1995).

68. *Ibid.*

69. *Ibid.*

70. The Hindu Right has no consistent position on freedom of expression. While the BJP has been careful not to take a pro-censorship position, and advocates, for example, a free press, the Hindu Right has no qualms calling for the suppression of speech that it finds offensive. The internal inconsistencies in the position of the Hindu Right can be seen in comparing and contrasting two other recent controversies: Sahmat and *Saamna*. Sahmat, a cultural organization established in 1991 to promote secularism primarily through art and music, organized an exhibit in 1993 which displayed diverse versions of the Ram legend. The exhibit included a passage from an ancient text—the *Dasratha Jataka* (400–200 BC)—which describes Sita and Ram as sister and brother. The BJP objected to the passage, which in their view suggested that Ram and Sita had an incestuous relationship, and created a national controversy around the issue. The panel on which the text was exhibited was confiscated, and Sahmat was prosecuted under the *Indian Penal Code* for promoting religious enmity and disharmony (sections 153(a) and 153(b)). *Saamna* is a Marathi daily newspaper, associated with the Shiv Sena, the more militant section of the Hindu Right. Two petitioners—J. B. D'Souza, a former state chief secretary and Dilip Thakore, a former editor—filed a writ in 1993

seeking an order for mandamus from the Bombay High Court to direct the government to prosecute Bal Thackeray (the head of the Shiv Sena) and Sanjay Raut (the editor of the *Saamna*) under sections 153(a) and 153(b) of the *Indian Penal Code* for promoting religious enmity and disharmony. The Bombay High Court rejected the petition in September 1994, on the grounds that the articles in question did not violate the law. In the case of Sahmat, the Hindu Right supported the use of the criminal law to censor speech that violated their version of religious tradition. But, in the case of *Saamna*, the Hindu Right decried the violation of their freedom of expression. For a more detailed discussion of these and other controversies regarding expression, see Ratna Kapur, 'Who Draws the Line? Feminist Reflections on Speech and Censorship in India', (Forthcoming *Economic and Political Weekly*, 1996) which is part of a larger work in progress on feminism and the politics of speech in India.

71. VHP advertisement in *Indian Express*, as cited in Ammu Joseph and Kalpana Sharma, 'Between the Lines: Women's Issues in English Language Newspapers', *Economic and Political Weekly* (26 October 1991) at 80.

72. See Kumkum Sangari and Sudesh Vaid, 'Introduction', in Sangari and Vaid, eds., *Recasting Women: Essays in Indian Colonial History* (New Delhi: Kali, 1989) 88; Tanika Sarkar, 'Rhetoric Against Age of Consent: Resisting Colonial Reason and Death of Child Wife', *Economic and Political Weekly* (4 September 1993) 1869; Lata Mani, 'Contentious Traditions: The Debate on Sati in Colonial India', in Kum Kum Sanaari and Sudesh Vaid, eds., *Recasting Women: Essays in Indian Colonial History* (New Delhi: Kali, 1989).

73. Uma Chakravarti, 'Whatever Happened to the Vedic Dasi? Orientalism, Nationalism, and a Script for the Past', in Sangari and Vaid, eds., *Recasting Women: Essays in Indian Colonial History* (New Delhi: Kali, 1989) 27.

74. See Chakravarti, *ibid*. See also Mani *supra note* 72.

75. Mani *supra* note 72 at 116.

76. See, e.g., Romila Thapar, 'Imagined Religious Communuties?: Ancient History and the Modern Search for a Hindu Identity (1989) 23:2 *Modern Asian Studies* 222.

77. Mani, *supra* note 72.

78. Golwalkar, *supra* note 17.

79. See Partha Chatterjee, 'The Nationalist Resolution of the Women's Question', in Sangari and Vaid, eds., *Recasting Women: Essays in Indian Colonial History* (New Delhi: Kali, 1989). See also Sarkar, *supra* note 60.

80. See Chatterjee, *supra* note 79 at 245–47.

81. Uma Bharati, quoted in 'The Hindu Woman Rises', *Organiser* (22 May 1994) at 1.

82. Tanika Sarkar's work has raised some questions of the extent to which this 'modern but not western' identity has been embraced by women within the ranks of the Hindu right. In analyzing the articles and views expressed in *Jagriti*, the journal of the Rashtra Sevika Samiti, she has observed: 'It is interesting to see that while the more authoritative statements—Golwalkar, RSS strictures, and Samiti's official accounts—applaud the new Hindu women for resisting Western modernism, women's own articles, when they deal with their everyday problems and perceptions, are little concerned about Western modernity' (in Basu et al., *supra* note 3 at 85). Sarkar's work suggests that the message of 'modern but not western' is not yet one that is hegemonic, in so far as it may not yet be embraced as part of the common sense of the women of the Hindu Right. Yet, the message is one that is increasingly repeated in the official pronouncements of the women's wings.

83. Nira Yuval-Davis and Floya Anthias, eds., *Woman-Nation-State* (New York: St Martin's Press, 1989) at 9.

84. *Supra* note 44.
85. Rajeswari Sunder Rajan, *Real and Imagined Women: Gender, Culture and Post-colonialism* (London: Routledge, 1993) at 133.
86. *Supra* note 30 at 120.
87. Sinha, *supra* note 31.
88. Joshi, *supra* note 34. Joshi argues that the West has nothing to offer Indian women, who should turn instead to their own history: 'Historically, the social relationships and institutions in India are patterned in such a manner, that a balanced evolving structure of social amity is created.... The Indian woman has always contributed in every way, to the growth of a social order. From the Vedic period to the struggle for India's freedom, till now, the Indian woman has played a key role in the family and outside and makes a sincere effort to keep the home protected. This institution has fallen apart in the West resulting in shattered individuality, where in society, the relationships are based on selfishness, not selflessness...the concept of women's emancipation in countries where Eve is considered to be a creation from Adam's rib can have no comparison with the Indian concept of Ardhnarishwar (half part as man and half part as women make the individual a form of God)'.
89. K. R. Malkani, *The RSS Story* (New Delhi: Impex India, 1980) at 172 and 175.
90. Partha Chatterjee, *supra* note 79.
91. Sarkar, *supra* note 40 at 22.
92. *Ibid.*
93. *The State, Religious Fundamentalism and Women: Trends in South Asia* (Working Paper—Subseries on Women, History and Development: Trends in South Asia) by Amrita Chhachhi (The Hague: Institute of Social Studies, 1988).
94. The Hindu Right's economic approach is still being fought out. On the one hand, the BJP has officially adopted 'swadeshi'—a form of economic nationalism boycotting multinational manufactured products, particularly in consumer products. On the other hand, the Shiv Sena government in Maharashtra, has not accepted 'swadeshi'. Yet, the Shiv Sena's on-going battle with the multinational Enron is illustrative of the tensions within its own position. The government 'threw them out' on the basis of economic nationalism. But it subsequently renegotiated a 'better' deal for Maharashtra with Enron.
95. Janine Brodie, *Politics on the Margins: Restructuring and the Canadian Women's Movement* (Halifax: Fernwood, 1995) at 53. See also Janine Brodie, 'Shifting the Boundaries: Gender and the Politics of Restructuring', in Isabella Bakker, ed., *The Strategic Silence* (London: Zed, 1994).
96. Chati, as quoted in 'The Hindu Woman Rises', *supra* note 81.
97. Valentine Moghadam, ed., *Identity Politics and Women: Cultural Reassertions and Feminisms in International Perspective* (Boulder, Colorado: Westview, 1994) at 16.
98. Tanika Sarkar's work on women in the Samiti has revealed that the Samitis work with women in and through their families, never in opposition to their families. Women's participation in the Samitis is completely contingent on their families' consent. 'Parental consent and discipline are revered as the ultimate court of decision, and Samitis see themselves as an arm of, rather than brake on, family control' (*supra* note 40 at 21). See also Sarkar, *supra* note 26.
99. Sarkar, *supra* note 26.
100. Basu et al., *supra* note 3 at 84–85.
101. Sarkar, *supra* note 40.
102. Pornography, along with prostitution and promiscuity, are frequently identified by fundamentalist movements as immoral threats from western culture. See generally, Moghadam, *supra* note 97.

103. The way in which women within the Hindu Right are articulating issues in and through the lens of familial ideology bears a strong resemblance to women's participation in right wing movements more generally. Women come into politics with a particular vision of their roles as wives and mothers—roles in which they are valued and affirmed—which in turn shapes their political demands. See generally Moghadam, *supra* note 97. On women in the anti-abortion movement in the United States, see Kristin Luker, *Abortion and the Politics of Motherhood* (Berkley: University of California Press, 1989). Luker demonstrates that women first involved in the anti-abortion movement in the late 1970s were overwhelmingly housewives who were defending a vision of women as wives, and particularly as mothers, which reflected the reality of their own lives. As Rebecca Klatch has argued, '[f]ar from suffering from false consciousness, in fact, social conservative women are well aware of their interests and act to defend their status as women' ('Women of the New Right in the United States: Family, Feminism and Politics', in Moghadam, *supra* note 97).

104. Shelley Gavigan, 'A Parent(ly) Knot: Can Heather Have Two Mommies?', paper presented at the Institute for Feminist Legal Studies Seminar Series, Osgoode Hall Law School, Toronto, September 1994, at 9. A shorter version of this paper appears in Didi Herman and Cari Stychin, eds., *Legal Inversions* (Chicago, Chicago University Press, 1996). As Gavigan further writes, the 'utility of ideology as an analytical concept is that it helps us understand the appeal and hold on our captured hearts and constrained imaginations, and the fact that one's sense of social reality finds resonance'. Gavigan relies on and develops the work of Terry Eagleton, *Ideology* (London and New York: Verso, 1991), and Doug Hay 'Property, Authority and the Criminal Law', in Doug Hay et al., *Albion's Fatal Tree: Crime and Society in Eighteenth Century England* (New York: Pantheon, 1975).

105. Gavigan, *ibid.*

106. Susan Boyd, 'Child Custody, Ideologies, and Employment' (1989) 3 *Canadian Journal of Women and the Law* 111; Susan Boyd, 'From Gender Specificity to Gender Neutrality? Ideologies in Canadian Custody Law', in Carol Smart and Selma Sevenhuijsen, eds., *Child Custody and the Politics of Gender* (London: Routledge, 1989) 126; Brenda Cossman, 'Family Inside/Out' (1994) 44 *University of Toronto Law Journal* 1.

5

Feminist Legal Revisions: Strategies for Engaging with Law

Imagination is the faculty of transforming the experience of what is into a projection of what could be, the faculty that frees thought to form ideals and norms.

Iris Marion Young
Justice and the Politics of Difference*

Then she would turn to me and say, 'You *are* going to transform this world, aren't you? You are going to create a planet without walls and without frontiers, where the gatekeepers have off every day of the year'. Long silences would follow her speeches, but the beauty of her images would linger on, and float around the courtyard like perfumes, like dreams. Invisible, but so powerful.

Fatima Mernissi
Dreams of Trespass: Tales of a Harem Girlhood†

We have seen the extent to which familial ideology informs the legal regulation of women, both inside and outside of the family. In chapter 2, we explored the ways in which this familial ideology constitutes and reconstitutes women as economically dependent wives and mothers, and sustains their subordination within the family. In chapter 3, we examined the extent to which constitutional challenges to legal discrimination against women have been limited by familial ideology. Attempts to resort

---

* Princeton: Princeton University Press, 1990.
† Massachusetts: Addison-Wesley Publishing Co., 1994.

to constitutional equality rights discourse have often been defeated by assumptions of women's natural roles and responsibilities within the family. In chapter 4, we have further seen the extent to which legal discourse is being used to advance the political agendas of reactionary social movements. The Hindu Right is appropriating the discourses of equality and secularism to further their own Hindutva campaign—a campaign which includes the rearticulation of women's roles and identities as wives and mothers within the family.

The question that we must now consider is, in light of all these limitations, how can law be used, if at all, to advance the women's movement. Can law and legal discourse be a subversive site? As we have seen, law is limited in important respects. Yet, relinquishing the terrain of law would be to surrender a powerful site in discursive struggles for ideological hegemony. Law remains an important discourse in the construction of gender and communal identity. Relinquishing law would be to leave the terrain to communalist and other patriarchal discourses. Feminists must continue to engage with law, and the broader discursive struggles over the construction of identity. But, we must do so in a way that reflects the complex and contradictory ways in which law regulates and constitutes women. We will argue that law can play an important role in feminist struggles. However, we believe that this role can only be realized with a fundamental shift in the way that we conceptualize law. Law has not been able to provide definitive answers to the problems that women confront in their lives. Nor do we believe that law will ever be able to do so. We believe, on the contrary, that we must stop thinking about law exclusively in these terms. As we argued in chapter 1, engagements with law should be reconceptualized as discursive struggles, where competing normative visions of the world are fought out. Feminist engagement with law can be seen as an effort to transform the meaning of equality, gender and gender difference. It is part of an effort to challenge dominant meanings, and the construction of women therein and supplant these meanings with alternative visions about women's roles and identities in the world. Law's role should be reconceptualized as including one of process. It may be the process of engaging with law—of litigation, of law reform, of legal literacy—that will offer the most to feminist struggles, and that may be able to most empower women. It is the process of engaging with law that may be able to best promote women's participation in decision-making. Instead of measuring strategic engagements with law only in terms of the legal result, winning or losing, law's role can be seen as, and measured against the extent to which it is successful in creating democratic space for women's participation in political, social, economic and cultural life.

In this chapter, we revisit this question of the role of law in social change. We begin by reviewing the debate over the role of rights in social movements. We argue that this rights debate has produced a more sophisticated and complicated understanding of both the possibilities and limitations of rights discourse in struggles for social change, which must inform our strategic engagement with law. Despite the limitations, law remains an important site of feminist struggle. In the subsequent sections, we then set out strategies for engaging with law at three different levels: litigation, law reform and legal literacy. We attempt to bring our understanding of the limitations and possibilities of law to each of these levels of engagement.

The Rights Debate: Can Rights Discourse Advance the Political Agendas of Social Movements

Debates have raged on the role that law can play in challenging existing social relations, and particularly, in improving the social, economic and political conditions of disadvantaged groups. This is a debate between progressive legal scholars and activists who reject the liberal notion of law's neutrality and objectivity; it is a debate between those who believe that law plays an important role in maintaining unequal power relations. The point of disagreement among these scholars and activists is whether law can be flipped on itself, that is, whether the same discourse that sustains the subordination of women and other disadvantaged groups can be used to challenge this subordination. It is, in the often quoted words of Audre Lorde, a debate over whether the master's tools can be used to dismantle the master's house.[1]

This debate has focused on the role of rights discourse and, particularly, of constitutional rights discourse in the struggles of disadvantaged groups. Critical legal scholars in the United States, and socialist legal scholars in Canada and Britain, although differing in significant ways, have questioned the efficacy of rights discourse in these struggles.[2] For a number of different reasons, it is argued that rights discourse is ultimately unable to represent the interests of marginalized and disadvantaged groups. Some critical legal scholars have argued that rights are individualistic and formalistic and thus unable to address the systemic and structural ways in which disadvantaged groups are oppressed. Some argue that constitutional rights are negative by nature, that is, these rights are, at best, capable of restricting state power, not conferring positive benefits.[3] Others have focused on the abstract nature of rights claims, and the ways in which rights discourse deprive struggles of their political character. In Canada, this critique, known as the legalization of politics school, has argued that rights discourse is deeply embedded in the dominant discourse of liberal legalism—a discourse within which power relations are obscured, and political claims are decontextualized and deradicalized.[4]

This critique of the utility of rights discourse has been met with considerable resistance. Some black and feminist writers have attempted to defend the role of rights in struggles for social change.[5] Patricia Williams argues, for example, that rights discourse remains important for those people who have never had rights. She argues that rights remain an important political signifier for black women and other disadvantaged groups.[6] Elizabeth Schneider similarly argues that rights discourse has been an important and effective political strategy for the women's movement. Her vision of the role of rights within these strategies, however, is a reconceptualized one. She argues that the arbitrary distinction between law and politics must be deconstructed, and that rights claims must be seen within the broader context of political strategy.[7] According to Schneider, rights can be important in consciousness-raising, in mobilizing marginalized groups, and in providing these groups with a powerful language with which to voice and legitimize their demands. Like Williams, she accords considerable significance to the symbolic power of rights claims in current political discourse and sees this representational power as efficacious in feminist struggles for social change.

Along similar lines, some Canadian feminists have attempted to develop an approach to sexual equality rights in particular, that undermines the abstract nature of rights discourse. The Women's Legal Education and Action Fund (LEAF)—an organization of feminist lawyers and activists set up in 1985 to promote and litigate sexual equality constitutional challenges—has developed a 'contextualized approach to sexual equality'. This approach begins with, and argues from, women's experience as a subordinated group. This insistence on contextualizing equality rights within the specificity of women's subordination is seen as an effective way to counter the decontextualizing and abstract nature of rights discourse, and as an important way to advance women's equality.[8]

Other feminist and legal scholars remain more skeptical about the role of rights discourse, even in its reconceptualized vision. Carol Smart, for example, while recognizing the important role that rights struggles in the past have played for the women's movement, particularly in winning formal equality rights, argues that 'the rhetoric of rights has become exhausted and may even be detrimental'.[9] She argues that casting political claims in rights discourse can 'oversimplify complex power relations', and give the impression that acquiring rights has in fact resolved power differentials.[10] Smart further argues that rights specifically intended to benefit disadvantaged individuals and groups 'can be appropriated by the more powerful'.[11] Judy Fudge, writing within the legalization of politics framework, has similarly challenged the role of rights in feminist mobilization, arguing that rights discourse can also mobilize conservative, anti-feminist groups.[12] She argues that there is nothing in rights discourse that 'precludes its use as a political symbol by a wider variety of groups which seek to attack state intervention designed to ameliorate hardships imposed by market ordering or socially embedded racist or sexist attitudes'.[13] Fudge argues that it is therefore not possible to evaluate rights strategies only in terms of mobilization. Rather, she argues that it is essential to consider the ways in which rights strategies may transform the political discourse. And in her view, this transformation is often depoliticizing.

As the rights debate continues to develop, feminists and other progressive scholars continue to complicate their analysis of the role of rights discourse in social movements. The question has become less one of which 'side' of the debate is right, and more one of applying the insights of the debate to particular strategies and campaigns in which social movements have deployed rights discourse. Kimberle Crenshaw, for example, has examined how the use of rights discourse by African-Americans has affected the nature of their political demands.[14] She has argued that while rights discourse was useful in attacking the denial of formal equality to African-Americans, it has also served to 'absorb, redefine and limit the language of protest'.[15] Judy Fudge has similarly explored the way in which the political demands of feminists struggles in relation to sexual violence have been transformed through the use of rights discourse.[16] Other progressive legal scholars have similarly argued for the need to recognize that rights discourse must be contextualized within broader social relations, including unequal relations of power. Joel Bakan has argued, for example, that it is important in evaluating the potential of rights in the discursive struggles of social movements to recognize that: '...rights discourse is not some free floating set of signifiers; it is connected at the root to historical and social forces, and existing social structures and institutions they have produced. Though rights discourse may not be conceptually fixed, it is historically and geographically anchored'.[17]

What are we to make of these debates? What is the role of law in social change? And more specifically, what are we to make of the role of law in the context of Indian women's struggles for social change? In the context of India, there is a history of disadvantaged groups resorting to law as part of their broader political struggle for empowerment. The people who will be displaced by the construction of the Narmada Dam, for example, have articulated their demands in the language of rights. They have resorted to the courts from time to time as part of their overall political strategy to prevent the construction of the dam. Rights discourse has played a role in mobilizing disempowered groups such as tribals (adivasis), and in raising their political awareness. A review of the most significant rape cases decided during the course of the past two decades—Rameeza Bee,[18] Mathura,[19] Suman Rani[20]—reveals that the litigant was invariably a working class, informally educated, rural woman. Although these cases did not always produce happy endings, particularly for the individual women involved, history nevertheless indicates how law has been resorted to by disadvantaged groups as part of their broader political strategy. Most recently, gay men have resorted to rights as a way to challenge the formal discrimination that continues to exist against such groups in law. In particular, the demands include the repeal of section 377 of the *Indian Penal Code*. Even though the provision is rarely used, the struggle for its repeal represents an ideological battle. The criminalization of certain types of sexual activity and the valourization of others becomes the basis for determining who is and is not eligible for state benefits and entitlements. Rights discourse is serving to forge a political identity for a group that has remained invisible and marginalized in the context of Indian society. At the same time, it is important to recognize that the use of rights discourse has not lead inexorably to radical social change. These struggles have been, at best, partially successful in challenging dominant social meanings, and have made considerably less inroad in changing social relations of inequality.

In our view, the rights debate can help us understand this complex and contradictory role of law. Rights strategies do seem to offer social movements useful tools for challenging the exclusion of disadvantaged groups. At the same time, it is important to heed the warnings of those who are somewhat more equivocal about this role. Rights are not 'free floating signifiers' that can simply be deployed at will to bring about social change. Rights discourse may be useful in the discursive struggles of social movements, but the extent of its power must be measured against the very real constraints of particular social and material contexts. Rights discourse may change and deradicalize the political content of a social movement. Rights discourse may be unable to displace other ideologically dominant discourses and the material structures in which these discourses are inscribed. Rights discourse may indeed provide an important and empowering language, but that is only the beginning rather than the end of the analysis of its potential in social movements.

We are of the view that these rights debates have advanced the understanding of both the limits of law and the possible uses of law in light of those limitations. Feminist legal scholars and activists are now forced to think about the role that law can play in struggles for empowerment in more complicated ways. Our study has suggested that all of the insights of the rights debate are partially valid. We have seen, for example, the extent to which equality rights discourse has been unable to challenge and transform underlying structural inequalities, like the sexual division of labour, that constitute and sustain women's subordination. We have also seen that legal discourse has been effectively appropriated by, and used to mobilize, reactionary social movements. Law is limited in important respects: it can depoliticize campaigns and undermine women's struggles for social change. Yet, in the first chapter we have also seen the importance of law and rights discourse in mobilizing the women's movement. Law can mobilize women, it can provide a language to challenge discriminatory laws and practices, and legitimize the struggle for formal equality rights. We have seen that the role of law is contradictory and that, in important respects, both sides of the rights debate are right.

In our view, law remains an important site of struggle. Law has been, and can continue to be, a site of discursive struggle with a subversive potential. It is a terrain on which the women's movement has challenged dominant constructions of gender, sexuality, and family. It is a terrain of contested meanings, where the women's movement has won important victories, particularly in condemning violence against women. Campaigns for law reform have provided opportunities for women to raise public awareness about issues that were previously unrecognized and/or simply accepted as a natural, unspoken part of life. Campaigns for law reform have forced those issues onto the public agenda, and challenged the construction of these issues as natural, incurable and/or private. At the same time, we have seen that the outcome of these campaigns has more often than not been highly contradictory. The use of rights discourse has come up against dominant and resistant discourses which have affected the outcome of these campaigns. While law is an important site of struggle, it is also one within which there are very real and material constraints.

We also believe that it is important to see these campaigns as vehicles to women's participation. Legal campaigns have been sites for fostering women's participation. The rights debate has further underscored the insights from the women's movement that it may be the process of engaging with law—be it litigation, law reform or legal literacy—that also offers promise to feminist struggles, and that may contribute to women's empowerment. It may be the process of engaging with law that can empower women to participate in decision-making and in the broader contest for meaning. As such, the reconceptualization of law may require a shift in emphasis—from outcome to process—a shift in which the value of participation takes on primacy. The history of the movement for women's rights has been a history of promoting women's full and equal participation in the world around them. In the struggle for formal equality, laws have been sought and enacted to remove legal obstacles to women's participation. From the right to hold property, to the right to widow remarriage, to the right to vote, legal reforms seeking to remove obstacles facing women have been sought. Similarly, attention to issues of violence against women, from sati in the nineteenth century to rape, dowry and domestic violence at the end of the twentieth century, can be seen as part of attempts to remove barriers to women's participation as full and equal members of their families and their communities. Affirmative action programmes—reservations for women in education, employment, politics—can again be seen as part of the efforts to overcome past disadvantage and promote women's participation in the world around them. The value of participation is thus hardly a novel objective in thinking about law and law reform. However, the way in which law can foster participation can be reconceptualized. As the women's movement has recognized, none of these laws has been sufficient to secure women's participation. While these reforms have been important in removing obstacles to participation and in progressively securing formal equality for women, they have not been able to secure substantive equality due to problems of access and chronic under-enforcement.

Although the campaigns to reform these laws may have been important catalysts in mobilizing women, the participation value of these laws dramatically drop once the reform is achieved. As the women's movement has begun to articulate, we need to recognize that the real value of the law reform—of the strategic engagement with law—may be in the campaign itself. It is as much the process of law, as the end result of law, that may be empowering for women. It is during moments of strategic engagement that women are most engaged. It is during these moments that women come together, form coalitions, articulate their political demands, and participate in contests over meaning. It is during these moments that women are engaged with law as discursive struggle—that they are actively seeking to displace previously dominant meaning with meanings that more closely approximate and capture their political vision. It is during these moments that law becomes a site of political contest, and potentially of political participation.

When revisioned in this light, these strategic engagements with law can be celebrated in their own right, rather than simply measured against an elusive standard of whether the law reform in question has improved women's lives. These engagements are not, however, without their attendant risks, not the least of which is the disillusionment that may follow in their wake. Perhaps the best way to minimize these risks is to take them seriously, and integrate them into the strategies. A consideration of these risks must form part of the reconceptualization of the role of law in feminist struggles, a reconceptualization which insists on beginning from a firm understanding of the limitations of law.

Improving women's lives through law is not an inconsequential objective—it should remain the explicit objective of strategic campaigns. However, neither litigation nor law reform in the past have lived up to the promise of social change. At best, such reform has been a symbolic contribution to the articulation of new social values and norms. This too is not insignificant, and must necessarily form a part of the women's movement's political agenda. The point is simply that feminists ought not to be discouraged or frustrated that these legal engagements, even when they are successful, do not bring about significant change in women's lives. The change is at best incremental—and can perhaps only be measured in terms of the changing social values that the reform embodies.

Legal strategies cannot and should not be abandoned in women's struggles. Rather, the more difficult question that will continue to present itself is when and how recourse to the law will be strategically viable. This shift towards a more complex and contextually specific analysis must involve broadening the debate. Breaking down the distinction between law and politics, and locating law within broader political struggles must include moving beyond what is often a narrow focus on constitutional rights discourse. An evaluation of the role of rights claims in social change must also include a consideration of the role of legislative rights, of law reform and of legal literacy strategies. Indeed, the distinction between law reform strategies and litigation strategies is an important one that has not been made sufficiently explicit in the debate. As Bartholomew and Hunt describe: '...law reform strategies [are] designed to transform rights-claims into legally recognised and politically enforceable legal or constitutional rights [whereas] ...litigation strategies employ court action, either defensively or aggressively as a means of advancing their rights claims'.[21] Strategies of invoking specific legislative rights, or of campaigning for new legislative rights may be of equal or greater importance in particular contexts. Further, the role of legal literacy has been all but ignored in these debates on the role of law in empowering disadvantaged groups. As we will argue, legal literacy strategies may have a dynamic role to play in these struggles. In evaluating the role of law, then, it is important to consider the law in all of these dimensions.

At the same time, it is important that rights discourse not be uncritically accepted as the focus of these struggles. Any attempt to use law must be informed by an understanding of the limitations and dangers of legal strategies. There must be a process of ongoing interrogation of if, when and how rights claims ought to be used. This process must include a consideration of how feminist litigation, law reform and legal literacy strategies can be made accountable to the broader social movement. Feminists must begin by locating legal claims within the political struggles of social movements. Shorter term objectives of both litigation and law reform strategies must not be allowed to dictate or undermine the long term political objectives of these struggles. Rather, the legal claims must be driven by, and accountable to, the more general and less specifically legal objectives of the social movement. These linkages are essential to prevent the struggles from being both isolated and reified in the legal forum, as well as to ensure that the social movement is not itself legalized, that is, that its agenda is not established by lawyers and individual litigants, but rather by the women within the social movement.[22] Otherwise, the effect of resorting to rights and law might well be de-mobilization rather than mobilization. To the extent that the value of process and participation has become central in this reconceptualization of the role of law, these linkages are essential. To ensure effective participation in any strategic engagement these linkages must be established prior to the development of a particular campaign, rather than simply tacked on as an afterthought. Real participation must involve some degree of participation in the initial decision-making and formulation stage of a legal strategy, not simply in the popular campaigns to which the strategy may give rise.

If legal discourse is potentially transformative, that is, if it has the potential to deradicalize the political claims of social movements, then it is essential to remain attentive to the ways in which political claims are translated into legal discourse. Feminists need to consider the extent to which political claims are being diluted in this process, whether there are ways to minimize the effect of this deradicalization by carefully choosing the language used, and whether those involved are prepared to accept the deradicalization of their claims in light of the particular objectives in any particular context. There may be times when political movements are unwilling to accept the transformative nature of legal discourse, and will choose not to pursue a legal claim. There may, however, be other times when the movement believes that the language it uses, both inside and outside the legal forums, will not jeopardize the nature of its political claims, and may in fact advance its struggles. Moreover, the transformative nature of legal discourse may play out in very different ways in the context of different legal strategies, that is, it may be more or less dangerous in the context of law reform and/or legal literacy. Feminists need to consider the risks within the context of specific legal strategies. Finally, the only way to guard against this danger of depoliticization is to recognize that it exists, and to remain vigilant in evaluating and reevaluating legal strategies. Feminists must also remain open, at all times, to the possibility that a legal strategy may not be the best option.

The following discussion is divided into three sections, which correspond to three different strategic uses of law: litigation, law reform and legal literacy. We will attempt to apply our insights on the contradictory role of law to each of these strategies for engaging with law. We will examine the ways in which a strategic engagement with law can in practice be made more complicated, and thus, be made to more fully embrace the contradictory nature of law in struggles for social change. Our efforts to classify these strategic uses of law, like all efforts at classification, is problematic, in so far as it may obscure the important relationships between and among these different forms of strategic engagement with law. For example, although constitutional rights litigation is a very different form of engagement with law as compared to legal literacy, both forms of engagement may be motivated by similar objectives. It may be necessary to engage in legal literacy before proceeding to litigation, and/or it may be possible to use litigation as a component of legal literacy. In the sections that follow, we will try to highlight and explore these and other connections between and among the different forms of strategic engagement with law.

Litigation

Litigation may have a role to play in advancing the political agenda of women's struggles for social change. But it is important that litigation strategies be rendered considerably more complex. Indeed, litigation is fraught with the many hazards and difficulties of feminist engagement. Lawyers and judges, by the very rules of the game, are the central players, and litigants must rely upon the professional skills and knowledge of their lawyers. It is hardly a model of participation and empowerment. However, we believe that it may still be an important forum for feminist engagement and that it may be possible to develop strategies that can better promote participation in the process. Further, we believe that litigation can be an important part of political strategies of the women's movement precisely because we believe that judicial decisions are important. As Jody Freeman has argued: 'Judicial decisions proclaim "truths" in the course of resolving particular disputes. Even if only indirectly or diffusely, judicial pronouncements can reinforce and alter social views'.[23] Freeman argues that 'it is important to challenge established meanings in legal discourse' in and through litigation 'because representations of reality are created and fixed in the form of judicial decisions and are then absorbed into the fabric of society, with broad and unpredictable effects'.[24]

In this section, we will discuss some of the factors that must be considered in developing and designing feminist litigation strategies. In the first section, we will consider the different forms that litigation can take and the different factors that may go into different forms of litigation. In the second section, we consider some of the difficult questions of responsibility and accountability that are raised by feminist litigation strategies which challenge the traditional solicitor/client relationship. In the third section, we will examine the content of litigation and some of the ways that we can complicate the nature of our legal arguments. In the fourth section, we raise the question of evaluation. Complicating our litigation strategies must also include complicating the way in which we evaluate the results of our strategies.

■ Multiple For(*u*)ms

In beginning to complicate our legal claims, we need to deconstruct the monolithic image of litigation. Litigation can take many different forms. Legal proceedings can be of a civil or criminal nature. The parties, procedures and remedies vary significantly between those two types of proceedings. Civil litigation involves a conflict between two or more private parties, whereas criminal litigation involves the state prosecution of individuals charged with criminal offenses. An equally significant distinction for the purposes of thinking about feminist litigation strategies is between defensive and offensive litigation. Offensive strategies involve initiating a legal claim, whereas defensive strategies involve defending or replying to a claim that is initiated elsewhere. Offensive litigation can

296SUBVERSIVE SITES

involve trying to enforce an existing legal right, or it can involve
challenging the constitutionality of a discriminatory rule or practice.
Defensive litigation can also involve trying to enforce or defend an
existing legal right, or it can involve trying to defend a rule or practice
from a constitutional challenge. There are, in other words, many different
ways of going to, or ending up in, court.

The criminal/civil and the offensive/defensive distinctions are cross-
cutting. Civil proceedings can be of an offensive or defensive nature. A
woman may initiate a legal proceeding, or she may have to respond to
a legal proceeding initiated by another party against her. For example,
she may bring an application for divorce, or she may be forced to respond
to her husband's application for divorce. Criminal proceedings can similarly be of either an offensive or defensive nature. Women may initiate
criminal proceedings by bringing a charge against a person who has
committed a crime against them. Alternatively, women may be accused
of a criminal offense, and forced to defend themselves against a state
prosecution.

There are very important differences in these forms of litigation. Choice
is perhaps the most significant factor. In offensive strategies, women can,
by and large, decide whether or not they should go to court. In defensive
strategies, the decision to initiate legal proceedings was made by another
party, and women have little choice but to defend themselves. The extent
of this choice, and of control over the legal proceedings vary in criminal
and civil cases. In civil cases, the individual directs the litigation. In
criminal cases, however, the individual only exercises choice in relation
to the initial decision to lay the complaint. The subsequent decision of
if, when, and how to prosecute rests with the state.

It is also important to recognize that there are important differences
within offensive litigation strategies. A legal proceeding can be initiated,
for example, to make an application for maintenance. Or, a legal proceeding can be initiated to challenge the constitutionality of maintenance
provisions. The former is an individual case—an attempt to secure a
remedy in an individual case. The latter has implications far beyond the
individual case. It can become a test case, which may affect the legal
regulation of a broad number of women. The decision to bring an
individual application for maintenance may involve a very different set
of factors than the decision to bring a constitutional challenge. There are
similar choices to be made within the context of defensive litigation. For
example in responding to an application for divorce or in defending
against a criminal prosecution, a woman may decide to bring a constitutional challenge to the civil or criminal provision in question. Such a
decision may transform the legal proceeding from an individual case to

a test case, and thereby significantly increase the social and political importance of the case.

It is also important to recognize that it is not only constitutional challenges that may become test cases affecting the legal regulation of women more generally. An individual application or defense can assume heightened importance if it raises a difficult, and as yet untested or unresolved point of law. An individual petition appealed to the Supreme Court may not only resolve the individual conflict but may further establish the law as it will affect all similar conflicts. A Supreme Court decision in an application for maintenance may resolve a point of law that will in turn affect all women seeking maintenance in a similar situation. It was, for example, an individual petition for maintenance under section 125 of the *Civil Procedure Code* which in the Shah Bano case became a question of the maintenance rights of all Muslim women, and which precipitated an unprecedented political controversy over Muslim personal law.

The implication of the case for the individual, the extent of the choice involved, and the precedential and symbolic value of the case are all important variables that must be considered in designing and evaluating feminist litigation strategies. As we will explore in the sections that follow, the extent of accountability may rise in accordance with the extent of choice exercised or with the precedential value of the case. Alternatively, questions of accountability or of mobilization may be inversely proportional to the risk to the personal liberty of the individual involved. We will explore these and other questions of the relationship between the form of litigation and strategic considerations of accountability, legal argument, and evaluation.

■ Representation and Accountability

Feminist litigation strategies raise some difficult questions of responsibility, representation, and accountability. According to traditional legal models of professional responsibility, lawyers are accountable to their clients. The rules of professional conduct are contained in the Bar Council of India rules, formulated under the *Advocates Act, 1961*. Section II of Chapter 2 on the Standards of Professional Conduct and Etiquette sets out a lawyer's duties to his or her client. Rule 24 states 'An advocate shall not do anything whereby he abuses or takes advantage of the confidence reposed in him by his client'. Further, section 35 of the *Advocates Act* provides that 'A lawyer must not, except with the client's consent, at any time disclose confidential information or use it otherwise than on behalf of the client'. Within this model, rights and responsibilities have been clearly established in the solicitor/client relationship. The lawyer takes instructions from the client, and the client alone, to whom she owes the responsibility to make the best possible arguments. All communications between a lawyer and her client are privileged.

Feminist litigation strategies present some difficult challenges to this traditional model of responsibility and representation. Women's organizations have come to play important roles in developing cases and supporting litigants. Women lawyers and activists are involved in framing the issues and setting the theoretical basis for the claim, with a view to the broader political agenda of the women's movement. This involvement raises a host of issues in relation to professional responsibility: how do these women's organizations fit within the traditional solicitor/client relationship? From who does the lawyer take instructions? Which communications are privileged? Which communications could be made subject to an order for disclosure? These dilemmas are heightened in cases in which feminist lawyers are involved, alongside activists, in shaping and supporting the case. Which lawyer is representing the client? How does the client relate to the various lawyers? Does the client's understanding and expectations correspond to the professional responsibility of the lawyers involved in the case?

Within the context of test case litigation, in which a women's organization adopts a particular case in an effort to move forward the political agenda of the women's movement, difficult questions arise in relation to client autonomy. Is the real client the individual aggrieved or the women's organization(s)? When women's organizations are playing the major role in framing the legal issue and developing the legal arguments, from whom are the lawyers to take instructions? To what extent are the women's organizations entitled to speak on behalf of the client in communications with the lawyers? How can the lawyers uphold their responsibility to protect the autonomy of their client if they are taking instructions from an organization with a political agenda. Who, in other words, is representing whom?

Some of these dilemmas have been encountered in the context of public interest litigation in the United States. Many public interest organizations interested in pursuing a test case or law reform litigation to advance their particular political agenda, such as the National Association for the Advancement of Coloured People (NAACP) and the American Civil Liberties Union (ACLU), carefully select their plaintiffs on the basis of their fit with the organization's objectives. The litigation is in turn directed in accordance with the organization's political agenda. Such politically driven litigation has raised a number of ethical considerations including the possibility of conflict in lawyer–client relationships. As some commentators have noted, there is a significant risk to a client's autonomy.[25] In such cases, clients loose their ability to direct the litigation. Decisions and priorities, normally set by clients, are often made by the lawyers, in accordance with the commitments and policies of the public interest organization. There is also the possibility of conflicts of interest between public interest lawyers and their clients in the resolution of the case. For example, a defendant, facing the prospect of a losing decision, may make an offer to settle. From the client's point of view the offer may be attractive. But from the public interest organization's point of view, waiting for a more positive decision would be the more desirable choice. Some commentators have observed these conflicts as a product of the fact that public interest lawyers and organizations have both clients and constituencies. While representing specific clients, public interest lawyers/organizations are, at the same time, advocates for 'a more loosely defined constituency or community'.[26] Others have suggested that in some cases, it is difficult to ascertain who the client actually is:

> A striking and significant aspect of the practice of public interest law is the frequency with which the lawyer's 'client' cannot be adequately described as the individual or organised group named as the client in a particular matter.[27]

Rather than the named plaintiff, it may be the public interest organization or its broader constituency that is more accurately described as the client.[28]

The potential conflicts within public interest litigation are not readily resolved, but rather, must be carefully negotiated on a case by case basis. Recognizing the possibility of such a conflict is an important first step in creating the space within which the conflict can be negotiated. The American critical race theorist, Derrick Bell, has issued an insightful warning: '[i]t is essential that lawyers "lawyer" and not attempt to lead client and class'.[29] Bell's words are a powerful reminder to public interest lawyers and, by extension, to feminist lawyers that their role is to take instructions from their clients. They may have an important role to play in devising innovative legal arguments, negotiating technical and political obstacles, and even helping organize clients and constituencies. But regardless of their political commitment, feminist lawyers and legal activists engaged in the project of trying to bring about social change through litigation must not forget their professional responsibilities.

We have argued that feminist engagement with law must be accountable to the broader social movement. This raises additional questions of how to achieve this kind of accountability and of how this accountability relates to the professional accountability of lawyers. These different lines of accountability raise the potential for conflicts of interests. The operating assumption has been that the interest of the various parties will correspond. But, what if, as is sometimes the case with public interest organizations, these interests do not correspond. What if the woman wants to accept a settlement, but the women's organization supporting her would prefer that she forego the settlement, and await a judgement that they hope will go in her favour; or what if the individual litigant wants to win at any cost, and therefore is willing to put forward an argument that the activists consider to be damaging to their political agenda? For example, in a case involving maintenance or divorce, should an individual woman make arguments that play directly into familial ideology by arguing that she was a good Hindu wife, and thereby increase her chance of success in the courts? Or, in the interest of not reinforcing an ideology that is damaging to women, should the individual litigant refrain from such argumentation? As we have discussed in previous chapters, familial ideology is highly contradictory. Although it constitutes women in subordinate subject positions, women whose lives correspond to the roles and identities of wives and mothers may be looked upon favourably by the courts, where women who deviate even slightly from those roles and identities may be penalized. An individual litigant who appeals to familial ideology may thereby be reinforcing the construction of women as wives and mothers, and the highly problematic norms and standards against which women are judged. How are these dilemmas between the short-term interest of the individual litigant, and the longer term objectives of political transformation to be negotiated and resolved?

This potential for a conflict of interest between the individual client and the social movement only further heightens the dilemmas of accountability. Does the lawyer take instruction from the individual litigant, or from the litigation committee? Who is the client? What happens to solicitor/client privilege? These questions highlight the importance of setting out the rights, rules and responsibilities of the various parties to the litigation. The rules of professional conduct may seem formal, abstract and apolitical to activists and other non-lawyers. There is no doubt some truth to this assessment. The rules can be difficult to accommodate with a more explicitly political engagement with law, and many rules need to be re-evaluated from the very standpoint of law as politics. Yet, many of the rules are important in guiding the behaviour of lawyers and in protecting the interests of the individual client.[30] The rules are a powerful reminder of the lawyer's accountability to her client; that it is the client and not the lawyer who should be directing the course of the litigation. To the extent that the traditional model of professional respon-sibility and accountability is challenged by feminist litigation strategies, feminists may need to develop their own guidelines on negotiating these conflicts and dilemmas.

Feminist legal scholars and litigators have begun to interrogate some of these questions and dilemmas. Martha Minow has considered the meaning of representation in law.[31] She explores what it means for anyone to represent someone else: '...who may speak for another? What is the difference between symbolizing or standing for another, on the one hand, and advancing the interests of another? Which should a representative pursue?'[32] Relying on the work of Hanna Pitkin, Minow reviews several different approaches to representation.[33] For example, in one definition, representation 'refers to the notion of likeness, mirror, map or portrait'.[34] As Minow explains, in this approach, representation 'depends not on authority, accountability, or any kind of acting, but instead on the rep-resentative's characteristics and ability to 'stand for' those he repre-sents'.[35] As Minow describes, this approach to representation is problematic in so far as perfect imitation or symmetry is impossible and any deviation from such accuracy raises dilemmas. Quoting from Pitkin: 'As soon as correspondence is less than perfect, we must begin to question what sorts of features and characteristics are relevant to action, and how good the correspondence is with regard to just those features'.[36] Since correspondence is always less than perfect, this approach ultimately begs the question of the actual meaning of representation.

Another approach to representation reviewed by Minow is one of a number of analogies to roles in which 'an individual may provide, care or speak for another'.[37] 'Actor, trustee, deputy, agent, steward—these are all notions with different shades of meaning pertinent to the idea of speaking for another'.[38] As Minow notes, this approach is also charac-terized by its own internal tension: '...the selection of which of these terms to accept as an analogy replicates the central ambiguity within the notion of representation itself: should the representative do what the represented party wants or what the representative thinks best'.[39] Neither of these two extremes can be appropriate for a representative since to do only what a represented party wants 'converts the representative into a mere conveyor of information'; on the other hand, to do only what a representative thinks best 'risks eliminating any connection, obligation or accountability to the represented party'.[40]

Naomi Cahn considers some of these dilemmas of representation within the specific context of feminist litigation.[41] Cahn argues, on the one hand, for the need for lawyers to listen to their clients' stories. But, Cahn notes that at the same time the lawyer 'needs to balance the clients' story with her perception of her own role',[42] a balance which may produce a number of tensions:

> If the lawyer is committed to political goals of feminism, what if the client has different goals? Should the primary objective be relief for the individual client or the establishment of a new legal right?...What role should the attorney play?...How do we ensure that the attorney's own experiences, which may be useful to litigation, are neither excluded nor exaggerated?...How should the lawyer shape the complexity of her client's story for presentation at trial?[43]

These are but a few of the difficult questions and dilemmas raised for the feminist representative. And as Cahn and others have concluded, there are no simple answers or formulas to the questions. Feminist lawyers can only begin to struggle with the dilemmas by recognizing that these *are* dilemmas; that representation is anything but a straightforward concept, and that these tensions in the role of the representative will have to be negotiated, carefully and contingently.

■ Legal Arguments

The way in which we frame our legal arguments goes to the heart of complicating our legal claims. Sometimes the nature of the legal argument is straightforward—an application for divorce or maintenance on a well-established ground. But, often the nature of claims are, or should be, more complicated. If we believe, for example, that adultery laws not only discriminate against women but also reinforce familial ideology, should we be framing applications for divorce on the ground of adultery? Since constitutional challenges to the adultery laws have repeatedly failed, there seems to be little hope, at the present moment, in successfully challenging these laws. In light of the unlikelihood of a successful challenge is there any alternative available to women? Should women simply be refusing to base their legal arguments on the ground of adultery? These questions in turn raise questions of the kind of litigation involved. A woman whose husband has brought an application for divorce on the basis of adultery has little choice but to respond. Alternatively, a woman who wants a divorce may find adultery the most practical ground to get out of her marriage. Do feminist lawyers or activists have any right to tell individual women that they should not be making these claims? In the context of individual applications for individual remedies, presumably they do not. Yet, in the context of test case litigation, this might become an appropriate consideration. At the same time, this distinction is not watertight. It is not always possible to predict with any accuracy when individual applications may become test cases or national campaigns. By the time an individual legal claim has become a national campaign, it may be too late to reframe the legal arguments. Constitutional challenges, on the other hand, can with some certainty be predicted to attract at least some public attention. We may be wise to work with the assumption that these cases almost always hold the potential to become test cases and/or national campaigns and should be approached accordingly. In so doing, we can begin by acknowledging a broader sense of accountability in the construction of legal arguments.

Constitutional challenges to legislation that discriminates against women raise some of the more difficult questions of how arguments should be framed. These difficulties are only further heightened in the context of challenges to family laws. In the current atmosphere of communalism, any attempt at bringing a constitutional claim that a particular custom, rule or tradition within a religious community violates women's equality rights risks fuelling the fires of communalism, and thus reinforcing the very political forces that the women's movement seeks to defeat. At first glance, it might seem wise to relinquish the terrain of law. Attempts to engage with law, either through constitutional or legislative rights discourse will only accentuate the conflicts. Yet, as we have argued, this would be to abandon a powerful site in the discursive struggles over the meaning of fundamental legal and political concepts, as well as one of the sites in the struggle to define the identity and status of women. Instead of abandoning this terrain, we need to consider how to most effectively counter the discursive strategies of the Hindu Right. How can we use legal strategies to challenge women's subordinate position, particularly in the current context of communalism and the rise of the Hindu Right?

In this section, we will discuss two concepts which may be of considerable assistance in framing feminist legal arguments: (*a*) substantive equality and (*b*) intersectionality. In our view, these concepts can make an important contribution to complicating feminist legal arguments to better capture the complexity of women's lives.

Substantive Equality

Equality has been a cornerstone in the political and legal struggles of the women's movement. Yet, as the preceding chapters have revealed, there is no uniform understanding of equality. Judicial approaches have been predominantly informed by a formal understanding of equality which insists on the formal equal treatment of those who are similarly situated. As we have discussed, the construction of women as different has often made it difficult for women to claim their equality rights, particularly within the family. The construction of women as wives and mothers through familial ideology operates to justify their differential treatment in law. In an approach that is not entirely dissimilar, we have seen that the Hindu Right is similarly advocating a model of formal equality in the context of religious minorities. And although advocating a rather different understanding of equality within the context of women as harmony in diversity, the Hindu Right similarly deploys the construction of women as wives and mothers to justify and celebrate their differential treatment in law. Neither the formal model of equality nor the harmony in diversity model of equality has been able to displace the dominant familial ideology.

Some feminist legal scholars have argued that we should abandon the concept of equality altogether. They have suggested that the hegemony of the formal model of equality, and its exclusive focus on sameness, is unable to accommodate the lived reality of women's lives.[44] Martha Fineman has argued in the context of American legal culture, with its doctrinal formulation of equality as sameness, that:

> While the initial adherence to an equality concept might have been necessary in taking the first steps toward trying to change the law and legal institutions, equality has proven insufficient as a concept with which to both assess and address the position of women under law. Equality may still have some use in circumscribed circumstances, such as in the context of arguing about measures when women and men stand in relatively equal positions (e.g., equal pay for equal work or equal voting rights), but there are many situations where positions are too unequal for equality to be of use.[45]

Fineman suggests that although the concept of equality may still have some purchase, it should no longer be the 'paramount organising principle of feminist legal thought'.[46]

While we agree that a formal model of equality is indeed unable to address the reality of historic and systemic discrimination, we do not believe that a rejection of this particular approach to equality necessitates that the discourse of equality be abandoned altogether. Rather, in our view, there is at least room to explore an alternative conceptualization of equality. Feminists engaged with law must turn their minds to the concept of equality and begin to more clearly articulate their normative vision of this fundamental constitutional right. In chapter 3, we suggested that a substantive model of equality may be better suited to advance women's political and legal demands for social change. As we have discussed, a substantive model of equality directs attention to the question of social disadvantage. In the context of sex discrimination, a substantive model of equality would consider whether the rule or practice in question contributes to women's social, economic or political inequality, or contributes to overcoming that inequality. This approach has the advantage of avoiding the sameness and difference debate, and the trap that gender difference presents to women's equality rights. By redirecting attention to the question of disadvantage and subordination, a substantive approach to equality creates space within which assumptions about gender difference can be interrogated and challenged. A substantive model of equality opens a discursive space within which questions of gender difference can be contested. The mere perception of a difference would no longer operate to close down any further analysis. Rather, a substantive model of equality directs attention to the relationship between difference and disadvantage; to a critical analysis of the socially constructed nature of gender difference, and to the extent to which assumptions of gender difference can operate to reinforce women's social, economic and political subordination. As we noted in the conclusion to chapter 3, a substantive model of equality will not automatically displace familial ideology and its construction of women as wives and mothers. The very grip of familial ideology lies in the extent to which these roles have been universalized and naturalized; rendered in effect a part of the collective common sense. But, in creating a space within which assumptions about gender difference can be contested, a substantive model of equality may provide a framework for chipping away at particular manifestations of familial ideology.

In respect of this alternative conception of equality, the Canadian experience provides an interesting contrast to the American experience. In Canada, LEAF has advanced this substantive equality for women through its purposive or contextualized approach to sexual equality. LEAF has argued that the purpose of the equality rights guarantees is 'to promote a society in which the hitherto powerless, excluded, and disadvantaged enjoy the valued social interests (such as dignity, respect, access to resources, physical security, membership in community, and power) available to the powerful'.[47] In its legal arguments, it has attempted to demonstrate in very specific contexts the extent to which '[w]omen suffer from social subordination, systemic abuse and deprivation of social power, resources and responsibility'.[48] And LEAF's efforts have been reasonably successful. The Supreme Court of Canada, in its leading equality rights decision, accepted many of LEAF's arguments. In *Andrews* v. *Law Society of British Columbia*,[49] the Supreme Court rejected the formal model of equality as embodied in the similarly situated test, and its focus on sameness. Instead, the main focus of an equality analysis should be 'the impact of the law on the individual concerned'. According to the court, discrimination is not a question of sameness and difference but rather, 'may be described as a distinction, whether intentional or not but based on grounds relating to personal characteristics of the individual or group, which has the effect of imposing burdens, obligations, or disadvantages on such individual or group not imposed upon others, or which withholds or limits access to opportunities, benefits, and advantages available to other members of society'.[50] The court accepted the view that equality rights must focus on the question of disadvantage, rather than simply on sameness and difference.[51]

It is difficult to predict whether similar arguments in favour of a substantive model of equality could be successful in the context of Indian constitutional law. Not unlike the American legal culture, equality in India has largely been conceptualized as sameness. However, as we have suggested in chapter 3, some inroads have been made toward a more substantive vision of equality. There is considerable room for manoeuvre within the language of compensatory discrimination that has emerged from the Supreme Court, particularly in relation to its more recent interpretations of Article 16. In our view, feminists engaged with law need to further explore this alternative vision and consider ways of pushing at the boundaries of existing constitutional formulations.

Multiple Discrimination and Intersectionality

In considering how to make legal arguments more complex, feminists engaged with law must consider the question of multiple discrimination. Legal and political demands have tended to be framed, for good reason, in terms of women's rights and discrimination on the basis of sex. The problem with this formulation is that women do not experience discrimination exclusively on the basis of sex. Rather, women may also experience discrimination on the basis of race, religion, ethnicity, caste, physical ability and/or sexual identity. To focus only on sex discrimination is to obscure the ways in which women—particularly women in minority and disadvantaged communities—experience multiple forms of subordination. To focus only on sex discrimination tends to reflect only the experience of those women who do not experience other forms of subordination, such as religious, ethnic or caste subordination. Moreover, these various forms of subordination and discrimination are not discrete and separate, but rather, intricately connected. The way in which a Muslim women experiences discrimination is intricately connected to both her identity as a woman and her identity as a Muslim. The way in which a lower caste woman experiences discrimination is intricately connected to her location in structures of both gender and caste subordination. Similarly, a lesbian woman experiences discrimination on the basis of her sexual identity as well as her gender identity.

Feminists engaged with law must begin to examine the ways in which women in different communities are discriminated against in different and often multiple ways. Discrimination law which has tended to focus on singular categories of discrimination must be able to reflect the complexities of women's oppression. The concept of intersectionality is intended to address this issue in law.[52] As Kimberle Crenshaw, who first developed the concept, describes, the fundamental inquiry of intersectionality is how simultaneous membership 'within at least two groups that are subjected to broad societal subordination bear[s] upon problems traditionally viewed as monocausal', that is, as resulting from a single cause, commonly either gender or racial discrimination.[53] Intersectionality is intended to capture the ways in which individuals may be discriminated against on multiple and simultaneous grounds; in Crenshaw's words, the ways in which a woman may be 'situated within overlapping structures of subordination', and the ways in which any particular disadvantage or disability is sometimes compounded by yet another disadvantage emanating from or reflecting the dynamics of a separate system of subordination. An analysis sensitive to structural intersection explores the lives of those at the bottom of multiple hierarchies to determine how the dynamics of each hierarchy exacerbates and compounds the consequences of another.[54] A woman may experience discrimination on the basis of gender and religion, or gender and caste, at the same time. And the discrimination that she faces is more than simply adding two or more different kinds of discrimination together. Intersectional discrimination refers to the ways in which each of the multiple grounds for discrimination becomes intertwined and inseparable. It becomes impossible to single out one form of discrimination.

A Muslim woman in India, for instance, does not simply experience discrimination in the same way as Muslim men. Nor is she discriminated against like all other women (that is, Hindu women). Nor is her discrimination simply the sum of these parts: discrimination against Muslims plus discrimination against women. Her experience of discrimination is a product of the interaction between gender, religion and community. The discrimination she experiences is as a Muslim woman. It is, for example, as a Muslim woman that she is disentitled from access to maintenance under section 125 of the *Code of Criminal Procedure* (not as a Muslim, or as a woman per se). It is as a Muslim woman that she is targeted by the Hindu Right (not as a Muslim, or as a woman). The grounds of discrimination operate simultaneously and inseparably; the grounds are interconnected and overlapping. To attempt to identify a single or a primary ground of discrimination would be to undermine the multiple and intersecting nature of the oppression.[55]

This analysis is helpful in revealing the dangers of pursuing strategies based exclusively on gender identity and gender oppression. To speak only of discrimination on the basis of sex or gender is to obscure the multiple and intersecting experiences of discrimination for many women. We cannot speak of the discrimination against Hindu women and Muslim women in the same breath, because of the fundamental differences in the ways in which these women are oppressed. Both groups of women may be oppressed. But the intersection of patriarchal and communal discourses are different. It might be possible to identify obvious ways in which Hindu women are discriminated against on the basis of gender within the dominant culture. It is less obvious to identify the ways in which Hindu women are oppressed by their community, as the Hindu community is the norm against which other community standards are measured. It constitutes part of the dominant ideology. Its pervasiveness renders it invisible. Muslim women, however, are more obviously discriminated against on the basis of both gender and community, that is, they are discriminated against as women and they are discriminated against as Muslims. The ways in which these forms of discrimination interact make it impossible to single out one form of discrimination over the other. We must not resort to discursive strategies based exclusively on gender identity, but rather adopt more complex notions of identity.

Such a discursive strategy is not entirely without precedent. In considering how to make our legal claims more complicated, the women's movement has much to learn from its own history. The women's movement faces very similar challenges to those it faced in the nationalist and anti-colonialist struggles. Women's status was an important site on which colonialism was justified. The women's movement could have worked against the anti-colonialist struggle by insisting on the patriarchal nature of Indian society and on the violation of their rights within the customs, rules and traditions of their communities. But, while insisting that their issues be included, these women were equally insistent on a careful analysis of the interlocking nature and causes of women's oppression—both patriarchy and imperialism were intricately woven together.[56] In much the same way, the contemporary women's movement needs to resist the temptation of basing its discursive strategies exclusively on gender. The need to develop more complex notions of identity and subordination is all the more urgent in the current context of heightened communal tensions, and the continuing ascension of the Hindu Right.

As recent history has revealed, legal strategies intending to highlight the violation of the rights of Muslim women can easily fan communalist flames. As discussed in chapter 4, the Hindu Right has been quick to appropriate such 'women's rights' issues, in advancing its ongoing assault on the rights of minorities. The condemnation of the practices of a religious and ethnic minority, as sexist and patriarchal can play into both the discursive strategies of the Hindu Right, and the feelings of vulnerability and persecution of the minority community. It may be that a more complex notion of identity and discrimination can assist feminists in negotiating these dilemmas. Feminist discursive strategies could insist on the multiple forms of oppression that Muslim women experience. Arguments could be developed which attempt to illustrate the intersecting nature of these multiple forms of oppression—arguments which insist equally on the structures of gender and religious subordination that affect Muslim women's lives.

The concept of intersectionality allows us to reflect on this multiple and intersecting oppression in law. It allows us to make more specific claims, which can more accurately represent the material specificity of women's oppression. A litigation strategy based on the concept of intersectionality is not, however, without its attendant risks. If the courts have still proven to be unable to grasp more 'simple' forms of discrimination against women, it may seem unwise to further complicate the nature of these claims. Yet, to fail to complicate these claims is to obscure the multiple and diverse ways in which women are oppressed, and to privilege gender discrimination above and beyond these other interactive grounds of discrimination. It may be that claims based on intersectionality can begin to deconstruct the homogeneity of women in legal discourse.

While challenges informed by intersectionality may be more difficult to convey to courts, there is no guarantee that litigation strategies based on gender discrimination alone will be successful. As we discussed in chapter 3, sex discrimination challenges have not been particularly successful. And even when the cases have succeeded in upholding, or striking down, the impugned legislation, the results in these cases have often been informed by and served to reinforce problematic constructions of women. Homogenous constructions of women as mothers and wives have been reinforced. Moreover, we need to consider the implication of continuing to make claims on the basis of a homogenous construction of women in the context of the upsurge of the Hindu Right.[57]

In developing legal strategies, feminists engaged with law must recognize that no single approach or strategy can be deployed to address the multiple ways in which women are oppressed. Adopting an intersectional analysis to discrimination may lead feminists engaged with law to consider the possibility of pursuing different legal strategies for different women. This strategy would help reflect the diversity and multiplicity of discrimination and oppression. Beyond the different nature of the legal arguments, it may be necessary for women to pursue different legal strategies. For example, in the current context of the continuing upsurge of the Hindu Right, it may be very different for a Hindu woman to bring a constitutional challenge to a discriminatory aspect of Hindu personal law than it would be for a Muslim woman to bring a similar challenge to Muslim personal law. As we discussed in chapter 4, the Hindu Right has begun to appropriate many issues traditionally associated within the secular women's movement. The discursive strategy, however, has been one in which the authority of the patriarchal family is not challenged. A challenge to a particular Hindu family law might invoke the wrath of the Hindu Right, or at least its more conservative and orthodox elements. The more radical the challenge to the family, the less likely the Hindu Right would be able to appropriate the challenge for its own purposes. A challenge to a Muslim personal law is, however, a very different story. The Hindu Right is only too willing to adopt such challenges in furtherance of their efforts at demonizing the Muslim community.

By advocating different strategies for different women, it might be argued that we are reinforcing the discrimination against women in minority communities. In other words, if women within the dominant Hindu community are free to pursue their legal claims in courts, while women within minority Muslim communities are warned against such action, are we not advocating a double standard and reinforcing the inferior position of women within Muslim communities? This is an important consideration, in so far as it is important to recognize the various ways in which the strategies we adopt may reinscribe the very problems we are trying to transcend. We do not mean to suggest that Muslim women should not go to court; only that it is more complicated for them because of the very nature of the multiple oppression they face, and the role of the state in that oppression. Muslim women may well be more suspicious of the state, and thus less likely to look to it for redress. Feminists engaged with law need to recognize that Muslim and Hindu women are not equal, they are not beginning from a level playing field. It is not that Muslim women are more oppressed as women, but that there are different implications that arise from different subject positions. These different subject positions need to be considered when formulating legal and non-legal strategies. It is not for feminist legal scholars to decide whether Shahnaz Shaikh or Shah Bano should go to court or not. Rather, the task for feminist legal scholars is to help reveal the full range of problems that may arise from such a decision, not only in terms of what the court might say, but also in terms of the social meaning that will be given to these strategies, particularly in a communalized environment. The more women understand about the implication of a decision to go to court, the implications of a victory or loss, the social meaning that might be given to these decisions, in addition to what the decision itself says, the better situated women will be to formulate their strategies and anticipate the consequences of such strategies. If women have all of this information, it will help them decide what to say and what not to say. If women know a decision will play into the hands of the BJP, as happened in the case of Shah Bano, it is better than not knowing it. It will influence the way in which women will make arguments in court, and allow them to formulate their claims in a way that will minimize the damage. It can allow women to more effectively strategize around the communal implications of the case, both inside and outside the court. If women know that the Hindu Right is likely to try to present itself as an ally in this struggle, then they will be in a better position to publicly explode this myth of alliance, and reveal the important differences between their positions. We are not advocating that women relinquish the use of law and legal argument, but rather, that they can better understand and anticipate the courts response and the communal implications of what they say and what the court says. By recognizing the different locations of these women in relation to the state, legal discourse, and the dominant society, the women's movement, with the assistance of feminist legal scholars may be better able to formulate strategies that address the specificity of these positions.

■ Evaluation

A final dimension of a feminist litigation strategy is to complicate the evaluation of a particular legal claim. This question of evaluation is an important aspect of complicating our understanding of law, and the ways in which it can be deployed as part of feminism's discursive struggles for social change. Evaluation is intricately connected to the objectives of the litigation strategy—objectives which should be set out at the design stage. If the objective of the litigation strategy is simply to readdress an individual complaint, then the relative success of the strategy can be evaluated on the straightforward basis of whether the complaint has been satisfactorily resolved. Has the complainant received what she wanted? Did she win custody of her children? Did she get a divorce? Maintenance? Did she defeat her husband's application for restitution of conjugal rights? If, however, the objectives of the litigation strategy include advancing the political agenda of the women's movement, then the strategy must be evaluated within a much broader context. The problem, of course, is that many legal claims do not, from their initial stage, fit neatly and categorically within one approach or the other. A case that was intended to individual readdress can easily become part of broader political campaigns. And an unsuccessful individual case is part and parcel of the overall political agenda of the women's movement.

In setting out objectives, and in evaluating whether litigation has met those objectives, it is important to think beyond the narrow legal question. We cannot evaluate the impact of a particular strategic engagement in terms of whether the particular campaign—be it a constitutional challenge or a law reform initiative—is successful on its face. Rather, legal claims must be located within the broader political struggle of the women's movement. We need to consider the impact of the legal claim on the women's movement. For example, has the legal campaign been effective in consciousness-raising and mobilization within the women's movement? Moreover, has the legal campaign been sufficiently accountable to the broader social movement, or has the social movement become dependent on the legal experts?[58]

We must, at the same time, consider the impact of the legal campaign on other social movements. Rights discourse can be equally mobilizing for progressive and non-progressive causes, and in fact, the Hindu Right is proving to be just as effective in mobilizing around rights as feminists.[59] It may not be enough to mobilize a women's movement that is dominated by Hindus around a particular rights campaign, if in the process this rights claim is mobilizing the Hindu Right as well. The question is thus not simply whether mobilization has occurred, but who it has mobilized. If the strategy has not mobilized the particular group on whose behalf the campaign has been launched, then its strategic value must be questioned. In the context of the Shah Bano case, the women's movement (which is dominated by Hindus), the Hindu Right (in favour of her claim), and the conservative and orthodox Muslim community (against her claim) were all mobilized. Muslim women, although not a homogenous group, were noticeably absent. And Shah Bano herself was ultimately demobilized.

We must also consider the broader social and political meaning of the legal campaign, that is, of the outcome of the discursive struggles between these different social movements competing over the meaning to be ascribed to the campaign. It is important, indeed essential, that an evaluation of a particular feminist litigation strategy include an analysis of these discursive struggles. For example, when a decision is pronounced in the courtroom, it may be cast in the discourse of liberalism and secularism. But outside of the courtroom, the discourse of the decision is communalized. The engagement with law must consider the broader context of representational politics, that is, the way in which the campaign is constituted in cultural discourses. As we have suggested, the Shah Bano case must be evaluated not merely in terms of this constitutional decision, and the subsequent law reform but rather, within the context of discursive struggles over the meaning of secularism, the relationship between religion and politics, the protection of minority communities, and the role and identity of women. Within this broader representational context, we can begin to see the ways in which law, despite its own liberal and secular discourse, is translated into communalist discourse and as such operates as an obstacle to empowerment. This potential for the communalization of legal discourse is an example of the contradictory nature of law and legal discourse. A victory in the courts may take on a very different social meaning, and may serve to mobilize and strengthen resistant discourses. It is but one example of being up against the limits of law.

Through all of this, we must not lose sight of the individual complainant. Notwithstanding all of these broader questions of the impact of the litigation strategy on the political agenda of the women's movement, we must remember that an individual was behind this case. An evaluation of the relative success of the case must include a consideration of whether the individual got want she wanted and at what personal cost. We need to return to the question of representation, and consider whether the needs of the individual litigant were adequately represented. Was she able to effectively participate in designing the legal strategy? Was she given an opportunity to tell her story? Or, was she lost in the legal shuffle?

Finally, an evaluation of a feminist litigation strategy must be open to the recognition that the outcome is, more likely than not, contradictory. While it is often important to proudly proclaim victories, as part of the broader discursive struggle over the social meaning of the decision, it is at the same time necessary for those involved in the litigation to take a more reflective and critical look at the outcome. As we have argued throughout this volume, feminist engagement with law has been contradictory. Many victories have been won, but these victories are rarely unequivocal; they are rarely on the terms that feminist activists had hoped. In evaluating particular litigation strategies, we must be willing to interrogate these contradictions, and not fall back into the 'either/or' trap of all or nothing thinking. And by shifting our expectations of law, it may be easier to recognize these contradictions without an overwhelming sense of defeat or disillusionment.

Law Reform

Campaigns for law reform have played an important role in the women's movement, past and present. As examined in chapter 1, social reformers in the nineteenth century, women in the independence movement, and contemporary feminist activists have all fought for law reform to eliminate discrimination against women, and to ensure that women's rights are protected. These campaigns for law reform have mobilized women, raised public awareness of discrimination and oppression, and succeeded in realizing many changes in the legal regulation of women.[60] Yet, after years of law reform, it often seems that little has changed. Despite the reforms to the rape law, women continue to be raped, the reporting rate remains low, and the acquittal rate of those that are reported is disturbingly high. The same can be said for virtually all areas of law reform. Despite the changes in the law, women's lives continue to be plagued by violence and socio-economic inequality. This gap between the formal rights of women and the continuing substantive inequality of women's lives can easily lead to a questioning of the value of law reform. Since nothing really changes, what is the point of lobbying for further change?

Archana Parashar has engaged with such critiques of the value of law reform and equality rights within the context of Indian women's struggles. She attempts to defend the continuing value of law reform, although she does so from a perspective that recognizes some of the limitations of law. Parashar argues that despite these incremental reforms, women in India still have not attained formal equality. She argues that the criticism of the potential of law reform has come from those who have already achieved equal legal rights—a criticism that in her view rings hollow for those who have not achieved equal legal rights. Echoing the position of Schneider and Williams, this is an important reminder of the importance of the struggle for and realization of formal equality rights for those disadvantaged groups who have been denied these rights.

In defending the role of law reform in feminist struggles for social change, Parashar argues that we must develop a more realistic appraisal of the limitations of law reform. She suggests that '...instead of dismissing law reform as a means of achieving equality for women, it is more productive to realise the limitations of law and have appropriate expectations that law reform by itself will be insufficient to change society and end women's oppression'.[61] In Parashar's view, much of the disillusionment with law reform comes from 'inappropriate expectations' about its potential to bring about social change. She argues that it is important to recognize the factors that limit what state-enacted laws can achieve.

Legal rights operate within the context of the given politico-economic system. Law reform may not remove the structural inequalities of the system which make it difficult for individuals to realise those rights. Instead of unrealistically expecting that law can change the whole social system, and then being disappointed at its failure to do so, it is more productive to realise that law can induce or assist social change only to a certain extent.[62]

Parashar persuasively argues that law reform can serve an important symbolic function:

Enacted laws embody certain values and express the symbolic consensus of society to adhere to those values. Symbolic legislation can be of liberating value as it can provide a focus around which forces of change can mobilise. For example, the endorsement of international conventions by national governments does not ipso facto make them domestic law of their countries, yet they provide activists with a valuable focus, people can remind the government of its commitment to certain principles and at times even compel it to act in accordance with these principles. Symbolic laws, therefore, may not directly bring about social change but may help create conditions which are conducive to such change. The Indian Dowry Prohibition Act, 1961, as initially enacted did not result in any prosecutions but its existence on the statute book helped focus attention on the widespread prevalence of the practice of dowry. The ineffectiveness of this law generated discussion and provided the necessary starting point for further action, including efforts to suitably modify the law, and it has ultimately been used more effectively to check the practice of dowry.[63]

Parashar's analysis of the role of law reform suggests that law reform can continue to be important in women's struggles, provided that women begin with an understanding of its limitations, and reconceptualize what law reform can reasonably be expected to achieve.

The struggle for law reform must continue to be an important dimension of the women's movement's engagement with law. Formal equality rights are important. The recognition and condemnation of the violations that women experience—the crimes and discrimination committed against women—continue to be important in discursive struggles. While these laws may not be enforceable or accessible to most or many Indian women, as we argued in chapter 1, these laws may nevertheless have an important symbolic value. It is in this symbolic, or discursive value, that law plays an ideological role in producing consensus. As Stuart Hall,

Carol Smart, and others have argued, law does not operate only as a coercive institution or power. Law also operates on the ideological level, in the 'production of consent'. It plays a 'positive and educative function which orchestrates public opinion'.[64] It is in this respect that law reform continues to play an important role in discursive struggles for ideological hegemony. Law reform can be reconceptualized as a process of creating a social consensus that certain forms of behaviour are unacceptable and not simply about the creation of individual rights, purportedly universally accessible to redress individual violations. By revisioning law reform campaigns as discursive struggles, where competing normative visions of the world are fought out, we can begin to understand feminist engagement as an effort to destabilize and displace previously dominant meanings of gender. Feminist campaigns for law reform can be seen as contestations of women's roles, responsibilities and identities, as feminists attempt to redefine social attitudes and acceptable social behaviours. For example, the campaign over rape law reform in the early 1980s can be seen as an effort to redefine the very meaning of rape, and to radically renegotiate prevailing understandings of the distinction between consensual and non-consensual sex. The women's movement, in campaigning for particular reforms to the *Indian Penal Code*, sought to redefine not only the legal meaning of rape, but also its social meaning. The law reform campaign over dowry can similarly be seen as an effort to redefine the social meaning of dowry. It was an effort to expose social practices that had previously been shrouded in the privacy of the family. The campaign sought a renegotiation in the public/private distinction, by seeking legal intervention in the private practices of the family. The very understanding of the family as private was, once again, challenged, as the women's movement sought to both expose and unequivocally condemn the violence that occurs within the family.

Law reform campaigns can also be reconceptualized as moments of fostering women's participation. The history and experience of the women's movement has demonstrated that it has been during law reform campaigns that women have been most effectively empowered to engage with and participate in political life. It is during these moments that women from a broad range of backgrounds have come together to form coalitions, to articulate their political demands, and to actively participate in discursive contestations over law. It is during these law reform campaigns that large constituencies of women are engaged with law as discursive struggle, as they seek to displace previously dominant meanings with meanings that better capture their political vision. It is during these moments that law becomes a site of political contestation and political participation, and that women have been most effectively empowered to engage in politics.

This understanding of the discursive and participatory value of law reform is not without its attendant risks. By reconceptualizing law as a site of discursive struggle, where meanings are contested and competing visions of the world are fought out, feminist engagement with law reform needs to consider the political implications of the interaction of different, and often conflicting discourses. We must consider the ways in which equality rights, and the liberal discourse of equality, will interact with communalist, familial, and other discourses, and produce quite unintended results.[65] A Uniform Civil Code, for example, may bring about equality for women within different communities. Feminists engaged in law must ask, however, how this struggle for equality rights is likely to interact with other ideological discourses, such as the communalist discourses of the Hindu Right. We have seen the extent to which any attempt at advocating for the legislative reform of these customs, rules or traditions through either a Uniform Civil Code, or more community-specific legislation runs the risk of promoting a more powerful communalist backlash. The campaign for a Uniform Civil Code, while mobilizing women, would also mobilize the Hindu Right (in support), and the conservative and orthodox within the Muslim community (in opposition).[66] Such a campaign may lead to a further polarization of communal sentiments, in which fundamentalists from one community are pitted against fundamentalists from another community. This polarization reinforces the very categories of communalism that need to be challenged and deconstructed, and as in the Shah Bano controversy, leaves moderates and progressives, particularly within minority communities, with nowhere to stand.

Particular attention needs to be given to the impact of formal equality rights on familial ideology. As we have demonstrated in chapter 3, winning equality rights within the family does not necessarily displace familial ideology. Formal equality rights for women and familial ideology are not necessarily mutually exclusive. Rather, familial ideology, and the constitution of gendered roles and identities within the family, can effectively undermine women's equality rights. These gendered roles and identities are used to justify the continuing differential, and often disadvantageous, treatment of women. This relationship between equality and familial ideology must also be considered in the context of law reform. Feminist legal scholars have explored the impact of the realization of formal equality rights within the family, and have shown that winning equality rights can change rather than eradicate the ways in which women are oppressed through law.[67] The advent of the liberal ideology of equality within the family has not always displaced familial ideology. For example, as we considered in chapter 2, while Hindu personal laws have been reformed, and women's equality rights realized in many aspects of this personal law, familial ideology continues to inform the interpretation and effect of these laws.

In making specific recommendations for law reform, it is important to consider the ways in which women are constituted in and through familial ideology. If at least part of the power of law reform lies in its normative value—in its discursive power to constitute and reconstitute the world around us—then it is essential that the discursive power of law reform be directed to challenge and not simply reinforce the traditional ways in which women are constituted in and through the family. It might be easier to argue for equality rights in the family in a way that does not challenge the traditional role and identity of women in the family. But the successful enactment of equality rights within such a framework would not go very far in the discursive struggles to redefine gender identity. Feminists engaged in law may decide, in any given law reform campaign, that the gains justify the limiting rhetoric; that it is strategic to deploy the familial ideology in support of the law reform campaign. Or feminists may decide that the risks outweigh the potential gains. We can only be in a position to evaluate this strategic consideration if we recognize that it is a strategic consideration; we can only measure the extent of the danger if we recognize that the danger exists.

Feminist strategies for law reform should also explore the homogenizing nature of legal discourse. As we have argued, the legal regulation of women assumes the homogeneity of the category of women. This discourse obscures both the diversity between and among women, and the material specificity of women's oppression. Law reform strategies not only require that we translate our demands for change into legal discourse; it further requires that we formulate very specific recommendations to amend particular legal provisions. At this stage, it is not the more fluid and open ended language of rights that we must adopt, but rather, the technical language of legislative drafting—a language that has not traditionally held out enormous promise for deconstructing the homogeneity of its subjects and classifications. The strategy of law reform thus seems to require that we play into, rather than challenge, the homogeneous construction of women. The challenge for feminist strategies for law reform is, then, to imagine new ways to challenge this homogenizing nature of legal discourse. How can we formulate specific recommendations for law reform that take into account the material diversity and specificity of women? How can we bring more complex understandings of identity to law reform? How can we contextualize a process of generalization?

The Uniform Civil Code exemplifies the relationship between many of these dilemmas of engaging with law reform. One of the stated objectives of the campaign for the Uniform Civil Code is the equality of women in the legal regulation of the family. The objective is certainly laudable, but the strategy raises serious risks. As we have argued, the Uniform Civil Code has been a cause celebre for the Hindu Right, which rarely misses an opportunity to attack the Muslim community through an attack on Muslim personal law, and the treatment of women therein. Through its discourse of secularism and formal equality, the Hindu Right insists that all religious communities should be treated the same. Yet, as we argued in chapter 4, it does so in a way that does not challenge women's roles and wives in the family. Rather, the Hindu Right simultaneously deploys its understanding of gender equality, as harmony in diversity, to insist that while all women must be treated the same, they need not be treated the same as men. While the secular women's movement has attempted to counter the Hindu Right, by directing attention to women's disadvantage within the family and by giving its own more progressive content to the Uniform Civil Code, it is the Hindu Right's message rather than that of the secular women's movement which seems to be carrying the day. The increasing power of the Hindu Right may not, in and of itself, be reason to abandon any given strategy. But, there are reasons to be particularly cautious about the Uniform Civil Code. The critique of Muslim personal law from anyone located outside the Muslim community has become so explosive that it has become virtually impossible to engage in any such critique without, however unintentionally, playing into the discursive strategies of the Hindu Right. There is reason to question whether this insistence on sameness, on the formally equal treatment of all religious and ethnic communities is the only or best way to achieve gender equality. There is little question that many dimensions of personal laws—Hindu, Muslim and Christian alike—are in need of reform. Archana Parashar has persuasively argued in her study, the personal laws of minority communities are particularly in need of reform, since these laws were not subject to the same major reform as Hindu personal laws in the 1950s. As we discussed in chapter 2, there are certainly many personal laws that discriminate against women, either on the face of the law or in its judicial interpretation. But, a recognition of the need for reform does not inexorably lead us to the Uniform Civil Code. From the perspective of promoting women's substantive equality, the reform of personal laws from within communities would be at least an equally viable alternative. This is the position taken by the All India Muslim Women's Association on the reform of Muslim personal law.

Promoting women's substantive equality involves the elimination of historic and systemic disadvantage, to facilitate their full and equal participation in social, political, economic and cultural life. It need not involve the erasure of all differences among women. A substantive model of equality would therefore, insist less on the formally equal treatment of all women, and more on the removal of the substantive inequalities facing women. In erasing the legal significance of religious, ethnic, and community differences, the discourse of the Uniform Civil Code would reconstitute women as an even more homogenous group. It would erase not only those differences in legal regulation which have contributed to women's disadvantage and discrimination, but also those differences that are integral to many women's cultural identity. Although the delineation between disadvantage and cultural identity is a highly contested one, within which conservative and orthodox voices would argue that any change whatsoever would violate a community's cultural identity, it may still be important to try to renegotiate those boundaries.

Recently, some groups have begun to explore new options for reform that attempt to promote women's substantive equality. They have sought to shift the terms of the highly polarized debate around the Uniform Civil Code, recognizing the limitations of lobbying for such a Code or promoting reform of the personal law from within the community. For example, the Peoples Movement for Secularism (PMS), a Delhi based group comprising of academics and activists, has proposed a strategy for pursuing law reform on the issue of personal laws.[68] The PMS proposal represents an interesting development in the debate on the reform of personal laws in so far as it significantly broadens the analysis beyond an exclusive focus on the discourse of women's equality, at the same time as it remains committed to the principle of promoting this equality. The proposal begins by reviewing the problems and limitations of a Uniform Civil Code in the 40s and 50s to promote national integration and including its use more recently by the Hindu Right as a means to attack religious minorities, particularly Muslims, and impose a homogenous cultural identity based on Hindu norms. The proposal highlights the extent to which women's rights have been continuously marginalized in these debates. At the same time, PMS argues that reform of the personal laws from within a community also has serious limitations. This kind of reform similarly falls into the trap of regarding the community as an homogenous entity, obscuring differences within the community. Furthermore, it subordinates individual rights, which include women's rights, to the interests or rights of 'the community', which is male headed.

PMS thus proposes that the debate be shifted to a wider discussion on women's equal rights in both the public and private space. It advocates reform that would cover the rights of women within the family as well as in the workplace, establishing a legal regime which would be equally applicable to all those born as or who become Indian citizens. In order not to negate the religious identity of any community, an individual would have the right to opt out of this secular law and choose to be governed by his or her personal law. The proposal attempts to take into account the way in which the Uniform Civil Code had been appropriated by the Hindu Right, and offers a strategy that attempts to reclaim the reform of personal laws on a feminist terrain. Although it does not ultimately transcend the homogenizing nature of legal discourse, it does seem to try to take it, along with the limitations of law and formal equality, into account. Despite some of the problems that remain to be worked out—such as the precise workings of a reverse optionality clause and the broader question of its political viability, the PMS proposal is in our view an important step forward in feminist law reform strategies in trying to think differently and creatively about engaging with law.

Finally, it is important to recognize that campaigns for law reform, deeply imbued in the rhetoric of individual rights, can create false expectations. Individuals who participate in the campaign, directly or indirectly, can come to believe that the passage of a particular piece of legislation will improve the position of women as individuals. These false expectations easily lead to disappointment and disillusionment with the legal system. The realization of a particular law reform can create the impression that the problem has been resolved, and that individual women whose rights are violated will have access to appropriate legal remedies. A successful campaign for law reform can mobilize a large number of people in the process, only to create a false sense of security and complacency in its aftermath.

We encounter a paradox in the strategic engagement with law reform. It is the resonance of the powerful rhetoric of individual rights and liberal equality that can mobilize large numbers of women, and other disenfranchized groups in campaigns for law reform. It is this powerful discourse that can force the state to recognize the political demands for change. It is, however, this same discourse that creates false expectations. This is not a simple or superficial problem, but rather, is deeply embedded in the discourse of law. It is a discourse that constitutes subjects as legal citizens; as individuals with rights and responsibilities. The act of participating in campaigns for law reform can be conceptually transformative, as participating subjects come to see the world around them through the liberal legal discourse of the campaign.

It is important to reiterate that we are not arguing against the value of law reform. We are simply attempting to reveal the many dilemmas and limitations of this process, in the hope that a more comprehensive understanding of these dilemmas and limitations can lead to a more strategic and effective engagement with this process. The better we understand the limitations of the legal strategy in which we are involved, the better prepared we will be to directly confront these limitations within our broader political strategies. A particular legal strategy for law reform is always only one small component of these broader political strategies.

Legal Literacy

Legal literacy has often been advocated as a means of realizing formal rights. Lack of awareness about law is seen as a major factor in the gap between the formal rights of women and other disadvantaged groups, and the continuing social and economic inequality of these groups. At its most general, legal literacy is education about law. There are, however, several different understandings of the objectives and methodologies of legal literacy. At least three distinct approaches to legal literacy can be identified: (a) access to justice; (b) mobilization; and (c) empowerment.[69] In this section, we will review these different approaches, and evaluate their relative strengths and weaknesses. We will examine some of the limitations and dangers inherent in the legal literacy process itself, and attempt to set out some preliminary strategies for pursuing legal literacy that can avoid these limitations.

■ Approaches to Legal Literacy

Access to Justice
The access to justice model is perhaps the most prevalent approach to legal literacy. According to this approach, legal literacy involves educating people about their legal rights, so that they will be in a position to enforce these rights. Legal literacy for women is education for women about their legal rights. Access to this information is seen as the first, and often the most significant step ensuring women's access to the law. An example of this approach can be seen in a course of legal literacy for women organized by the National Law School of India. The central objectives of this course include: '(a) to enable people to know of their rights and duties under law with a view to avoid discrimination,

victimization and exploitation; (b) to promote responsible citizenship towards the growth of a healthy democracy under the rule of law and respect for individual rights; (c) to facilitate access to legal remedies in case of injustice'.[70] The objectives of legal literacy are framed within the liberal discourse of law, with its focus on the individual. Individual access to law must begin with individual awareness of law. The problem of access is thus framed, in liberal terms, as an individual rather than structural problem. If individuals are informed of their rights, then they will be better able to seek access to the legal system to enforce these rights. Awareness is not the only obstacle to access to justice within this liberal understanding: legal aid, family courts, and other issues of individual accessibility are also promoted.[71]

This approach to legal literacy addresses a real and pressing problem that women face in accessing the legal system and enforcing their rights. Women do lack knowledge of their rights under law. And without knowledge of these rights, there is no question of enforcement or redressal of a violation of these rights. A recent example of this approach is found in the series entitled 'Our Laws' produced by a non-governmental organization at the behest of the government.[72] The compilation explains through the use of both visuals and texts, the rights available to women under different laws, such as the labour laws, the personal laws and the rape laws. Another booklet (on domestic violence), which marks the first of a series, has also been produced and provides legal information and advice on how to use the law and its provisions to claim rights.[73] These materials provide important and accessible information about the legal system, and the rights guaranteed to women. More recently, the government is working on a National Dissemination Plan which will attempt to weave legal information into the training curricula of grassroots functionaries such as the village level health workers, school teachers, land record keepers, police and forest staff as well as the local panchayat (local self-government units). It has stated in a recent report that organizational assistance to enable women to act upon the information they receive by establishing local networks and accessing other related support mechanisms, will be given top priority.[74]

These developments are certainly welcomed, in providing women with greater information about their legal rights, and moderately improving some women's access to the legal system. As an approach to legal literacy, however, this access to justice model is limited in some important respects. This approach to legal literacy focuses on individual access to individual rights. The problem, and the solution, is seen in individual terms. Beyond women's lack of awareness, the problem is seen as one for individual women to come forward and claim their rights as individuals.

As with all liberal understandings of law, this approach does not examine underlying structural inequalities. There is no consideration of the structural obstacles that women or other disadvantaged groups have faced, and continue to face, in relation to the legal system. There is no consideration of the role that law has played in constituting and reconstituting the subordination of women. Accordingly, there is no interrogation of the limitations of law in overcoming this subordination.

This access to justice model mirrors the discourse of law, in which subjects are constituted as individual legal citizens, with individual rights and responsibilities. The assumptions informing this approach are the assumptions of legal discourse—of universality, neutrality, objectivity and equality. All individuals are equally endowed with legal rights, which are equally enforceable. This approach does not consider the ways in which this ideology of individualism and equality operates to obscure and legitimate these underlying structural inequalities.[75] Nor does it consider the potential impact of this understanding of law and legal literacy on its subjects. Without any analysis of the limitations of law, this approach can create and reinforce unrealistic expectations of law. Women are taught to believe in the false promises of law, rather than challenge and engage these promises. The very process of legal literacy, within this model, becomes part of the process of constituting legal subjects. This access to justice model thus risks reinforcing both the ideological hegemony of legal discourse, and the ways in which this discourse contributes to the subordination of women.

Mobilization

Some women's and other progressive groups working with law and legal literacy have suggested that law can be an important catalyst—that it can mobilize people into action.[76] In this approach, legal literacy is not understood as an educational process which will improve individual access to justice, but rather, as a tool in collective mobilization for social and political action. Within this framework, legal literacy is important as a first step in mobilizing people in and through law.[77]

This approach to legal literacy represents a significant shift in the understanding of the role of law in social change. It moves beyond the individualism of the access to justice model, and recognizes the need for collective responses to more structural problems of collective disadvantage. Law is located within the broader context of political strategies. However, this mobilization approach to legal literacy is not unproblematic. It is based on mobilizing women in support of a political agenda that has already been established. Rather than empowering the participants to determine their own political and legal agenda, this approach seeks to mobilize people to participate in an ongoing political struggle. It risks cultivating dependency on activists and lawyers to both set agendas and run campaigns, rather than empowering women to make their own choices and set their own priorities.

Second, the emphasis on mobilization does not sufficiently emphasize or address the limitations of law. No doubt, some discussion of the limitations of particular laws would necessarily form part of the project of legal literacy. For example, the focus might be on the failure of the state to enforce particular rights, or on the failure of particular laws to protect the interests of women. The educational process would therefore involve highlighting the inadequacies of existing legal structures or provisions. However, the objective of the education process is mobilization—to collectively demand that their rights are enforced; or to collectively demand law reform. As a result, this approach might not provide a full sense of the limitations of law reform in the political struggle for which mobilization is sought. In the women's movement, for example, the campaigns for reform of the rape laws have used legal literacy to solicit and mobilize more widespread support. These campaigns have played an important role in raising awareness of the gross inadequacies of rape law and the need for reform, as well as effectively mobilizing and politicizing large numbers of women. The failure to consider the limitations of law, including the limitations of law reform, however, has risked reinforcing the hegemony of legal discourse. Notwithstanding the more collective focus of this approach, women may still be encouraged to see the law as the solution to their problems.

Rather than attempt to decentre law, these campaigns have risked reinforcing the centrality of law in transcending women's oppression, and the illusion that law can deliver on its promises. There is little question that this is not the intention of the activists involved in these campaigns, most of whom are far more ambivalent about the role of law. Yet, in the midst of political campaigns, participants invariably get caught up in the exigencies of political rhetoric. Indeed, it may seem politically counterproductive to engage in long discussions on the limitations of the reform being sought. Without attention to these limitations, however, women may be mobilized on the false pretences of law: that law will address these problems; that law reform can correct the injustices that women face in their lives. This mobilization approach, notwithstanding its more sophisticated understanding of law as politics, may unwittingly cultivate a dependency on law, and thereby serve to reinforce the ideological hegemony of law. While mobilization is an important objective of law, and of legal literacy, it is not sufficient in and of itself.

Empowerment

A third approach to legal literacy which has only recently begun to emerge emphasizes the process of empowerment. Drawing on the insights of critical pedagogy some activists and writers have begun to argue that the objective of legal literacy should be the development of critical consciousness, that is, the ability to think critically about the power relationships affecting their lives, and ultimately, to take action to challenge and transform these relations.[78] Margaret Schuler and Sakuntala Kadirgamar-Rajasingham have defined legal literacy within this approach as 'the process of acquiring critical awareness about rights and law, the ability to assert rights, and the capacity to mobilize for change'.[79] Within an empowerment approach to legal literacy, the object of the educator is not simply to provide information about legal rights, but rather, to actively engage the participants, contextualize the learning process with their own lives and provide the legal and technical tools for the participants to decide if and how law can be useful in their struggles for social transformation.[80]

Critical pedagogy, particularly in the context of the third world, has been fundamentally shaped by the groundbreaking work of Paulo Freire on literacy.[81] Freire has developed an emancipatory approach to literacy, in which literacy is conceptualized not simply as the acquisition of a technical skill of reading and writing, but rather, an inherently political project. Literacy should endeavour to create critical consciousness, that is, to create a critical awareness of, and an ability to critically intervene in and transform, the world in which we live. In this view, both teachers and students are active agents, engaged in the process of constructing and reconstructing meaning about the world around them. As Henry Giroux describes Freire's approach to emancipatory literacy:

> ...the issue of literacy and power does not begin and end with the process of learning how to read and write critically; instead, it begins with the fact of one's existence as part of a historically constructed practice with specific relations of power. That is, human beings within particular social and cultural formations are the starting point for analysing not only how they actively construct their own experiences within ongoing relations of power but also how the social construction of such experiences provides them with the opportunity to give meaning and expression to their own needs and voices as part of a project of self and social empowerment.[82]

In Freire's critical pedagogy, the object of literacy is not simply that individuals learn to read the written word, but rather, that they learn to read the world around them. It begins with an affirmation of their consciousness, culture and experiences as knowledge, and attempts to contextualize this experience and knowledge within the context of the broader social relations in which they live.[83]

Henry Giroux has attempted to further develop this Frierian understanding of literacy, applying Marxist and critical theory to the study of schooling and education in the West.[84] In Giroux's critical theory of education, schools are understood as a means of social and cultural reproduction, as well as sites of the production of individual subjectivities. In developing his theory of critical or radical pedagogy, Giroux is attentive to both the possibilities of critique, and the limitations of critique within specific historical and materials structures. In his view, radical pedagogy must endeavour to transform 'subjectivity as it is constituted in the individual's needs, drives, passions, and intelligence, as well as changing the political, economic, and social foundations of the wider society'.[85] In Giroux's view, critical literacy involves a learning process that: '...not only empowers people through a combination of pedagogical skills and critical analysis, it also becomes a vehicle for examining how cultural definitions of gender, race, class, and subjectivity are constituted as both historical and social constructs'.[86]

Margaret Schuler has begun to apply these insights of critical pedagogy to legal literacy.[87] She attempts to integrate the insights of Freire's approach to critical conscientization, and Giroux's understanding of critical literacy as cultural politics. She argues that 'these ideas about conscientisation, consciousness raising and critical consciousness provide the foundation for a dynamic and effective approach to legal literacy'.[88]

> Within this framework, critical legal literacy is also a form of cultural politics concerned with reading, understanding and transforming the cultural values and social norms embodied in the law. With regard to women, legal literacy becomes a 'cultural politics of gender' concerned with understanding the social, political, cultural and psychological dimensions of women's oppression, its expression in law, and effective action for change.[89]

She argues that legal literacy must seen as '...about developing capacities in women that allow them to use the law and rights as a political resource and to gain the skill and power needed to effect positive social change within the family and the broader cultural, social, and political community'.[90] Following from the insights of critical pedagogy, as developed by Schuler, feminist approaches to legal literacy must promote the development of critical consciousness about women's subordinate position in society and the role of law in reinforcing that subordination, and ultimately, develop strategies for challenging and transforming these relations. Women must be allowed to reflect upon their lives, to connect legal information with their lives, to work towards an understanding of the violations that had occurred in their lives, and link these violations with broader structural causes such as class, caste or gender.[91] Within this approach, mobilization remains an important objective of legal literacy. It is not, however, the sole or primary objective. Rather, mobilization is seen within the overall educational process of empowerment. Within this approach, women and other disadvantaged groups must first understand the structures and institutions that affect their lives, so that they may then be in a position to set their own priorities and establish their own agendas for political action. In this respect, the empowerment approach to legal literacy has incorporated the strengths of the mobilization approach, without prioritizing mobilization as the sole objective of legal literacy.

■ Pushing at the Limits of Legal Literacy

The empowerment approach to legal literacy has begun to address the limitations of law, that is, to ensure that education about law includes education about the limitations of law in addressing structural oppression.[92] Some legal literacy projects informed by this approach have begun to examine the broader context of what actually happens in the legal system when women attempt to claim their rights. For example, the Youth for Unity and Voluntary Action (YUVA), based in Bombay, has developed an approach to legal literacy which most closely resembles this third model.[93] The organization set up a Legal Resource Centre run by a social worker and community workers, to deal with the rights violations that were taking place within the communities where they were working. The Centre has directed its attention to women's issues and rights. Its initial efforts at legal literacy were confined to information-giving by lawyers, but it soon became dissatisfied with these sessions. The Centre attempted to shift the focus of its training programmes to deal with specific issues of those within the community. Although law was addressed, it was not the main focus of the sessions.

Similarly, in the area of litigation, the Centre initially pursued cases in the conventional fashion of seeking relief from the court. However, the litigants expressed their frustration resulting from the dependency on the Centre that was created by this approach. The women needed a collective space where they could share their experiences not only of law, but also of their lives, and provide support for one another. The Centre thereafter abandoned its case by case approach, and focused its resources on creating a common space for women where they could plan their strategies collectively. A Women Litigants' Association was subsequently formed whose first objective was to improve the attitude and functioning of the family law court, where many women had suffered humiliation and experienced inefficiency. As a collective group they used methods of protest and petitioning to challenge the court process and its treatment of women litigants. Through this method they acquired visibility, and the court staff and process gradually became more attentive and responsive to their needs and issues.

Gradually, a process of continuous interaction between the workers of the Centre and the community women emerged. This interaction involved providing practical information about law and legal procedures, as well as a space for the women to reflect on the strengths and weaknesses of their strategies. Women engaged in critical analysis of their experiences with the justice system and the strengths and limits of using law as a means of empowerment. Subsequent residential training workshops were also organized to enable the Centre's workers and the litigants to interact and address one another outside of the exclusive context of legal problems and issues. The process of the Centre has been based on action and reflection which has proven to be quite effective in empowering women. Its initial experience revealed the problems of using law as a starting point for women's empowerment. The gradual shift towards starting with the experiences of the women placed the process of empowerment in the hands of the women. The Centre furnished a space in which critical reflection and analysis could take place and women could actively participate in the process of empowerment. This process created the possibility of challenging law and the legal system rather than remaining dependent on it and submissive to it. Organizations like YUVA have begun to address the gap between formal rights and substantive inequality. Attention has begun to be directed at the particular ways in which law contributes to women's oppression. Beyond pointing out explicitly discriminatory rules and practices, some legal literacy activists working within this framework are attempting to examine the gendered assumptions that continue to inform both legislation and judicial approaches to this legislation. The strategies have begun to reveal the gender biases, the class biases, and the religious and ethnic biases of the law.

The empowerment approach to legal literacy has thus gone a considerable distance in recognizing the limitations of law, and in transcending the limitations of both the access to justice and the mobilization approach to legal literacy. This examination of the limitations of law is an important development in legal literacy, and must be further pursued. In our view, it is essential that legal literacy informed by a framework of empowerment begin from, and include, this understanding of both the limits and possibilities of law. Strategies of legal literacy must provide a realistic account of the law, that explores legal discourse as a site of power, and the ways in which that power impacts on women. We must continue to push this analysis further, and ensure that this approach to legal literacy continues to examine the multiple and contradictory ways in which law constitutes and sustains the subordination of women. As legal literacy projects informed by this empowerment approach are developed, women and other disadvantaged groups must be educated about law as a powerful discourse which constitutes, sustains and naturalizes these structures of oppression.

It is also essential that we begin to interrogate the limitations and dangers inherent in the process of legal literacy itself. We have noted that both the access to justice approach, and the mobilization approach to legal literacy, by failing to consider the limitations of law, may reinforce the ideological hegemony of legal discourse. There is, however, no guarantee that an approach that begins to examine the limitations of law can avoid reinscribing the very discourse that it sets out to challenge. We need to consider the extent to which rights discourse, and more specifically, the process of educating women about their rights, is conceptually transformative. We must ask whether teaching people to think about rights, and articulate their political demands in terms of rights, transforms the way in which they think about and see the world around them. We have argued that law is a constituting discourse—it is one among many discourses that constitutes individuals to understand the world around them in certain ways. Law, as an ideologically dominant discourse, plays an important role in constituting and legitimating unequal power relations. Legal subjects are individual citizens, with individual rights and responsibilities, subject to the rule of law. To what extent does legal literacy become part of the Enlightenment project of law, that is, of constituting the subject as a legal subject, endowed with individual rights and responsibilities? Legal discourse constitutes women as rights bearers. It is a discourse deeply imbued with liberalism, which constitutes subjects as individuals. This is its radical potential, since women have never had rights, and never been individuals. But, this is also the danger of legal discourse. It is a discourse that teaches people to see themselves as legal subjects—it constitutes subjects with a particular understanding of themselves, with a particular understanding of their relationship to the state.

We need to consider the relationship between legal literacy and the rapid expansion of capitalist relations of production in India through the new economic policies. Indeed, it may not be coincidental that legal literacy strategies are becoming popular at precisely the same moment that the state is promoting its new economic policies. The constitution of the legal subject, endowed not only with legal rights, but with legal liabilities, occurs in and through basic legal discourses. The most basic of these legal discourses are not constitutional rights, but rather, the discourses of contracts, property and tort. It is these legal discourses which provide the basic framework of liberal legalism, and the necessary legal cornerstone of capitalist relations. It is important to consider then, the extent to which legal literacy projects may have the intention and/or the effect of bringing the unenfranchised within the rule of law, and in so doing, legitimizing the contemporary legal regime. In the case of the access to justice approach, this would appear to be an explicit objective of the legal literacy campaign. While both the mobilization and critical consciousness approaches begin from perspectives that challenge the unequal power relations created and sustained by the contemporary legal regime, it is important to examine whether the effect of these strategies is not in fact to legitimate and reinforce these inequalities. Even with the empowerment approach to legal literacy, there is a tension between teaching participants about the law, and not subjecting the participants to the ideology of legal discourse. Yet, this approach, with its emphasis on teaching women to think critically about the power relationship that affect their lives, is well-equipped to address the problem of the hegemonizing nature of legal discourse. Rather than accepting legal discourse on its own terms, this approach to legal literacy must unmask the ways in which this discourse constitutes, sustains, and naturalizes relationships of oppression. If law and legal literacy is intended to be a tool for empowerment, feminists engaged in legal literacy must remain vigilant that it does not become a constituting discourse. One of the objectives of legal literacy within this framework, then, must be to create some critical distance between the participants and the discourse of law. Women must be taught about law, without becoming the subjects of law. Women must be taught to think critically about legal discourse, and not simply to see the world through the lens of this discourse.

The struggle against the Hindu Right exemplifies this tension within and challenge to the empowerment approach to legal literacy. The Hindu Right is challenging the very institutions and discourses of secular democracy. Paradoxically, Hindutva is both laying claims to the discourses of secularism, equality and rights at the same time as it threatens to undermine the very secular commitment of Indian democracy. At this particular moment in history, when secularism is being challenged by the Hindu Right, who are providing meaningful discourses and participatory structures for women, the struggle against the forces of Hindutva requires the legitimization of the discourse of secularism. The dilemma, however, is how to legitimate the discourse of secularism without subjugating women to the discourse of liberalism which has historically informed secularism. A secular state is essential if women are to be able to make any claims regarding their rights to equality. And yet, we have seen the limitations of such legal claims, and the need to protect against the hegemonizing nature of legal discourse. Legal literacy must teach women to think critically about the discourses of secularism; to understand and engage with the competing discourses of secularism, the ways in which the Hindu Right is appropriating and subverting one of these discourses, the importance of defending secularism in the face of this threat, and the limitations of the discourses of secularism in women's struggles. Secularism is the necessary discursive foundation for all progressive social movements in India. As long as the Hindu Right remains a threat, secularism must be vigorously defended. Yet, its successful defense does no more than set the stage for women's engagement with law, and the continuing struggle for social change.

The objective of legal literacy must be to enable the participants to think critically about law and legal discourse. This objective is explicitly strategic, that is, it is intended to put women in a position to critically evaluate strategies for engaging with law and empower women to make their own decisions about if, when, and how rights claims ought to be pursued. In this respect, legal literacy may necessarily precede litigation and law reform as strategies. Legal literacy ought to be designed to foster women's participation, and create the critical consciousness that will in turn allow women to effectively participate in other strategic engagements with law. If participation in litigation and/or law reform strategies is to be meaningful, then women must come to these strategies with both a sense of empowerment to articulate their views and experiences, and the ability to think critically about the role of law in their lives.

To the extent that law's role in women's struggles has been reconceptualized as one that emphasizes participation, legal literacy becomes a necessary precondition for any further engagement. Feminist litigation strategies and/or feminist law reform strategies will only be effective in creating democratic space for women's participation in political, social, economic and cultural life if women come to these strategies with a degree of critical legal literacy. Without this critical legal literacy, feminist litigation and/or law reform strategies will, at best, be able to pay lip service to the value of participation, and at worse, will in fact further contribute to the disempowerment of women by creating expectations that law will never be able to meet.

Finally, it is important to emphasize that although legal literacy may be the critical point of departure for feminist engagements with law, we do not mean to reify the rule of legal literacy in struggles for social change. We would caution against attempting to use education about law alone to promote the kind of critical consciousness contemplated by this empowerment approach. Legal literacy programmes need to be part of broader based educational programmes for women, designed to promote critical education on a broad range of issues. It may be important that women first be exposed to basic feminist concepts such as gender, gender roles, and the relationship of those roles to women's oppression.[94] Legal literacy may assist in further developing a critical understanding of the way in which law itself operates to constitute these gender roles. But to begin with law would be to risk creating the false impression that law alone constructs these relationships. Beginning with law would risk creating and reinforcing the primacy and centrality of law, rather than understanding law as one among a number of structures that contribute to women's oppression.

Conclusion

In this chapter, we have suggested ways in which feminist strategies for engaging with law can be developed to better capture the complex and contradictory nature of law. In attempting to overcome the limitations of law identified in previous chapters, we have tried to deconstruct the assumed monolithic nature of law. We have at the same time attempted to reconstruct different ways in which feminists might want to think about pursuing multiple legal strategies. In terms of litigation strategies, we have outlined a host of issues and dilemmas which need more attention. Feminist lawyers need to address questions of accountability and professional ethics while dealing with a case that seeks to alter the ways in which women are constructed. Developing litigation strategies requires that lawyers and activists assess cases from the point of view of the individual litigant while at the same time considering its broader political implications. Legal arguments need to anticipate the relevance of adopting positions which may secure a victory for the individual, but reinforce the dominant construction of women in law as mothers and wives. We have suggested that it may be useful in litigation strategies to begin to develop and apply arguments that promote a substantive model of equality. We have also suggested that attention to the question of the intersection of different forms of discrimination may be crucial in developing legal arguments that better capture the complexity of law in women's lives.

In the context of law reform strategies, we have similarly suggested ways in which feminist strategies may be made more complex. Strategies need to be formulated with the knowledge that law is a site for competing ideologies. Feminists need to engage with law in an effort to challenge the dominant ideology which operates to reinforce the subordination of women. Campaigns for law reform have been, and can continue to be, a place for challenging and displacing previously dominant understandings of the world. Campaigns for law reform can be an important place for feminists to tell different stories about women—stories which may fundamentally challenge the roles and identities that have previously been accorded to women. Yet, in doing so, it will be important for feminists to anticipate a broad range of resisting discourses. As a site of discursive struggle, other groups with other agendas will similarly attempt to use law to advance their normative vision of the world. The relative success of different groups may seem to depend on the extent to which their stories cleave to previously dominant stories. The strategies of the Hindu Right, for example, in playing into dominant familial ideology with the roles it accords to women as wives and mothers, may be more successful because these strategies do not challenge the ideology that has been dominant in law. Feminists engaged with law will face real and serious dilemmas. It may, in these circumstances, seem easier to simply deploy the same ideological constructions. Yet, as we have tried to argue throughout this volume, it is precisely these ideological constructions that have contributed to the subordination of women in and through law. Feminists will need to confront these dilemmas head on, and try to construct and reconstruct creative legal arguments to negotiate their way through these dilemmas.

Finally, this chapter has highlighted the importance of legal literacy to feminist legal practice. We have drawn attention to the need to develop a legal literacy strategy that moves beyond the access to justice and mobilization approaches, and works towards women's empowerment. The focus on providing critical information and adopting an interactive process will assist in locating law's relevance within a broader political strategy. The previous chapters have illustrated how law can harm women, how it can be used by counterhegemonic forces of the right wing to reinforce women's traditional roles as wives and mothers. Law has also been used to put in place the new economic policies of the government, which is withdrawing rights previously enjoyed by women and rendering their situation more precarious and vulnerable to exploitation in the market as well as in the home. Legal literacy models need to expose these and other profound limitations of law. Legal literacy needs to break down assumptions that law is the solution or that it can alter the substantive reality of women's lives unless strategies are informed by a knowledge of what law can and cannot do.

We have not attempted to provide a formula or blueprint for feminist engagement with law, since we do not believe that such a formula or blueprint exists. Feminist legal strategies will have to respond to the materially specific contexts in which the legal and political issues arise. Each strategy will have to be carefully constructed, taking a host of variables into account. In this chapter, we have simply attempted to highlight some of the issues and variables that may need to be taken into account in developing these strategies, and to provide some concrete suggestions for making feminist legal arguments more complex. At the same time, throughout the chapter, we have tried to highlight some of the problems and dangers that we perceive with these strategies of litigation, law reform and legal literacy. We believe that it is only by remaining vigilant to the dangers that may reside in legal strategies that we may be able to minimize these dangers. Even within the context of legal literacy strategies, in which we see perhaps the greatest promise for law in feminist struggles for social change, we have tried to highlight the very real dangers and limitations of this process. Some may dismiss our concerns as alarmist or idealist. We do not believe that we are either. Our analysis of the complex and contradictory nature of law in the oppression of women and in challenging that oppression leads us directly to these concerns.

Can law be a subversive site? Our answer continues to be a tentative one—that law might, in some circumstances, be able to challenge dominant discourses that have contributed to and reinforced women's subordination. Throughout this volume, however, we have argued that any and all feminist engagement with law must begin from a thorough interrogation of the limitations of law. It is essential, in our view, that feminist legal strategies begin with a process of questioning whether—rather than simply assuming that—law can be a subversive site. As we have shown, there are many contexts in which law has not been a subversive site. Quite the contrary, law has often operated to reinforce unequal power relations between women and men. But, as we have suggested, this need not mean that feminists abandon the terrain of law. It does mean that feminists must radically rethink the nature of their strategic engagement on this terrain. Again and again, feminists must return to the question of the limitations of law and build their strategies from a foundation that recognizes these limitations. We must not shy away from the question of whether law can be a subversive site, because it is a question that will only ever be answered tentatively, partially, and in very particular contexts. We must not think that we have ever definitely answered the question of law's subversive potential, because in our view there is no definitive answer to this question. The subversive potential of law can only be discovered by constantly revisiting these hard questions, renegotiating the boundaries of law, and reimagining our strategies.

NOTES

1. Audre Lorde, *Sister Outsider: Essays and Speeches* (New York: Crossing Press, 1984).
2. See P. Gabel, 'The Phenomenology of Rights—Consciousness and the Pact of the Withdrawn Selves' (1984) 62 *Texas Law Review* 1563; N. Tushnet, 'An Essay on Rights' (1984) 62 *Texas Law Review* 1363.
3. Andrew Petter, 'Legitimating Sexual Inequality: Three Early Charter Cases' (1989) 34 *McGill Law Journal* 358; Alan C. Hutchinson and Andrew Petter, 'Private Rights/Public Wrongs: The Liberal Lie of the Charter' (1988) 38 *University of Toronto Law Review* 278.
4. Harry Glasbeek and Michael Mandel, 'The Legalization of Politics in Advanced Capitalism: The Canadian Charter of Rights and Freedoms' (1984) *Socialist Studies* 87 ('...the legal technique actually obscures issues by dealing with them in abstractions that are meant to disguise the political nature of the choices being made'.). See also Michael Mandel, *The Charter of Rights and the Legalization of Politics in Canada* (Toronto: Wall and Thompson, 1989).
5. Patricia Williams, 'Alchemical Notes: Reconstructing Ideals from Deconstructed Rights' (1987) 22 *Harvard Civil Rights—Civil Liberties Review* 418; Patricia Williams, *The Alchemy of Race and Rights* (Cambridge: Harvard University Press, 1991); Elizabeth Schneider, 'The Dialectics of Rights and Politics: Perspectives From the Women's Movement' (1986) 61 *New York University Law Review* 589.
6. Williams, *The Alchemy of Race and Rights, supra* note 5 at 164: 'Rights feel new in the mouths of most black people...it is still deliciously empowering to say. It is the magic wand of visibility and invisibility, of inclusion and exclusion, of power and no power. The concept of rights, both positive and negative, is the marker of our citizenship, our relation to others'.
7. Amy Bartholomew and Alan Hunt in "What's Wrong with Rights?" (1990) 9 *Law & Inequality* 1 at 50, have argued for a reconceptualization of rights that similarly locate rights within political strategies. They argue that '[a] twofold approach is needed: first, a conceptualization of rights that captures their unsettled characteristics, and second, a theory of rights that explicitly addresses the question of political strategy'. They argue at 51–52 that such a reconceptualization will emphasize 'the historically constructed materiality' of rights, which will in turn 'facilitate the development of a politics of rights which is attentive to strategic questions about the selection of rights and rights-claims, and the work involved in transforming existing discourses to serve new political objectives'. See also Alan Hunt, 'Rights and Social Movements: Counter-Hegemonic Strategies' (1990) 17 *Journal of Law and Society* 309.

8. For a general discussion of LEAF, see Sherene Razack, *Canadian Feminism and the Law* (Toronto: Second Story, 1991).

9. Carol Smart, *Feminism and the Power of Law* (London: Routledge, 1989) at 139.

10. *Ibid.* at 144.

11. *Ibid.* at 145.

12. Judy Fudge, 'The Efficacy of Entrenching of Bill of Rights Upon Political Discourse' (1989) 17 *International Journal of the Sociology of Law* 445. See also Judy Fudge, 'What Do We Mean by Law and Social Transformation?' (1990) 5 *Canadian Journal of Law and Society* 48; and Judy Fudge, 'The Public/Private Distinction: The Possibilities of and Limits to the Use of Charter Litigation to Further Feminist Struggles' (1987) 25 *Osgoode Hall Law Journal* 485. See also Judy Fudge and Harry Glasbeek, 'The Politics of Rights: A Politics With Little Class' (1992) 1 *Social and Legal Studies* 45.

13. Fudge, 'The Efficacy of Entrenching a Bill of Rights', *supra* note 12 at 448.

14. Kimberle Crenshaw, 'Race, Reform and Retrenchment: Transformation and Legitimation in Anti-Discrimination Law' (1988) 101 *Harvard Law Review* 1331.

15. *Ibid.*

16. Fudge, *supra* note 12. Didi Herman in *Rights of Passage: Struggles for Lesbian and Gay Legal Equality* (Toronto; University of Toronto Press, 1994) has similarly explored the effect of rights discourse on gay and lesbian struggles. She has argued that although rights discourse was useful in the mobilization of gay men and lesbians, and in the affirmation of previously marginalized identities, she is critical of the particular way in which formal equality informed this discourse and had the effect of reinforcing the idea that gay men and lesbians are abnormal members of an immutably sexual minority. Elsewhere in her writings, Herman has been highly critical of the position of Judy Fudge and Harry Glasbeek for what in her view is their dismissal of the role of rights discourse in social movement. In 'Beyond the Rights Debate' (1993) *Social and Legal Studies* 25, Herman argues that Fudge and Glasbeek too easily dismiss the potential of rights discourse for marginalized groups. Ironically, despite the theoretical differences between their positions, Fudge's and Herman's analysis of the impact of the use of rights discourse on the nature of political demands of social movements bears certain strong similarities.

17. Joel Bakan and Michael Smith, 'Rights, Nationalism and Social Movements in Canadian Constitutional Politics' (1995) 4 *Social and Legal Studies* 275, at 291. See also Joel Bakan 'Constitutional Interpretation and Social Change: You Can't Always Get What You Want (Nor What You Need)' (1991) 70 *Canadian Bar Review* 307.

18. The rape campaigns that emerged following the Rameeza Bee case is discussed in chapter 1.

19. *Tukaram* v. *State of Maharashtra*, A 1979 SC 185.

20. *Prem Chand* v. *State of Haryana*, A 1989 SC 937.

21. Bartholomew and Hunt, *supra* note 7 at 56.

22. Brenda Cossman, 'Dancing in the Dark: A Review of Gwen Brodsky and Shelagh Day' (1990) 10 *Windsor Yearbook for Access to Justice* 223.

23. Jody Freeman, 'Defining Family in *Mossop* v. *DSS*: The Challenge of Anti Essentialism and Interactive Discrimination for Human Rights Litigation' (1994) 44 *University of Toronto Law Journal* 41 at 60.

24. *Ibid.* at 89.

25. Martha Hausman, 'The Ethics of Lawyering in the Public Interest: Using Client and Lawyer Autonomy as a Guidepost' (1990–91) 4 *Georgetown Journal of Legal Ethics* 383.

26. 'The New Public Interest Lawyers' Comment (1970) 79 *Yale Law Journal* 1069 at 1124.
27. *Ibid.* at 1129.
28. *Ibid.* at 1124. See also Judith Mossoff, 'Do Orthodox Rules of Lawyering Permit the Public Interest Advocate to Do the Right Thing?: A Case Study of HIV-Infected Prisoners' (1992) 30 *Alberta Law Review* 1258 at 1274.
29. Derrick Bell Jr., 'Serving Two Masters: Integration Ideals and Client Interests in School Desegregation Litigation' (1976) 85 *Yale Law Journal* 470 at 512.
30. Solicitor–client privilege is perhaps the most obvious, in terms of protecting the interests of the client.
31. Martha Minow, 'From Class Action to Miss Saigon: The Concept of Representation in Law' (1991) 39 *Cleveland State Law Report* 269.
32. *Ibid.* at 277–78.
33. *Ibid.* at 280–84; Minow reviews the work of Hanna Feinchel Pitkin in *The Concept of Representation* (Berkely: University of California Press, 1967).
34. *Ibid.* at 281.
35. *Ibid.*
36. Pitkin, as cited in Minow, *supra* note 31 at 282.
37. Minow, *supra* note 31 at 282.
38. *Ibid.* at 282–83.
39. *Ibid.* at 283.
40. *Ibid.*
41. Naomi Cahn, 'Defining Feminist Litigation' (1991) 14 *Harvard Women's Law Journal* 1.
42. *Ibid.* at 18–19.
43. *Ibid.* at 19.
44. See for example, Martha Fineman, *The Illusion of Equality: The Rhetoric and Reality of Divorce Reform* (Chicago: University of Chicago Press, 1991).
45. Martha Fineman, *The Neutered Mother, The Sexual Family and other Twentieth Century Tragedies* (New York: Routledge, 1995) at 41.
46. *Ibid.* at 42.
47. Helena Orton, 'Litigating for Equality: LEAF's Approach to Section 15 of the *Charter*', in Karen Busby, Lisa Fainstein, and Holly Penner, eds., *Equality Issues in Family Law: Considerations for Test Case Litigation* (Winnipeg, Man.: Legal Research Institute of the University of Manitoba, 1990) 7 at 9.
48. Catharine MacKinnon, 'LEAF's Theory of Equality: Breaking New Ground' (1990) 3:2 *LEAFlines* 1 at 1–2.
49. [1989] 1 S.C.R. 143, 56 D.L.R. (4th) 1.
50. *Ibid.* at 174 S.C.R.; at 18 D.L.R. (per McIntyre J.).
51. LEAF's contextualized approach to sexual equality has not been entirely unproblematic. As several commentators have pointed out, LEAF's approach to sexual equality, in emphasizing women's experiences of gender subordination, has tended to obscure important differences among women such as differences of race, ethnicity, caste and sexual orientation. See Razack, *supra* note 8; Lise Gotell, 'Litigating Feminist 'Truth': An Anti-Foundational Critique' (1995) 4 *Social & Legal Studies* 99. In its efforts to demonstrate women's shared experience in relation to issues such as reproductive control, maternity leave, pregnancy discrimination, rape, and sex harassment, LEAF has tended to construct women as a monolithic and homogeneous category. The ways in which issues of reproductive control, or sexual assault may affect different women differently was overlooked in LEAF's early approach. In recent years, however, LEAF

has begun to direct its attention to those issues of difference, and to address the particular experiences of women of colour, First Nations women, women with disabilities, and lesbian women. It has, in effect, begun to try to further complicate its own contextualized approach to sexual equality and put forward legal arguments that can better capture the diversity of women's experiences of subordination. See Gotell, *ibid.* In the next section, we turn to consider the implications of multiple discrimination for feminist litigation strategies in India.

52. See Kimberle Crenshaw, *Words that Wound: Critical Race Theory, Assaultive Speech, and the First Amendment* (Boulder, Co.: Westview Press, 1993): Peggy Smith, 'Separate Identities: Black Women, Work and Tide VII' (1991) 14 *Harvard Women's Law Journal* 21; Nitya Duclos (Iyer), 'Disappearing Women: Racial Minority Women in Human Rights Cases' 5 *Canadian Journal of Women and Law* 40.
53. Crenshaw, *supra* note 52 at 114.
54. *Ibid.*
55. It is not only in relation to gender and religion/community that these grounds of discrimination intersect. The discrimination experienced by a dalit woman, for example, is also qualitatively different from the experience of discrimination against dalit men, or non-dalit women.
56. Joanna Liddle and Rama Joshi, 'Gender and Imperialism in British India', *Economic and Political Weekly* (26 October 1985) 43.
57. It is important to consider how these arguments may play out in the context of the Hindu Right. On the one hand, the Hindu Right constructs Hindu and Muslim women very differently; on the other hand, its political rhetoric argues that women should be the same—and in effect, that Muslim women should be demuslimized, and treated just like Hindu women. If the women's movement continues to base claims on a homogeneous gender identity, this might play directly into the strategies of the Hindu Right, that is, that women should be the same. But, there is also the fact that communalist discourse constructs Muslim women and Hindu women very differently (while arguing that they should be the same). Is this a reason to argue that women are the same? But, in fact, they are not the same. Even the way in which the Hindu Right discourse is trying to constitute these women through different discourses illustrates the extent of the differences. It is difficult to see the strategic advantages of arguing on the basis of a homogenous gender identity. This homogenous discourse cannot get at the ways in which the Hindu Right are using both gender and community to advance their agendas.
58. Cossman, *supra* note 22.
59. Ratna Kapur, 'Feminism, Fundamentalism and Rights Rhetoric' (1992) 5:1 *Indian Journal of Social Science* 33.
60. Nandita Gandhi, 'Impact of Religion on Women's Rights in Asia', *Economic and Political Weekly* (23 January 1988).
61. Archana Parashar, *Women and Family Law Reforms in India: Uniform Civil Code and Gender Equality* (New Delhi: Sage, 1992) at 30.
62. *Ibid.*
63. *Ibid.* at 33.
64. Carol Smart, *The Ties that Bind: Law, Marriage and the Reproduction of Patriarchal Relations* (London: Routledge and Kegan Paul, 1984) at 21. See also Stuart Hall et al., eds., *Policing the Crisis: Mugging, the State, and Law and Order* (London: MacMillan, 1978).
65. As Parashar, *supra* note 61, has rightly argued, compliance or non-compliance with the law is not the only measure of effectiveness. Rather, she argues: 'An assessment

of the effectiveness of any law requires an unambiguous statement of the aims of the particular law and of the desired result. Furthermore, any measure of effectiveness has to take account the unintended consequences of the law'.

66. It is not only the conservative and orthodox within the Muslim community who have opposed the Uniform Civil Code. More progressive voices within the Muslim community, such as the Muslim Women's Association have opposed a Uniform Civil Code, preferring instead to pursue reform of Muslim personal laws within the Muslim community.

67. See Susan Boyd, 'Child Custody, Ideologies and Employment' (1989) 3 *Canadian Journal of Women and Law* 111; 'Child Custody and Working Mothers', in S. Martin and K. Mahoney, eds., *Equality and Judicial Neutrality* (Toronto: Carswell, 1987) 168.

68. See 'Civil Codes and Personal Laws: Reversing the Option', Working Group on Women's Rights, Peoples Movement for Secularism, presented at the Indian Association of Women's Studies Conference, 28 December 1995 (on record with PMS). Other examples presented at the conference which are taking into consideration the impact of the increasingly communal environment on law generally, and the debate on the Uniform Civil Code in particular, see, 'Protection of Women's Economic Rights Through Specific Legislations and Reform from Within—Dual Strategy for Law Reform', Majlis (available on record with Majlis, Bombay), arguing in favour of a focus on legislation concerning women's economic rights as well as reform from within the personal laws; and the Draft Resolution of All India Democratic Women's Association, National Convention, 9–10 December 1995, New Delhi *Equal Rights, Equal Laws*, arguing in favour of piecemeal reform towards women's equality which would include lobbying for legislation where none exists, such as on domestic violence, matrimonial property rights and compulsory registration of marriage (available on record with All India Democratic Women's Association, New Delhi).

69. These three approaches are not unrelated. The mobilization approach, for example, borrows from, and builds upon the access to justice model, by insisting on the importance of information to educate and mobilize people, which is in turn seen as a vehicle for the realization of, and access to, justice. Similarly, the critical consciousness model builds upon the mobilization approach. While in this approach it is not sufficient to mobilize people without first creating critical consciousness, the objective of the approach remains mobilization and empowerment to demand and realize access to justice.

70. Madhava Menon, 'Introduction to the Indian Legal System and Legal Awareness' (part of a course organized by the National Law School of India).

71. *Ibid.*

72. Produced and published by the Multiple Action Research Group for the Department of Women and Child, Ministry of Human Resource Development, Government of India, 1992.

73. Lawyers' Collective, *Domestic Violence: Legal Aid Handbook* (New Delhi: Kali, 1992).

74. Draft of the Country Paper for the Fourth World Conference on Women, Beijing, 1995 (Department of Women and Child, Ministry of Human Resource Development, Government of India, 3 June 1994) at 60–61. See also India, Committee on the Status of Women in India, *Toward Equality: Report of the Committee on the Status of Women in India* (New Delhi: Ministry of Education and Social Welfare, 1975).

75. Indeed, reinforcing the rule of law, and the legitimacy of legal discourse seems to be an explicit objective of some access to justice legal literacy projects. The National

Law School of India's 'Legal Literacy for Women' course includes as a stated objective: '...to help remove popular dissatisfaction with law and legal processes by 'de-mystifying' them and by increasing people's participation'.

76. See Nandita Gandhi and Nandita Shah, *Issues at Stake: Theory and Practice in the Contemporary Women's Movement in India* (New Delhi: Kali, 1992) at 270.

77. See Jim Paul and Clarence Dias, *Developing Law and Legal Resources for Alternative People Centred Development: A Human Rights Approach* (New York: ICLD, 1985) (on mobilization through law/human rights). See also Margaret Schuler, 'Legal Literacy and Empowerment of Women,' in *My Rights, Who Control?* (Asia Pacific Forum on Women, Law and Development, 1989).

78. Paolo Freire, *The Pedagogy of the Oppressed* (New York: Seabury Press, 1970).

79. Margaret Schuler and Sakuntala Kadirgamar-Rajasingham, 'Legal Literacy: A Tool for Women's Empowerment', in Margaret Schuler and Sakuntala Kadirgamar-Rajasingham, eds., *Legal Literacy: A Tool for Women's Empowerment* (New York: UNIFEM, 1992).

80. *Ibid.*

81. Freire, *supra* note 78.

82. Giroux, 'Introduction' in Paulo Freire and Donaldo Macedo, eds., *Literacy: Reading the Word and the World* (South Hadley: Bergin & Garvey, 1987) at 7.

83. Kathleen Weiler, *Women Teaching For Change: Gender, Class and Power* (New York: Bergin & Garvey, 1988). Freire requires that teachers be reflective of their own consciousness, the ideological biases of this consciousness, and the social relations which has produced this consciousness. In Freire's model, 'both students and teachers must seek to understand the forces of hegemony within their own consciousness as well as in the structured, historical circumstances in which they find themselves'.

84. See generally Henry Giroux, *Ideology, Culture and the Process of Schooling* (Philadelphia: Temple University Press, 1981).

85. Henry Giroux, *Theory, Resistance, and Education* (South Hadley: Bergin & Garvey, 1983) at 22.

86. Giroux, *supra* note 82 at 6.

87. Schuler and Kadirgamar-Rajasingham, *supra* note 79.

88. *Ibid.* at 45.

89. *Ibid.* at 23.

90. *Ibid.* at 49. As Freire, and others commenting on Freire's work have made clear, there is no simple formula to the operationalization of this approach to critical consciousness. Giroux has stated:

Freire's work is not meant to offer radical recipes for instant forms of critical pedagogy; rather, it is a series of theoretical signposts that need to be decoded and critically appropriated within the specific contexts in which they might be useful.

Henry Giroux, 'Introduction', in Paolo Freire, *The Politics of Education: Culture, Power and Liberation*, trans. Donaldo Macedo (Granby, Mass.: Bergin & Garvey, 1985) at xviii–xix.

91. See Ratna Kapur, 'From Theory to Practice: Reflections on Legal Literacy with Women in India', in Schuler and Kadirgamar-Rajasingham, eds., *Legal Literacy: A Tool for Women's Empowerment*, *supra* note 79 at 93.

92. See Schuler and Kadirgamar-Rajasingham, *supra* note 79. See also Kapur, *ibid.*

93. Youth for Unity and Voluntary Action (YUVA), an NGO based in Bombay has been conducting legal literacy programmes for women and other disadvantaged groups

within this kind of empowerment framework. YUVA established a Legal Resource Centre in 1987 to address rights violations within the communities of workers colonies and pavement dwellers that it works with. The Centre's primary objectives are: (*a*) to provide legal education, (*b*) to demystify law to make it accessible to people, (*c*) to intervene on behalf of powerless groups by means of public interest litigation and (*d*) to strengthen ongoing struggles. With specific reference to women, the Centre has been attempting to help women establish their legal identity through registration cards and helping widows file claims after riot situations to secure compensation in their name. It has also intervened on behalf of women in family law cases. For other examples of legal literacy within this empowerment framework, see *Report by Action for World Solidarity: How to do Legal Literacy* (Bangalore, 1991); and *Report on Training Methodologies*, by Jagori (Rishikesh, 6–13 April 1993).

94. See Kapur *supra* at 91.

Table of Cases

Index